FINE ARTS, MUSIC AND LITERATURE

COPYRIGHT AND THE MUSIC MARKETPLACE

ANALYSIS, CHALLENGES, AND RECOMMENDATIONS FOR IMPROVEMENT

FINE ARTS, MUSIC AND LITERATURE

Additional books in this series can be found on Nova's website
under the Series tab.

Additional e-books in this series can be found on Nova's website
under the e-book tab.

FINE ARTS, MUSIC AND LITERATURE

COPYRIGHT AND THE MUSIC MARKETPLACE

ANALYSIS, CHALLENGES, AND RECOMMENDATIONS FOR IMPROVEMENT

KEITH TURNER
EDITOR

Copyright © 2015 by Nova Science Publishers, Inc.

All rights reserved. No part of this book may be reproduced, stored in a retrieval system or transmitted in any form or by any means: electronic, electrostatic, magnetic, tape, mechanical photocopying, recording or otherwise without the written permission of the Publisher.

We have partnered with Copyright Clearance Center to make it easy for you to obtain permissions to reuse content from this publication. Simply navigate to this publication's page on Nova's website and locate the "Get Permission" button below the title description. This button is linked directly to the title's permission page on copyright.com. Alternatively, you can visit copyright.com and search by title, ISBN, or ISSN.

For further questions about using the service on copyright.com, please contact:
Copyright Clearance Center
Phone: +1-(978) 750-8400   Fax: +1-(978) 750-4470   E-mail: info@copyright.com.

NOTICE TO THE READER

The Publisher has taken reasonable care in the preparation of this book, but makes no expressed or implied warranty of any kind and assumes no responsibility for any errors or omissions. No liability is assumed for incidental or consequential damages in connection with or arising out of information contained in this book. The Publisher shall not be liable for any special, consequential, or exemplary damages resulting, in whole or in part, from the readers' use of, or reliance upon, this material. Any parts of this book based on government reports are so indicated and copyright is claimed for those parts to the extent applicable to compilations of such works.

Independent verification should be sought for any data, advice or recommendations contained in this book. In addition, no responsibility is assumed by the publisher for any injury and/or damage to persons or property arising from any methods, products, instructions, ideas or otherwise contained in this publication.

This publication is designed to provide accurate and authoritative information with regard to the subject matter covered herein. It is sold with the clear understanding that the Publisher is not engaged in rendering legal or any other professional services. If legal or any other expert assistance is required, the services of a competent person should be sought. FROM A DECLARATION OF PARTICIPANTS JOINTLY ADOPTED BY A COMMITTEE OF THE AMERICAN BAR ASSOCIATION AND A COMMITTEE OF PUBLISHERS.

Additional color graphics may be available in the e-book version of this book.

Library of Congress Cataloging-in-Publication Data

ISBN: 978-1-63482-869-7

Published by Nova Science Publishers, Inc. † New York

CONTENTS

Preface		vii
Chapter 1	Copyright and the Music Marketplace *Office of the General Counsel, U.S. Copyright Office*	1
Chapter 2	Testimony of Lee Thomas Miller, President, Nashville Songwriters Association International. Hearing on "Music Licensing Under Title 17 Part One"	179
Chapter 3	Statement of Neil Portnow, President and CEO, The Recording Academy. Hearing on "Music Licensing Under Title 17 Part One"	181
Chapter 4	Testimony of David M. Israelite, President and Chief Executive Officer, National Music Publishers' Association. Hearing on "Music Licensing Under Title 17 Part One"	187
Chapter 5	Statement of Michael O'Neill, Chief Executive Officer, BMI. Hearing on "Music Licensing Under Title 17 Part One"	195
Chapter 6	Testimony of Rosanne Cash, Singer, Songwriter, on behalf of the American Music Association. Hearing on "Music Licensing Under Title 17 Part Two"	205
Chapter 7	Statement of Cary Sherman, Chairman and CEO, Recording Industry Association of America. Hearing on "Music Licensing Under Title 17 Part Two"	209
Chapter 8	Statement of Charles M. Warfield, Jr., Senior Advisor, YMF Media, LLC. Hearing on "Music Licensing Under Title 17 Part Two"	217
Chapter 9	Statement of Paul Williams, President and Chairman of the Board, American Society of Composers, Authors and Publishers (ASCAP). Hearing on "Music Licensing Under Title 17 Part Two"	225
Chapter 10	Testimony of Chris Harrison, Vice President, Business Affairs, Pandora Media Inc. Hearing on "Music Licensing Under Title 17 Part Two"	237
Index		247

PREFACE

The United States has the most innovative and influential music culture in the world, but much of the legal framework for licensing of music dates back to the early part of the twentieth century, long before the digital revolution in music. Our licensing system is founded on a view that the music marketplace requires a unique level of government regulation, much of it reflected in statutory licensing provisions of the Copyright Act. The Copyright Office believes that the time is ripe to question the existing paradigm for the licensing of musical works and sound recordings and consider meaningful change. This book provides an analysis, discusses challenges and recommendations for improvement of the copyright laws in the music marketplace.

Chapter 1 – Few would dispute that music is culturally essential and economically important to the world we live in, but the reality is that both music creators and the innovators that support them are increasingly doing business in a legal quagmire. As this report makes clear, this state of affairs neither furthers the copyright law nor befits a nation as creative as the United States.

The Copyright Office has previously highlighted the outmoded rules for the licensing of musical works and sound recordings as an area in significant need of reform. Moreover, the Office has underscored the need for a comprehensive approach to copyright review and revision generally. This is especially true in the case of music licensing—the problems in the music marketplace need to be evaluated as a whole, rather than as isolated or individual concerns of particular stakeholders.

While this view is hardly a surprising one for the U.S. Copyright Office, it is no simple matter to get one's arms around our complex system of music licensing, or to formulate potential avenues for change. For this reason, in early 2014, the Office undertook this study—with all industry participants invited to participate—to broadly consider the existing music marketplace.

This report is the result of that effort. In addition to identifying the shortcomings of the current methods of licensing music in the United States, it offers an in-depth analysis of the law and industry practices, as well as a series of balanced recommendations to improve the music marketplace.

Chapter 2 – This is the Testimony of Lee Thomas Miller, President, Nashville Songwriters Association International.

Chapter 3 – This is the Statement of Neil Portnow, President and CEO, The Recording Academy.

Chapter 4 – This is the Testimony of David M. Israelite, President and Chief Executive Officer, National Music Publishers' Association.

Chapter 5 – This is the Statement of Michael O'Neill, Chief Executive Officer, BMI.

Chapter 6 - This is the Testimony of Rosanne Cash, Singer, Songwriter, on behalf of the American Music Association.

Chapter 7 – This is the Statement of Cary Sherman, Chairman and CEO, Recording Industry Association of America.

Chapter 8 – This is the Statement of Charles M. Warfield, Jr., Senior Advisor, YMF Media, LLC.

Chapter 9 – This is the Statement of Paul Williams, President and Chairman of the Board, American Society of Composers, Authors and Publishers (ASCAP).

Chapter 10 – This is the Testimony of Chris Harrison, Vice President, Business Affairs, Pandora Media Inc.

In: Copyright and the Music Marketplace
Editor: Keith Turner

ISBN: 978-1-63482-869-7
© 2015 Nova Science Publishers, Inc.

Chapter 1

COPYRIGHT AND THE MUSIC MARKETPLACE[*]

Office of the General Counsel, U.S. Copyright Office

EXECUTIVE SUMMARY

The United States has the most innovative and influential music culture in the world, but much of the legal framework for licensing of music dates back to the early part of the twentieth century, long before the digital revolution in music. Our licensing system is founded on a view that the music marketplace requires a unique level of government regulation, much of it reflected in statutory licensing provisions of the Copyright Act. The Copyright Office believes that the time is ripe to question the existing paradigm for the licensing of musical works and sound recordings and consider meaningful change.

There is a widespread perception that our licensing system is broken. Songwriters and recording artists are concerned that they cannot make a living under the existing structure, which raises serious and systemic concerns for the future. Music publishers and performance rights organizations are frustrated that so much of their licensing activity is subject to government control, so they are constrained in the marketplace. Record labels and digital services complain that the licensing process is burdensome and inefficient, making it difficult to innovate.

While there is general consensus that the system needs attention, there is less agreement as to what should be done. In this report, after reviewing the existing framework and stakeholders' views, the Copyright Office offers a series of guiding principles and preliminary recommendations for change. The Office's proposals are meant to be contemplated together, rather than individually. With this approach, the Office seeks to present a series of balanced tradeoffs among the interested parties to create a fairer, more efficient, and more rational system for all.

---

[*] This is an edited, reformatted and augmented version of a report issued by the United States Copyright Office, Februrary 2015.

A. Guiding Principles

The Copyright Office's study revealed broad consensus among study participants on four key principles:

- Music creators should be fairly compensated for their contributions.
- The licensing process should be more efficient.
- Market participants should have access to authoritative data to identify and license sound recordings and musical works.
- Usage and payment information should be transparent and accessible to rightsowners.

In addition to the above, based on the record in the proceeding, the Office has identified several additional principles that it believes should also guide any process of reform.
These are:

- Government licensing processes should aspire to treat like uses of music alike.
- Government supervision should enable voluntary transactions while still supporting collective solutions.
- Ratesetting and enforcement of antitrust laws should be separately managed and addressed.
- A single, market-oriented ratesetting standard should apply to all music uses under statutory licenses.

The Office was guided by all of the above principles in developing its recommendations, which are summarized below.

B. Licensing Parity and Fair Compensation

Questions of licensing parity and fair compensation are closely tied to the relative treatment of music rights and rightsholders under the law. The Copyright Office believes that any overhaul of our music licensing system should strive to achieve greater consistency in the way it regulates (or does not regulate) analogous platforms and uses. With that goal in mind, the Office recommends the following:

- *Regulate musical works and sound recordings in a consistent manner.* The Office believes that, at least in the digital realm, sound recordings and the underlying musical works should stand on more equal footing. The Copyright Office's approach would offer a free market alternative to musical work owners, in the form of an opt-out right to withdraw specific categories of rights from government oversight in key areas where sound recording owners enjoy such benefits—namely, interactive streaming uses and downloads.
- *Extend the public performance right in sound recordings to terrestrial radio broadcasts.* As the Copyright Office has stated repeatedly for many years, the United

States should adopt a terrestrial performance right for sound recordings. Apart from being inequitable to rightsholders—including by curtailing the reciprocal flow of royalties into the United States—the exemption of terrestrial radio from royalty obligations harms competing satellite and internet radio providers who must pay for the use of sound recordings. Assuming Congress adopts a terrestrial performance right, it would seem only logical that terrestrial uses should be included under the section 112 and 114 licenses that govern internet and satellite radio.

- *Fully federalize pre-1972 sound recordings.* As it concluded in its 2011 report on the topic, the Copyright Office believes that pre-1972 recordings—currently protected only under state law—should be brought within the scope of federal copyright law, with the same rights, exceptions, and limitations as more recently created sound recordings. The lack of federal protection for pre-1972 sound recordings impedes a fair marketplace. Record labels and artists are not paid for performances of these works by digital services, which (at least until recent court rulings under state law) were considered free from copyright liability on the sound recording side. At the same time, the owners of the musical works embodied in these sound recordings are paid for the same uses.

- *Adopt a uniform market-based ratesetting standard for all government rates.* While in some cases the law provides that the ratesetting authority should attempt to emulate a free market, in other cases it imposes a more policy- oriented approach that has led to below-market rates. There is no policy justification for a standard that requires music creators to subsidize those who seek to profit from their works. Accordingly, the Office calls for adoption of a single rate standard—whether denominated "willing buyer/willing seller" or "fair market value"—that is designed to achieve rates that would be negotiated in an unconstrained market.

C. Government's Role in Music Licensing

The government's involvement in the music marketplace is unusual and expansive relative to other kinds of works created and disseminated under the Copyright Act. In many cases, it compels copyright owners to license their works at government-set rates. Regulation of music publishers and songwriters is particularly pervasive: the two most significant areas of their market (mechanical and performance licensing) are subject to mandatory licensing and ratesetting. Antitrust concerns have been the traditional rationale for government intervention. To be sure, where particular actors engage in anticompetitive conduct in violation of antitrust laws, that conduct should be addressed. But compulsory licensing does more than that—it removes choice and control from all copyright owners that seek to protect and maximize the value of their assets.

Regardless of the historical justifications for government intervention, the Copyright Office believes that in today's world, certain aspects of the compulsory licensing processes can and should be relaxed. The below recommendations offer some ideas for how that might be accomplished in the various areas of the market where there is government involvement.

Performing Rights Organizations ("PROs") and the Consent Decrees

Many important issues have been raised in the Department of Justice's ("DOJ's") parallel consideration of the American Society of Composers, Authors and Publishers ("ASCAP") and Broadcast Music, Inc. ("BMI") consent decrees. The Office endorses that review, and—in light of the significant impact of the decrees in today's performance-driven music market—hopes it will result in a productive reconsideration of the 75-year-old decrees. At the same time, the Copyright Office observes that it is Congress, not the DOJ, that has the ability to address the full range of issues that encumber our music licensing system, which go far beyond the consent decrees. In the area of performance rights, the Office offers the following recommendations:

- *Migrate all ratesetting to the Copyright Royalty Board ("CRB").* The Copyright Office believes that allegations of anticompetitive conduct are worthy of evaluation (and, if appropriate, remedial action) separate and apart from the determination of fair rates for musical works. Each of these two critical policy objectives merits government attention in its own right. Accordingly, the Office proposes that the function of establishing rates for the public performance of musical works—currently the province of federal district courts under the consent decrees—be migrated to the CRB. Industry ratesetting is, of course, a primary function of the CRB, and the CRB has the benefit of experience assessing a broader spectrum of rate-related questions than the federal rate courts, as well as specific expertise in copyright law and economics.

- *Repeal section 114(i).* Regardless of whether PRO ratesetting is migrated to the CRB, as further discussed below, the Copyright Office endorses the proposal that the prohibition in section 114(i) that currently prevents ratesetting tribunals from considering sound recording performance royalties be eliminated. Originally designed as a protective measure to benefit songwriters and publishers, it appears to be having the opposite effect.

- *Streamline interim ratesetting and require immediate payment of royalties.* Under the consent decrees, anyone who applies for a license has the right to perform musical works in a PRO's repertoire—without paying the PRO any compensation—pending the completion of negotiations or rate court proceedings resulting in an interim or final fee. The problem is exacerbated by the substantial burden and expense of litigating even an interim rate in federal court. The Copyright Office believes that to the extent a licensing entity is required to grant a license upon request, there should be a streamlined mechanism to set an interim royalty rate, and that the licensee should have to start paying immediately.

- *Permit opt-out from PROs for interactive streaming.* The Office believes that music publishers should be able to withdraw specific categories of licensing rights from their authorizations to the PROs. At least for now, the Office believes that withdrawal of performance rights should be limited to digital rights equivalent to those that the record labels are free to negotiate outside of sections 112 and 114—essentially, interactive streaming rights for digital services. Publishers that chose to opt out would be required to provide a list of their withdrawn works and other pertinent information to a central source, such as the general music rights organization ("GMRO") discussed below. In addition, the Office believes that songwriters affiliated with that publisher should retain the option of receiving their writer's share of royalties directly through their chosen licensing collective.

- *Allow bundled licensing of mechanical and performance rights.* Industry participants support increased bundling of rights—i.e., reproduction, distribution, and performance rights—in unified licenses to facilitate greater licensing efficiency. Although bundling of sound recording rights occurs as a matter of course, various legal restrictions have prevented that same development on the musical work side. The Office believes that the government should pursue appropriate changes to the legal framework to encourage bundled licensing, which could eliminate redundant resources on the part of both licensors and licensees. This could include allowing the PROs and other entities to become music rights organizations ("MROs"), which would be authorized to license both performance and mechanical rights.

Mechanical Licensing and Section 115

Study participants highlighted the serious shortcomings of the 106-year old compulsory license for "mechanical" reproductions of musical works (*e.g.*, CDs, vinyl records and downloads) in section 115. On the copyright owner side, parties complained that the mandatory nature of the license does not permit them to control their works or seek higher royalties. On the licensee side, parties criticized section 115's requirement of song-by-song licensing, a daunting task in a world where online providers seek licenses for millions of works. In light of these concerns, the Office offers the following recommendations:

- *Permit collective licensing of mechanical rights but with an opt-out right for interactive streaming and download uses.* The Office is sympathetic to music publishers' arguments for elimination of the compulsory license in section 115 in favor of free market negotiations. But in light of the diffuse ownership of musical works, it seems clear that some sort of collective system would be necessary even in section 115's absence. The Office thus believes that, rather than eliminating section 115 altogether, section 115 should instead become the basis of a more flexible collective licensing system that will presumptively cover all mechanical uses except to the extent individual music publishers choose to opt out. At least initially, the mechanical opt-out right would extend to interactive streaming rights and downloading activities—uses where sound recording owners operate in the free market (but not physical goods, which have somewhat distinct licensing practices). As envisioned by the Office, the collective system would include MROs (as noted, with the ability to represent both performance and mechanical rights), a GMRO (that would collect for works or shares not represented by an MRO or covered by a direct deal), and individual publishers that choose to opt out. Licensees could thus achieve end-to-end coverage through the combination of MROs, the GMRO, and direct licensors.

- *Establish blanket licensing for digital uses under section 115.* To further facilitate the rights clearance process and eliminate user concerns about liability to unknown rightsowners, the Office believes that mechanical licensing, like performance licensing, should be offered on a blanket basis by those that administer it. This would mean that a licensee would need only to file a single notice with an MRO to obtain a repertoire-wide performance and mechanical license from that licensing entity. The move to a blanket system would allow marketplace entrants to launch their services—and begin paying royalties—more quickly.

- *CRB ratesetting on an "as-needed" basis.* The Office believes that the CRB should continue to set rates under the section 115 license, though with an important modification: as is now the case with performance rights, rather than establish rates across the board every five years, the CRB would set rates for particular uses only on an as-needed basis when an MRO and licensee were unsuccessful in reaching agreement. Other interested parties (such as other MROs and other users) could choose to join the relevant proceeding, in which case those parties would be bound by the CRB-determined rate.

- *Ensure copyright owners possess audit rights.* Publishers have long complained about the lack of an audit right under section 115. In that regard, section 115 is an outlier—such audit rights have been recognized under other statutory licenses. The Office believes that the mechanical licensing system should be amended to provide for an express audit right, with the particular logistics to be implemented through regulation.

- *Maintain audiovisual uses in the free market.* Record companies proposed extending compulsory blanket licensing to certain consumer audiovisual products—such as music videos, album cover videos, and lyric videos—uses that have traditionally required a synchronization license negotiated in the free market. The Office is sympathetic to the labels' concerns, but cannot at this time recommend that consumer synch uses be incorporated into a government- supervised licensing regime. The Office does not perceive a market failure that justifies creation of a new compulsory license, and the market appears to be responding to licensing needs for consumer audiovisual products.

Section 112 and 114 Licenses

One of the few things that seems to be working reasonably well in our licensing system is the statutory license regime under sections 112 and 114, which permits qualifying digital services to engage in noninteractive streaming activities at a CRB-determined (or otherwise agreed) rate. Although the differing ratesetting standards for these licenses—as well as some of the rates established under those standards—have been a source of controversy, from the record in this study, the licensing framework itself is generally well regarded. Notwithstanding the comparatively positive reviews of the section 112 and 114 licenses, there are a few relatively minor improvements that the Office believes should be considered:

- *Consider ratesetting distinction between custom and noncustom radio.* In 2009, the Second Circuit ruled that personalized radio services are eligible for the section 112 and 114 licenses. Although the Office has some reservations about that interpretation, there appears to be no overwhelming call to remove custom radio from the statutory regime. Nonetheless, within that regime, it may be appropriate to distinguish between custom and noncustom radio, as the substitutional effect of personalized radio on potentially competing interactive streaming services may be greater than that of services offering a completely noncustomized experience. While the issue could be addressed legislatively, this does not appear to be necessary, as the CRB has the discretion to set different rate tiers today when the record supports such an outcome.

- *Allow fine-tuning of technical aspects of the license through the exercise of regulatory authority.* Internet services have criticized a number of the detailed limitations that section 114 imposes on compulsory licensees. These include the so-called "sound recording performance complement," a restriction that limits the frequency with which songs from the same album or by the same artist may be played by the service, as well as a prohibition against announcing upcoming selections. But for the fact that they appear in the statute itself, such details would seem to be more appropriately the province of regulation. As suggested more generally below, Congress may wish to commit nuances like these to administrative oversight by the Copyright Office.
- *Consider permitting SoundExchange to process record producer payments.* Record producers—who make valuable creative contributions to sound recordings—are not among the parties entitled by statute to direct payment by SoundExchange. In some cases, an artist may provide a letter of direction requesting SoundExchange to pay the producer's share of income from the artist royalties collected by SoundExchange, which SoundExchange will honor. It has been suggested that this informal practice be recognized through a statutory amendment. Though it would be beneficial to hear more from artists on this issue, the Office agrees that in many instances producers are integral creators and that the proposal therefore merits consideration.
- *Allow SoundExchange to terminate noncompliant licensees.* Unlike section 115, sections 112 and 114 do not include a right to terminate a licensee that fails to account for and pay royalties. The Office does not see a justification for continued licensing of a user that is not meeting its obligations, and agrees that the section 112 and 114 statutory licenses should be amended to include a termination provision akin to that in section 115.

Public Broadcaster Statutory License

- *Create a unified statutory licensing scheme for public broadcasters.* Public broadcasters must engage in a multitude of negotiations and ratesetting proceedings in different fora to clear rights for their over-the-air and online activities. Especially in light of the relatively low royalty rates paid by public broadcasters, Office suggests that the ratesetting processes applicable to public broadcasters be consolidated within a unified license structure under section 118 under the auspices of the CRB, where they would likely be much more efficiently resolved.

D. Licensing Efficiency and Transparency

The Office believes that accurate, comprehensive, and accessible data, and increased transparency, are essential to a better functioning music licensing system. Authoritative data would benefit all participants in the marketplace for sound recordings and musical works, and facilitate a more efficient system. In addition, it is essential to make reliable usage and payment information available to rightsholders. To achieve these twin goals, the Office offers the following recommendations:

- *Establish incentives through the statutory licensing scheme for existing market players to create an authoritative public database.* The Copyright Office believes that any solution to the music data problem should not be built by the government but should instead leverage existing industry resources. Accordingly, the Office recommends that the government establish incentives through the statutory licensing regime to encourage private actors to coordinate their efforts and contribute to a publicly accessible and authoritative database, including by encouraging the adoption and dissemination of universal data standards. To facilitate this process, the Copyright Office should provide regulatory oversight regarding standards and goals.
- *Establish transparency in direct deals.* Throughout the study, a paramount concern of songwriters and recording artists has been transparency in the reporting and payment of writer and artist shares of royalties, especially in the context of direct deals negotiated by publishers and labels outside of the PROs and SoundExchange, which may involve substantial advances or equity arrangements. These concerns should be addressed as part of any updated licensing framework, especially one that allows publishers to opt out of the statutory licensing system and pursue direct negotiations. In the case of direct deals for rights covered by an MRO or SoundExchange, the Office recommends allowing songwriters and artists to elect to receive their shares of royalties from the licensee through their chosen licensing entity.

E. An Updated Music Licensing System

To implement the principles and recommendations laid out above, the Copyright Office is proposing an updated framework for the licensing of musical works. The basic components of this proposal are as follows:

- *MROs.* Under the Office's proposal, except to the extent they chose to opt out of the blanket statutory system, publishers and songwriters would license their public performance and mechanical rights through MROs.
  - An MRO could be any entity representing the musical works of publishers and songwriters with a market share in the mechanical and/or performance market above a certain minimum threshold, for example, 5%. Existing rights organizations, such as ASCAP, BMI, HFA and others, could thus qualify as MROs.
  - Each MRO would enjoy an antitrust exemption to negotiate performance and mechanical licenses collectively on behalf of its members—as would licensee groups negotiating with the MROs—with the CRB available to establish a rate in

case of a dispute. But MROs could not coordinate with one another and would be subject to at least routine antitrust oversight.
- Each MRO would be required to supply a complete list of the publishers, works, percentage shares and rights it represented, as well as the MRO's licensing contact information, to the GMRO, and would be obligated to keep that information current. MROs would not have to share all of their data for purposes of the public database. For example, there would be no need for an MRO to provide contact information for its members (other than those that opted out) since the MRO would be responsible for distributing royalties under the licenses it issued.
- MROs would also be responsible for notifying the GMRO of any members that had exercised opt-out rights by providing the relevant opt- out information, including where a direct license might be sought, so potential licensees would know where to go for license authority.
- *GMRO.* Even though most licensing activity would be carried out by the MROs and directly licensing publishers, the hub of the new licensing structure would be the "general" MRO or GMRO. The GMRO would have certain important responsibilities:
    - First, the GMRO would be responsible for maintaining a publicly accessible database of musical works represented by each MRO, which would incorporate data supplied by the MROs and other authoritative sources. The GMRO would actively gather missing data, reconcile conflicting data, and correct flawed data, and would also provide a process to handle competing ownership claims. In addition to musical work data, the GMRO would also incorporate sound recording data— presumably from SoundExchange—into the public database, and be responsible for developing additional data that matched sound recordings with musical works to facilitate more efficient licensing.
    - Second, the GMRO would also serve as the default licensing and collection agent for musical works (or shares of works) that licensees were unable to associate with an MRO or opt-out publisher. Services with usage-based payment obligations would transmit records of use for unmatched works, along with associated payments and an administrative fee, to the GMRO. The GMRO would then attempt to identify the MRO or individual copyright owners and, if successful, pay the royalties out. If unsuccessful, the GMRO would add the usage record to a public unclaimed royalties list and hold the funds for some period of time—*e.g.*, three years—to see if a claimant came forward. As is the case with SoundExchange, after that period, the GMRO could use any remaining unclaimed funds to help offset the costs of its operations.
- *GMRO funding and resources.* The Copyright Office believes that both copyright owners and users should provide support for the GMRO, as both groups will benefit from its activities. Under the Office's proposal, every MRO, as well as SoundExchange, would be required to contribute key elements of data to create and maintain a centralized music database. MROs would be responsible for allocating

and distributing the vast majority of royalties. In exchange for these contributions on the part of copyright owners, the Office believes that most direct financial support for the GMRO should come from fees charged to users of the section 112, 114 and 115 licenses. Thus, although licensees would be paying royalties to MROs and individual publishers directly—and SoundExchange as well—they would have a separate obligation to pay a licensing surcharge to the GMRO. The surcharge to be paid by statutory licensees could be determined by the CRB based on the GMRO's costs (and without consideration of royalty rates) through a separate administrative process. The surcharge would be offset by administrative fees and other sources of income for the GMRO, including any "black box" funds unclaimed by copyright owners.

- *Copyright Royalty Board improvements.* Under the Copyright Office's proposal, ratesetting by the CRB would shift from a five-year cycle to a system under which the CRB would step in only as necessary when an MRO or SoundExchange and a licensee could not agree on a rate. The new model would create opportunities for combined ratesetting proceedings for noninteractive services (*e.g.*, internet, terrestrial, and satellite radio) encompassing both sound recordings and musical works. The Office recommends other procedural adjustments to the CRB as well—including adjustments to the statutorily prescribed litigation process and its settlement procedures. It would also be worthwhile to remove unnecessary procedural details in the statute that are better left to regulation by the CRB.

- *Regulatory implementation.* The Copyright Office recommends that if Congress acts to restructure the music licensing system, it would be most productive for the legislation to set out the essential elements of the updated system but leave the details to be implemented through regulation by the Copyright Office and, in ratesetting matters, the CRB. Such a construct would likely be more realistic to enact than a highly detailed statutory prescription—especially in the case of music licensing, where the particulars can be overwhelming.

- *Further evaluation.* Should Congress choose to embark upon a series of changes to the licensing system as described above, the Office recommends that the new system be evaluated by the Copyright Office after it has been in operation for a period of several years. Assuming the new licensing framework includes an opt-out mechanism, the efficacy of that process would be of particular interest. Congress could choose to narrow or expand opt-out rights as appropriate.

I. INTRODUCTION

The United States has the most innovative and influential music culture in the world, but our system for enabling the paid use of music—and ensuring compensation for its creators—lags far behind. The structures that evolved in the previous century to facilitate the lawful exploitation of musical works and sound recordings, while perhaps adequate for the era of discs and tapes, are under significant stress. From a copyright perspective, we are trying to deliver bits and bytes through a Victrola.

It is a testament to the irresistible power of music that industry and market participants have done their best to adapt the old methods, including pre-digital government policies, to embrace current technologies and consumer expectations. But the costs of failing to update our outmoded licensing methods are escalating. Even when distributors are perfectly willing to pay licensing fees, they may find it difficult to identify the owners of the music they use. Those seeking to launch new delivery platforms are constrained—and sometimes even defeated—by the complexities and expense of convoluted clearance processes. Perhaps most concerning is that many deeply talented songwriters and developing artists now question whether a career in music is realistic under the current regime.

As might be expected, many of the issues raised by the participants in this study of the music marketplace revolved around government mandates, in particular the role of the antitrust consent decrees governing the licensing of performance rights in musical works by performing rights organizations ("PROs"), the section 115 "mechanical" license for the reproduction and distribution of musical works, and the section 112 and 114 licenses for the digital performance of sound recordings.

There is a profound conviction on the part of music publishers and songwriters that government regulation of the rates for the reproduction, distribution, and public performance of musical works has significantly depressed the rates that would otherwise be paid for those uses in an unrestricted marketplace. The standards employed for the section 115 and PRO ratesetting proceedings—section 801(b)(1)'s four- factor test for mechanical uses and the "reasonable fee" standard of the consent decrees (which cannot take into account sound recording performance rates)—are perceived as producing below-market rates, especially when compared to rates paid for analogous uses of sound recordings. On the other side of the fence, licensees urge that government oversight is essential to forestall alleged monopolistic practices on the part of the PROs and large music publishers.

The PROs are viewed as both as a blessing and a threat. Licensees laud the efficiencies of the blanket licenses they offer while at the same time bemoaning the societies' perceived bargaining position as a result of that very breadth. Songwriters, for their part, are deeply concerned about the potential loss of transparency in reporting and payment, should major publishers opt to withdraw from the PROs and license performance rights directly—as some publishers have suggested they may do in a quest for higher rates than those set by the rate courts under the consent decrees.

With respect to the section 112 and 114 licenses for the performance of sound recordings, the debate has centered on the disparate rate standards for differing classes of digital users—the more malleable 801(b)(1) standard that is applied to satellite radio versus the willing buyer/willing seller standard for competing online radio services—as well as the overall burden and expense of the CRB ratesetting process. Internet radio providers complain that the CRB process has yielded rates that have required them to seek congressional intervention.

There are differing opinions as to how to handle pre-1972 sound recordings, which are currently outside of the ambit of federal copyright law but protected in varying degrees under differing state regimes. Some concur with the Copyright Office's 2011 recommendation that pre-1972 recordings should be brought fully within the scope of federal copyright protection, but others argue for a more limited fix or no fix at all. Meanwhile, since the inception of the study, three courts have held that the public performance of pre-1972 recordings is subject to protection under applicable state law, further complicating the licensing landscape.

And last but not least is the longstanding issue of whether terrestrial radio broadcasters should continue to be exempted under the Copyright Act from paying royalties for the performances of sound recordings that drive their multibillion dollar industry—a debate that has been sharpened as online radio services seek to compete with their terrestrial counterparts.

At the same time, stakeholders widely acknowledge that there is a need for universal data standards to facilitate the identification of musical works and sound recordings, and the licensing process generally. In particular, there is broad recognition of the necessity for reliable data to match sound recordings to the musical works they embody. But there is discord as to how to address these problems. Some market participants are willing to share the data they accumulate with the world, while others are reluctant to do so.

Despite the wide range of viewpoints expressed in the course of this study, the Office's review of the issues has confirmed one overarching point: that our music licensing system is in need of repair. The question, then, is how to fix it, in light of the often conflicting objectives of longtime industry participants with vested interests in traditional business models and infrastructure; digital distributors that do not produce or own music and for which music represents merely a cost of doing business; consumers whose appetite for music through varied platforms and devices only continues to grow; and individual creators whose very livelihoods are at stake. This report seeks to chart a path forward.

Given their complexity and significance, many of the issues addressed below would themselves be worthy of a separate report. But instead of focusing on each particular licensing process as an isolated problem, the goal of this study is to illuminate the system as a whole—including interrelated issues and concerns—to see if there may be a balanced set of changes that could provide benefits to all. Rather than present a detailed legislative proposal, then, with all of the intricacy that would entail, the report instead suggests some key principles and modifications that the Copyright Office believes would be useful in framing a better system.

The ideas described below are thus intended to serve as a useful framework for continuing discussion of how we might reinvent our music licensing system, rather than a fully developed answer. As Congress considers a range of potential amendments to our copyright laws, the Office hopes that interested parties will take advantage of this unique opportunity to improve our music licensing process for the digital age.

A. Study History

In April 2013, Congress, led by the House Judiciary Committee, began a comprehensive review of the nation's copyright laws to evaluate "whether the laws are still working in the digital age."[1] The myriad issues affecting the music industry have been a significant focus of that review.[2]

The Office initiated this study to illuminate critical concerns of the music marketplace and to identify potential avenues for change. On March 17, 2014, the Office published an initial Notice of Inquiry in the Federal Register (the "First Notice") requesting public comment on twenty-four subjects affecting the existing music licensing environment.[3]

The Office received 84 written comments in response to its notice, spanning a broad spectrum of interested parties, including music industry associations, service providers and technology companies, legal scholars, public interest groups, and individual artists and creators.[4]

In June 2014, the Office conducted three two-day public roundtables in Nashville, Los Angeles, and New York City.[5] The roundtables provided participants with the opportunity to share their views on the topics identified in the First Notice and other issues pertaining to our music licensing system and how it might be improved.

In addition, on July 23, 2014, the Office published a second Notice of Inquiry ("Second Notice") requesting further comments on a number of significant issues raised in earlier comments and discussed at the roundtables.[6] The Office received 51 substantive written comments in response to the Second Notice, again representing a wide variety of viewpoints, on these subjects.[7]

B. Licensing and Ratesetting Charts

The Office has prepared a series of charts to illustrate our current systems for licensing of musical works and sound recordings and the ratesetting procedures under the several statutory licenses, as well as how those processes would be altered as a result of the modifications proposed by the Office. These appear at the back of the study in Appendix D. The Office hopes that these charts will prove helpful to readers as they make their way through this report.

II. MUSIC LICENSING LANDSCAPE

Our rules for music licensing are complex and daunting even for those familiar with the terrain. To begin with, our licensing structures must address two different species of copyright—the sound recording and the musical work—residing in a single product. Each of these separate copyrights, in turn, itself represents several different exclusive rights that may be separately licensed, including the rights of reproduction, distribution, public performance, as well as the right to synchronize works with visual content.

The situation is further complicated by the fact that many licensing transactions are regulated by the government. But the government rules have not been implemented in a unified or systematic fashion. Instead, they represent a series of statutory and judicial mandates that came into effect at various points during the last century to address particular concerns of the day. And still more challenging is that not all licensing is conducted according to these government-mandated protocols. Some licensing is permitted to transpire in the private marketplace without government oversight. In addition, there are voluntary workarounds to the government processes—more efficient alternatives that have grown up like trees around the government rules and are now deeply rooted.

This section provides an introduction to our music licensing system and those who participate in it.[8] Before turning to the challenges we face and how they might be addressed, it is important to understand where we are and how we got here.

A. Copyright Overview

1. Brief History of Copyright Protection for Music

Congress passed the first federal copyright act in 1790.[9] That act did not provide express protection for musical compositions (or "musical works" in the parlance of the current Copyright Act), though such works could be registered as "books."[10] Then, in 1831, Congress amended the law to provide expressly that musical works were subject to federal copyright protection.[11]

The 1831 amendment, however, provided owners of musical works with only the exclusive right to reproduce and distribute their compositions, i.e., to print and sell sheet music, because, "[a]t the time, performances were considered the vehicle by which to spur the sale of sheet music."[12] In 1897, Congress expanded the rights of music owners to include the exclusive right to publicly perform their works.[13] With the 1909 Copyright Act, federal copyright protection for musical works was further extended by adding an exclusive right to make "mechanical" reproductions of songs in "phonorecords"—in those days, piano rolls, but in the modern era, vinyl records and CDs. At the same time, Congress limited the new phonorecord right by enacting a compulsory license for this use, a topic that is addressed in greater depth below.[14] And in 1995, Congress confirmed that an owner's exclusive right to reproduce and distribute phonorecords of musical works extends to digital phonorecord deliveries ("DPDs")—that is, the transmission of digital files embodying musical works.[15]

Over time, new technologies changed the way people consumed music, from buying and playing sheet music, to enjoying player pianos, to listening to sound recordings on a phonograph or stereo system.[16] But it was not until 1971, several decades after the widespread introduction of phonorecords, that Congress recognized artists' sound recordings as a distinct class of copyrighted works that were themselves deserving of federal copyright protection.[17] This federal protection, however, was limited to sound recordings fixed on or after February 15, 1972, and, until more recently, protected only the exclusive rights of reproduction, distribution, and preparation of derivative works. No exclusive right of public performance was granted.[18] Then, in 1995, Congress granted sound recording owners a limited public performance right for digital audio transmissions—though, as discussed below, that right was made subject to compulsory licensing under sections 112 and 114 of the Copyright Act.[19]

2. Musical Works versus Sound Recordings

As the above history indicates, a musical recording encompasses two distinct works of authorship: the musical work, which is the underlying composition created by the songwriter or composer along with any accompanying lyrics, and the sound recording, which is the particular performance of the musical work that has been fixed in a recording medium such as CD or digital file. Because of this overlap, musical works and sound recordings are frequently confused. It is important to keep in mind, however, that these are separately copyrightable works.

A musical work can be in the form of sheet music, i.e., notes and lyrics written on a page, or embodied in a phonorecord, i.e.,i,n a recording of the song.[20] A sound recording comprises the fixed sounds that make up the recording. The musical work and sound recording are separately protected, and can be separately owned, under copyright law.

3. Key Players in the Music Marketplace

Musical works and sound recordings can be—and often are—created, owned, and managed by different entities.

a. Songwriters

The authors of a musical work are composers, lyricists and/or songwriters.[21] A songwriter may contribute music, lyrics, or both.

The Songwriters Guild of America ("SGA") and Nashville Songwriters Association International ("NSAI") are well-known trade organizations that represent the general interests of songwriters. Another group, the Society of Composers and Lyricists ("SCL"), represents the interests of songwriters working specifically in the motion picture and television industries.

b. Music Publishers

Songwriters often enter into publishing agreements with music publishers. Under such an arrangement, the publisher may pay an advance to the songwriter against future royalty collections to help finance the songwriter's writing efforts. In addition, the publisher promotes and licenses the songwriter's works and collects royalties on the songwriter's behalf. In exchange, the songwriter assigns a portion of the copyright in the compositions he or she writes during the deal term to the publisher—traditionally 50%, but sometimes less—and the publisher is compensated by receiving a royalty share.[22] In some cases, a musical work has a single songwriter and a single publisher, and dividing royalties is relatively straightforward. But many songs have multiple songwriters, each with his or her own publisher and publishing deal. In such cases, it may be challenging to determine royalty shares—or "splits"—among the various parties.[23]

The three "major" music publishers—Sony/ATV Music Publishing ("Sony/ATV"), Warner/Chappell Music, and Universal Music Publishing Group ("UMPG")—together control over 60% of the music publishing market.[24] There are also a handful of mid-sized music publishers, such as Kobalt Music Group and BMG Chrysalis, and thousands of smaller music publishers, among them self-published songwriters. The National Music Publishers Association ("NMPA") and the Association of Independent Music Publishers ("AIMP") are two major trade organizations representing the interests of music publishers.[25] Another group, Interested Parties Advancing Copyright ("IPAC"), was established in Nashville in 2014 and includes independent publishers, administrators, business managers, and entertainment attorneys.[26]

c. Performing Rights Organizations ("PROs")

Songwriters and publishers almost always associate themselves with a PRO, which is responsible for licensing their public performance rights. The two largest PROs—the American Society of Composers, Authors and Publishers ("ASCAP") and Broadcast Music, Inc. ("BMI")—together represent around over 90% of the songs available for licensing in the United States.[27] ASCAP and BMI operate on a not-for-profit basis and, as discussed below, are subject to antitrust consent decrees that impose constraints on their membership and licensing practices. In ASCAP's case, this includes an express prohibition on licensing any rights other than public performance rights.

In addition to these larger PROs, there are two considerably smaller, for-profit PROs that license performance rights outside of direct government oversight. Nashville-based SESAC, Inc. was founded in the 1930s.[28] SESAC's market share of the performance rights market is unclear, but appears to be at least 5% and possibly higher.[29] Global Music Rights ("GMR"), a newcomer to the scene established in 2013, handles performance rights licensing for a select group of songwriters.[30] While ASCAP and BMI's consent decrees prohibit them from excluding potential members who are able to meet fairly minimal criteria,[31] SESAC and GMR have no such restriction and add new members by invitation only.[32]

d. Mechanical Rights Administrators

As examined in more depth below, the right to make and distribute phonorecords of musical works—i.e., the mechanical right—is subject to compulsory licensing under section 115 of the Act. But in practice, because of the administrative burdens imposed by the license—including service of a notice on the copyright owner and monthly reporting of royalties on a song-by-song basis—mechanical licensing is often handled via third-party administrators.[33] The oldest and largest such organization is the Harry Fox Agency, Inc. ("HFA"), which was established by the NMPA in 1927 and today represents over 48,000 publishers in licensing and collection activities.[34] Mechanical licenses issued by HFA incorporate the terms of section 115, but with certain variations from the statutory provisions.[35] Another entity that assists with mechanical licensing is Music Reports, Inc. ("MRI"), which prepares and serves statutory notices on behalf of its clients and administers monthly royalty payments in keeping with the requirements of section 115.[36] Mechanical licenses are also issued and administered directly by music publishers in many instances.

e. Recording Artists and Producers

The creators of sound recordings typically include recording artists—that is, the singer or members of the band who are featured in the recording. The recording process is often managed by a producer, who supervises and contributes overall artistic vision to the project. Other "nonfeatured" musicians and vocalists may add their talents to the recording as well. Except with respect to digital performance rights falling under the section 114 statutory license,[37] featured artists are typically paid under their record company contracts, while nonfeatured performers are usually compensated at an hourly rate based on their work on specific projects.[38] Producers may be paid a flat fee for their efforts and/or may be paid a royalty share by the featured artist out of the artist's earnings.[39]

The organization SoundExchange collects and pays royalties to featured and nonfeatured artists (as well as to record companies) for noninteractive streaming uses under the section 112 and 114 statutory licenses, and advocates for their interests in relation to those uses.[40] The Recording Academy, also known as the National Academy of Recording Arts and Sciences ("NARAS")—the organization responsible for the GRAMMY awards—represents musicians, producers, recording engineers, and other recording professionals on a wide range of industry matters.[41] The Future of Music Coalition ("FMC") advocates on behalf of individual music creators.[42] The American Federation of Musicians of the United States and Canada ("AFM") and Screen Actors Guild-American Federation of Television and Radio Artists ("SAG-AFTRA") are labor unions that represent the interests of nonfeatured musicians and vocalists.[43]

f. Record Companies

Most commercially successful sound recordings are the product of contractual relationships between recording artists and record labels.[44] Though levels of responsibility vary according to the specifics of individual recording contracts, a record label's usual role is to finance the production of sound recordings, promote the recordings (and sometimes the recording artists themselves), and arrange to distribute the recordings via physical and digital distribution channels.[45] Except in the case of noninteractive streaming uses that qualify for the section 112 and 114 licenses, record labels typically handle the licensing for the sound recordings they own.

In modern industry parlance, there are two classes of record labels: "major" labels and "independent" labels.[46] There are currently three major record labels: Universal Music Group ("UMG"), Sony Music Entertainment, Inc. ("SME"), and Warner Music Group ("WMG").[47] Independent labels are entities that are not wholly owned by one of the three major record labels. In the United States, there are currently hundreds of independent labels, which account for roughly 35% of domestic recording industry revenues.[48]

One notable feature of the modern music marketplace is the extent of common corporate ownership of major record labels and major music publishers: UMPG is owned by UMG (which in turn is owned by French media conglomerate Vivendi); the Sony Corporation owns SME and half of Sony/ATV; and Warner/Chappell Music is a division of WMG.[49]

The Recording Industry Association of America ("RIAA") and the American Association of Independent Music ("A2IM") are the two primary trade organizations representing the interests of record labels. The International Federation of the Phonographic Industry ("IFPI") represents record labels globally.[50] As noted above, SoundExchange—originally a division of the RIAA and later spun off as an independent entity[51]—represents the interests of the record labels in relation to the section 112 and 114 licenses.

g. Music Providers

There are a number of organizations that represent the interests of the thousands of music broadcasters and distributors—including radio and television stations, digital music companies, and physical and online record stores.

The National Association of Broadcasters ("NAB") is the main trade organization representing terrestrial (AM/FM) radio and television broadcasters.[52] Broadcasters have also established a number of "music license committees" that collectively negotiate licensing arrangements with the PROs. These include the Radio Music License Committee ("RMLC"),[53] the Television Music License Committee ("TMLC"),[54] the National Religious Broadcasters Music License Committee ("NRBMLC") and the National Religious Broadcasters Noncommercial Music License Committee ("NRBNMLC").[55] National Public Radio ("NPR") operates and advocates on behalf of public radio stations.

The Digital Media Association ("DiMA") is a national trade organization that advocates for digital music and media companies, such as Pandora, Rhapsody, Apple, and YouTube.[56]

CTIA–The Wireless Association ("CTIA")[57] represents the wireless communications industry, and the Computer and Communications Industry Association ("CCIA") represents a broad range of technology companies.[58]

Music Business Association ("Music Biz"), formerly the National Association of Recording Merchandisers, includes many physical and digital distributors of music in its membership.[59]

h. Consumers

Last but not least, there are music fans. As digital technologies continue to evolve, individual users interact with music more and more in ways that implicate copyright— they copy it, share it, and remix it with other content.

A number of groups represent the interests of music consumers in policy matters, including Public Knowledge and the Consumer Federation of America ("CFA").[60]

B. Licensing Musical Works

1. Exclusive Rights in Musical Works

The owner of a musical work possesses exclusive rights under the Copyright Act, including the right to authorize others to exploit the following exclusive rights: the right to make and distribute copies (*e.g.*, sheet music) or phonorecords (*e.g.*, CDs and digital audio files) of the work (the so-called "mechanical" right);[61] the right to create derivative works (*e.g.*, a new work based on an existing composition);[62] the right to display the work publicly (*e.g.*, by posting lyrics on a website);[63] and the right to perform the work publicly (*e.g.*, in a live venue or broadcast).[64] Although it is not specified in section 106 of the Act, as a matter of business practice, the music industry also recognizes the right to synchronize musical works to visual content (*e.g.*,in a music video). The synchronization (or "synch" right) is a species of the reproduction right and may also implicate the derivative work right.[65]

The music industry relies on different entities to license and administer rights in musical works, principally because of a variety of legal restrictions and industry practices that have grown up over time. This balkanized licensing scheme was not overly problematic during the analog age, when determining the boundaries between rights was relatively straightforward. In pre-digital days, radio and record distributors represented distinct commercial channels with different licensing needs. Today, however, digital providers often merge these roles. As a result, the demarcations between traditional licensing categories are no longer as clear— especially with respect to the relation between reproduction and distribution rights, on the one hand, and public performance, on the other. The current complexity of the music licensing marketplace is attributable at least in part to the blurring of the traditional lines of exploitation.

2. Reproduction and Distribution Rights

a. Historical Background

Until the early twentieth century, owners of musical works were compensated primarily through the reproduction and distribution of sheet music. Sales of sheet music were a significant source of revenue for music publishers for a long time.[66] And prices for sheet music were, as they are today, set in the free market.[67]

By the early 1900s, however, technological advances made music available for the first time via "mechanical" renderings of songs captured in player piano rolls and phonograph records.[68] Although music publishers insisted that physical embodiments of their works were copies, the Supreme Court held otherwise in the 1908 case *White-Smith Music Publishing v. Apollo*, reasoning that such reproductions were not in a form that human beings could "see and read."[69]

With the enactment of the 1909 Copyright Act, however, Congress overrode the Court's decision and recognized copyright owners' exclusive right to make and distribute, and authorize the making and distribution, of phonorecords—i.e., mechanical reproductions—of musical works.[70] At the same time, Congress was concerned about a lack of competition in the marketplace—in particular, it was alleged that the Aeolian Company, a manufacturer of player pianos, was seeking to buy up exclusive rights from publishers to create a monopoly for piano rolls.[71] To address that concern, Congress simultaneously created a compulsory license for mechanical reproductions of musical works—the first compulsory license in U.S. copyright law—establishing a statutory rate of 2 cents per copy.[72]

Though it has been amended several times, the 1909 compulsory license, originally set forth in section 1(e) of the Act,[73] continues in force today. In the Copyright Act of 1976, Congress recodified the compulsory license in section 115, and raised the statutory rate to 2.75 cents.[74] At that time, Congress also created the Copyright Royalty Tribunal ("CRT")—with five commissioners appointed by the President—to adjust the royalty rate thereafter.[75] The CRT was replaced in 1993 by the Copyright Arbitration Royalty Panel ("CARP") system; rather than permanent appointees, the CARP arbitrators were convened for specific rate proceedings.[76] The CARP system, in turn, was replaced in 2004 by the current system, the Copyright Royalty Board ("CRB"), which is composed of three administrative judges appointed by the Librarian of Congress.[77]

In 1995, Congress enacted the Digital Performance Right in Sound Recordings Act of 1995 ("DPRSRA"), which, in addition to granting a digital performance right for sound recordings, amended section 115 to expressly cover the reproduction and distribution of musical works by digital transmission, or DPDs.[78] The 1995 legislation recognized what is often referred to as "pass-through" licensing for DPDs, in that it allows a section 115 licensee, such as a record label, to authorize a third-party service to distribute DPDs of the works covered under its license.[79]

Significantly, the express recognition of digital transmissions of musical works as a right covered by section 115 led to a lengthy rulemaking proceeding commenced by the Copyright Office in 2001 to determine the scope and application of the section 115 compulsory license with respect to various uses, which included the question whether interactive streaming services were required to procure mechanical licenses under section 115 in addition to performance licenses.[80] In 2008, recognizing that streaming services make and rely upon server copies and other reproductions of musical works in order to operate, the Office concluded that streaming services could utilize the section 115 compulsory licensing process to cover the reproductions made to facilitate streaming.[81] In 2009, the CRB adopted the first statutory rates and terms for interactive streaming services.[82] As a result of these developments, on-demand streaming services seek both mechanical and PRO licenses for the musical works they use.

b. Mechanical Rights Licensing

Statutory Licensing

Under section 115, those who seek to make and distribute reproductions of a musical work may obtain a license to do so by serving a notice of intent ("NOI") on the copyright owner, no later than thirty days after making, and before distributing, any phonorecords.[83] Once a person has served the NOI, the person must provide statements of account and pay the statutorily prescribed royalties on a monthly basis.[84] If the name and address of the owner of the work cannot be identified from the public records of the Copyright Office, the user may file the NOI with the Office.[85] In that case, the user must pay a filing fee to the Office but does not need to deposit royalties.[86]

The compulsory license under section 115 is available only after a recording has been made and distributed to the public under the authority of the copyright owner.[87] Consequently, the initial recording of a musical work, or "first use," does not fall under the compulsory license, and the copyright owner has the authority to determine whether and how the work is first reproduced and distributed. Once a work is eligible for statutory licensing, section 115 limits the way the work can be exploited. A section 115 license includes the right to make a musical arrangement of the song but does not permit the user to change the basic melody or fundamental character of the work.[88]

As noted above, the CRB is the administrative body responsible for establishing statutory rates and terms under the section 115 license, a process that by statute takes place every five years.[89] While copyright owners and users are free to negotiate voluntary licenses that depart from the statutory rates and terms, in practical effect the CRB-set rate acts as a ceiling for what the owner may charge. Rates for the license are established under a standard set forth in section 801(b)(1) of the Copyright Act, which requires the CRB to weigh several policy-oriented objectives:

(A) To maximize the availability of creative works to the public.
(B) To afford the copyright owner a fair return for his creative work and the copyright user a fair income under existing economic conditions.
(C) To reflect the relative roles of the copyright owner and the copyright user in the product made available to the public with respect to relative creative contribution, technological contribution, capital investment, cost, risk, and contribution to the opening of new markets for creative expression and media for their communication.
(D) To minimize any disruptive impact on the structure of the industries involved and on generally prevailing industry practices.[90]

The rates currently applicable under section 115 were the result of an industry-wide negotiated agreement that was submitted to the CRB as a settlement of the most recent ratesetting proceeding.[91] The current rate to make and distribute permanent downloads or physical phonorecords of a musical work is 9.1 cents per copy.[92] For ringtones, the rate is 24 cents per use.[93] The royalty rate to make reproductions of musical works in connection with interactive streaming, limited download services, and certain other services is a percentage of the service's revenue ranging from 10.5% to 12%, subject to certain minimum royalty floors, and after deducting royalties paid by the service for the public performance of those works.[94] It may seem counterintuitive that ringtones— which typically use only short excerpts of musical works—have a significantly higher royalty rate than full-length reproductions. Because ringtones abbreviate the full-length work, it was not immediately clear whether ringtones were eligible for the section 115 license. As a result, many ringtone sellers entered into privately negotiated licensing arrangements with publishers at rates well above the statutory rate for the full use of the song.[95] In 2006, the Copyright Office resolved the section 115 issue, opining that ringtones were subject to compulsory licensing.[96] But in the ensuing ratesetting proceeding before the CRB, music publishers were able to introduce the previously negotiated agreements as marketplace benchmarks, and as a result secured a much higher rate for ringtones than the rate for full songs.[97]

Voluntary Licenses

Section 115 provides that a license that is voluntarily negotiated between a copyright owner and user will be given effect in lieu of the rates and terms set by the CRB.[98] Although the use of the section 115 statutory license has increased in recent years with the advent of digital providers seeking to clear large quantities of licenses, mechanical licensing is still largely accomplished through voluntary licenses that are issued through a mechanical licensing agency such as HFA or by the publisher directly.[99] While HFA and other licensors typically incorporate the key elements of section 115 into their direct licenses, they may also vary those terms to some degree, such as by permitting quarterly accountings rather than the monthly statements required under the statute.[100] That said, as observed above, the terms of the statutory license act as a ghost in the attic, effectively establishing the maximum amount a copyright owner can seek under a negotiated mechanical license.[101]

Recent Reform Efforts

The last significant legislative effort to modernize mechanical licensing took place nearly a decade ago. In 2006, Representatives Lamar Smith and Howard Berman introduced the Section 115 Reform Act ("SIRA").[102] SIRA would have created a blanket mechanical license for digital services, while leaving the remainder of section 115 intact for physical reproductions (and also not affecting performance rights).

SIRA included several notable features.[103] It would have established a "general designated agent" with the possibility of additional designated agents provided they represented at least 15% of the music publishing market. Copyright owners would elect to be represented by a designated agent, with the general designated agent representing any copyright owners that failed to make such an election. Each designated agent would have been required to maintain a searchable electronic database of musical works represented by that agent. The cost of establishing such databases would have been shared by designated agents and licensees, with cost-sharing amounts determined by the CRB. The CRB would also have established rates and terms for the license itself, and there would have been an interim ratesetting mechanism for new types of services. There were also provisions addressing distribution of unclaimed funds and audit rights. SIRA enjoyed support from key industry participants, including NMPA, DiMA, SGA, and the PROs.[104] Although the bill was forwarded to the full Judiciary Committee, due to opposition from other parties, it was not reported out.[105]

SIRA followed—and was perhaps an industry response to—an earlier 2005 proposal from the Copyright Office. Then-Register of Copyrights Marybeth Peters testified before

Congress to propose a "21st Century Music Reform Act."[106] Among other things, that proposal would have effectively repealed the section 115 statutory license, and would have authorized the establishment of "music rights organizations" ("MROs") that could license both performance and mechanical rights on a blanket basis. The proposal also conditioned an MRO's recovery of statutory damages on the MRO having made publicly available the list of works it was authorized to license. While industry participants agreed in principle with the basic goals of the Copyright Office's proposal, they expressed concerns about many of its specifics, including the lack of a limit on the number of MROs, antitrust issues, and administrative burdens.[107]

3. Public Performance Rights

a. The PROs

As mentioned above, although musical compositions were expressly made subject to copyright protection starting in 1831, Congress did not grant music creators the exclusive right to publicly perform their compositions until 1897.[108] Though this right represented a new way for copyright owners to derive profit from their musical works, the sheer number and fleeting nature of public performances made it impossible for copyright owners to individually negotiate with each user for every use, or detect every case of infringement.[109] ASCAP was established in 1914, followed by other PROs, to address the logistical issue of how to license and collect payment for the public performance of musical works in a wide range of settings.[110]

Today, the PROs provide various different types of licenses depending upon the nature of the use. Anyone who publicly performs a musical work may obtain a license from a PRO, including terrestrial, satellite and internet radio stations, broadcast and cable television stations, online services, bars, restaurants, live performance venues, and commercial establishments that play background music.

Most commonly, licensees obtain a blanket license, which allows the licensee to publicly perform any of the musical works in a PRO's repertoire for a flat fee or a percentage of total revenues.[111] Some users opt for a blanket license due to its broad coverage of musical works and relative simplicity as compared to other types of licenses. Large commercial establishments such as bars, restaurants, concert venues, stores, and hotels often enter into blanket licenses to cover their uses, paying either a percentage of gross revenues or an annual flat fee, depending on the establishment and the type and amount of use.[112] Terrestrial radio stations obtain blanket licenses from PROs as well, usually by means of the RMLC.[113] Many television stations, through the TMLC, also obtain blanket licenses.[114]

Less commonly used licenses include the per-program or per-segment license, which allows the licensee to publicly perform any of the musical works in the PRO's repertoire for specified programs or parts of their programming, in exchange for a flat fee or a percentage of that program's advertising revenue.[115] Unlike a blanket license, the per-program or per-segment license requires more detailed reporting information, including program titles, the specific music selections used, and usage dates, making the license more burdensome for the licensee to administer.[116]

Users can also license music directly from music publishers through a direct license or a source license. A direct license is simply a license agreement directly negotiated between the copyright owner and the user who intends to publicly perform the musical work. Source licenses are commonly used in the motion picture industry, because the PROs are prohibited from licensing public performance rights directly to movie theater owners.[117] Instead, film producers license public performance rights for the music used in films at the same time as the synchronization rights, and pass the performance rights along to the theaters that will be showing their films.[118] In the context of motion pictures, source licenses do not typically encompass non-theatrical performances, such as on television. Thus, television stations, cable companies, and online services such as Netflix and Hulu must obtain public performance licenses from the PROs to cover the public performance of musical works in the shows and movies they transmit to end users.[119]

b. Antitrust Oversight

Basic Antitrust Principles

Unlike the mechanical right, the public performance of musical works is not subject to compulsory licensing under the Copyright Act. But, as described below, ASCAP and BMI are subject to government antitrust regulation through longstanding consent decrees. And while neither SESAC nor GMR is subject to such direct antitrust regulation, each, of course, must abide by generally applicable antitrust law, which is enforceable by the government or through private causes of action. SESAC, for example, has recently been the subject of private antitrust suits, as discussed below. A detailed explanation of the antitrust rationale that underlies the PRO consent decrees is beyond the scope of this study. But a brief discussion of some basic antitrust principles may be helpful in understanding the motivation behind the decrees.

Section 1 of the Sherman Antitrust Act prohibits "[e]very contract, combination in the form of trust or otherwise, or conspiracy, in restraint of trade or commerce among the several [s]tates."[120] As the Supreme Court has opined, however, "Congress could not have intended a literal interpretation of the word 'every,'" and as a result, courts "analyze[] most restraints under the so-called 'rule of reason.'"[121] The rule of reason test requires a court to not only find a restraint of trade, but also determine whether that restraint is unreasonable.[122] The Supreme Court has also recognized, however, that "[o]nce experience with a particular kind of restraint enables the Court to predict with confidence that the rule of reason will condemn it, it has applied a conclusive presumption that the restraint is unreasonable."[123] Thus, certain arrangements— including price-fixing agreements—are deemed per se violations of section 1.[124]

A "tying" arrangement is another kind of business practice that raises antitrust concerns. A tying arrangement is "an agreement by a party to sell one product but only on the condition that the buyer also purchases a different (or tied) product."[125] Such arrangements are unlawful "if the seller has 'appreciable economic power' in the tying product market and if the arrangement affects a substantial volume of commerce in the tied market."[126] But as the Federal Trade Commission ("FTC") observes, "[t]he law on tying is changing."[127] While the Supreme Court "has treated some tie-ins as per se illegal in the past, lower courts have started to apply the more flexible 'rule of reason' to assess the competitive effects of tied sales."[128]

Department of Justice Consent Decrees

Since 1941, ASCAP and BMI's licensing practices have been subject to antitrust consent decrees overseen by the Antitrust Division of the DOJ and enforced by federal district courts in New York City.[129] Those consent decrees were implemented in reaction to alleged anticompetitive practices of ASCAP and BMI. Specifically, when originally formed, both PROs acquired the exclusive right to negotiate members' public performance rights, and forbade their members from entering into direct licensing arrangements. Additionally, both offered only blanket licenses covering all of the music in their respective repertoires.[130]

In the 1930s, the DOJ's Antitrust Division investigated ASCAP for anticompetitive conduct—specifically that ASCAP's licensing arrangements constituted price-fixing and/or unlawful tying.[131] The government subsequently filed federal court actions in 1934 and 1941, arguing that the exclusive blanket license—as the only license offered at the time—was an unlawful restraint of trade and that ASCAP was charging arbitrary prices as a result of an illegal copyright pool.[132] While the first case was never fully litigated after the government was granted a mid-trial continuance, the latter action was settled with the imposition of a consent decree in 1941.[133] That consent decree has been modified twice, first in 1950 and most recently in 2001.[134] The United States also pursued antitrust claims against BMI, resulting in a similar consent decree in 1941.[135] The 1941 BMI consent decree was superseded by a new decree in 1966, which was last amended in 1994.[136]

Although the ASCAP and BMI consent decrees are not identical, they share many of the same features. As most relevant here, the PROs may only acquire nonexclusive rights to license members' public performance rights; must grant a license to any user that applies, on terms that do not discriminate against similarly situated licensees; and must accept any songwriter or music publisher that applies to be a member, as long as the writer or publisher meets certain minimum standards.[137]

ASCAP and BMI are also required to offer alternative licenses to the blanket license. One option is the adjustable fee blanket license, a blanket license with a carve-out that reduces the flat fee to account for music directly licensed from PRO members. Under the consent decrees, ASCAP and BMI must also provide, when requested, "through-to- the-audience" licenses to broadcast networks that cover performances not only by the networks themselves, but also by affiliated stations that further transmit those performances downstream.[138] ASCAP and BMI are also required to provide per-program and per-segment licenses, as are described above.[139]

ASCAP is expressly barred from licensing any rights other than its members' public performance rights (i.e., ASCAP may not license mechanical or synchronization rights).[140] Although BMI's consent decree lacks a similar prohibition, in practice BMI does not license any rights other than public performance rights.[141]

Finally, and perhaps most significantly, prospective licensees that are unable to agree to a royalty rate with ASCAP or BMI may seek a determination of a reasonable license fee from one of two federal district court judges in the Southern District of New York.[142] The rate court procedures are discussed in greater detail below.

In response to requests by ASCAP and BMI to modify certain provisions of their decrees, the DOJ's Antitrust Division announced in June 2014 that it would be evaluating the consent decrees, and has solicited and received extensive public comments on whether and how the decrees might be amended.[143] Specifically, both ASCAP and BMI seek to modify the consent decrees to permit partial grants of rights, to replace the current ratesetting process with expedited arbitration, and to allow ASCAP and BMI to provide bundled licenses that include multiple rights in musical works.[144] The DOJ has expressed its intent to "examine the operation and effectiveness of the Consent Decrees," particularly in light of the changes in the way music has been delivered and consumed since the most recent amendments to those decrees.[145] At the same time, the DOJ is conducting a related investigation to determine whether there has been a coordinated effort among music publishers and PROs to raise royalty rates.[146]

Key Antitrust Cases

In addition to the DOJ actions that led to the adoption of the consent decrees, PRO practices have been the subject of private antitrust actions, including a number related to the consent decrees. The decisions in these cases serve to highlight courts' approach to the collective licensing of public performance rights and administration of the consent decrees.

In the 1979 Supreme Court case of *BMI v CBS*, CBS had sued ASCAP and BMI, alleging that the blanket license violated antitrust laws by constituting "illegal price fixing, an unlawful tying arrangement, a concerted refusal to deal, and a misuse of copyrights."[147] Rather than declaring the blanket licenses per se unlawful, the Court held that they should be evaluated under a "rule of reason" test, observing that a blanket license could be useful to address the problem of negotiating thousands of individual licenses. The Court also noted as relevant the fact that there were no "legal, practical, or conspiratorial impediment[s]" to obtaining direct licenses, indicating licensees have a real choice in the direct license as an alternative to the blanket license.[148] On remand, the court of appeals upheld the blanket license under the rule of reason, explaining that it did not unreasonably restrain competition because CBS could feasibly obtain direct licenses from copyright owners.[149]

After the *BMI v. CBS* litigation, a number of other courts examined the blanket license, and sustained it against antitrust challenges under rule-of-reason analysis. In *Buffalo Broadcasting v. ASCAP*, the Second Circuit concluded that, in the context of local television stations, the blanket license did not violate the Sherman Act because per-program licenses, direct licenses, and source licenses were realistic alternatives to the blanket license.[150] A federal district court in the District of Columbia reached a similar conclusion with respect to cable stations.[151]

More recent litigation has involved royalty rate disputes. In 2012, the Second Circuit addressed rate disputes involving ASCAP and BMI, on the one hand, and DMX, a background music service, on the other, regarding the rate to be paid for an adjustable-fee blanket license.[152] In arguing for a lower rate, DMX pointed to direct licenses it had entered into with a number of copyright owners, most of them smaller publishers, on relatively favorable terms for DMX.[153] DMX, however, also relied on a direct license from Sony/ATV, a major music publisher. That deal gave Sony/ATV a pro rata share of the same annual rate as other smaller publishers, but also provided Sony a $2.4 million advance and a $300,000 administrative fee.[154] The court found this and the other direct deals entered into by DMX to be persuasive benchmarks and that the rate courts reasonably considered DMX's direct licenses in their rate determinations. Although the PROs argued that the substantial advance paid to Sony/ATV rendered that license an inadequate basis to set rates for the remainder of publishers covered by PRO licenses, the court of appeals affirmed the rates adopted by the rate courts.[155]

There has also been recent litigation between the PROs and Pandora, the internet radio service. In 2011 and 2013, respectively, in response to demands by their major publisher members, ASCAP and BMI both amended their rules to allow music publishers to withdraw from PRO representation the right to license their public performance rights for "new media" uses—i.e., digital streaming services—while still allowing the PROs to license to other outlets on their behalf.[156] As a result, Pandora—faced with a potential loss of PRO licensing authority for the major publishers' catalogs—proceeded to negotiate licenses directly with EMI Music Publishing Ltd. ("EMI"),[157] Sony/ATV and UMPG at varying rates that brought the publishers higher fees than those they were receiving under the PRO system. Pandora, however, challenged the publisher's partial withdrawal of rights before both the ASCAP and BMI rate courts. In each case—though applying slightly differing logic—the court ruled that under the terms of the consent decrees, music publishers could not withdraw selected rights; rather, a publisher's song catalog must be either "all in" or "all out" of the PRO.[158]

Following these rulings, the district court held a bench trial and issued a decision on the merits of the rate dispute between ASCAP and Pandora.[159] Relying on Pandora's negotiated agreements with the major publishers as benchmarks, ASCAP sought a rate of 1.85% of revenues for 2011-2012, 2.50% for 2013, and 3.00% for 2014-2015.[160] The court determined that a rate of 1.85% of revenues with no increase was appropriate for the entire period. In so concluding, the court rejected ASCAP's reliance on the higher-priced licensing agreements with the major publishers, concluding that Sony/ATV and UMPG had engaged in improper negotiation tactics, such as declining to provide lists of the works the publishers represented so that Pandora could remove those works from its service in the event of a failure to reach agreement.[161] The *Pandora* decision is addressed in greater depth in Part IV.

SESAC has also recently been the target of antitrust suits by local television stations and the RMLC, both of which have accused SESAC of engaging in anticompetitive conduct by taking steps to make its blanket license the only viable option for these users, such as by unreasonably and steeply raising the cost of the per-program license and imposing penalties on publishers that engage in direct licensing.[162] In October 2014, the local television stations and SESAC agreed to a settlement in which SESAC agreed to pay $58.5 million to the television stations and to provide a per-program license in addition to a blanket license beginning January 1, 2016.[163] The RMLC suit against SESAC remains pending.

c. Consent Decree Procedures

As noted, ASCAP and BMI are required by their consent decrees to grant a nonexclusive license to publicly perform all of the works in their repertoires to any potential licensee who makes a written application.[164] An entity that seeks a public performance license begins the process by submitting such a request to the PRO. In the absence of an established rate for the applicant's use, the PRO and the applicant may then engage in negotiations regarding the appropriate rate.[165] Significantly, however, under both consent decrees, the mere submission of the application gives the applicant the right immediately to being using the musical works in the PROs' repertoires without payment of any fee or compensation during the pendency of negotiations or a ratesetting proceeding.[166]

If the PRO and licensee are unable to agree on a fee, either party may apply for a determination of a reasonable fee by the applicable rate court.[167] The term "rate court" is a bit of a misnomer, however; as noted above, rate disputes are handled by the federal district judge in the Southern District of New York who has been assigned ongoing responsibility for administration of the relevant consent decree.[168] Currently, the ASCAP decree and ratesetting cases are overseen by Judge Denise Cote, and Judge Louis L. Stanton oversees these matters with respect to BMI.

In a rate court proceeding, the PRO has the burden of proving that the royalty rate it seeks is "reasonable," and if the court determines that the proposed rate is not reasonable, it will determine a reasonable rate itself.[169] In determining a reasonable fee, the rate court is tasked with assessing the fair market value of the license, i.e., "what a license applicant would pay in an arm's length transaction."[170] But antitrust concerns also play a direct role: according to the Second Circuit, the rate courts are also obligated to "tak[e] into account the fact that the PRO, as a monopolist, exercises disproportionate power over the market for music rights."[171]

Since negotiations between PROs and potential licensees—as well as rate court proceedings—can be lengthy, an applicant or a PRO may apply to the rate court to fix an interim rate, pending final determination of the applicable rate. Under the two decrees, such interim fees are supposed to be set by the court within three to four months.[172] Once the rate court fixes the interim rate, the licensee must pay the interim fee retroactively to the date of its license application.[173] Final royalty rates are also applied retroactively.[174]

Significantly, section 114(i) of the Copyright Act prohibits the rate court from considering the licensing fees paid for digital performances of sound recordings in its ratesetting proceedings for the public performance of musical works.[175] This provision was included when Congress created a public performance right for sound recordings with the 1995 enactment of the DPRSRA.[176] In theory, it was intended to protect royalties for the public performance of musical works from being diminished as a result of the grant of a public performance right for sound recordings in digital contexts.[177]

4. Statutory License for Public and Noncommercial Broadcasting

The activities of public and noncommercial educational broadcasters are subject to a hodgepodge of music licensing protocols. Section 118 provides a statutory license that covers such entities' public performances of musical works and reproductions and distributions that enable such performances.[178] The section 118 license, however, applies only to over-the-air broadcasts.[179] Noncommercial broadcasters must clear digital performance rights for musical works (*e.g.*, for internet radio) with the PROs under the provisions of the consent decrees as applicable.[180]

In addition, the section 118 license does not extend to the use of sound recordings by noncommercial broadcasters. For certain reproduction, distribution, and derivative rights for sound recordings, noncommercial broadcasters rely on the exemption in section 114(b), which applies to music "included in educational television and radio programs . . . distributed or transmitted through public broadcasting entities."[181] The 114(b) exemption does not apply to digital performances and related reproductions, however.[182] For those uses, noncommercial broadcasters must obtain section 112 and 114 statutory licenses (discussed below).[183]

C. Licensing Sound Recordings

1. Exclusive Rights in Sound Recordings

The owner of a sound recording fixed after February 15, 1972 possesses a number of exclusive rights under the Copyright Act, including the right to make and distribute copies or phonorecords (*e.g.*, CDs and DPDs) of the work;[184] the right to create derivative works (*e.g.*, a new work based on an existing recording);[185] and the right to perform the work publicly by means of a digital audio transmission (*e.g.*, via internet or satellite radio).[186] The Act exempts public performances of sound recordings by terrestrial radio stations.[187]

2. Reproduction and Distribution Rights

Except in the limited case of noninteractive streaming services that qualify for compulsory licensing under sections 112 and 114, licenses to reproduce and distribute sound recordings—such as those necessary to make and distribute CDs, transmit DPDs and ringtones, or operate an interactive music service—are obtained through direct negotiation between a licensee and the sound recording owner (usually a record label) in the open market.[188]

3. Public Performance Rights

a. Lack of Terrestrial Performance Right

In the 1995 DPRSRA, Congress gave sound recording owners an exclusive public performance right, but one limited to digital audio transmissions, and created the section 112 and 114 statutory licenses to cover satellite radio and noninteractive subscription providers engaged in digital performances.[189] In 1998, Congress extended the compulsory license provisions to include subscription internet radio services.[190] It also expanded the exemption for ephemeral copies for over-the-air broadcasts and created the section 112(e) statutory license.[191] Traditional over-the-air broadcasts, however, are expressly exempted from the sound recording performance right.[192]

Congress drew this legal distinction based on perceived differences between digital and traditional services, believing at the time that traditional broadcasters posed "no threat" to the recording industry, in contrast to digital transmission services.[193] A longstanding justification for the lack of a sound recording performance right has been the promotional effect that traditional airplay is said to have on the sale of sound recordings.[194] In the traditional view of the market, broadcasters and labels representing copyright owners enjoy a mutually beneficial relationship whereby terrestrial radio stations exploit sound recordings to attract the listener pools that generate advertising dollars, and, in return, sound recording owners receive exposure that promotes record and other sales.[195]

As discussed in Section III, apart from the fact that sound recordings help generate billions of dollars annually for terrestrial radio stations, there are significant questions as to whether the traditional view of the market—even if persuasive in earlier times— remains credible today. Notably, in 2014, with 298 million active listeners, terrestrial radio had "more than double the total of Pandora (79 million), Sirius XM (27 million) and Spotify (14 million) combined."[196]

Internationally, the United States is an outlier. Virtually all industrialized nations recognize a more complete public performance right for sound recordings than does the United States.[197] The failure of U.S. law to do the same causes U.S. record companies and artists to forgo an estimated $70-100 million in royalties for foreign exploitations of their works due to the lack of reciprocity.[198]

Significantly, however, in recent years, the nation's largest broadcast company, iHeartMedia (formerly Clear Channel), has entered into licensing agreements with WMG and a number of independent record labels (including Big Machine Records, the record label of Taylor Swift, Rascal Flats, and Tim McGraw) covering both terrestrial and internet radio.[199] While the current CRB rate for streamed radio is a per-play rate, these arrangements apparently feature a percentage-based or other alternative rate structure for both digital and terrestrial uses.[200] Although the terms of these deals remain private, reports indicate that iHeartMedia agreed to pay the smaller labels based on an industry rate of 1% of advertising revenues for terrestrial uses, and perhaps a larger sum to WMG.[201]

In recent years there have also been various legislative efforts to provide for a more complete public performance right,[202] as well as numerous congressional hearings focused on expanding the right to cover traditional broadcast transmissions.[203] The Copyright Office has long supported, and continues to support, the creation of a more complete sound recording performance right.[204]

b. Section 112 and 114 Licenses

The section 114 statutory license allows different types of noninteractive digital music services—free and paid internet radio services,[205] "preexisting" satellite radio services,[206] and "preexisting" music subscription services[207]—to perform sound recordings upon compliance with the statutory license requirements, including the payment of royalties as determined by the CRB.[208] In addition, recognizing that such digital services must make server reproductions of sound recordings—sometimes called "ephemeral" copies—to facilitate their digital transmissions, Congress established a related statutory license under section 112 to authorize the creation of these copies.[209] Rates and terms for the section 112 license are also established by the CRB.

The section 112 and 114 licenses for sound recordings are subject to a number of technical limitations. For instance, services relying on the section 114 statutory license are prohibited from publishing an advance program schedule or otherwise announcing or identifying in advance when a specific song, album or artist will be played.[210] Another example is the "sound recording performance complement," which limits the number tracks from a single album or by a particular artist that may be played during a 3-hour period.[211]

Payment and reporting of royalties under the section 112 and 114 licenses are made to a single non-profit agent: SoundExchange.[212] SoundExchange was established by the RIAA in 2000 and in 2003 was spun off as an independent entity.[213] The Copyright Act specifies how royalties collected under section 114 are to be distributed: 50% goes to the copyright owner of the sound recording, typically a record label; 45% goes to the featured recording artist or artists; 2½% goes to an agent representing nonfeatured musicians who perform on sound recordings; and 2½% to an agent representing nonfeatured vocalists who perform on sound recordings.[214] Section 112 fees are paid by SoundExchange directly to the sound recording owner.[215] Prior to distributing royalty payments, SoundExchange deducts the reasonable costs incurred in carrying out its responsibilities.[216]

Notably, the Act does not include record producers in the statutorily defined royalty split. As a result, record producers must rely on contracts with one of the parties specified in the statute, often the featured recording artist, in order to receive royalties from digital performances.[217] To help facilitate these contracts, SoundExchange has begun processing direct payments to producers based upon written direction from the featured artist.[218]

Since SoundExchange became an independent entity in 2003, it has distributed over $2 billion to artists and labels.[219] The collective engages in outreach to identify and locate artists and labels who may be due royalties from the funds that is has collected.[220] Nonetheless, significant amounts of unclaimed funds have accumulated over time.[221] Press accounts indicate that SoundExchange had unclaimed royalties of approximately $96 million as of the end of 2013.[222] Under the applicable regulations, SoundExchange retains all undistributed royalties for not less than three years, and thereafter may release them to offset its administrative costs and/or to engage in ratesetting and enforcement activities.[223]

Interactive/Noninteractive Distinction

The statutory licensing framework applies only to noninteractive (i.e., radio-style) services; interactive or on-demand services are not covered.[224] The distinction between interactive and noninteractive services has been the matter of some debate. The statute provides that an interactive service is one that enables a member of the public to receive either "a transmission of a program specially created for the recipient," or "on request, a transmission of a particular sound recording, whether or not as part of a program, which is selected by or on behalf of the recipient."[225]

The statutory definition leads to the question whether so-called "personalized" or "custom" music streaming services—services that tailor the music they play to individual user preferences—transmit programs that are "specially created for the recipient." In *Arista Records LLC v. Launch Media, Inc.* ("*Launch Media*"), the Second Circuit held that one such service that played songs for users based on users' individual ratings was not interactive because the service did not displace music sales.[226] Following the *Launch Media* decision, personalized music streaming services such as Pandora and Rdio obtain statutory licenses as noninteractive services for their public performance of sound recordings. The CRB-established rates do not currently distinguish between such customized services and other services that simply transmit undifferentiated, radio-style programming over the internet.

Ratesetting Standards

Notably, under section 114, the rate standard applicable to "preexisting" satellite radio and music subscription services (i.e., those services that existed as of July 31, 1998) differs from that for other services such as internet radio and newer subscription services.[227] This distinction is a legislative artifact. The section 114 statutory license was first created with the enactment of the DPRSRA in 1995, and at the time it applied only to satellite radio and subscription music services. Royalty rates and terms under the more limited 1995 license were governed by the four-factor policy-oriented standard in section 801(b)(1) of the Act—that is, the same standard that had long applied to the section 115 license for musical works.[228] With the enactment of the DMCA in 1998, Congress expanded the section 114 license to include internet radio, created a new statutory license for associated ephemeral recordings in section 112, and created a new ratesetting standard—the "willing buyer/willing seller"—standard. Congress, however, grandfathered preexisting services (i.e., those that existed before the DMCA's enactment) under the old royalty ratesetting standard.

Accordingly, because of the staggered enactment of the section 112 and 114 licenses, royalty rates for a limited set of older services—Sirius XM, as the only preexisting satellite service, and Music Choice and Muzak, as the only preexisting subscription services—are governed by the four-factor standard in section 801(b) of the Act.[229] Meanwhile, for all internet radio and other newer digital music services, and for all ephemeral recordings regardless of the service, the CRB is to establish rates and terms "that most clearly represent the rates and terms that would have been negotiated in the marketplace between a willing buyer and a willing seller."[230] As explained in Section III, the continuing propriety of that disparity is a matter of dispute among stakeholders.

CRB Ratesetting Proceedings

The statutory rates that apply under the section 112, 114 and 115 licenses are established by the CRB.[231] CRB ratesetting proceedings for the section 112, 114, and 115 licenses take place at five-year intervals, and the timing of these proceedings is set by statute.[232]

The CRB is composed of three judges, and Congress imposed strict qualifications for these positions. Each CRB judge is required to have at least seven years of legal experience.[233] The chief copyright royalty judge must have a minimum of five years of experience in adjudications, arbitrations, or court trials. As for the other two judges, one must have significant knowledge of copyright law and the other must have significant knowledge of economics.[234] The Register of Copyrights also plays a role in ratesetting, in that she is responsible for reviewing the CRB's determinations to ensure they are free from material legal error, and may also be called upon to address material questions of substantive law that impact the proceedings.[235] Final ratesetting determinations are appealable to the United States Court of Appeals for the District of Columbia Circuit.[236]

Congress intended the ratesetting process to permit voluntary industry agreements when possible.[237] For example, Congress provided antitrust exemptions to statutory licensees and copyright owners of sound recordings, so that they could designate common agents to collectively negotiate and agree upon royalty rates.[238] The statute also allows for settlement of ratesetting disputes, and mandates a three-month "voluntary negotiation period" at the start of each proceeding before the parties submit their cases.[239] If a settlement is reached among some or all of the participating parties, the Act empowers the CRB to adopt that settlement "as a basis for statutory terms and rates" that will apply to all parties under the statutory license.[240] Notably, however, the Act does not require the CRB to immediately act on such settlements. In the past, the CRB has deferred the adoption of partial settlements until the end of the full ratesetting proceeding.[241]

Absent a settlement, the CRB must proceed to determine the rates and terms of the statutory license. Although the CRB has some flexibility in organizing its procedures, many aspects of its proceedings are dictated by the statute.[242] In many instances, these procedures depart from practices used in ordinary civil litigation. For instance, participating parties must file their written direct cases in support of their requested rates—including witness testimony and supporting exhibits—before any discovery has been taken.[243] Additionally, the statute requires separate direct and rebuttal phases of ratesetting hearings, effectively resulting in two trials.[244] These procedures cannot be altered by the CRB even upon stipulation of the parties.

Royalty Rates

In general, the CRB (like the CARP before it) has adopted "per-performance" rates for internet radio, rather than the percentage-of-revenue rates that are typical in PRO licenses.[245] That per-stream approach has proven controversial. After the CRB's "Webcasting II" decision in 2007, a number of internet radio services and broadcasters complained that the per-performance rates were unsustainable. These concerns led Congress to pass legislation giving SoundExchange the authority to negotiate and agree to alternative royalty schemes that could be binding on all copyright owners and others entitled to royalty payments in lieu of the CRB-set rates.[246] Similar complaints after the CARP's 1998 webcasting decision led Congress to enact analogous legislation in 2002.[247]

In the wake of Congress' actions, SoundExchange reached agreement with a number of internet radio services, in general adopting royalty rates that were more closely aligned with the services' revenues. For example, in 2009, SoundExchange negotiated rates with large commercial "pureplay" internet radio services (i.e., services like Pandora that only transmit over the internet).[248] Under that agreement, those services agreed to pay the greater of 25% of gross revenues or specified per performance rates.[249]

c. Privately Negotiated Licenses

A streaming service that does not fall under the section 112 and 114 licenses—i.e., an interactive service—must negotiate a license with a record company in order to use the label's sound recordings.[250] Since direct licenses are agreed upon at the discretion of the copyright owner and the potential licensee, the license terms can be vastly different from those that apply under the statutory regime. It is common for a music service seeking a sound recording license from a label to pay a substantial advance against future royalties, and sometimes an administrative fee.[251] Other types of consideration may also be involved. For example, the major labels acquired a reported combined 18% equity stake in the on-demand streaming service Spotify allegedly based, at least in part, on their willingness to grant Spotify rights to use their sound recordings on its service.[252]

4. Pre-1972 Sound Recordings

When Congress acted in 1971 to grant federal copyright protection to sound recordings, it extended federal protection prospectively, to recordings created on or after February 15, 1972.[253] Sound recordings fixed before February 15, 1972 are protected by a patchwork of differing state laws.[254]

The disparate treatment of pre-1972 sound recordings under federal versus state law has given rise to a number of significant policy concerns, including issues about the preservation and use of older recordings without the benefit of federally recognized limitations on copyright owners' exclusive rights.[255] These issues were extensively addressed in a 2011 Copyright Office report on potential federalization of copyright for pre-1972 recordings.[256]

In its report, the Office surveyed state laws and determined that "the protections that state law provides for pre-1972 sound recordings are inconsistent and sometimes vague and difficult to discern."[257] In addition, the Office's report concluded that state law did not provide adequate protection for uses that would be considered fair uses under federal law.[258] The Office therefore recommended that pre-1972 recordings be brought within the federal copyright system, which would offer uniform protection to their owners as well as appropriate exceptions and limitations for the benefit of users.

Since the Office's report was released, there have been some notable developments in this area. A significant question has arisen concerning whether state law protection extends to the public performance of pre-1972 recordings.[259] In the context of their negotiated deals with record labels, some major services, including YouTube and Spotify, obtain licenses that cover the use—including the performance—of pre-1972 sound recordings.[260] Some services that use the section 112 and 114 statutory licenses, such as Music Choice,[261] make payments to SoundExchange for use of pre-1972 works pursuant to the same statutory rates and terms applicable under sections 112 and 114.[262] Others, including Sirius XM and Spotify, do not pay royalties either to copyright owners directly or to SoundExchange for performances of pre-1972 sound recordings.[263]

Recently, three courts—two in California and one in New York—have held that the unauthorized public performance of pre-1972 sound recordings violates applicable state law. In the initial case, a California federal district court ruled that Sirius XM infringed rights guaranteed to plaintiffs by state statute.[264] A state court in California subsequently adopted the federal court's reading of the California statute in a second action against Sirius XM.[265] Following these decisions, in a third case against Sirius XM, a federal district court in New York has indicated that the public performance of pre-1972 sound recordings constitutes common law copyright infringement and unfair competition under New York law.[266] Notably, the reasoning employed in these decisions is not expressly limited to digital performances (i.e., internet streaming and satellite radio); they thus could have potentially broad implications for terrestrial radio (currently exempt under federal law for the public performance of sound recordings) as well. In the meantime, similar lawsuits have been filed against other digital providers, including Pandora, Google, Apple's Beats service, and Rdio, alleging the unauthorized use of pre-1972 recordings.[267]

Another issue that has been the subject of recent litigation is whether the DMCA safe-harbor provisions extend to pre-1972 sound recordings.[268] Under section 512(c), an internet service provider is not liable for "infringement of copyright by reason of the storage at the direction of a user of" infringing material, provided that the service meets certain statutory conditions, including take-down requirements.[269] Meanwhile, a separate provision of the Act, section 301(c), preserves state law protection for pre-1972 sound recordings, stating that "any rights or remedies under the common law or statute of any state shall not be annulled or limited by this title until February 15, 2067."[270] In its 2011 report, the Office examined the interplay between these two provisions, and concluded that the DMCA safe harbors did not apply to pre-1972 sound recordings.[271] Although one decision predating the Office's report found that the DMCA safe harbors do apply to pre-1972 sound recordings,[272] more recent decisions have agreed with the Copyright Office that the safe harbors are a creature of federal law and do not limit state law protections.[273]

D. Synchronization Rights

To incorporate music into an audiovisual work—such as a film, video television program, or video game—the creator of that work must obtain synchronization licenses from both the owner of the musical work and the owner of the sound recording. Synchronization (often shortened to "synch") refers to the use of music in "timed- relation" to visual content.[274] Although the Copyright Act does not refer explicitly to a synchronization right, it is generally understood to be an aspect of music owners' reproduction and/or derivative work rights.[275]

The licensing of music for audiovisual works, unlike that for other uses, occurs in the free market for both musical works and sound recordings. The synch market thus stands as a useful counterpoint to the regulated licensing markets discussed above. A notable feature of the synch market is the relatively even balance between royalties paid for the musical works rights and those paid for the sound recording rights. Musical work and sound recording owners are generally paid equally—50/50—under individually negotiated synch licenses.[276]

The synchronization market for uses in commercial works such as film, television programs, and video games appears reasonably efficient and flexible. In addition to in- house resources, a number of intermediaries help handle licensing for those who wish to use music in a new creative work. Music supervisors working for production companies facilitate selection, negotiation, and delivery of music for use in audiovisual productions.[277] Companies such as Greenlight, Dashbox, Cue Songs, and Rumblefish provide online services that offer different songs for synchronization purposes.[278]

An evolving aspect in the music licensing marketplace is the exploitation of music videos that record labels produce to accompany new releases. Traditionally, any royalties for these videos were nominal, as they were created largely to promote sales of records through music video channels such as MTV.[279] But more recently, as videos have become among the most common ways in which consumers wish to enjoy music,[280] there is strong interest in developing this market. Record labels seek to license these professionally created videos—which incorporate musical works—to online providers such as YouTube and Vevo.[281]

In the early 2000s major record labels and publishers entered into "New Digital Media Agreements" ("NDMAs") to allow labels efficiently to obtain licenses from their major publisher counterparts so they can pursue new digital products and exploit music videos in online markets.[282] These licensing arrangements, in turn, became a model for a more recent 2012 agreement between UMG and NMPA that allowed UMG to seek similar rights from smaller independent publishers on an "opt-in" basis. The licensing arrangement includes rights for the use of musical works in "MTV-style" videos, live concert footage, and similar exploitations.[283]

Like the major record labels, larger music publishers have entered into direct licensing relationships with the on-demand video provider YouTube that allow them some amount of control over the use of user-uploaded videos incorporating their music and provide for payment of royalties.[284] Following the settlement of infringement litigation by a class of independent music publishers against YouTube in 2011,[285] NMPA and its licensing subsidiary HFA announced an agreement with YouTube in which smaller publishers could choose to license their musical works to YouTube by opting in to prescribed licensing terms. Those who choose to participate in the arrangement grant YouTube the right to "reproduce, distribute and to prepare derivative works (including synchronization rights)" for videos posted by YouTube's users.[286] The license does not, however, cover the public performance right. Music publishers who opt into the YouTube deal receive royalties from YouTube and have some ability to manage the use of their music through HFA, which administers the relationship and can access YouTube's content identification tools on behalf of individual publishers.[287] Over 3,000 music publishers have entered into this licensing arrangement with YouTube.[288]

Another developing area is the market for so-called "micro-licenses" for music that is used in videos of modest economic value, such as wedding videos and corporate presentations. In the past, income received by rightsholders from licensing such uses might not overcome administrative or other costs. But the market is moving to take advantage of technological developments—especially online applications—that make micro-licensing more viable. This includes the aforementioned services like Rumblefish, but also efforts by NMPA, HFA, and RIAA to license more synchronization rights through programs that allow individual copyright owners to effectuate small licensing transactions.[289]

E. Licensing Efficiency and Transparency

New digital services face a formidable challenge when attempting to license music. One study showed that acquiring the necessary rights to offer a marketable digital music offering[290] requires roughly 18 months of effort, with some entities never able to successfully negotiate the licenses needed to launch their services.[291] One of the key reasons for this complexity is the lack of an "authoritative list of rights holders and the recordings/works they represent."[292]

As discussed in detail in Section III, it is widely acknowledged that reliable, up-to-date information about copyrighted works is a critical prerequisite for efficient licensing in the modern music marketplace. Both copyright owners and music services must be able to uniquely identify particular sound recordings and underlying musical works, along with the dynamic and often fractured ownership status of these distinct works. In addition, they need to be able to pair sound recordings with the musical works they embody. While the industry has made some progress on this front, much remains to be done.

1. Data Standards

One of the initial considerations regarding management of reliable and up-to-date copyright information for musical works and sound recording copyrights is the use of standard identifiers. Fortunately, the music industry already employs a variety of standard identifiers recognized by the International Organization for Standardization ("ISO"), the international standard-setting body. The ISO has established two key standards for the identification of works themselves—the International Standard Music Work Code ("ISWC") for musical works, and the International Standard Recording Code ("ISRC") for sound recordings.[293]

The ISWC represents a unique, permanent, and internationally recognized reference number for the identification of musical works. The standard was developed by the International Confederation of Societies of Authors and Composers ("CISAC"). In the U.S. and Canada, ASCAP is the appointed agency that assigns ISWCs, and works with other representatives of songwriters and publishers to assign ISWCs. As relevant here, to obtain an ISWC, a publisher must provide the following minimum: at least one original title for the work; all songwriters of the work identified by their Interested Parties Information ("IPI") code (discussed below); and whether the work is derived from an existing work.[294] One significant issue with ISWCs, then, is that they cannot be assigned until all the songwriters on a musical work are identified. This has the benefit of assuring that data are complete before an identifier is attached. But it also leads to a substantial lag time before the ISWC for a particular musical work can be assigned— unfortunately, this can occur well after a record is released, so that digital files embodying the individual tracks often will not include ISWCs identifying the underlying musical works.[295] ASCAP and BMI—which also use proprietary numbering systems to track works internally—add ISWCs to their databases as those codes are assigned.[296]

The ISRC was created as a unique, permanent, and internationally recognized reference number for the identification of sound and music video recordings. ISRCs are assigned at the track—rather than album—level. The ISO has appointed IFPI as the international ISRC agency. IFPI in turn, designates national or regional agencies to manage the issuance of ISRCs within a specific country or region. The U.S. ISRC agency is RIAA. RIAA authorizes individual record labels to assign ISRCs to their own recordings.[297] ISRCs are required to be included on digital files provided for the iTunes store and by many other digital platforms.

There are some shortcomings with the ISRC system. First, there is no single definitive U.S. database for ISRCs. Instead, each sound recording owner must maintain its own ISRC records and metadata.[298] Notably, however, SoundExchange, is currently compiling a database of sound recordings performed under the section 112 and 114 licenses, and expects to have good identification and ownership information, including ISRCs, for approximately 14 million recordings in the relatively near term.[299]

In addition, in the case of multiple owners, ISRCs do not require a complete list of owners before assignment of ISRCs. Instead, the ISRC website recommends that multiple owners simply designate one of the owners to assign the ISRC.[300]

The ISO has adopted two other codes to identify the individuals or entities associated with particular works. The IPI code allows a musical work to be associated with the various parties that are involved in its creation, marketing, and administration. IPI codes apply to composers, authors, composer/authors, arrangers, publishers, administrators, and sub-publishers. The codes are assigned by CISAC and are necessary to obtain an ISWC.[301]

The International Standard Name Identifier ("ISNI") is akin to the IPI, but while the IPI scheme is limited to musical works, ISNI is designed to be a global identification system for creators of *all* types of copyrighted works, including authors, songwriters, recording artists, and publishers. The ISNI International Agency was founded in 2010 to develop the standard, with the goal of eventually replacing existing, disparate identification standards, including the IPI.[302] ISNIs are assigned by an international network of registration agencies which rely upon a centralized database to assign and track ISNI identifiers.[303] Over 8 million identities have been registered so far across multiple classes of creators and works.[304] At the moment, however, it appears that most ISNIs are being assigned to literary authors in Europe. It also seems that the number of registration agencies globally remains limited, with only one agency so far in the United States.[305]

The music industry also employs identifiers not associated with ISO, including Universal Product Codes ("UPC"). In the music context, a UPC is a set of numbers, along with a corresponding barcode, that identify a finished music product. A different UPC is usually necessary for each product or version of a product to distinguish among, for example, albums, digital singles, or remixed versions of sound recordings. UPCs are generally required by most major physical retailers, and are now required by the iTunes store and other digital platforms. Record labels generally acquire UPCs from GS1 US, a nonprofit group that sets standards for international commerce. UPCs can also be obtained for free or at a nominal cost from a music distributor such as CD Baby or TuneCore.[306]

In addition to standards that have been or are being developed by international standard-setting entities, there are also private initiatives for identifying music and its owners, for example, through the use of digital acoustic fingerprinting and similar technologies. Examples include Gracenote, Shazam, and The Echo Nest—and perhaps most notably, YouTube. An acoustic fingerprint is a digital rendering of the acoustical properties of a particular sound recording, typically one embodied in a digital file such as an mp3 file. That fingerprint can be stored and searched for matches to other digital music files.[307] An acoustic fingerprint does not, on its own, provide ownership or authorship information, but it can be associated with metadata—such as the standardized identifiers discussed above—that does. One advantage of using digital fingerprints is that while it is relatively trivial to strip metadata such as ISRCs and ISWCs from individual music files, it is arguably more difficult to alter a file's acoustic fingerprint without changing the quality of the audio.[308]

2. Public Data

The U.S. Copyright Office operates a public registration system, which maintains information that can help to identify musical works, sound recordings, and their owners. The registration database, however, is not a comprehensive resource for this purpose. Copyright registration is not mandatory, and so registration records are far from complete. In addition, even when a work has been registered, the registration record is static and thus will not reflect a change in ownership.[309]

The database that houses the Office's registration records is not currently designed to identify or locate works through the use of standard identifiers, such as those described above, and such identifiers are not required in the registration process.[310] As a result, a relatively small number of registration records for musical works and sound recordings reflect these standard identifiers.[311]

Apart from the original registration, some, but not all, copyright owners choose to record assignments and transfers of ownership through the Copyright Office's recordation process. Again, however, such records are far from complete.[312] Nor, due to the historical separation of the registration and recordation systems, is information about recorded documents reliably linked to registration records.[313]

3. Non-Government Databases

Several entities actively develop and maintain their own discrete databases, many of which include standard identifiers and other metadata used by the music industry to track sound recordings and musical works.

As noted above, the RIAA does not keep a central database of sound recordings associated with ISRCs, and so the most comprehensive U.S. sound recording database is likely that of SoundExchange. SoundExchange maintains a database of sound recordings whose uses have been reported to it under the section 112 and 114 licenses, together with information regarding the associated recording artists and labels. This database is not currently publicly accessible or available to be used for licensing purposes.[314]

In the realm of musical works, HFA maintains an extensive database of ownership information and provides an online tool enabling the public to search for songwriter and publisher data for all songs that have been registered by its member publishers.[315] ASCAP, BMI, and SESAC each also have databases covering the compositions in their repertoires that are available to the public through their respective websites.[316] In addition, ASCAP and BMI—along with the Society of Composers, Authors and Music Publishers of Canada ("SOCAN")—are currently collaborating to create a common, authoritative resource for the musical works represented by the several organizations. The joint initiative, called MusicMark, will enable publishers to submit a single file for registration of a song and revise ownership data across the PROs simultaneously, even if the work was co-written by members of different societies. Each PRO will then integrate the registration data into its own repertoire database. By enabling PRO members to more efficiently register musical works through a single interface—including works co-written by songwriters who are members of different PROs—MusicMark should provide a more accurate and synchronized view of copyright information for works in the repertoires of the participating PROs.[317]

While each of these databases represents an important and valuable component of the U.S. music marketplace, because they are separate and separately controlled, they do not offer a comprehensive licensing resource. The HFA and PRO databases are currently searchable by the public only manually, on an individual song basis.[318] In addition, these organizations do not warrant the accuracy or completeness of the information they provide (perhaps because they are relying upon representations by third parties concerning authorship and ownership).[319] Finally, it is unclear what effect publisher withdrawal from the PROs in favor of direct administration of the relevant rights—should it come to pass—might have on the efficacy of the PRO databases.[320]

4. International Efforts

One example of international efforts to address data information deficiencies is (or was) the planned Global Repertoire Database ("GRD") for musical works, to be developed by a working group spearheaded and funded by music publishers and collective management organizations in the EU with the support of the World Intellectual Property Organization ("WIPO"). The GRD was intended to provide a comprehensive and authoritative source of data about the ownership and administration of musical works throughout the world. Its supporters anticipated enabling registrations directly from publishers, composers and collective management organizations, and maintaining a database of those registrations, with procedures to resolve ownership disputes. Unfortunately, despite the acknowledged need for solutions in data sharing, support for the project has waned and the GRD effort has been put on hold (at least for the time being).[321]

A similar effort remains underway with respect to sound recordings. Phonographic Performance Ltd ("PPL"), the U.K. collective rights organization, is building a Global Recordings Database and has so far compiled ownership data on over 5.6 million recordings released in the United Kingdom. PPL intends to expand its efforts by working with major record companies and a range of overseas music licensing companies to include worldwide data.[322]

Another initiative is the U.K.'s Copyright Hub, a web portal connected to a network of rightsholders that aims to make it easier for people to track down and license copyrighted works.[323] At present, the Copyright Hub's functionality is fairly basic, offering helpful information about copyright law and website links to licensing organizations. The plan is to change from a signposting tool into an inquiry router that sends queries to rights managers' databases, and returns results to Hub users.[324] In addition, further development may enable creators to register rights information with third-party registries linked to the Hub.[325]

5. Data Sharing Initiatives

As explained above, data regarding the creation, ownership, and administration of sound recordings and musical works are currently maintained in discrete and independently administered databases. A number of initiatives have attempted to overcome this situation by developing standards related to the communication of information about works among disparate sources. In particular, these initiatives are aimed at allowing relevant information and metadata to be efficiently communicated in a common format so that each party requiring access to the data can understand and automatically process that data without excessive administrative costs.

One such initiative is Digital Data Exchange ("DDEX"), an industry consortium consisting of media companies, music licensing entities, digital service providers and others.[326] DDEX has developed standardized formats in which rights and licensing information is represented and communicated.[327] For example, DDEX offers digital sales reports standards that are being used in the U.K. to provide standard reporting formats between digital music services and the U.K. PRO, PRS for Music.[328] By employing DDEX messaging standards, entities wishing to transact with multiple companies can avoid handling multiple formats and delivery methods.[329]

A similar initiative is WIPO's proposed International Music Registry ("IMR"), which seeks to provide a single access point to the different rights management systems used around the world. WIPO is currently conducting a series of stakeholder discussions on the IMR's scope and structure.[330]

III. CHALLENGES OF THE CURRENT SYSTEM

Perhaps not surprisingly in light of its bewildering array of rights and practices, those who participated in the study identified many significant obstacles in the current music licensing marketplace. As detailed below, stakeholders have a wide range of opinions concerning how best to address them.

Despite the areas of controversy, however, on a somewhat brighter note, study participants were able to articulate some broad areas of consensus as to the overarching principles that should guide any revision of our licensing system, as follows: First, music creators need to be fairly compensated for their efforts.[331] Second, the licensing process needs to be more efficient, including through bundling of necessary rights.[332] Third, market participants need access to authoritative data to identify and license the music they use.[333] And fourth, usage and payment information should be transparent and accessible to rights owners.[334] Many of the stakeholders' omments reflect these important goals.

A. Compensation and Licensing Disparities

1. Effect of Market Trends on Creator Income

According to the Supreme Court, copyright is intended to increase the "harvest of knowledge" by assuring creators "a fair return for their labors."[335] And, as noted above, industry participants are in general agreement that a well-functioning music licensing system should adequately compensate those who create and record songs.[336] There is, however, substantial debate as to whether the current music licensing system is achieving this goal and, if it is not, the reasons why it is failing creators.

In recent years, many music creators have decried what they see as a precipitous decline in their income.[337] Understanding the reasons for this apparent decrease requires a basic understanding of creators' various income streams. Songwriters have three primary sources of income, which they generally share with music publishers: mechanical royalties, synchronization royalties, and performance royalties. Recording artists receive a share of revenues from their record labels for the sale of physical and digital albums and singles, sound recording synchronization royalties, and digital performance royalties. In addition, recording artists may derive income from live performances, the sale of merchandise, and other sources.[338]

a. From Physical Formats to Downloads to Streaming

In recent years there has been a profound shift in the way music is consumed—from purchases of physical albums, to downloads of digital singles, to on-demand access through digital streaming services. These shifts in music consumption patterns have led to corresponding changes in the relative mix of income streams to copyright owners—in particular, an increased reliance on performance royalties as compared to reproduction and distribution royalties.[339]

For example, the below charts from the RIAA illustrate the shift from U.S. physical sales to digital downloads and other sources of revenue from 2004 to 2013. They reflect remarkable change in less than a decade:[340]

Other data from the RIAA show how streaming, in particular, has boomed in recent years:[341]

NMPA submitted data showing a similar shift.[342] In 2012, NMPA reported that 30% of U.S. music publisher revenues came from performance royalties, 36% from mechanical royalties, 28% from synch royalties, and 6% from other sources.[343] Two years later, NMPA reported that 52% of music publisher revenues came from public performance royalties, while only 23% came from mechanical royalties, 20% from synch licenses, and 5% from other sources.[344] Other recent sales data show that streaming is continuing its surge—according to Nielsen, the number of on-demand streams in the United States grew 54% from 2013 to 2014, with "over 164 billion songs streamed on-demand through audio and video platforms."[345]

The meteoric rise of streaming has corresponded with a sharp decline in physical and digital download sales. In 2014, according to Nielsen data, total U.S. album sales (in both physical and digital formats) fell by 11.2%, and digital download sales decreased 12.5%, from the year before.[346] Of course, this has been accompanied by a commensurate drop in mechanical revenues for music publishers and songwriters. According to NSAI, "[m]any songwriters report a reduction of 60 to 70% or more" in mechanical royalties, and those royalties "continue to decrease by an alarming rate."[347] Many believe that in the not-too-distant future, interactive streaming will eclipse digital downloads to become the dominant means by which consumers access music.[348]

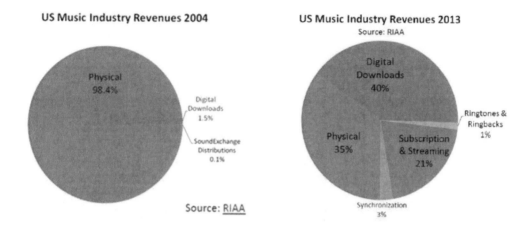

Other data from the RIAA show how streaming, in particular, has boomed in recent years:[341]

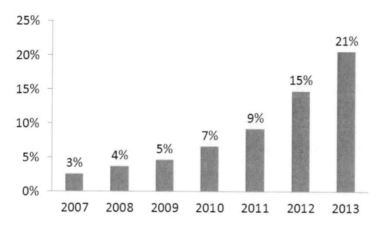

Meanwhile, since the late 1990s, there has been a marked decline in industry revenues overall.[349] RIAA observes that, since 1999, total U.S. recorded music retail revenues have dropped about 53%.[350] As relative newcomer Spotify summed up the situation, "the majority of revenue in the industry has evaporated."[351]

What is a matter of some debate among stakeholders, however, is the actual cause of this striking decline. Some commenters view the reduction in overall revenue and creator income as the result of ordinary market forces. For example, NAB suggested that general market factors—including an extended recession, a decline in consumer discretionary spending, and increased competition for consumers' shrinking entertainment budgets—have all contributed to reduced creator income.[352] Other stakeholders identified industry-specific market trends as a reason for the decline, such as increased competition driving down the value of synch licenses.[353]

Others attribute at least a good portion of the decrease to the shift from album sales to individual song purchases.[354] IPAC explained this dynamic in the context of mechanical royalties:

> Dramatically lower album sales is the primary market development that has led to songwriters reporting significant income declines in recent years. During the heyday of the CD, album cuts made almost as much money in mechanical royalties as the most popular single on the CD. Today's music industry is seeing significantly fewer full album purchases and significantly more individual song purchases. As a result, mechanical royalty income generated from the songs on an album has declined dramatically, leading to the decline in songwriter income.[355]

But IPAC also observed that this trend has been exacerbated by the shift to streaming, which it claims generates lower royalties for copyright owners,[356] a topic that is addressed next.

b. Impact of Music Streaming Models

A major area of debate is whether digital music streaming services fairly compensate rightsholders, particularly music publishers and songwriters. Digital streaming providers assert that they provide copyright owners with entirely new revenue streams by paying performance royalties to both sound recording and musical work owners for interactive and noninteractive services.[357] With respect to sound recording royalties specifically, DiMA noted that "[d]igital radio alone paid out $590.4 million in royalties to artists and rightsholders last year."[358]

Copyright owners, as well as the RIAA, acknowledge the increase in performance royalties.[359] ASCAP and BMI in recent years have both announced record-high collections and royalty distributions.[360] But notwithstanding the overall increase in performance royalties, many copyright owners believe that "the downward spiral of record sales and therefore artist and mechanical royalties has not yet been compensated by the increase in streaming revenue."[361] In other words, increases in performance revenues have not made up for the dramatic decrease in sales.

Significantly, the leading interactive streaming audio service, Spotify, believes that the "rapid decline [in industry revenue] is not due to a fall in music consumption but to a shift in music listening behavior towards formats that do not generate significant income for artists."[362] ASCAP observed that "technological developments have significantly increased the use of musical works, yet significantly decreased the income earned by songwriters."[363] Songwriters increasingly worry about their income (or lack thereof) from digital streaming services, especially those that they regard as poorly "monetized"—i.e., ad-supported services that do not require a subscription fee or generate a large amount of advertising revenue.

A growing number of high-profile songwriter/artists—including Taylor Swift and Thom Yorke—are leveraging their sound recording rights to remove their music from Spotify, principally out of concern that Spotify's free ad-supported tier of service does not fairly compensate them for their songs.[364] As Swift put it succinctly: "I think that people should feel that there is a value to what musicians have created, and that's that."[365]

Songwriter concerns are vividly illustrated by the following tweet by Bette Midler:

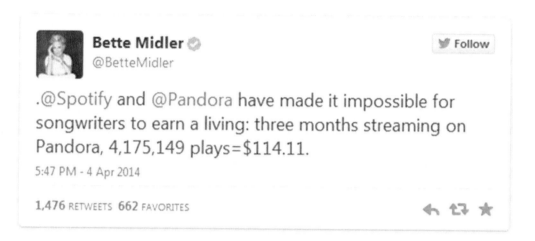

Other songwriters have made similarly bleak claims.[366] For instance, the songwriter Aloe Blacc recently reported:

> Avicii's release "Wake Me Up!" that I co-wrote and sing, for example, was the most streamed song in Spotify history and the 13th most played song on Pandora since its release in 2013, with more than 168 million streams in the US. And yet, that yielded only $12,359 in Pandora domestic royalties—which were then split among three songwriters and our publishers. In return for co-writing a major hit song, I've earned less than $4,000 domestically from the largest digital music service.[367]

Notably, songwriters who are not also recording artists with some measure of control over their recordings typically do not have the option to withdraw their works from low-paying services, because—due to the combination of the section 115 compulsory license and the ASCAP and BMI consent decrees—they have no choice other than to permit the exploitation of their musical works by such providers. And even recording artists cannot remove their music from noninteractive digital services like Pandora that qualify for the section 112 and 114 compulsory licenses.

For their part, the digital music services deny that they are the cause of the decline in songwriter income. These services note that they pay royalties for the public performance of sound recordings, while terrestrial radio does not, and so the total royalties they pay to both sound recording and musical work owners must be considered.[368] Accordingly, Pandora challenged the numbers cited by Midler and Blacc by publicizing the total amounts paid for all rights to perform the songs, including sound recording rights—stating that they paid $6,400 in royalties in Midler's case and over $250,000 for the plays of "Wake Me Up!".[369]

Digital music services emphasize that they "pay the lion's share of their revenues over to rights owners,"[370] and suggest that the songwriter concerns are more accurately traced to the division of total royalties between sound recording owners and musical work owners.[371] From the services' perspective, total content costs are the relevant consideration. They assert that they are "agnostic" as to how that total is divided among various rightsholders.[372]

Digital music services and broadcasters also contend that, to the extent individual creators believe they are not receiving adequate income, the blame might lie with intermediaries. DiMA stated that "there is little transparency about what happens to the significant royalties generated from digital music services after they are paid to record labels, music publishers, and PROs, and processed under the financial terms of recording artists' and songwriters' own private arrangements with rightsowners."[373] DiMA thus alleged that, rather than being paid out to individual creators, "a significant portion of the royalties received are retained by [intermediaries] for their own account, or applied toward the recoupment of advances paid to recording artists and songwriters."[374] SAG-AFTRA and AFM, which represent individual artists, expressed a similar worry that direct licensing deals "can create uncertainty regarding which benefits of the deal are subject to being shared with Artists at all." They noted in particular that "[d]irect license deals increasingly have been reported to include 'breakage'—advance payments or guaranteed payments in excess of the per-performance royalty earned under the license—equity shares, promotion or other non-usage based elements" and that even if such amounts are shared with artists, they "may be subject to recoupment and less transparent than payments under the compulsory license."[375]

c. Non-Performing Songwriters

While all creators have been affected by the shift from full-album sales to digital streaming models, songwriters who are not also performing artists appear to have been especially hard hit. Unlike songwriter-artists, "pure" songwriters who write works for others to perform do not have the potential to make up for lost income through touring or merchandise sales.

According to NSAI, since 2000, the number of full-time songwriters in Nashville has fallen by 80%.[376] NSAI further observes that two decades ago, there were some 3,000 to 4,000 publishing deals available for songwriters in Nashville; that number has since dropped to 300 to 400.[377] A publishing deal is crucial, as it "essentially pays a songwriter an annual salary to write songs."[378] Without such a deal, it may be impossible for a songwriter to finance his or her creative efforts. A recent article in *The Teennessean* concludes that the result of the shift away from album sales to streaming "has been the collapse of Nashville's musical middle class."[379]

d. Additional Considerations

Piracy

In addition, a broad range of stakeholders—with the exception of the CFA and Public Knowledge[380]—pointed to piracy as a continuing challenge that depresses revenues for both legal music providers and rightsholders. But piracy was not a significant focus of discussion. Unlike in the Napster era, stakeholders now seem resigned to this marketplace condition and the perhaps irreversible impact it has had on the industry. RIAA—which abandoned its lawsuits against individual file-sharers several years ago[381]—observed that piracy "certainly is in the background when you talk about whether digital music services are earning enough money or paying enough money, competing against free remains a problem."[382] DiMA agreed that "the truth is that any legitimate digital service right now competes with free."[383] This sentiment was echoed by Spotify as well: "We are competing with piracy. It's a reality that we all face on every level of the ecosystem. We are all competing with free."[384]

Impact of DMCA Safe Harbors

While piracy may now be considered as an accepted background fact, the same cannot be said of the DMCA safe harbors, codified in section 512 of the Copyright Act, which remain highly controversial. Section 512 curtails liability for online providers for infringing user-posted content provided that they remove such content expeditiously in response to a copyright owner's takedown notice.[385] Although the operation of the DMCA safe harbors is beyond the scope of this study, the Office briefly notes these DMCA concerns since they were so frequently expressed.[386]

Many copyright owners blame the DMCA's safe harbor regime for allowing digital providers the opportunity to profit from the unauthorized use of copyrighted music without paying licensing fees.[387] One composer, Hélène Muddiman, likened the situation to a company giving away someone else's CDs at a fairground and making money by advertising to the people in line.[388] Music publisher Jason Rys contended that "due to the DMCA there's nothing you can realistically do to stop your songs from appearing on YouTube."[389]

In addition to complaining that the notice and takedown regime created under the DMCA results in an impossible game of "whack-a-mole"—since removed content is frequently reposted, requiring the owner to serve another takedown notice[390]—some stakeholders also point out that the digital companies' ability to exploit infringing content unless and until a notice is sent affords these providers significant added leverage in licensing negotiations, since content owners must either agree to a license or devote significant resources to an unending takedown process. This dynamic, in turn, is thought to have a "depressive effect" on royalty rates.[391]

For their part, digital services stress the considerable effort that is required to respond to copyright owners' slew of takedown notices. The number of takedown requests submitted to Google, for example, continues to climb and suggests a staggering amount of online infringement. In 2010, Google received approximately 3 million DMCA takedown requests; in 2014, that number was 345 million—over 940,000 takedown requests every day.[392]

2. Disparate Treatment of Analogous Rights and Uses

Closely tied to the issue of fair compensation is the disparate legal treatment of sound recordings and musical works, both vis-à-vis each other and across different delivery platforms. Many participants regard these disparities as unwarranted, and blame them for the unfairness and inefficiency in the music licensing system.

a. Inconsistent Ratesetting Standards

As explained above, ratesetting standards under the statutory licenses and consent decrees differ based on the right and use at issue. The CRB establishes rates for mechanical reproductions of musical works under section 115 under the four-factor, public policy-oriented standard in section 801(b)(1) of the Copyright Act.[393] Under the ASCAP and BMI consent decrees, the rate courts establish rates for the public performance of musical works under a "fair market value" analysis which attempts to determine the price that a willing buyer and willing seller would agree to in an arm's length transaction, but gives substantial weight to antitrust concerns.[394]

As also described above, rates for the digital performance of sound recordings under section 114 are set under different standards, depending on the type of use. Royalty rates for a limited set of older services—Sirius XM, as the only preexisting satellite service, and Music Choice and Muzak, as the only preexisting subscription services—are governed by the same four-factor standard in section 801(b)(1) as mechanical reproductions of musical works subject to compulsory licensing under section 115.[395] Meanwhile, royalty rates for all internet radio and newer noninteractive subscription services, and for all ephemeral recordings under section 112 regardless of the type of service, are established under the so-called "willing buyer/willing seller" standard, which many believe yields more market-oriented rates than those established under section 801(b)(1).[396]

Most stakeholders seem to acknowledge that it is problematic for the law to impose differing ratesetting standards, especially for businesses that provide similar services.[397] As DiMA noted, "[t]he 'playing field' regarding ratesetting standards is not level, and the result is fundamental inequity."[398] Depending upon whether they wish to see higher or lower royalty rates, however, these same stakeholders disagree as to which ratesetting standard should apply.

Music services and public interest groups support adoption of the 801(b)(1) standard for all statutory licenses, as the standard more likely to produce lower rates. Public Knowledge and CFA, for example, opined that the 801(b)(1) standard's balancing of policy considerations and focus on "creating economic incentives with the ultimate purpose of encouraging artists and platforms to create new works and bring those works to market" better aligns with the constitutional purpose of copyright law.[399] Similarly, Sirius XM pointed out that the 801(b)(1) standard provided more "latitude to consider the enumerated policy factors, including recognizing the 'relative contributions' of technological pioneers, and ensuring that both copyright owners and users are treated fairly."[400] It also noted that rates set under the standard have proven less susceptible to legal challenge or congressional modification.[401]

Taking a somewhat different tack, DiMA criticized the willing buyer/willing seller standard for "requir[ing] judges to set a rate based solely on *marketplacebenchmarks*," where "there is very little record evidence of market rates for directly licensed internet radio services that are not tied to a separate rights grant for additional service types and functionalities (such as direct licenses for interactive services)."[402] In a related vein, Spotify noted that under the willing buyer/willing seller standard, benchmark rates proffered by licensees "are often premised on the agreements entered into by only the largest of licensors . . . [who] demand

'Most Favored Nations' provisions to ensure that only the highest rates are utilized in the market as opposed to rates that would arise from true free market negotiations."[403]

In contrast, copyright owners and their representatives support the adoption of the willing buyer/willing seller standard for all rates across the board. They posit that the willing buyer/willing seller standard is fairer to music owners and creators, who cannot opt out of compulsory licenses.[404] BMI stated that it is "simple and self-evident" that creators should be paid at a fair market value rate.[405] Sony/ATV argued that the 801(b)(1) standard "creates artificially deflated rights," whereas a willing buyer/willing seller standard "will create fair market value" for copyright owners.[406] In sum, copyright owners strongly object to a ratesetting standard that does not aspire to free- market rates.

In this regard, a number of copyright owners, including NMPA, ASCAP, BMI, SESAC, and NARAS, expressed support for the Songwriter Equity Act ("SEA"), proposed legislation that would change the ratesetting criteria applicable to section 115 from the 801(b)(1) formula to the willing buyer/willing seller standard.[407]

b. Different Ratesetting Bodies

Another disparity in the ratesetting process involves the bodies that oversee the ratesetting proceedings. As discussed above, antitrust consent decrees entered into with the DOJ by ASCAP and BMI dictate that rates set for the public performance of musical works administered by those PROs are overseen by two judges of the U.S. District Court for the Southern District of New York that sit as rate courts for the respective consent decrees. Antitrust concerns play a predominant role in the setting of these rates.[408] In contrast, the CRB, which sets rates for the statutory licenses in sections 112, 114, and 115, does not set rates with antitrust concerns specifically in mind.[409] Instead, the CRB is designed to be an expert ratesetting body, and to bring to bear "a significant mastery of economics and marketplace factors as well as considerable knowledge of copyright law."[410]

A number of stakeholders criticized this divided ratesetting regime. Licensees pointed out that similar services must petition different bodies to obtain the rights necessary to engage in a single activity—for example, interactive streaming—leading to increased costs. When rates are set by different bodies at different times, there is a question as to how to adjust and harmonize the different rates.[411] Others raised fundamental structural and procedural concerns, such as the propriety of a single district court being tasked with an ongoing economic responsibility it is not specifically designed to handle, in comparison to a dedicated tribunal such as the CRB. Bob Kohn, author of a well-known treatise on music licensing, noted that "rate court proceedings have morphed from the nature of a fairness hearing for proposed rates to an actual rate setting process— something which the courts are not equipped to do, especially without jurisdiction over rate setting for mechanical reproductions of musical works and transmissions of sound recordings."[412]

Music services fear that fragmented consideration of royalty rates across different ratesetting bodies can lead to unsustainable results.[413] On this point, a representative from Spotify stated:

> One thing that is absolutely essential, though, is that any rate setting standard is not looked at in a vacuum. . . . If we have an increase in publishing rates, for example, that go up beyond, much higher than they are at the moment, then we could be in a situation where we pay out more than one hundred percent of our revenue, which is unsustainable.[414]

Adding to general concerns about disparate ratesetting processes is the fact that section 114(i) of the Copyright Act prevents the PRO rate courts from considering fees set by the CRB for digital performance of sound recordings, thus further encouraging balkanization.[415] Recognizing the shortcomings inherent in the current divided approach, some participants proposed unifying ratesetting proceedings for music licensing in a single body, observing that this could also lead to cost savings through the elimination of duplicative proceedings.[416]

c. Pre-1972 Sound Recordings

As explained above, legal uncertainties surround state law protection for pre-1972 sound recordings. This has led digital music providers to take different approaches as to the payment of royalties for the streaming of pre-1972 sound recordings—some pay, and some do not. In recent months, questions of whether and how to pay for such uses have become more immediate due to judicial decisions in California and New York upholding the right of pre-1972 sound recording owners to collect for performances of their works—and additional lawsuits are pending.[417]

As a general matter, some stakeholders support the full federalization of sound recordings—i.e., the total inclusion of pre-1972 sound recordings within the federal Copyright Act, subject to existing exceptions and limitations—while others have favored a more limited solution that would, for example, provide a payment mechanism under the section 112 and 114 licenses for noninteractive digital services with a safe harbor from state liability. In addition, it seems that some parties, particularly digital music services, might be content to operate without a federal statutory obligation to compensate pre-1972 sound recording owners. But these stakeholders at least acknowledge that a federal licensing scheme would be preferable to obtaining direct licenses under scattered state laws for each sound recording performed, which is no longer merely a hypothetical scenario.[418]

Full Federalization Considerations

Full federalization means that all rights and limitations in the Copyright Act applicable to post-1972 sound recordings would also apply to pre-1972 sound recordings.[419] The Copyright Office's 2011 report on the treatment of pre-1972 recordings recommends full federalization. Specifically, the Office concluded that this approach would "improve the certainty and consistency of copyright law, will likely encourage more preservation and access activities, and should not result in any appreciable harm to the economic interests of right holders."[420]

A range of study participants agree with the Office's view.[421] The prospect of receiving federally required compensation for pre-1972 exploitations is a driver for some; NARAS, which largely agreed with the Office's findings, observed that "older artists, who contributed greatly to our nation's cultural legacy, often rely on their recordings as their sole source of income."[422] Others consider access to the full spectrum of the Copyright Act's rights and limitations to be an important element of any solution. Some creators of pre-1972 sound recordings, for instance, believe they should have access to federal termination rights.[423] The Library of Congress (which submitted comments as an interested party) worried that preserving "millions of historic music and sound recordings" will be impossible under the current regime, where "pre-1972 recordings are subject to a variety of disparate state laws and state common law that . . . lack statutory language to exempt archival copying for preservation purposes."[424] Others, including digital music services, feel strongly that the fair use doctrine and DMCA safe harbor provisions should apply to pre-1972 recordings.[425]

Partial Federalization Alternative

Supporters of partial federalization, while open to consideration of a broader solution, believe that a measure requiring compensation for use of pre-1972 sound recordings should be enacted in the near term.[426] SoundExchange explained that full federalization "would raise a number of complicated issues," but resolving those issues should not delay providing legacy artists with fair compensation for the use of their works.[427] SoundExchange noted in particular that "the artists who created pre-1972 recordings are especially dependent on digital revenue streams, because they are often less likely than more current artists to be able to generate significant income from touring, product sales and other sources."[428] For those who support such an approach, obtaining royalties from digital performance services is of primary importance and partial federalization should be implemented as a short-term solution while issues of full federalization continue to be debated.[429]

Accordingly, some stakeholders advocated for Congress to simply expand the section 112 and 114 statutory licensing scheme to encompass pre-1972 sound recordings. According to these parties, bringing pre-1972 sound recordings within the scope of federal copyright protection in this manner would supply digital music services with an easy means to offer lawful public performances of those recordings while generating new sources of revenue for copyright owners.[430] Proponents of partial federalization have supported Congress' adoption of the Respecting Senior Performers as Essential Cultural Treasures Act (otherwise known as the "RESPECT Act"), legislation introduced in 2014 that would extend the section 112 and 114 licenses to cover pre-1972 recordings but at the same time provide protection from state law liability for such uses.[431]

d. Terrestrial Radio Exemption

As explained above, current law does not require traditional terrestrial—or "over-the-air"—radio broadcasters to compensate sound recording owners for the public performance of their recordings.[432] Digital music services, by contrast, must pay both sound recording owners and musical work owners for performances. The Copyright Office has long supported a full public performance right for sound recordings.

Recording artists and record labels argue that they are entitled to compensation from terrestrial radio stations in the same way that songwriters and publishers receive compensation when their songs are played on the radio.[433] They characterize the terrestrial broadcast exemption as an antiquated "loophole" that causes "glaring inequity."[434] They believe that the terrestrial radio industry does not adequately compensate sound recording owners for helping to generate billions of dollars in annual advertising revenues for radio services.[435] In this regard, they assert that the promotional effect of radio airplay on record sales claimed by broadcasters is overstated, and that sound recording owners should not be forced to forgo compensation in exchange for the suggestion of promotional value.[436]

In addition, copyright owners and digital streaming services together urge that current law gives terrestrial radio unwarranted competitive advantage over new, innovative entrants.[437] They note that wireless communications technologies have improved to the point where digital services are competing directly with traditional terrestrial radio, and consumers are using the same devices to receive digital and analog transmissions of the same recordings.[438] As one participant put it, "[t]o me it seems obvious that having an individual song play or performance on terrestrial radio in your car is fundamentally the same as a satellite radio Sirius XM play in your car as is a Pandora stream via a wireless cellphone tower through your car radio."[439]

Predictably, terrestrial broadcasters opposed a new requirement to pay performance royalties for sound recordings, likening such payments to a "tariff" aimed at subsidizing the recording industry.[440] They state that the terrestrial broadcast exemption represents a "reciprocal dynamic" by which "record labels and performing artists profit from the free exposure and promotion provided by radio airplay, while local radio stations receive revenues from advertisers that purchase airtime to sell their products and services."[441] As evidence of the high promotional value of broadcast radio, they point out that record companies spend millions of dollars annually trying to persuade radio stations to play or promote their recordings.[442]

Foreign performance royalties are an important consideration in this debate. Virtually all industrialized nations recognize a more robust sound recording performance right than the United States; according to proponents of the right, the United States stands out on the list of countries (among them Iran and North Korea) that do not.[443] Proponents further point out that the terrestrial radio exemption prevents U.S. sound recording owners and performers from collecting royalties for foreign radio broadcasts, as most countries do not require payment of performance royalties to American sound recording owners due to the lack of reciprocity.[444] According to one estimate, in addition to forgone domestic royalties, U.S. sound recording owners are deprived of between $70 and $100 million in foreign royalties each year.[445]

For their part, broadcast industry representatives dispute the amount of royalties sound recording owners are unable to recover as a result of the limited performance right.[446] They posit that U.S. expansion of the performance right will be insufficient to compel reciprocity, claiming many foreign nations will continue to balk at paying royalties unless the U.S. makes other conforming changes to its law as well.[447] They also maintain that many U.S. sound recording owners are already paid when their works are performed abroad, as foreign collection societies are sometimes willing (or even compelled) to pay for these uses.[448]

B. Government's Role in Music Licensing

1. PRO Consent Decrees

PROs, publishers, songwriters, and others criticized the ASCAP and BMI consent decrees on many fronts, arguing that the 75-year-old regime is outdated,[449] that PROs "can no longer meet the evolving needs of writers, publishers, music licensees and ultimately the consumers,"[450] and that while the "consent decrees were imposed to protect against anticompetitive behavior, they are now used to distort and manipulate the market for the benefit of a handful of powerful digital distribution companies that are the gatekeepers between music's creators and those who want to enjoy that music."[451] Licensees and others, however, believe that the consent decrees are vital to preventing anticompetitive conduct by the PROs and major publishers.[452] Some believe that direct antitrust regulation should be extended even further, to encompass all licensing of public performances of musical works.[453]

As noted above, the DOJ is undertaking a review of the consent decrees to examine their continued operation and effectiveness, and has solicited public comments, which reflect many of the same concerns that the Office heard during this study.[454] While the DOJ is focused on whether the consent decrees can or should be modified as a matter of antitrust policy, this study examines the impact of the decrees on the music licensing marketplace in general.

a. Royalty Rates

Under the consent decrees, any party may obtain permission from ASCAP or BMI to perform musical works upon the submission of an application. If, after the application is received, the PRO and user cannot agree to the licensing fee, either may apply to the applicable rate court for a determination of the rate.

In general, licensees expressed more confidence in the rate court process than did the PROs and copyright owners. For instance, DiMA opined that the "time-tested" rates have "consistently established royalty rates that appropriately approximate the 'fair market value' of particular licenses in different contexts."[455] CTIA observed that the rate courts are "essential to foster competitive market pricing for music performance rights."[456]

In contrast, PROs and copyright owners stated that the rate courts deflate public performance royalties below their true market value.[457] Songwriters and publishers believe that the rate court rates are inequitable to copyright owners, asserting that the rates they set are "below-market,"[458] "unfair and unrealistic[],"[459] and "artificially low."[460] In support of these claims, several stakeholders pointed to the 12 to 1 (some say 14 to 1) discrepancy between the rates set by the CRB for the public performance of sound recordings and rates set by rate courts for the public performance of musical works.[461]

Copyright owners complained that the "fair market value" standard employed by the rate courts is inadequate, with a "lack of clarity regarding what factors the rate court should consider . . . and the weight given to those factors."[462] A number of copyright owners highlighted section 114(i), which precludes consideration of rates set for sound recording performances by the rate courts, as one reason for below-value PRO performance rates.[463] In addition, ASCAP objected that "neither ASCAP nor BMI are free to refuse to license their repertories," leading to a lack of "competitive market transactions involving non-compelled sellers" to use as benchmarks for the government-regulated rate.[464]

b. Rate Court Proceedings

A common complaint about the rate court process is that it is expensive and time-consuming.[465] Netflix observed that "both the substantial costs of litigation and the business uncertainties inherent in court-determined approximations of what is a competitive rate impose unnecessary risks and costs on all parties."[466] Music Choice complained that "costs are disproportionately burdensome on individual licensees," whereas a PRO can spread its costs across copyright owners.[467] But ASCAP observed, "ASCAP and applicants have collectively expended well in excess of one hundred million dollars on litigation expenses related to rate court proceedings, much of that incurred since only 2009."[468] And attorney Christian Castle objected that "songwriters did not ask for [the process], cannot escape it, and are forced to participate."[469]

Federal copyright litigation is not only expensive but often lengthy,[470] and the rate courts are no exception. According to BMI, "a typical rate court case can take many years to be resolved, which includes the inevitable, potentially multi-year, appeal of the trial court's decision."[471] ASCAP noted that although the consent decree "mandates that proceedings must be trial-ready within one year of the filing of the initial petition, that deadline is rarely met."[472] As music attorney Dina LaPolt commented, the drawn-out proceedings create the perception that rate courts "cannot keep up with the pace set by the new digital marketplace."[473]

c. Interim Fees

Other concerns revolve around the fact that the rate for a particular license may not be established until long after the licensee begins using musical works. The ASCAP and BMI consent decrees allow music users to perform the PRO's repertoire upon the mere filing of an application for a license, without payment of any license fee.[474] As a general matter, songwriters, publishers, and PROs found it unfair that "the current rate court system . . . does not provide for an inexpensive, effective way to set interim fees to compensate creators while the long rate-setting process plays out."[475]

This feature potentially exposes the PROs to gamesmanship by applicants, as "the burden is on the PRO to make a motion for the imposition of an interim fee—a motion that is, like the rate court proceeding itself, expensive and time-consuming."[476] As ASCAP elaborated: "Even when an interim fee is paid, it is often at less than full value," leading many licensees to make "strategic choices to stay on interim terms until ASCAP determines it must commence an expensive rate court proceeding."[477] BMI observed that "it is not unheard of for an applicant to go out of business before a fee is ever set; as a result, the PROs (and, of course, in turn, our writers, composers and publishers) are never compensated for the use of their valuable repertoires."[478]

d. Inconsistent Regulation of PROs

Yet another concern is the disparate treatment of entities that license performance rights. The largest PROs, ASCAP and BMI, are subject to direct government oversight and regulated pricing under the consent decrees. Other entities that represent significant catalogs of works, however, such as SESAC and GMR—and major publishers, who may withdraw from the PROs to license public performance rights directly—are not. Some contend that the application of different rules to these different players creates an unwarranted competitive imbalance and opportunities for regulatory arbitrage.[479]

Licensees argued that SESAC, for example, has taken advantage of this discrepancy by engaging in anticompetitive behavior that is prohibited under the consent decrees.[480] As noted above, in 2014, RMLC and local television stations each separately sued SESAC seeking antitrust relief.[481] RMLC argued that SESAC's practices created "significant overcharges to radio stations for their uses of SESAC music,"[482] while the local television stations criticized SESAC for offering only a blanket license and refusing to provide licensees with repertoire information.[483] These suits were both allowed to proceed after the respective courts denied SESAC's motions to dismiss.[484] (The parties to the New York case brought by Meredith Corporation have since agreed to a settlement.[485])

SESAC disagreed that it has a competitive advantage, instead contending that because "the industry . . . arose in a culture that assumes that the rates set by the rate courts are accurate . . . SESAC must also accept those rates."[486] And copyright owners suggested that the rates obtained by SESAC and GMR outside of the consent decrees might be useful as market benchmarks in rate court proceedings.[487]

Even within the consent decree framework, there are regulatory discrepancies. The ASCAP and BMI decrees are administered by different district court judges, and in the past, there have been periods of time during which the ASCAP and BMI decrees included significantly different terms.[488] The decrees are still not entirely aligned. For example, the ASCAP consent decree expressly prohibits ASCAP from licensing any rights other than public performance rights, while the BMI consent decree contains no such provision. BMI has expressed the view that it may license other rights under its consent decree—but has yet to do so.[489] In short, "[n]othing obligates the rate courts to reach similar results on rate-setting or other issues."[490]

e. Parties' Proposals

Stakeholders suggested a broad range of solutions to the perceived shortcomings of the consent decrees governing ASCAP and BMI. The most salient proposals are discussed below.

Complete or Partial Withdrawal of Rights

As discussed above, the ASCAP and BMI rate courts recently concluded that, under the consent decrees, music publishers could not withdraw only "new media" (i.e., digital streaming) rights from the PROs to be licensed directly. As a result, the major publishers have petitioned the DOJ seeking modification of the consent decrees to allow for such partial withdrawals. As an alternative plan, major publishers are also evaluating whether to withdraw their works entirely from the PROs and directly negotiate public performance rates outside of the consent decree framework.[491]

A broad range of stakeholders expressed serious apprehension about complete publisher withdrawal, predicting "havoc" for the music industry.[492] BMI noted that complete withdrawal "is potentially catastrophic for smaller publishers and songwriters who depend on BMI for their livelihood, and for BMI's hundreds of thousands of customers who depend on BMI to fulfill their copyright obligations."[493] Significantly, Martin Bandier, chairman and CEO of Sony/ATV—one of the major publishers considering full withdrawal—similarly predicted that if Sony/ATV found it necessary to withdraw, such an outcome could be "catastrophic" for ASCAP and BMI.[494]

Part of the concern is that many administrative costs of running a PRO, such as negotiating licenses or monitoring radio stations, do not scale downward with a reduction in revenues; a royalty check costs the same amount to process whether it is large or small. ASCAP and BMI offset their administrative costs by charging a commission (roughly 13% of royalties paid in both cases[495]). If major publishers are to wholly withdraw, the commissions collected by the PROs from the substantial royalties generated by those catalogs would no longer be available to defray fixed overhead expenses. As a result, the remaining smaller members of these organizations would have to shoulder the full administrative costs, likely through significantly higher commissions.[496] Some commenters questioned whether the PROs would be able to continue in operation in such a circumstance.[497] A related concern is that smaller publishers might face unsustainable increases in licensing and transaction costs as independent entities, which could lead to greater consolidation in the music publishing market.[498]

Nonetheless, based on their public statements and comments during this study, at least two major publishers—UMPG and Sony/ATV—appear poised to withdraw.[499] In contrast to Sony/ATV, a representative from UMPG suggested that such an action would not be the end of the PROs:

> We could withdraw tomorrow, and it would be seamless. The landscape would not change that much. You're talking about introducing maybe a few additional players to the licensing process, Universal being one of them. The societies don't go away. The societies continue to exist for those writers and publishers who don't have the resources that we're fortunate enough to have to create infrastructures to deal with licensing and data management, but there are several solutions, they are all workable, and they don't impact the industry or the writer community negatively.[500]

As an alternative to full withdrawal, partial withdrawal of only new media rights remains a possibility if the rate courts' "all in or all out" interpretations of the consent decrees are reversed on appeal, or the DOJ concludes that it should support a modification of the decrees to permit it. The PROs and major publishers have advanced several arguments in favor of partial withdrawal, including their view that it would allow for fairer, market-based rates for new media uses, that it would allow for greater flexibility in licensing terms, and that directly negotiated licenses with digital services would provide a competitive benchmark in ratesetting proceedings governing non- withdrawing publishers.[501]

Licensees, however, stated that even partial withdrawal would undermine the protection of the consent decrees, and allow the withdrawing publishers to raise rates through the exercise of unfettered market power.[502] Music Choice claimed that for the brief period before the ASCAP rate court banned publishers' partial withdrawal, "negotiations with Sony and UMPG were oppressive, and resulted in substantially higher royalty rates."[503] Others echoed the concern that publishers would engage in anticompetitive behavior.[504]

Songwriters also have significant concerns about publisher withdrawals, specifically as to how the writer's share of performance royalties would be administered and paid. Songwriter contracts typically provide that the writer's share will be collected and paid through a PRO,[505] but many of these contracts likely do not contemplate publisher withdrawal from the PRO.[506] Songwriters fear that, if they instead receive payment through the publisher, they will be vulnerable to the publisher's less transparent accounting.[507] FMC suggested that "[a]ny further amendments to the consent decrees must be done with complete transparency and with a thoughtful consideration of the impact on songwriters' leverage and compensation."[508]

The SCL voiced concerns that withdrawal of publishers from U.S. PROs would cause problems for foreign songwriters, who enter into exclusive arrangements with their local performing rights society, which in turn authorize U.S. PROs to collect royalties on their behalf through reciprocal relationships. According to SCL, a U.S. publisher representing a foreign author's works under a sub-publishing agreement lacks the authority to withdraw that writers' rights from the U.S. PRO.[509] Questioned about this, David Kokakis of UMPG responded that his company has "considered the international implications" of withdrawal and does not "currently intend to disrupt that [reciprocity] model."[510] Kokakis maintained that "exploitation of foreign works in the United States . . . would continue to run through the [U.S.] societies."[511]

A number of study participants proposed continued reliance upon the PROs to collect and administer royalties from licensees even under directly negotiated deals.[512] According to ASCAP, when the major publishers sought to withdraw their new media rights, ASCAP entered into administration arrangements with the withdrawing publishers "that enabled the publishers to negotiate directly their digital rights in the free market, but leave the administration of such deals—receiving fees, processing music use information data, matching works to interested parties and paying all interested parties—to ASCAP" for a fee.[513] Such an arrangement might also address the concern that the withdrawing publishers would "lack the infrastructure to license and collect performance royalties from bars, restaurants or live performance venues."[514]

Elimination versus Expansion of Consent Decrees

During the course of this study, PROs, publishers, and songwriters have advocated for the sunset of the consent decrees that govern ASCAP and BMI.[515] ASCAP noted the anomaly that the decrees "continue[] into perpetuity regardless of the increased competition in the marketplace for licensing the public performance of musical works."[516] ASCAP thus views the decrees as "particularly punitive in nature when viewed in light of current DOJ policy," which mandates the inclusion of sunset provisions in standard consent decrees, and under which the DOJ "does not currently enter into consent decrees with terms longer than ten years."[517] ASCAP observed that the marketplace has undergone massive changes since its decree was first adopted in 1941, in that "ASCAP now faces vibrant competition, not only from BMI, but also from unregulated competitors such as SESAC, foreign PROs, and new market entrants, as well as from ASCAP's own publisher and writer members."[518] BMI similarly points out that "outmoded views of the purported monopoly power of regulated collectives such as BMI and ASCAP need to be discarded" as "digital technology has made it easier for creators and distributors, including unregulated competitors to PROs, to identify performances and their owners."[519]

In contrast, licensees fear that sunset of the consent decrees would lead not just to higher but "supracompetitive" rates that are all the more problematic when licensees have to pay performance royalties for both sound recordings and mechanical rights.[520] A wide range of licensees accordingly support the continuation of the consent decrees in essentially unchanged form.[521]

Some participants went further by suggesting that the restrictions imposed by the consent decrees should be extended to the smaller PROs not currently subject to direct supervision. For example, Netflix suggested that all PROs should be subject to the same ratesetting authority and that PROs could divide the shares of the royalty pools among themselves.[522] Participants also suggested that withdrawing major publishers should be subject to oversight and possibly a consent decree to protect against a concentration of market power.[523]

Rate Court Changes

The costs and length of rate court proceeding are frustrating for many. Some— including ASCAP and BMI—have suggested replacing the rate courts with an alternative dispute resolution process such as arbitration.[524] IPAC advocated for private negotiation followed by expedited mediation within prescribed time limits.[525]

Licensees, however, were skeptical. NAB stated that "[t]here is no reason to believe that, without drastic elimination of appropriate and essential discovery and appellate review, private arbitration will be any more efficient, speedy, or cost-effective than the rate courts."[526] FMC voiced a concern that sealed arbitration proceedings would threaten transparency.[527] Even while acknowledging the rate courts' flaws, a number of licensees supported the continuation of that regime, in part due to its procedural safeguards, including use of the Federal Rules of Civil Procedure and Evidence.[528] As one licensee opined, "the *process* of rate-setting under the ASCAP and BMI consent decrees—and the hypothetical competitive market standard for rate-setting applied in Rate Court cases—has worked reasonably well."[529]

PROs and publishers also seek to encourage interim payment of royalties pending the determination of a final rate. MMF and FAC suggested that "[a]t the very least US licensees should be required to make an interim payment pending the issuing of a final license with an agreed tariff."[530] BMI suggested that rather than invoking the burdensome rate court process to set an interim rate, the fee could be set at the rate the licensee paid under its last license or, for new users, the "going industry rate."[531]

Bundled Licensing

There appears to be broad agreement among stakeholders that PROs and other licensing entities should be able to bundle performance rights with reproduction and distribution rights, and potentially other rights, to meet the needs of modern music services.[532] NSAI, for example, opined that "[t]he most efficient path to digital service providers obtaining necessary licenses would be to allow the PRO's to license and collect mechanical royalties."[533]

Stakeholders offered conflicting methods by which bundled rights could be made available. For instance, NMPA suggested that bundled rights could be sought directly from the music publishers that own and administer the song in question.[534] But the PROs suggested that their existing structures could be leveraged to facilitate bundled licensing on a blanket basis, if only the consent decrees were amended.[535] Several parties also observed that allowing bundling of rights would align U.S. music licensing with collective practices in Europe.[536]

Elimination of Section 114(i)

Songwriters and publishers expressed support for the SEA, which, in addition to addressing the ratesetting standard under section 115, would amend section 114(i) to remove language prohibiting the rate courts and other bodies from considering the license fees payable for the public performance of sound recordings when determining rates to be paid for musical works.[537] Proponents of the SEA stated that rate courts should be able to consider all relevant evidence[538] and predicted that the courts, after considering the CRB-established sound recording rates, would increase performance rates for musical works so that they were more commensurate with rates paid for sound recordings.[539]

Music services opposed amending section 114(i) on the ground that eliminating the evidentiary exclusion of the CRB-set rate for sound recordings would increase rates for musical works without a proportional decrease of rates for sound recordings, leading to an overall escalation of total content costs to potentially unsustainable levels.[540] Some noted that those who now support the elimination of that provision are the same parties who sought it in the first place, as the provision was enacted out of copyright owners' concern that consideration of sound recording license fees might depress musical work rates.[541] Opponents further observed that music publishers themselves previously testified before the CRB that it was economically logical and necessary to maintain a distinction between musical work and sound recording rates, and are now simply questioning their prior judgment in light of the higher sound recording rates set by the CRB.[542]

2. Mechanical Rights Licensing

Many parties have called for either the complete elimination or modernization of section 115, citing issues such as the administrative challenges of the license, the inaccuracy and slowness of the ratesetting process, and frustration with government-mandated rates.

a. Royalty Rates and Standard

A broad range of parties expressed dissatisfaction with royalty rates established by the CRB. Music publishers and songwriters argue that the rates determined under the section 801(b)(1) standard applicable to section 115 are depressed as a result of the government ratesetting process and do not reflect the fair market value of musical works. While advocating for the elimination of the compulsory license, these parties also assert that at the very least mechanical rates should be established under the more market-oriented willing buyer/willing seller standard that applies under the section 112 and 114 licenses.[543]

Musical work owners explain that section 115 acts as a ceiling that does not allow them to seek higher royalties through voluntary negotiations.[544] Many point to the fact that the current 9.1 cent rate for phonorecords has not kept pace with inflation, since the original 2 cent rate set by statute in 1909 would be 51 cents today if adjusted for inflation.[545] In addition, a number of participants noted a 9 to 1 inequity of rates between sound recordings and musical works for downloads and CDs: when a song is downloaded from iTunes for $1.29, approximately 80 cents is allocated for the sound recording, but only 9.1 cents goes to the musical work.[546] By way of contrast, rates for privately negotiated synchronization licenses—which are not subject to government oversight—generally reflect a 1 to 1 ratio between musical works and sound recordings.[547]

Digital music services, however, disagree, contending that the statutory rates set under the section 801(b)(1) standard reflect fair market value, or higher.[548] According to them, the statutory rates provide a "useful benchmark for direct deals" by providing a framework by which to negotiate such deals.[549] They contend that the willing buyer/willing seller standard is faulty at best since "the 'market' the standard seeks to construct or emulate does not exist and often has never existed,"[550] whereas the section 801(b)(1) standard is "flexible" and more predictable and accounts for fairness in compensating copyright owners.[551]

Though record labels are in agreement with digital music services that the section 801(b)(1) standard does not result in rates lower than fair market value, they have also advocated changing the rate standard to the willing buyer/willing seller standard.[552] Record labels point to the importance of emphasizing fair market value as "the goal of any rate-setting process" and argue that harmonizing the statutory rate standards by bringing section 115 within the willing buyer/willing seller standard would achieve that goal.[553]

b. Administrative Burdens

Stakeholders expressed near universal concern about the inefficiencies of the mechanical licensing process. The section 115 statutory license creates a per-work licensing model; the same model is employed when seeking licenses through intermediaries such as HFA.[554] Licensees seeking to release individual records typically obtain a mechanical license for the specific product through HFA or directly from the publisher.[555] But digital services seeking large volumes—sometimes millions—of licenses are more likely to rely on the section 115 statutory license for at least some of their licensing needs. Consequently, digital providers expressed considerable frustration with the song-by-song licensing process.[556]

Although the statutory licensing process is more commonly relied upon now than it has been in the past, RIAA regarded this development as merely "an indication that musical work licensing is so broken that mass use of the compulsory license process is the best of a lot of bad options."[557] In addition to the burden of seeking licenses for individual works, licensees complain about the lack of readily available data concerning musical work ownership, as described further below.[558] Digital services asserted that the inaccessibility of ownership information leads to costly and burdensome efforts to identify the rightsholders and potentially incomplete or incorrect licenses, exposing them to the risk of statutory infringement damages despite diligent efforts.[559]

A number of licensees also objected to the detailed accounting and payment requirements imposed by section 115.[560] DiMA noted that for "direct license agreements for rights otherwise covered by the section 115 statutory licenses, it is customary for digital music services to pay rightsowners on a *quarterlybasis*."[561] The statute, however, requires accounting and payment on a monthly basis, which increases administrative burdens and out-of-pocket costs.

c. Perceived Unfairness

Many stakeholders are of the view that the section 115 license is unfair to copyright owners. As one submission summed it up: "The notifications, statements of account, license terms, lack of compliance, lack of audit provisions, lack of accountability, lack of transparency, 'one size fits all' royalty rates and inability to effectively enforce the terms of the license demonstrate a complete breakdown in the statutory licensing system from start to finish."[562]

Lack of Audit Rights

Though there may be significant practical limitations on copyright owners' ability to exercise audit rights due to the burden and expense of examining licensees,[563] the right to audit is nonetheless highly valued. Accordingly, there is a particular industry concern that section 115 does not provide music publishers with the right to verify the statements of account they receive from licensees.

Section 115 differs from other statutory licenses in the Copyright Act in providing for an "honor system" of self-reporting without a verification procedure.[564] Owners of musical works, therefore, have no choice other than to rely upon user-certified royalty statements that they may find difficult to trust.[565] Further complicating the situation is that a compulsory licensee may pay all royalties to one co-owner without any notification to the others.[566]

As one stakeholder put it, "[a]n audit right is particularly necessary in the music industry which has an admittedly long and storied history of dubious accounting practices and exploiting songwriters. Every songwriter deserves and should be entitled to a straight count; self-certification . . . is not sufficient."[567] Another stated, "it's trust but you can't verify . . . . [W]e've got to rely on the kindness of strangers that they're going to report accurately."[568]

For many musical work owners, the issue is not just trust, but fairness. As musician David Lowery explained, "I have seen instances where a supposed compulsory licensee has failed to comply with its payment obligations for years, ignored termination notices, and yet is still able to continue to receive the benefits of new statutory licenses for songwriters who await the same fate."[569] Or, as another songwriter advocate concluded: "Having been compelled by the government to license their songs to strangers, it seems only fair that the songwriter at least be able to confirm to their reasonable satisfaction that they are getting a straight count."[570]

While record companies seemed to offer some support for the ability of publishers and songwriters to audit mechanical uses,[571] digital services objected to any sort of verification process. In opposing an audit right, DiMA argued that the required statements of account already provide for a method of "self-auditing," and that auditing requirements would be burdensome and frustrate the value of the license itself.[572] In addition, due to the challenges of accounting for digital uses under different licensing schemes, DiMA believed auditing would cause even good-faith actors to appear noncompliant.[573]

A few parties offered specific proposals for an audit right under section 115. NMPA and HFA suggested amending section 115 to include a duty to exchange and update usage data on a continuous basis.[574] David Lowery suggested a system whereby the Copyright Office could investigate licensees that were not compliant with their duties under section 115.[575]

Administrative Issues

Publishers, songwriters, and licensing administrators emphasized the problem of noncompliant statutory licensees.[576] The required notices to obtain a statutory license are frequently deficient,[577] and licensees regularly fail to timely and accurately pay and report usage.[578] Due to the involuntary nature of the license, publishers and songwriters cannot easily avoid these risks, as "[n]othing in the Section 115 license scheme requires any consideration of the creditworthiness or trustworthiness of the compulsory licensee."[579] Many found the recourse provided by statute—termination of the license and costly infringement lawsuits—ineffective.[580]

Publishers also complained about regulatory provisions that permit payment of royalties and service of NOIs on a single co-owner of a work, with that co-owner then under an obligation to account to the other co-owners. As one commenter explained, "[t]his practice effectively shifts to the copyright owner the accounting and payment obligations of the user."[581]

At the same time, a number of parties asserted that the complex nature of the statutory licensing scheme was unfair to licensees. Some pointed to the complexity of the section 115 royalty regulations for digital services—and the fine distinctions they draw among different types of services—as a source of confusion as to what royalties need to be paid.[582] Digital services also highlighted the one-sided risk of costly statutory damages should they fail to ascertain that a first use of a work has occurred (rendering the work eligible for statutory licensing) and timely serve an NOI on the copyright owner, even where such determination is difficult due to lack of sufficient data.[583]

d. Parties' Proposals

Elimination of Statutory License

Songwriters and publishers appear almost universally to favor the elimination of the section 115 statutory license, albeit with an appropriate phase-out period.[584] They assert that the statutory regime creates an artificial *statuqsuo* that precludes a private market from developing.[585] Musical work owners predict that the elimination of a license would allow "a functioning licensing market . . . [to] flourish."[586]

Digital music services, however, assert that the section 115 license is both important and fair, as it "provides an *essential counter-balance to the unique market power of copyright rights owners* . . . by providing a mechanism for immediate license coverage, thereby negating the rights owner's prerogative to withhold the grant of a license."[587] Thus, some licensees view section 115 as a protection against monopoly power that allows the public to enjoy musical works while still compensating copyright owners.[588] Spotify argued that the free market is not stifled by the statutory license, but that section 115 instead acts as "an indispensable component to facilitating a vibrant marketplace for making millions of sound recordings available to the public on commercially reasonable terms."[589]

Blanket Licensing

In light of the widely perceived inefficiencies of song-by-song licensing of mechanical rights—particularly as compared to the collective approach of the PROs—a wide range of stakeholders suggested that a blanket system would be a superior means of licensing mechanical rights.[590] As RIAA noted, blanket licensing avoids the administrative costs associated with negotiating and managing large numbers of licenses of varying terms and provides a way for legitimate services to avoid infringement risk.[591] Similarly, the publisher ABKCO opined that blanket license agreements would facilitate the use of music and would help licensees fulfill notification and reporting obligations.[592] IPAC suggested that blanket licensing could be implemented through the creation of one or more licensing agencies.[593]

To highlight the complexity of licensing in the modern music marketplace, RIAA described the experience of one of its members, which had released "a very successful album," and "had to obtain for that album 1481 licenses for the release of three physical products, the 92 digital products, the 27 songs across the 51 songwriters" with a total of "89 shares."[594] One of those shares "represented [a] 1.5 percent interest in a song, and there were two publishers for that."[595] According to the RIAA, apart from multiple songwriter interests, one of the reasons for this explosion in licensing complexity is the increased complexity of the releases themselves—whereas in the past a record label release consisted of "a disk and some liner notes," today it comprises multiple digital formats, different kinds of audiovisual presentations, and different kinds of music services.[596]

In light of its belief that these problems "cannot be solved by piecemeal efforts," RIAA proposed fundamentally restructuring performance and mechanical licensing for musical works.[597] Under the RIAA proposal, record labels would receive a compulsory blanket license covering all rights (performance, mechanical, and synch) necessary for what RIAA calls "modern music products," including audiovisual products like music videos, videos with album art or liner notes, and lyric videos.[598] The rate court and CRB would be eliminated. Instead, the record labels and publishers would agree upon splits of revenues received by the record labels from their sale and licensing of recorded music. The record companies would have sole responsibility to sell and license those products; those deals would be negotiated by the labels in the marketplace (except for uses falling under the section 112 and 114 licenses).[599] RIAA believed that its proposal would achieve fair market rates for publishers and songwriters while retaining the benefits of a collective licensing system, such as simplified licensing and lower administrative costs.[600]

But publishers and songwriters vigorously resisted RIAA's proposal, arguing that it would merely shift control over musical works from songwriters and music publishers to record labels—since the labels would then be in charge of licensing decisions and royalty rates.[601] They also expressed concern about bringing audiovisual works or other rights currently outside of the compulsory system under a statutory blanket license.[602] NMPA characterized the RIAA's proposal as "seeking to expand the scope of the Sec. 115 compulsory license to authorize almost all forms of exploitation of a sound recording, including, among other things, record label created videos, and 'first use' rights."[603]

3. Sections 112 and 114

As compared to issues relating to the licensing of musical works, concerns regarding the section 112 and 114 statutory licenses were relatively modest.

a. Royalty Rates

Sound recording owners appear generally satisfied with the section 112 and 114 rates set under the willing buyer/willing seller standard.[604] A2IM, in particular, appreciates that the CRB's process treats all sound recordings the same for ratesetting purposes.[605]

CFA and Public Knowledge, however, assert that section 112 and 114 royalties are "much too high," pointing to the fact that Pandora had "yet to demonstrate sustained profitability."[606] DiMA similarly contended that the willing buyer/willing seller standard yields rates that are "high and unsustainable" and that numerous services, including those operated by AOL, Yahoo!, East Village Radio, Turntable.fm, Loudcity, RadioParadise, and 3 Wk, have exited the business as a result.[607]

DiMA also criticized the CRB's imposition of per-performance rates for internet radio, suggesting that such a rate structure should not be applied "in circumstances where the higher usage does not equate to higher revenues for the digital music service provider."[608] DiMA and others additionally observed that Congress felt compelled to offer relief to internet radio services complaining of high rates under the willing buyer/willing seller standard by passing the Small Webcaster Settlement Act of 2002 and the Webcaster Settlement Acts of 2008 and 2009 to allow for negotiated alternatives to the CRB-set rates.[609]

b. Interactive/Noninteractive Divide

Stakeholders expressed a number of concerns regarding eligibility for the section 112 and 114 licenses.

As discussed above, interactive services are not eligible for the statutory licenses under sections 112 and 114, though in the Second Circuit's 2009 *LaunchMedia* decision, the court concluded that a custom radio service—one that relies on user feedback to play a personalized selection of music—is not an "interactive" service.[610] As a result, custom radio services such as Pandora are treated as noninteractive and operate under section 112 and 114 licenses.

Copyright owners expressed concern that "customized Internet radio has approached interactivity in every sense of the word except under the outdated requirements of the statutory definition."[611] RIAA similarly opined that *Launch Media* "all but extinguished voluntary licensing of personalized streaming services at a premium [above] the statutory rate."[612] Notably, however, sound recording owners did not necessarily favor moving personalized services out of the statutory license.[613] Instead, they advocated for a "middle tier" of royalty rates for personalized radio services under the statutory license.[614]

Other participants argued for expansion of the statutory licensing framework to cover additional services.[615] For instance, A2IM favored "narrowing the definition of 'interactive service' to cover only those services that truly offer a full on-demand interactive experience."[616] SAG-AFTRA and AFM also supported such an expansion, as "[a]rtists will continue to benefit most fairly from [customized services] through receiving an equal share of the proceeds, paid to them directly and transparently by SoundExchange."[617]

In addition to the interactive/noninteractive distinction of section 114, concerns were raised about the sound recording performance complement—which limits the number of plays of a single featured artist or from a particular album in a three-hour period—as well as section 114's ban on the pre-announcement of songs.[618] Broadcasters said that these requirements frustrate simulcasting activities of terrestrial radio stations that do not adhere to these restrictions in their over-the-air broadcasts.[619] NAB contended that the sound recording performance complement "merely serve[s] as a bargaining chip for leverage in the negotiations with broadcasters, due solely to the undue burden such restrictions place on radio stations that seek to stream their broadcasts,"[620] and pointed out that record labels regularly grant broadcasters waivers of the restriction as evidence that the record labels do not need these provisions to protect their interests.[621] NPR noted the upstream effect of the limitation, explaining that because public radio has limited resources, it is forced to "create separate programming depending on the method by which it will be distributed."[622]

c. Technical Limitations of Section 112

A number of digital services criticized technical limitations on the availability of the section 112 license that applies to the ephemeral (i.e., server) copies needed to facilitate their transmissions.[623] For example, some licensees criticized the requirement that the licensee destroy such copies within six months' time as "unreasonable" and "archaic" and one that has no benefit for rightsholders.[624] NAB noted that this requirement is particularly illogical as server copies "are not meant to be temporary."[625] DiMA suggested that section 112 should be substantially updated to reflect modern realities of digital music services.[626] Others suggested that any ephemeral copies made in furtherance of a public performance should be exempted entirely.[627]

RIAA opposed a blanket exemption for ephemeral recordings, explaining that those recordings "have value" by providing services with "improved quality of service, operational efficiencies or other competitive advantages."[628] RIAA also observed that "[t]he current statutory scheme replicates marketplace agreements for sound recordings, in which licensees commonly acquire performance and related reproduction rights in a single transaction and pay a bundled royalty that covers both rights."[629]

d. Lack of Termination Provision

SoundExchange opined that while the section 112 and 114 licensing framework "generally works well," noncompliance with the statutory requirements—by irregular or inaccurate payments or missing or incomplete reporting—is "commonplace."[630] SoundExchange described its efforts to bring services into compliance, but also expressed its belief that the section 112 and 114 system needs "a clear mechanism for termination of statutory licenses for services that repeatedly fail to act in compliance with applicable requirements," such as the one that exists under section 115.[631]

e. Royalty Distribution Process

Unlike section 114—which provides a statutory formula for the direct distribution of royalties by SoundExchange to artists, record labels and musicians—the related section 112 license contains no such requirement. Some submissions suggested that the royalties collected by SoundExchange as the designated agent under the section 112 license should be distributed to artists directly, as under section 114, rather than through record labels.[632] Music Choice commented that, "[d]ue to the terms of their agreements with the record companies and various record company accounting practices . . . the vast majority of recording artists never see a penny of the portion of the performance royalty allocated to the Section 112 license."[633]

In addition, section 114 currently does not allocate a share of royalties to record producers, so there is no statutory mandate for direct payment to producers. Instead, individual contracts between recording artists and producers provide for producer compensation, which may include a share of royalties.[634] SoundExchange has begun processing direct payment of the producer's share of performance royalties on a voluntary basis when it receives written authorization from the featured artist.[635] NARAS has proposed to make this process a "consistent and permanent" feature of section 114.[636]

4. Public and Noncommercial Broadcasting

As discussed above, the activities of public and noncommercial educational broadcasters are subject to two different statutory licenses as well as PRO licensing and ratesetting. Noncommercial broadcasters complain about the divergent licensing mechanisms for the various music rights they must acquire. Noncommercial religious broadcasters observed that, to clear musical works rights, they could be required to participate in a CRB proceeding under section 118 for over-the-air transmissions, two rate court proceedings under the consent decrees for digital transmissions of ASCAP and BMI works, and private negotiation for digital transmissions of SESAC works.[637] In addition, ascertaining the rate for digital performances of sound recordings requires participation in yet another CRB ratesetting proceeding under section 114.[638]

Noncommercial broadcasters thus seek to expand the section 118 license to encompass "all music elements."[639] Noncommercial religious broadcasters proposed, in particular, "[f]olding digital transmissions of musical works into the existing section 118 license applicable to broadcast transmissions."[640] NPR advocated for a further step: broadening the section 118 license to encompass "all known and yet to be created distribution methods and technologies," including physical products and permanent digital downloads.[641]

Finally, noncommercial broadcasters seek to ensure that the policy-oriented 801(b)(1) ratesetting standard will apply to any expanded version of the section 118 license.[642]

5. Concerns Regarding CRB Procedures

As with the rate courts, many stakeholders expressed concern about the CRB ratesetting process—many of which are governed by detailed statutory provisions[643]—including specific concerns regarding discovery procedures, the settlement process, and bifurcated proceedings.

a. Inefficiencies and Expense

Copyright owners and licensees together complained about the inefficiency and high cost of proceedings before the CRB.[644] RIAA and SoundExchange suggested that one way to reduce costs would be to simplify the rate standards and move to a straightforward willing buyer/willing seller rate standard across the board.[645] SoundExchange noted that "[r]elative to a streamlined fair market value standard, every specific factor included in a rate standard increases cost and decreases predictability."[646]

Stakeholders also pointed to the bifurcated ratesetting procedures contemplated by statute—which references separate direct and rebuttal phases of ratesetting hearings[647]— as a significant and costly inefficiency,[648] creating a "'two ships passing in the night' quality to the proceedings."[649] There was broad support for eliminating the bifurcated nature of trials before the CRB because "[b]ifurcation offers no advantages or efficiencies in discovery, comprehension of complex issues, savings in judicial resources, or elimination of duplicative presentations of evidence."[650]

Another shortfall of the system is that the rate adjustment process occurs only once every five years. Parties representing both copyright owners and music users found the process slow and insufficiently responsive to new and developing technologies and services.[651] Because ratesetting occurs only on a periodic basis, copyright owners and users must attempt to predict and accommodate each type of service that might arise in the upcoming five-year period.[652] For instance, as RIAA recounted, "[t]he Section 115 rate-setting process . . . resulted in a rate schedule with 17 different rate categories, and in which publishers and songwriters can receive varying percentages of the relevant content royalty pool" based on those categories, causing the administration of payments to be "exceedingly complex."[653]

b. Settlement Obstacles

In theory, Congress designed the CRB procedures to facilitate and encourage settlement rather than administrative ratesetting by the CRB. Several stakeholders, however, noted practical and procedural hurdles they have encountered in finalizing settlements.

The most common stakeholder plea was to modify the CRB process so the Judges would act quickly on any settlement.[654] Stakeholders complained that even where a settlement is reached, the CRB has delayed ruling on the settlement,[655] sometimes adopting the settlement only after the proceedings were concluded.[656] RIAA also observed that delay of settlement has frustrated the business plans of services.[657] Music Choice concurred that delays during the voluntary negotiation period leave inadequate time for parties to conduct rate proceedings.[658]

To address these issues, SoundExchange proposed bypassing CRB approval of settlements by granting the section 112 and 114 designated agent (i.e., SoundExchange) the authority to enter into opt-in settlement agreements for a statutory license.[659] It further suggested that the CRB could be required to adopt a negotiated settlement even if it would not fully resolve a case.[660] SoundExchange also surmised that parties may be reluctant to settle because the negotiated rate may be used as a benchmark or otherwise in rate determinations, and suggested that parties be permitted to designate settlements as non-precedential.[661]

c. Discovery Process

Music services criticized the discovery process that applies to ratesetting proceedings before the CRB on two grounds. First, they observed that because the statute specifies that discovery occurs only *after* the submission of the parties' direct cases—contrary to the ordinary practice in civil litigation—"parties are required to assume what they will develop during discovery and hope that relevant information will be voluntarily revealed by their opponent in the opponent's written case."[662] Licensees believe that this process puts them at a disadvantage, because much of the information regarding benchmark rates is held by copyright owners.[663] In addition, the statutory procedures limit discovery to documents directly related to the direct statements.[664] Licensees suggested that this rule allows copyright owners to behave strategically in their own direct statement and thus limit discovery.[665]

Music providers also complained about the statutory limits on discovery.[666] While recognizing the hypothetical benefits of a streamlined discovery process, some observed that there are no actual cost savings and the restrictions are not fair.[667] According to licensees, the 60-day discovery window is too short,[668] and the statutory limit of 25 interrogatories and 10 depositions for all parties on each side is insufficient.[669] Other discovery-related suggestions included adoption of a standardized blanket protective order that would be implemented for "non-public, commercially-sensitive information produced in discovery and submitted as evidence."[670] NAB also supported use of the Federal Rules of Civil Procedure and Federal Rules of Evidence, with slight modifications, for CRB proceedings.[671]

In response to these concerns about discovery, copyright owners argued that the commenting parties "did not identify any instance in which the Judges believed the current procedures prevented a full record from being developed,"[672] and added that "open-ended discovery" would add to the complication, expense, or inefficiency of proceedings.[673] At the same time, copyright owners agreed that conducting discovery "up front" could be "helpful," along with eliminating the bifurcated nature of CRB proceedings.[674]

C. Licensing Efficiency and Transparency

1. Music Data

a. Lack of Reliable Public Data

Based on the record in this proceeding, there can be little doubt that the current music licensing landscape is severely hampered by the lack of publicly accessible, authoritative identification and ownership data.[675] There are several facets to this problem.

To begin with, there is a lack of comprehensive and reliable ownership data, particularly for musical works. As RIAA noted, "it is difficult to identify and keep track of musical work ownership due to changes when musical works and catalogs change hands."[676] Further complicating the situation is that the rights to musical works are often split among multiple songwriters, with differing publishers and PROs, making musical work data harder to track and maintain.[677]

In addition, digital music files often do not include the standard identifiers for the copyrighted works the files embody—i.e., the ISRC for the sound recording and the ISWC for the underlying musical work.[678] Even when the file includes the ISRC, as is now commonplace for new releases, the ISWC for the underlying musical work is often not yet assigned at the time of initial release.[679] And even after an ISWC has been obtained by the musical work owner, there is no comprehensive, publicly accessible database that can be used to match the ISRC to the ISWC.[680] Google noted that requiring licensors to supply data helps to "identify exactly what it is they are licensing . . . both from a deal implementation standpoint as well as a deal valuation standpoint," adding that "those sort of data requirements . . . work their way back up the chain, to the creators."[681]

Beyond the ISRC and ISWC, there is also a lack of universal and uniform data to identify songwriters and recording artists associated with individual works. While a global identifier for creators—the ISNI—has been certified by ISO to replace older systems employed by the PROs and others, it is not yet widely used.[682]

These shortcomings cause serious inefficiencies. Licensees expend significant effort attempting to identify particular sound recordings and the musical works they embody, as well as tracking down their copyright owners. Because there is no centralized data resource, stakeholders devote "significant resources to maintaining redundant and often inconsistent databases of musical work ownership and split information."[683] Digital services noted that the lack of an authoritative source of data exposes even well- intentioned actors to potential statutory damages for "inadvertently distributing works without requisite authorization."[684] According to DiMA, this risk is inequitable because copyright owners inadequately identify themselves and their works.[685]

Commenters also referenced the recent *Pandora* rate court decision, in which the court found that withdrawing publishers did not supply catalog data that would have allowed Pandora to pull their songs from its service.[686] Some were troubled by this tactic, and urged that, if this type of publisher withdrawal is allowed, the withdrawing publisher must be required to "provide immediate transparency as to the musical works that are no longer subject to license."[687]

On the licensor side of the equation, the lack of reliable data means that royalty payments may be delayed, misdirected, or never made.[688] SoundExchange highlighted in particular the problems caused when digital services fail to include standard identifiers in their reports of usage under the section 112 and 114 statutory licenses. It explained that basic data elements—featured artist name, track title, album name, and label name—"simply are not sufficient to distinguish unambiguously among the tens of millions of recordings actively being commercialized today."[689] Instead, "standard identifiers are the only practicable way to identify and accurately account for usage of all those recordings."[690]

RIAA similarly noted that "[a] flourishing musical work licensing marketplace requires both that potential licensees can get licensed and that royalties flow properly to music publishers and songwriters," and that "reliable and accessible information is critical to making that happen."[691] NMPA agreed, saying that a "database where we know the rights" would be valuable.[692] Flawed or missing data is not a problem unique to major labels or famous artists, and A2IM commented that inaccurate data is "especially problematic for the independent label community" because it is harder to identify lesser- known artists without accurate data.[693]

b. Parties' Views

In light of the concerns identified above, there appears to be widespread agreement that authoritative and comprehensive data related to the identity and ownership of works would substantially enhance transparency in the music licensing system, reduce transaction costs, and facilitate direct licensing through private negotiation in the open market.[694] There is, however, less harmony about the best way to achieve this goal.

Some suggested that the government should play a central role. DiMA, for example, proposed that the Copyright Office create and maintain a music database, while others called for the Office to identify and publicize data standards, and facilitate or require submission of such data in the registration or recordation process.[695] Others conceived of quasi-governmental solutions. FMC stated that Congress might consider creating a "nonprofit to oversee the development of a global registry database (or databases) that could be overseen by government, in cooperation with international bodies."[696] Several licensees suggested ASCAP and BMI should be required to provide better and more usable repertoire data.[697] Some proposed more market-based solutions, such as data expert Jim Griffin's proposal to emulate the registration system for websites, whereby the government would engage in standards-setting to encourage the creation of profit- seeking private registries, similar to domain name registries like GoDaddy.[698]

Others groups—principally representing copyright owners—believed that government involvement was unnecessary. In NMPA's view, if the market for creative works were unregulated and free of governmental price controls (including the section 115 license), "transactional hubs, syndication platforms and other supply chain management platforms" would develop to match buyers to sellers and to allocate and distribute revenues.[699] For their part, the PROs highlighted their online repertoire databases and efforts such as MusicMark to enhance access to reliable repertoire data.[700] The PROs acknowledged that their plans do not include making all of their data available to the public, however, stressing that they face significant confidentiality concerns.[701]

RIAA noted that assignment of ISRCs and ISWCs could be better coordinated (*e.g.*, by having the record company first recording a new song assign the ISRC and ISWC in tandem to ensure that the ISWC will be available to relevant stakeholders upon a song's release).[702] Stakeholders generally shared the view that such solutions are worth exploring.[703]

Both SoundExchange and RIAA observed that there are fewer problems with sound recording than musical work data.[704] According to them, sound recording identification and ownership information is generally available from product packaging, or from publicly available internet sources such as allmusic.com and discogs.com.[705] Additionally, digital services generally receive metadata from record companies and distributors providing music files.[706] RIAA pointed out that, unlike musical works, ownership of sound recordings is rarely divided among multiple co-owners, and record companies owning commercially significant recordings are less numerous than music publishers, with less frequent changes in ownership.[707]

SoundExchange additionally explained that it maintains robust identification and ownership information, including ISRCs for approximately 14 million sound recordings.[708] SoundExchange is actively exploring means by which it might provide statutory licensees with access to its database for statement of account purposes. For example, SoundExchange may offer music services the capability to search for ISRCs or supply music services with ISRCs that are missing from their reports of use.[709]

SoundExchange and RIAA together emphasized that licensees operating under the section 112 and 114 licenses should use available identifying information, particularly ISRCs, when reporting usage to SoundExchange.[710] Such an obligation would increase automatic matching of reported usage to known repertoire and facilitate accurate manual matching when necessary, thus enhancing the data maintained by SoundExchange.[711] Both parties noted that adoption of such a requirement would encourage broader use of the ISRC standard.[712]

2. Usage and Payment Transparency

Incomplete or inaccurate data frustrates the ability of creators and sellers of music to track how music is used and what payments are made. Even when accurate data is available, however, stakeholders had concerns about the effectiveness of music usage and payment tracking for payment allocation and about the lack of audit rights for certain licenses. At bottom, the issue in the music industry is that participants want reassurance that they are being treated fairly by other actors.[713]

a. Advances and Equity Deals

There was a growing concern that payments received by record companies and music publishers from new digital music services as part of direct deals are not being shared fairly with songwriters and recording artists.[714] SAG-AFTRA and AFM warned that while direct licensing deals between digital music services and record labels or publishers may result in more compensation from licensees, direct deals may actually result in lower payments to artists than under the statutory licensing scheme.[715]

A major objection to direct licensing is that labels and publishers do not necessarily share advance payments of royalties—in particular, unrecouped advances or "breakage" monies—with creators.[716] Advance payments of royalties can be significant; Google, for instance, reportedly paid more than $400 million to WMG under a recent three-year deal to license the label's music for YouTube and its subscription offerings.[717] In many cases, if an advance is not fully recouped (i.e., fully applied to royalties due) by the end of the license term, the excess fees are retained by the label or publisher rather than returned. The question is whether these funds are accounted for and paid out by the label or publisher to its artists or songwriters.

Some record labels and publishers may share unrecouped advances with performers and writers, but the practice is not universal.[718] And while well-established musicians may occasionally negotiate a right to collect on breakage,[719] others are not as successful.[720] Negotiating for these payments can be difficult, as artists and songwriters are not necessarily aware of deal terms. For example, SGA commented that without the testimony of an executive representing DMX in a BMI rate court proceeding, the songwriting community would never have known of a $2.4 million advance paid by DMX to Sony/ATV.[721]

Similarly suspect for creators are equity deals between major labels and digital services. It has been reported, for instance, that the major labels collectively acquired an 18% ownership interest in Spotify.[722] Referencing Spotify, as well as YouTube and Musicmaker, Perry Resnick, who conducts music audits, commented that "[m]any deals are not done unless the major labels receive a share of equity in the licensee, which also lowers the royalty rates paid for specific recordings, sometimes down to zero."[723] There seems to be no reliable practice, however, under which artists and songwriters are compensated for such equity arrangements.[724]

b. PRO Distributions

PROs create value by licensing, administering, and enforcing music creators' public performance rights. Yet some songwriters voiced concerns that part of this value is lost through inaccurate payment allocation. PROs frequently use sampling surveys to estimate how many times a song has been performed during a payment period, and rely upon those estimates to allocate royalties among their members.[725]

An alternative, and more comprehensive, form of measurement is census reporting, whereby licensees account for each use of a musical work (*e.g.*, each individual stream) to the collecting entity. Census reporting is more common for digital services, where it is easier to track individual performances.[726] ASCAP relies upon census data only when it is "economically feasible" to process.[727] For many uses—including terrestrial radio uses and some digital uses—ASCAP uses a sample survey.[728] BMI similarly relies upon extrapolated data to pay royalties in many instances.[729] Information concerning ASCAP's and BMI's distribution practices is publicly available on their websites.[730]

Some musicians and publishers commented that increased use of census data instead of surveys would result in more accurate payments by PROs to their members under blanket licenses. For instance, Music Services stated that survey-based distribution, particularly for radio and live performances, is "antiquated" and that "[m]any publishers and writers believe they are not receiving their fair share of the PRO pot."[731] Other participants observed that under a sampling system, musicians who do not have "mainstream" songs on the radio are underpaid.[732] Under this view, since sampling is more likely to identify hit songs, the PRO will likely undercount performances of works by emerging or fringe musicians.

In response, a representative from ASCAP sympathized, stating "ideally, yes, I wish everyone would get paid for every performance," but noted the administrative impracticality of identifying every use.[733] Others echoed this sentiment, commenting that even if uses could be precisely tracked, some would be so small that they would not be payable.[734] Nonetheless, ASCAP notes that "[a]s new technologies make surveying a given medium such as broadcast radio economically efficient, we implement those technologies to move closer to a full census."[735] For its part, BMI commented that there is competition between PROs for members and the market will sufficiently drive distribution methodologies.[736]

Despite these concerns, songwriters generally expressed confidence in the PROs.[737] The PROs are seen as relatively transparent[738] and protecting the writers' share of performance royalties.[739] SGA noted that "licensing through the PROs . . . has benefited and given protection to the community of American music creators for over one hundred years" by "provid[ing] music creators with the crucial assurance that an important source of revenue will be paid directly to them by the PRO."[740] Similarly, in NSAI's estimation, "ASCAP and BMI essentially act as not-for-profit collection arms for songwriters and composers."[741]

c. "Pass-through" Licensing

As noted above, under section 115, compulsory licensees can authorize third-party streaming services to transmit downloads and streams of musical works. Songwriters and publishers complain vigorously about this system.[742] SGA pointed out that pass-through licensing "creates a situation in which the creators and owners of musical compositions have no privity of contract with online music distribution giants such as Apple iTunes, and must therefore rely on sometimes adversarial record company 'intermediaries' for the monitoring and payment of royalties earned via online download usage."[743] Another commenter explained that "pass-through licensing, where record labels can license mechanical rights directly on publishers' behalf and without publishers' input, leaves songwriters with no clue as to whether or not they are properly paid."[744]

Stakeholders appear largely to agree that the pass-through approach—which mimics the traditional physical model, where record labels ship product to stores and report sales back to publishers—is unnecessary in the digital environment, since it is feasible for music owners to have a direct relationship with consumer-facing distributors. Significantly, even RIAA, a presumed beneficiary of the section 115 pass-through license, appears to favor the end of this pass-through licensing: "The major record companies generally support in principle the elimination of pass-through licensing . . . within the context of a structure that makes it unnecessary."[745]

IV. ANALYSIS AND RECOMMENDATIONS

It may be the very power of music that has led to its disparate treatment under the law. The songs we enjoy in our early years resonate for the rest of our lives. Human beings have a deep psychological attachment to music that often seems to approach a sense of ownership; people want to possess and share the songs they love. Perhaps this passion is one of the reasons music has been subject to special statutory treatment under the law.

Regardless of what has animated our century-old embrace of government regulation of music, the Copyright Office believes that the time is ripe to question the existing paradigm and consider meaningful change. In recent years, we have seen piecemeal efforts to address particular issues through focused legislation: there have been bills directed to the lack of a terrestrial performance right for sound recordings, ratesetting inequities, and payment for pre-1972 sound recordings. Each has targeted a specific issue or issues within the existing system. In the current environment, however, these sorts of limited proposals—standing alone—seem unlikely to generate broad enough support to become law. It is for this reason, perhaps, that some members of Congress have recently indicated interest in a more holistic approach.[746]

How ambitious should any such approach be? As a number of commenters remarked during the course of this study, if we were to do it all again, we would never design the system that we have today. But as tempting as it may be to daydream about a new model built from scratch, such a course would seem to be logistically and politically unrealistic. We must take the world as we find it, and seek to shape something new from the material we have on hand.

In this section, based on the information and commentary gathered in the study, the Office analyzes critical areas of concern and—considering the record and merits of disparate viewpoints—suggests ways to reshape our music licensing system to better meet the demands of the digital era. Following a discussion of the role of government in the music marketplace, the Office outlines a series of interrelated changes that might be implemented to modernize our struggling system. The recommendations below seek to capitalize on the value that existing institutions and methods could continue to provide under an updated framework.

Rather than presenting a detailed plan, the Office's recommendations should be understood as high-level and preliminary in nature—more of a sketch than a completed picture. It is also important that the proposals be contemplated together, rather than in isolation. The Office seeks to present a series of balanced tradeoffs among the interested parties to create a fairer, more efficient, and rational system for all.

A. Guiding Principles

The Copyright Office appreciates and agrees with the four grounding principles that were articulated by many during the course of this study, as discussed above. These are:

- Music creators should be fairly compensated for their contributions
- The licensing process should be more efficient

- Market participants should have access to authoritative data to identify and license sound recordings and musical works
- Usage and payment information should be transparent and accessible to rightsowners

As much as there may be consensus on these points, however, the opposite could be said of stakeholders' views as to how best to achieve them. Having considered the plethora of issues that plague our current licensing system—and how they might practically be addressed—the Office has identified some additional principles that it believes should also guide any process of reform. These are:

- Government licensing processes should aspire to treat like uses of music alike
- Government supervision should enable voluntary transactions while still supporting collective solutions
- Ratesetting and enforcement of antitrust laws should be separately managed and addressed
- A single, market-oriented ratesetting standard should apply to all music uses under statutory licenses

Each of these principles is explored below in the context of the Office's overall recommendations.

B. Licensing Parity and Fair Compensation

Questions of licensing parity and fair compensation are closely tied to the relative treatment of music rights and rightsholders under the law.[747] The Office believes that any overhaul of our music licensing system should strive to achieve greater consistency in the way it regulates (or does not regulate) analogous platforms and uses. In addition to rewarding those distribution models that are most resource-efficient and appealing to consumers, evenhanded treatment will encourage more equitable compensation for creators.

From today's vantage point, at least, the impact of our current system on different classes of copyright owners and users—favoring some while disadvantaging others— seems to be more the product of historical happenstance than conscious design. To the extent our policies require copyright owners to subsidize certain business models through reduced royalties, as copyright owners claim, this is not the result of a present- day judgment that it is a fair way to treat creators, or promotes the values of our copyright system. The same can be said of policies that impose higher royalty obligations on one business model over competing platforms.

The policy rationales that animated the creation of the section 115 compulsory license, the PRO consent decrees, and even the section 112 and 114 framework for digital performances, are now decades behind us. The Office believes that the current widespread perception that the system is outmoded and broken may provide an opportunity to review and rationalize the playing field.

1. Equitable Treatment of Rights and Uses

As suggested above, the Copyright Office believes that an important element of a robust and fair music marketplace is to treat equivalent uses of sound recordings and musical works—and competing platforms—alike, or as alike as can practically be achieved.

a. Musical Works versus Sound Recordings

Which is more important, the song or the sound recording? "It all begins with a song," runs the oft-cited refrain;[748] but then again, the song is brought to life through a sound recording. While there is, of course, no definitive answer to this question, as reflected throughout this report, the law nonetheless treats sound recordings and musical works differently.

In the case of noninteractive streaming uses, sound recordings are subject to compulsory licensing at government-set rates. But apart from this, sound recordings are licensed by their owners in the free market.

As for musical works, while synch uses (including consumer-generated videos) are not subject to government oversight,[749] the other core segments of the market (mechanical reproduction and performance uses) are regulated. As indicated above, a recurring complaint from publishers and songwriters is that significantly higher rates are paid for sound recordings than for musical works in the online world—whether those rates are set by the CRB or by one of the rate courts. At least some of this disparity appears to arise from publishers' inability to negotiate free from government constraint where record companies can.

In keeping with the guiding philosophy that government should aspire to treat like uses of music alike, the Office believes this should change, at least in the digital realm. That is, where sound recording owners have the ability to negotiate digital rates in the open market, so should owners of musical works.

Although the path to enabling this type of parity is complicated by the divergent licensing frameworks for mechanical and performance rights on the musical work side, the Office's approach would offer a free market alternative to musical work owners, in the form of an opt-out right, in the most significant areas where sound recording owners enjoy unfettered digital rights—namely, interactive streaming uses and downloads. And where sound recording owners are subject to statutory ratesetting—i.e., in the case of noninteractive streaming—musical works would remain regulated. To further promote uniformity of approach, as discussed below, the Office is recommending that all music ratesetting activities—whether on the sound recording or musical work side— take place before the CRB.

The Office believes that treating analogous uses alike in the digital environment is more likely to yield equitable rates as between sound recordings and musical works—or will at least make that goal more attainable.[750] This does not mean that the Office assumes that the rates for sound recordings and musical works necessarily should be equal. Rather, the goal is to encourage evenhanded consideration of both rates by a single body, under a common standard, to achieve a fair result.

The benefits of parallel treatment would not be limited to licensing at government-set rates. Where a music publisher had chosen to opt out of the statutory license to negotiate a direct deal, both the publisher and the sound recording owner would have the same ability to make their case to the licensee. The licensee would then be in a position to assess the value of each right and proceed accordingly, as happens in the synch market today.

Finally, such an approach would also allow for the possibility of achieving an all-in rate—and simplified rate structure—covering both sound recordings and musical works for noninteractive uses under the section 112 and 114 licenses (including terrestrial radio, which the Office proposes be brought under those licenses, as discussed below).[751] As suggested by the record labels, it might be possible for labels and publishers to agree to a royalty split as between them—or have the split set in an initial phase of a CRB proceeding—and then proceed together as allies in litigating the rates to be paid by statutory licensees.[752]

b. Terrestrial Radio

In the case of terrestrial radio, federal law exempts what is currently a 17 billion dollar industry[753] from paying those who contribute the sound recordings that are responsible for its success.[754] Apart from being inequitable to rightsholders—including by curtailing the reciprocal flow of such royalties into the United States—the exemption of terrestrial radio from royalty obligations harms competing satellite and internet radio providers who must pay for the use of sound recordings. In a world that is more and more about performance and less about record sales, the inability to obtain a return from terrestrial radio increases the pressure on paying sources. The market-distorting impact of the terrestrial radio exemption probably cannot be overstated.

The Office has long supported the creation of a full sound recording performance right, advocating for Congress to expand the existing right so it is commensurate with the performance right afforded to other classes of works under federal copyright law.[755] As one of the few remaining industrialized countries that does not recognize a terrestrial radio performance right, the United States stands in stark contrast to peer nations.[756] In her recent testimony before Congress, the Register of Copyrights described the terrestrial performance right issue as "ripe for resolution,"[757] recommending that any congressional efforts to update the Copyright Act include a legislative answer.[758]

Radio broadcasters argue that a sound recording performance royalty would unfairly impose a "tariff" to subsidize the recording industry at the expense of broadcasters— their opinion, the limited performance right and lack of royalties in terrestrial radio have not impacted the "growth or supremacy of the United States recording industry."[759] This argument would seem to ring hollow, however, given the current challenges faced by that industry.

Radio broadcasters also point to the promotional effect of traditional airplay on sales of sound recordings as a reason for maintaining the status quo. Undoubtedly, sound recording owners recognize value in radio airplay, in particular for new releases.[760] But any such value must be considered and weighed in the context of the overall earnings of the broadcast industry. Significantly, as consumer preferences shift away from music ownership, the potential for sales is becoming less relevant, and the promotional value of radio less apparent.

In this regard, the creation of a terrestrial sound recording performance right need not overlook or negate the question of promotional value, because this factor can be taken into account by a ratesetting authority, or in private negotiations, to arrive at an appropriate royalty rate. Such an approach would appear to be a rational solution because it seems fair to assume that a willing buyer and willing seller would do the same.[761]

c. Pre-1972 Sound Recordings

Another area where the law diverges in the way it treats sound recordings and musical works is the lack of federal protection for pre-1972 sound recordings, many of which remain commercially valuable. This, too, impedes a fair marketplace. Satellite and internet radio services appear to rely heavily on pre-1972 recordings in curating their playlists, presumably because (at least until recent court rulings) these selections have been viewed as free from copyright liability on the sound recording side.[762] At the same time, the owners of the musical works embodied in these sound recordings are paid for the same uses.

The Office is of the view that pre-1972 recordings should be brought under the protection of federal copyright law. Such a change would serve the interests of licensing parity by eliminating another market distortion. In addition, it would allow for a federal compensation mechanism for the artists responsible for pre-1972 works.

In 2009, Congress instructed the Office to conduct a study on the "desirability and means" of extending federal copyright protection to pre-1972 sound recordings.[763] After considering input from stakeholders, the Office concluded that pre-1972 sound recordings should be brought under federal copyright law with the same rights, exceptions, and limitations as sound recordings created on or after February 15, 1972.[764] In the Office's view, full federalization of pre-1972 sound recordings (with special provisions to address ownership issues, terms of protection, and registration) would improve the certainty and consistency of copyright law, encourage more preservation and access activities, and provide the owners of pre-1972 sound recordings with the benefits of any future amendments to the Copyright Act.[765]

The Office has not changed its mind. Indeed, since the Office issued its 2011 report, there have been significant developments under both California and New York state law which underscore the need for a unified federal approach to sound recordings. As a result of lawsuits brought by pre-1972 sound recording owners against Sirius XM and Pandora, there have been trial court decisions in California and New York upholding claims that performances of the plaintiffs' sound recordings in those jurisdictions are protected under applicable state law.[766] Subject to any further judicial developments, this means that the defendant services need to obtain licenses from sound recording owners to perform the recordings. But because the requirement to do so is based on state, rather than federal law, users may not rely upon the section 112 and 114 licenses for this purpose.

The legal question of state protection of pre-1972 sound recording performance rights will undoubtedly continue to percolate in other states as well.[767] In addition, there is the significant related question of whether and how the pre-1972 rulings may be applied to performances by terrestrial broadcasters, which of course currently enjoy an exemption under federal law. This aspect of the story has yet to unfold.

In the last Congress, SoundExchange, joined by others, pursued legislation known as the RESPECT Act that would expand the jurisdiction of that organization to collect royalties for pre-1972 performances and provide a safe harbor from state liability for paying services.[768] But this proposed amendment to federal law would not offer the full panoply of federal copyright protection to pre-1972 rightsowners, nor would it allow for application of the DMCA harbors or rights-balancing exceptions such as fair use. In addition, there are important policy considerations relating to the preservation of older works and access to "out-of-print" recordings still subject to state protection that the RESPECT Act does not address.

For these reasons, while the Copyright Office recognizes the potential value of enacting a relatively expedient fix to make sure older artists get paid and to eliminate liability concerns of digital services seeking to exploit pre-1972 recordings, it continues to believe that full federalization remains the best alternative.

2. Consistent Ratesetting Standards

Where the government has stepped in to establish rates for the use of music, it has likewise acted in an inconsistent fashion. While in some cases the law provides that the ratesetting authority should attempt to emulate the free market, in other cases it imposes a more policy-oriented approach.[769]

In this regard, the ratesetting standards under the section 112 and 114 licenses have been a persistent source of unhappiness for both music owners and users. This is hardly surprising, as these licenses prescribe different rate standards for competing platforms— internet radio versus satellite radio—thus allowing both sides to complain.

Satellite radio and "pre-existing" subscription services (such as those provided through cable television) are able to benefit from the four-factor section 801(b)(1) test, which allows the CRB to ponder broader concerns than what negotiating parties might consider in the marketplace—for example, whether a contemplated rate will result in "disruptive impact on the structure of the industries involved and on generally prevailing industry practices."[770] Many interpret the section 801(b)(1) language as enabling the ratesetting body to protect the vested interests of licensees by establishing rates lower than what would (at least theoretically) prevail in the free market.

Rates for the reproduction and distribution of musical works in digital and physical formats are also set under the more policy-oriented 801(b)(1) standard. This is a significant point of contention for music publishers and songwriters, who have been lobbying for legislation to substitute the willing buyer/willing seller standard.[771]

By contrast, rates paid by internet radio services are set by the CRB according to a "willing buyer/willing seller" rate standard. Most perceive the willing buyer/willing seller standard to be more market-oriented in its approach.[772] But internet radio providers have twice taken their case to Congress to override the rates set by the CRB under that rubric,[773] and Congress has given them the opportunity to negotiate substitute agreements with SoundExchange.[774]

As for public performance rights in musical works, by virtue of the consent decrees, ASCAP and BMI are subject to a "reasonable fee" approach, which seeks to approximate hypothetical "fair market value."[775] Though the term "reasonable fee" is not defined in either consent decree, each places the burden of proof on the PRO to establish that its proposed rates are reasonable.[776] The PROs attempt to meet this burden by offering negotiated rates as benchmarks, which economic evidence may or may not be accepted by the court after considering its relevance—often through the lens of quasi-antitrust analysis.[777]

While there are those who might argue that the particular wording of a discretionary rate standard will not have much impact on a results-oriented tribunal, there is at least some evidence to the contrary. For example, in 2008, in establishing rates for satellite radio services, the CRB found it "appropriate to adopt a rate . . . that is lower than the upper boundary most strongly indicated by marketplace data," stating that they did so "in order to satisfy 801(b) policy considerations related to the minimization of disruption that are not adequately addressed by the benchmark market data alone."[778] In any event, there appears to be a shared perception among many industry participants—both those that chafe at the section 801(b)(1) standard and those that like it—that the standard yields lower rates.[779]

The Office believes that all government ratesetting processes should be conducted under a single standard, especially since the original justifications for differential treatment of particular uses and business models appear to have fallen away. There is no longer a threatened piano roll monopoly, and satellite radio is a mature business. Further, however that rate standard is formulated—i.e., whether it is articulated as "willing buyer/willing seller" or "fair market value"—it should be designed to achieve to the greatest extent possible the rates that would be negotiated in an unconstrained market. To the extent that it enumerates specific factors, they should be ones that might reasonably be considered by copyright proprietors and licensees in the real world. In the Office's view, there is no policy justification to demand that music creators subsidize those who seek to profit from their works.

Under such a unified standard, the CRB or other ratesetting body would be encouraged to consider all potentially useful benchmarks—including for analogous uses of related rights (*e.g.*, fees paid for the comparable use of sound recordings when considering musical work rates[780])—in conducting its analysis. But again, it should take into account only those factors that might be expected to influence parties who negotiated rates in the open market. These might include, for example, the substitutional impact of one model on other sources of revenue, or whether a service may promote sales of sound recordings or musical works through other channels.[781] But upon arriving at rates believed to reflect what would be agreed in the open market, those rates would not be discounted on the basis of abstract policy concerns such as "disruptive" impact on prevailing industry practices or solicitude for existing business models notwithstanding their competitive viability in the marketplace.

C. Role of Government in Music Licensing

Government regulation of music has focused on the interrelated concerns of access, pricing and competition. As noted above, section 115—the first compulsory license in our copyright law—was enacted to prevent a single piano roll company from exercising exclusive control over song copyrights. The PRO consent decrees are the result of the government's attempt to balance the efficiencies of collective licensing with concerns about anticompetitive conduct. More recently, Congress chose to extend the public performance right for digital uses of sound recordings on the condition that certain of those uses would be subject to compulsory licensing under sections 112 and 114 of the Copyright Act, thus further extending the practice of regulatory oversight.

As a result of these policy determinations, an administrative tribunal, the CRB, sets the fees paid for the reproduction and distribution of musical works, as well as the royalties due for radio-style digital performance of sound recordings. Two federal judges in New York City are responsible for establishing the fees for the public performance of musical works across traditional and digital platforms. For better or worse, these decades-old regimes are deeply embedded in our licensing infrastructure.[782]

Viewed in the abstract, it is almost hard to believe that the U.S. government sets prices for music. In today's world, there is virtually no equivalent for this type of federal intervention—at least outside of the copyright arena.[783] The closest example is the retransmission by cable and satellite providers of copyrighted television programming (including the music embodied in that programming), which is also subject to compulsory licensing under the Copyright Act and government-set rates.[784] But retransmission rights represent a much more limited segment of the overall revenues for the television industry than do the core music markets subject to government ratesetting, and even there, broadcasters are permitted separately to negotiate non- government-controlled fees for access to the signals that carry the copyrighted works.[785]

1. Antitrust Considerations

As explained above in discussing the section 115 statutory license and PRO consent decrees, much of the rationale—indeed, the original rationale—for government regulation of the music marketplace revolves around antitrust concerns. The government has long wanted to ensure that the market is not unduly influenced by monopoly power. Thus, Congress' uneasiness with the dominant position of the Aeolian piano roll company in 1909 led it to enact a compulsory license for musical works so others could compete with that company.

Concerns about potential monopoly effects are heightened when would-be competitors decide on the prices to be charged for products or products are required to be purchased together, as is the case when musical works are licensed by multiple owners on a blanket basis through ASCAP or BMI. The government, including the Supreme Court, has acknowledged the social benefits of this type of collective blanket licensing, and has endorsed it under a "rule of reason" approach rather than finding it per se unlawful.[786] But the government has also, since the World War II era, subjected ASCAP and BMI to extensive regulation under their respective consent decrees.

It is worth noting that the longevity of these two decrees represents a rather extreme exception to the modern DOJ guidelines which, since 1979, have required that such decrees terminate, generally after a period of no longer than ten years.[787] More recently, in March 2014, the DOJ announced a policy to facilitate the "fast track" review and termination of most perpetual or "legacy" decrees.[788] Under that policy, the DOJ will "advise courts that pre-1980 'legacy' decrees, except in limited circumstances, are presumptively no longer in the public interest."[789] The DOJ has suggested, however, that among those "limited circumstances" is "when there is a long-standing reliance by industry participants on the decree."[790] The revised DOJ policy would thus appear to exclude the PRO decrees.

The word "monopoly" came up many times in the written and oral presentations of participants in this study in discussing the continuing significance of the decrees and antitrust oversight. But it is important to understand that there are two distinct types of "monopoly" being referenced, and each requires separate analysis.

The first type of "monopoly" refers to alleged anticompetitive practices on the part of the PROs, and also sometimes of the major publishers and record labels with significant market share. Here the concern is that licensees—for example, a television network or online service—have insufficient leverage to negotiate appropriate licensing fees with the licensor.[791] Excessive market power is the linchpin of antitrust analysis, whether in a government-initiated enforcement action or private litigation;[792] typically, however—and as discussed below in connection with the *Pandora* litigation—the remedies for civil antitrust violations do not involve long-term government price controls. Such remedies instead tend to focus on injunctive relief to address the particular anticompetitive behavior in question and/or the payment of one-time fines.[793]

The second type of monopoly referenced by participants is a wholly different one, namely, the limited "monopoly" in an individual work that is conferred by virtue of the exclusive rights granted under the Copyright Act. Even though it is not a product of collective activity, these exclusive rights probably play no less of a significant role in debates about music licensing. Many licensees—for example, large online providers— believe they must have access to complete, or virtually complete, catalogs of sound recordings and musical works in order to compete in the marketplace. A compulsory license—at least in theory—can make that possible.

But compulsory licensing removes choice and control from copyright owners who seek to protect and maximize the value of their assets. An increasingly vocal number of copyright owners believe they should be able to withhold their works from low-paying or otherwise objectionable digital services, in part because such services may cannibalize sales or higher-paying subscription models. Taylor Swift's widely publicized decision to pull her catalog from the leading streaming provider Spotify because she did not want her songs available on Spotify's free tier of service has been widely reported, and other artists appear to be following suit.[794] Similarly, artist manager Irving Azoff of GMR has reportedly threatened YouTube with a billion-dollar lawsuit if they do not remove his clients' repertoire from their site.[795] In order to take such action—and demand higher compensation—the use cannot be subject to mandatory licensing.[796] But for those under a compulsory license or a consent decree, it is not possible to say no.

In this regard, it is interesting to compare music to other types of copyrighted works, for example, television shows and movies. Like music, a particular television show or movie may not be a fully satisfying substitute for another—or a substitute at all. But consumers do not expect to be able to access every television show through Hulu, or every movie through Netflix. It is understood that different services can and will offer different content.

Even within the music universe, the law treats sound recordings and musical works differently with respect to the right to say no. We seem to accept the fact that a licensee offering downloads or interactive streaming will need to negotiate deals with major and independent record labels, or forgo the content. On the musical work side, however, government policy has subjected these same uses to government-mandated licensing.

Even given greater latitude to make licensing decisions, it would seem that musical work owners would be strongly incentivized to license services that they believed would pay a reasonable return. This seems to be true of the record labels, which have authorized a wide range of download and interactive music services outside of a mandatory licensing regime.[797] But the labels are not required to license services that show little promise or value. Why is this demanded of music publishers and songwriters?

The Office believes that the question of whether music copyright owners should be able to choose whether to agree to a license is an especially critical one. Understandably, those seeking permission to use music appreciate the security of compulsory licensing processes and certainty of government-set rates—as buyers of content likely would in any context.[798] But modern competition law does not view the rights enjoyed by copyright owners as intrinsically anathema to efficient markets. As the DOJ itself has explained, "antitrust doctrine does not presume the existence of market power from the mere presence of an intellectual property right."[799]

As a general matter, the Office believes that certain aspects of our compulsory licensing processes can and should be relaxed. But this does not mean that antitrust concerns should be overlooked. Many pertinent considerations have been raised in the DOJ's parallel consideration of the ASCAP and BMI consent decrees. The Office strongly endorses that review, and—in light of the significant impact of the decrees in today's performance-driven music market—hopes it will result in a productive reconsideration of the 75-year-old decrees. At the same time, the Office observes that it is Congress, not the DOJ, that has the ability to address the full range of issues that encumber our music licensing system, which go far beyond the consent decrees.

2. The PROs and the Consent Decrees

Since the first part of the twentieth century, ASCAP and BMI have provided critical services to songwriters and music publishers on the one hand, and myriad licensees on the other, in facilitating the licensing of public performance rights in musical works. SESAC, though smaller, has also played an important role in this area, administering performance rights for a select group of clients. More recently, GMR has come onto the scene as a fourth contender in the performance rights arena with an impressive client roster. Each of these organizations offers repertoire-wide—or "blanket"—licenses for the musical works they represent, with the four together essentially representing the entire spectrum of musical works available for licensing in the U.S., including many foreign works. Blanket licenses are available for a wide range of uses, including terrestrial, satellite, and internet radio, on-demand music streaming services, website and television uses, the performance of recorded music in bars, restaurants, and other commercial establishments, and live performances as well.

As detailed above, both ASCAP and BMI, unlike their smaller competitors SESAC and GMR, are subject to continuing consent decrees. The decrees, overseen by federal district courts in New York City (typically referred to as the "rate courts"), were last updated before the rise of licensed digital music services—in the case of BMI, in 1994, and in the case of ASCAP, in 2001. The consent decrees impose significant government- mandated constraints on the manner in which ASCAP and BMI may operate. Among other things, ASCAP and BMI are required to grant a license to any user who requests one, without payment of royalties until a royalty rate is set by negotiation or following litigation before the rate court. Under its decree, ASCAP may not issue mechanical licenses for the reproduction or distribution of musical works; while the BMI consent decree is silent on this point, BMI has not itself issued mechanical licenses. Except to the extent a licensee seeks a narrower license—such as a "per-program" license or a blanket license with "carveouts" for directly licensed works—ASCAP and BMI are required to license all works in their repertoire.

a. Pandora Analysis

Publisher Withdrawals

In 2013, as part of pending ratesetting litigation with the internet radio service Pandora, both the ASCAP and BMI rate courts—applying slightly different logic—interpreted the consent decrees as prohibiting music publishers from withdrawing authorization to license their songs for particular types of uses.[800] Major music publishers had sought to withdraw their "new media" (i.e., online and mobile usage)[801] rights from the PROs in an effort to negotiate with Pandora directly to achieve higher rates than what they believed they would otherwise be awarded in court.[802]

Following their decisions to withdrawal, EMI agreed to a rate equivalent to the existing ASCAP rate of 1.85% for services like Pandora (but without deductions for ASCAP's fees); Sony/ATV negotiated for a prorated share of an industrywide rate of 5% (which translated to a 2.28% implied rate for ASCAP); and UMG obtained a prorated share of 7.5% (or a 3.42% ASCAP rate).[803] Subsequently, however, the two rate courts held that these publishers could not selectively withdraw specific rights from ASCAP or BMI to be negotiated independently. Instead, the publishers had to be "all in" or "all out."[804]

In the wake of these decisions, the three publishers who had sought to withdraw, (now two, as Sony/ATV has since become affiliated with EMI), are, for the moment, back "in," and ASCAP and BMI have petitioned the DOJ to modify their decrees to allow these sorts of partial withdrawals by their publisher members. With the petitions pending, however, both Sony/ATV and UMPG—which together represent some 50% of the music publishing market[805]—have made it clear that they may well choose to withdraw *all* rights from the PROs in the future.

The specter of across-the-board withdrawal by the major publishers from ASCAP and BMI is concerning to many in the music sector. The three major publishers—Sony/ATV, UMPG, and Warner/Chappell—together represent approximately 63% of the U.S. music publishing market,[806] and the songwriters they represent (as well as the publishers themselves) currently license the vast majority of their performance rights through the PROs.[807] The Office agrees that the full withdrawal of leading publishers from ASCAP and BMI would likely significantly disrupt the music market by fundamentally altering the licensing and payment process for the public performance of musical works without an established framework to replace it, at least in the short run.

On the user side, as might be predicted, many strongly prefer the government-supervised PRO system over the unregulated negotiation of rights, and oppose the movement toward withdrawal. While many licensees—such as commercial radio and television stations represented by RMLC and TMLC—are successful in negotiating (rather than litigating) rates with ASCAP and BMI under the current regime, it is reassuring to them to know that they can turn to a federal court if they view it as a better option. Like the radio and television sectors, digital services, including Pandora (whose recent rate court litigation is discussed below), also strongly favor government oversight of music publishers' licensing practices.

Notably, although SESAC is not subject to a consent decree, television and radio licensees recently sued that organization in separate actions for alleged anticompetitive licensing practices.[808] SESAC settled the television case by agreeing to reimburse the television station plaintiffs almost $60 million in licensing fees[809] (the radio case remains pending). Without opining on their merits, the Office observes that these cases illustrate the importance and corrective potential of private enforcement actions outside of the consent decree environment.

Concerns about the impact of large publisher withdrawals are not limited to the user side. Songwriters, too, are apprehensive. According to longstanding industry practice, songwriters are paid their "writer's share" of performance royalties directly by the PROs; these monies do not flow through the publishers. In a world of direct licensing, publishers would not be required to adhere to established standards for the reporting and payment of royalties, such as those employed by ASCAP and BMI. Songwriters worry that direct licensing could thus result in a system with much less accountability and transparency than they currently enjoy under the PROs.

There is a particular concern about publishers' treatment of advance payments and licensing fees by music services, as such monies may not be accounted for by the publisher in a transparent fashion. This, in turn, raises a question in songwriters' minds as to whether withdrawal would exacerbate this problem.[810] In addition, apart from any contractual issues in relation to American songwriters, non-U.S. writers who assign their rights exclusively to their local societies—which in turn enter into contractual relationships with ASCAP and BMI to collect royalties on their behalf in the United States—do not see how they can properly be subject to U.S. publisher withdrawal.[811] On top of all this, a precipitous decline in overall royalty throughput would almost certainly result in markedly increased—and perhaps prohibitive—administrative costs for those who remained affiliated with ASCAP and BMI.

An interesting question is whether significantly decreased market shares on the part of ASCAP and BMI due to major publisher withdrawals would, paradoxically, obviate the need for ongoing government control of those organizations. From a practical perspective, one might question why ASCAP and BMI would remain subject to significant government controls if larger market competitors (i.e., the major publishers) were not subject to such supervision. We assume that the DOJ may address this issue in its forthcoming analysis.

Rate Decision

Following the rulings on withdrawal, the ASCAP court, in a lengthy opinion, proceeded to determine a "reasonable fee" of 1.85% for Pandora, applying a "hypothetical" "fair market value" standard.[812] In so doing, the court was dismissive of the publishers' frustrations with the rate court process and their "envy" of the much higher rates being paid by Pandora to sound recording owners (over 50% of revenues versus the publishers' combined market share of 4%)[813]—which sound recording rates in any event the court could not consider as a result of the statutory bar in section 114(i).[814]

The court sharply criticized Sony/ATV's and UMPG's efforts to negotiate higher rates with Pandora outside of the confines of the consent decree that could then serve as benchmarks in the rate court proceeding. Finding the publishers' tactics objectionable—especially in light of the fact that Pandora could face large-scale copyright liability if it failed to conclude licenses—it rejected the outside agreements as suitable benchmarks.[815] Among other things, the court took issue with Sony/ATV's and UMPG's failure to provide lists of the compositions they owned to Pandora so Pandora could remove their respective works from its service if necessary.[816]

While the court's opinion suggests that Sony/ATV and UMPG may have engaged in anticompetitive behavior by "purposefully set[ting] out" to "create higher benchmarks," and also expressed concern about the publishers' "coordinated" behavior in withdrawing new media rights—as well as their aggressive negotiation strategies—the court ultimately concluded that it had "no need to explore which if any of [their] actions was wrongful or legitimate."[817] In this regard, while it was not the only aspect of the publishers' conduct that troubled the court, it is hard to see how the mere desire to seek higher royalty rates could constitute an antitrust violation—or the fact that the CEO of Sony/ATV appeared in a news article "in shirt sleeves with a large cigar in his mouth" to boast of the higher rate he had negotiated with Pandora.[818]

Undoubtedly, the *Pandora* court believed itself to be carrying out the purpose of the ASCAP decree, and the decree, of course, is meant to address antitrust concerns. But the opinion is notable for its focus on the behavior of a handful of actors instead of an empirically based economic analysis of the proper rate for Pandora. For example, rejecting ASCAP's arguments that the court should consider Pandora's commercial success as part of its inquiry, the court opined that "market share or revenue metrics are poor foundations on which to construct a reasonable fee."[819] Yet it seems that these factors might well be considered by parties in an actual market negotiation.

Additionally, even assuming for the sake of argument that Sony/ATV's and UMPG's negotiation tactics had unequivocally been found by the court to cross the line from forceful negotiations to anticompetitive conduct, it must be remembered that the rate set by the court applies not only to those companies, but to all other publisher and songwriter members of ASCAP as well. Such a court-ordered rate is also likely to heavily influence the market for the other PROs, and hence the industry as a whole. A question arises, then, as to whether the court's repudiation of specific conduct on the part of some by rejecting the possibility of a higher rate represents a fair outcome for the rest of the industry.

Availability of Song Data

As a general matter, the Office concurs with the apparent view of the *Pandora* court that a service should be able to ascertain what works are covered under a license so as to permit the service to remove unauthorized works if necessary. Infringement liability should not arise from a game of "gotcha." Since the *Pandora* decision, it appears that both Sony/ATV and UMPG have made efforts to make their song data available to licensees.[820] In addition to such voluntary efforts, the Office believes that government policies should strongly incentivize the public availability of song ownership data for works in the marketplace, a topic that is addressed in more depth below.

b. PRO Ratesetting Process

This above section reviews the *Pandora* decision in some detail because it illuminates an important policy concern: namely, whether we should continue to blend antitrust oversight with industry rate proceedings as envisioned under the consent decrees. In the *Pandora* litigation, this approach appears to have yielded a mixture of competition and ratesetting considerations, without a satisfying analysis of either. The Office is of the view that allegations of anticompetitive conduct are worthy of evaluation (and, if appropriate, remedial action) separate and apart from the question of a fair rate—and vice versa. Each of these two critical policy objectives merits government attention in its own right.[821]

The Office therefore proposes that the ratesetting aspects of PRO oversight be separated from whatever government supervision is determined still to be necessary to address antitrust concerns.

Migrate to Copyright Royalty Board

Assuming PRO ratesetting is separated from any ongoing antitrust oversight, the Office proposes that the function of establishing rates be migrated to the CRB.[822] Industry ratesetting is, of course, a primary function of the CRB, and the CRB has the benefit of experience assessing a broader spectrum of rate-related questions than the federal rates courts. Significantly, the CRB sets rates on the sound recording side as well as for musical works. It also has in-house economic expertise. While, as discussed below, interested parties appear to agree that the statutory framework governing the CRB's procedures could stand some improvement, on the whole it seems only logical to consolidate music ratesetting proceedings in a single specialized tribunal.

In offering the suggestion that the CRB assume responsibility for the rates applicable to the public performance of musical works, the Office does not mean to suggest that the CRB should not question the legitimacy of particular benchmarks if there is reason to do so (as the CRB in fact routinely does in ratesetting proceedings). But the ultimate aim of the proceeding should be a fair rate for the industry as a whole, rather than the enforcement of antitrust policy. The Office believes that a process focused on industry economics rather than antitrust analysis offers a more auspicious framework to establish broadly applicable rates.

Under the Office's proposal, discussed in more detail below, the CRB, like the rate courts, would step in to set a rate only when it could not be agreed as between the relevant parties. Such ratesetting activities would not need to occur on a five-year schedule, as under the current CRB system, but would be commenced on an as-needed basis, like today's proceedings before the ASCAP and BMI rate courts. Additional parties seeking to resolve the same rate issue could be offered the opportunity to join the proceeding. Assuming the experience were similar to that of the rate courts, the vast majority of rates would be agreed voluntarily rather than litigated.

Assuming the ratesetting authority for the public performance of musical works were transferred from the rate courts to the CRB, a question arises as to whether the separation of ratesetting and antitrust responsibilities would provide the occasion to sunset the decrees and adopt a more modern approach to antitrust oversight in this area. Under a more flexible approach, the DOJ would investigate and address potential anticompetitive behavior on an as-needed basis, rather than continue to impose presumptive restrictions under the consent decrees. As noted above, private enforcement actions, as well, could play a role in policing alleged misconduct. We leave such questions of antitrust policy for the DOJ to answer.

Section 114(i)

Regardless of whether PRO ratesetting is migrated to the CRB, as further discussed below, the Copyright Office endorses the proposal—embodied in the proposed SEA legislation[823]—that the prohibition in 114(i) that currently prevents ratesetting tribunals from considering sound recording performance royalties be eliminated. Originally designed as a protective measure to benefit songwriters and publishers, it appears to be having the opposite effect. Contrary to the suggestion of the *Pandora* court,[824] the Office does not understand why, absent such a restriction, it might not be relevant to consider sound recording royalties in establishing a fair rate for the use of musical works should a ratesetting authority be so inclined.[825]

Interim Fees

Under the consent decrees, anyone who applies for a license receives one. There is no requirement of immediate payment. As discussed above, an applicant has the right to perform musical works in a PRO's repertoire pending the completion of negotiations or rate court proceedings resulting in an interim or final fee.[826] Since the consent decrees do not provide for immediate and concurrent payment for uses made during these periods—and do not establish a timeframe for the commencement of a rate court proceeding—an applicant is able to publicly perform a PRO's catalog of works for an indefinite period without paying.[827] Needless to say, commercial entities do not typically receive a steady supply of product for months or years based on a mere letter request. But such is the case with music.

The problem is exacerbated by the substantial burden and expense of litigating a rate in federal court—a contingency both sides seek to avoid. Licensees may pay nothing or greatly reduced fees for years as negotiations drag on, while still enjoying all of the benefits of a license. The Office agrees with those commenters who have suggested that this system—under which services may launch and continue to operate without an agreed rate—significantly increases the leverage of licensees at the expense of the PROs and their members.[828] Because the licensee already has access to the works it needs, there is no urgency to agree to a rate.

Once again, the Office does not see why music is treated differently from the goods of other suppliers in the marketplace. A fair and rational system should require licensees to pay at least an interim rate from the inception of their service, subject to a true-up when a final rate is negotiated with the PRO or established by the ratesetting authority.

Notably, both the ASCAP and BMI consent decrees include a process for the rate court to set interim rates. In practice, however, it seems that this option—which, at least for BMI, entails up to four months of discovery and motion practice[829]—is not commonly exercised. Likely this is due to parties' reluctance to undertake the considerable burden and expense of federal court litigation, especially when the result is only a temporary one.[830]

The Office is of the view that to the extent a licensing entity is required to grant a license upon request, there should be a viable (not merely theoretical) mechanism—for example, a brief, single-day hearing before the ratesetting authority (*e.g.*, the CRB)—to set an interim royalty rate without undue burden or expense. While nothing is ever as simple as it seems, the Office believes that a workable system should be feasible. For example, a licensee could be required to share a written description of the material aspects of its proposed service, after which both parties would proffer lists of relevant rates already in effect, which together would serve as guidance for the decisionmaker. It should not be necessary to have an elaborate procedure when the temporary rate can be adjusted retroactively. In addition to being more equitable for music owners, the Office believes requiring licensees to pay an interim rate would provide greater incentive to resolve rates through voluntary negotiations at the outset.

c. Partial Withdrawal of Rights

A primary focus of the commentary to the Copyright Office—and to the DOJ in its review of the consent decrees—is music publishers' ability (or inability) to withdraw specific categories of licensing rights from their authorizations to the PROs. The purpose of such withdrawals would be to allow music owners to negotiate in the marketplace for the exploitation of their songs—or, if not satisfied with the price offered, to withhold their songs from particular services. This has an analog in much of the discussion surrounding section 115, another area where publishers and songwriters seek the ability to escape from mandatory licensing.

As noted above, except in the case of internet radio providers that qualify for the section 112 and 114 statutory licenses, record companies are free to negotiate with potential licensees in the open market. But for music publishers, it is the exception rather than the norm, as the licensing of both mechanical and performance licenses is largely subject to government mandate.

There is substantial evidence to support the view that government-regulated licensing processes imposed on publishers and songwriters have resulted in depressed rates, at least in comparison to noncompulsory rates for the same uses on the sound recording side. Setting aside efficiency concerns, the Office does not see a principled reason why sound recording owners are permitted to negotiate interactive streaming rates directly while musical work owners are not. The Office is therefore sympathetic to the publishers' position that they should be permitted to withdrawal certain rights from the PROs to permit market negotiations. The Office believes that partial withdrawal—in the form of a limited right to "opt out"—should be made available to those who want it. This view is reinforced by the possibility of wholesale defections by major (and perhaps other) publishers from ASCAP and BMI if government controls are not relaxed, and the potential chaos that would likely follow.

Any such opt-out process would need to be carefully managed to ensure licensees did not face undue burdens in the licensing process as a result. At least for now, the Office believes that withdrawal of performance rights should be limited to digital rights equivalent to those that the record labels are free to negotiate outside of section 112 and 114—essentially, interactive streaming rights for new media services. In the case of such a partial withdrawal, the publisher would be free to pursue a direct deal for the rights in question (or, if not satisfied with a licensee's offer, withhold songs from the service in question).

Publishers who chose to opt out would need publicly to identify the particular uses subject to withdrawal, the licensing organization from which they were being withdrawn, each of the affected works, where a direct license might be sought, and other pertinent information.[831] As discussed below, it is the Office's recommendation that a non-profit general music rights organization ("GMRO") be designated by the Copyright Office to receive, maintain and offer access to this information. The Office additionally proposes that the current PROs be permitted to expand to become to become music rights organizations ("MROs") that would be capable of administering not just performance rights but mechanical and perhaps other musical work rights as well.[832]

While the publisher would presumably choose to be paid directly by the licensee under any resulting outside licensing arrangement rather than through an MRO, in order to ensure songwriters' confidence in the accounting and payment process, the Office believes that songwriters affiliated with that publisher should retain the option of receiving their writer's share of royalties directly from the licensee through their chosen MRO.[833]

Finally, to the extent publishers failed to affiliate with an MRO, their performance rights would fall under the default licensing authority of the GMRO, which, as described below, would collect royalties and distribute them to publisher claimants. The combination of direct deals, MRO-issued licenses, and the GMRO backstop would allow licensees to secure full licensing coverage for necessary performance rights.

d. Bundled Licensing

During the study, industry stakeholders broadly supported increased bundling of rights to facilitate greater licensing efficiency. On the sound recording side of the equation, this does not appear to be much of an issue. To the extent noninteractive services procure licenses under section 112 and 114, they obtain both digital performance rights and the reproduction rights (*e.g.*, server copy rights) needed to engage in the streaming process. When services negotiate licenses outside of the statutory scheme, the labels are free to bundle all necessary rights together.

On the musical work side, however, the story is different. Licenses for the reproductions necessary to support an interactive streaming service are issued under section 115, whereas licenses for the streamed performances of the works are obtained from the PROs. In 2008, following a lengthy Copyright Office administrative proceeding and industrywide settlement, the CRB adopted regulations that effectively establish bundled rates for various types of streaming activities, under which the total cost of licensees' PRO performance licenses is deducted from the overall percentage rate applicable to the relevant service under section 115.[834] But while the royalty rate problem may have been addressed, an interactive service must still obtain separate mechanical and performance licenses and report complex accounting information under these two different licensing regimes (song-by-song licensing under section 115 versus blanket licensing by the PROs).

In 2005, former Register of Copyrights Marybeth Peters proposed moving from a dualistic approach for the licensing of musical works for mechanical and performance purposes to a system of integrated music rights organizations, or MROs.[835] At the time—when mechanical royalties represented a more significant income stream then they do today—music publishers and songwriters expressed considerable skepticism about such a bundled approach.[836] Today, in an era where mechanical royalties are becoming more marginal, Register Peters' proposal appears prescient, and enjoys support among publishers, songwriters and—not surprisingly—digital licensees.[837] It now seems apparent that the government should pursue appropriate changes to our legal framework to encourage bundled licensing, which could eliminate redundant resources on the part of both licensors and licensees.

As touched upon above, the most obvious step in this regard would be to allow existing music licensing organizations to expand to fill this role—the PROs would be permitted to take on mechanical licensing, and mechanical licensing entities such as HFA or MRI could integrate performance rights into their businesses. To satisfy reporting and payment obligations under songwriter or other agreements that distinguish between these rights, some sort of allocation of income as between the two rights would likely be required. This perhaps could be addressed by the CRB in establishing bundled rates (as under the section 112 and 114 licenses), or by the individual MROs in administering negotiated licenses.[838]

3. Mechanical Licensing and Section 115

As sales of CDs continue to slip away, mechanical licensing revenues for the reproduction and distribution of musical works under section 115—once the primary source of income for publishers and songwriters—likewise continue to decline.[839] Although sales of digital downloads through services like Apple iTunes have bolstered mechanical royalties in recent years, even DPD sales have fallen off with the rise of streaming services such as Spotify. Even so, mechanical revenues still currently represent about 23% of income for musical works (as compared to 52% generated by performances, 20% by synch uses, and 5% by other uses).[840] Of the mechanical share, a small amount is generated by the server and other reproductions of musical works required for online providers to operate interactive streaming services which, as noted above, also pay performance royalties.

Commenting parties have focused on two primary areas of concern with respect to the 106-year old compulsory license embodied in section 115. The first, put forth by music publishers and songwriters, is that the compulsory license does not permit them to control the use of their works or seek higher royalties. Relatedly, rightsowners also complain about the lack of an audit right under section 115 and practical inability to enforce reporting or payment obligations against recalcitrant licensees.

The second overarching concern with respect to section 115 is its song-by-song licensing requirement, which dates back to the original incarnation of the compulsory license in 1909. Song-by-song licensing is viewed by music users as an administratively daunting—if not sisyphean—task in a world where online providers seek licenses for millions of works.

a. Free Market Negotiation versus Collective Administration

One of the most challenging issues to arise in this study has been whether musical work owners should be liberated from the section 115 compulsory licensing regime. Citing the significantly higher rates paid to sound recording owners for uses where musical work owners are regulated and sound recording owners are not—and the contrasting example of the unregulated synch licensing market, where in many cases licensing fees are evenly apportioned—music publishers and songwriters have made a convincing case that government regulation likely yields rates below those they would enjoy in a free market. Motivated by concerns similar to those raised in connection with the consent decrees, many musical work owners would like to see an end to section 115. The Office—which, as noted, believes that compulsory licensing should exist only when clearly needed to address a market failure—is sympathetic to these claims.

On the other hand, in comparison to the record industry—where three major companies can issue licenses for much of the most sought-after content, with independent labels representing the balance[841]—U.S. musical work ownership is more diffusely distributed over a greater number of entities and self-published songwriters.[842] Unlike sound recordings—which are typically wholly owned by an individual label—many musical works are controlled by two, three or even more publishers. Notwithstanding the default rules of joint copyright ownership, publishers and songwriters frequently have understandings that they are not free to license each other's respective shares.[843] And there are millions of musical works in the marketplace. Spotify, for instance, reports that it offers some 30 million songs on its service.[844]

Understandably, as described above, digital music providers are intensely opposed to a system that would require individual licensing negotiations with thousands of musical work owners. Even publisher proponents of the proposal to sunset section 115 do not deny that it would be extraordinarily difficult for services to negotiate with myriad small copyright owners for all of the mechanical licenses they seek, and concede that there must be some sort of collective system to facilitate licensing from smaller rightsowners.[845] But apart from the optimistic view that should section 115 be retired, new entities will spring forth to meet this need, there is little detail concerning how a collective solution would reliably be implemented.

The difficulty, then, is how to reconcile the competing values of free market negotiation and collective management of rights. Each represents an express goal of reform: fair compensation to creators, on the one hand, and licensing efficiency, on the other. A middle path may provide the best answer.

Publisher Opt-Out Right

The Office believes that rather than eliminating section 115 altogether, section 115 should instead become the basis of a more flexible collective licensing system that will presumptively cover all mechanical uses except to the extent individual rightsowners choose to opt out. At least initially, the mechanical opt-out right would extend to the uses that could be withdrawn from blanket performance licenses—that is, to interactive streaming rights—and, in addition, to downloading activities[846] (which, by judicial interpretation, do not implicate the public performance right[847]). To reiterate, these are uses where sound recording owners operate in the free market but publishers do not.[848]

Full Market Coverage

As envisioned by the Office, the collective system would comprise MROs (as noted, with the ability to represent both performance and mechanical rights) acting on behalf of their respective publisher members; individual publishers (including self-published songwriters) representing their own mechanical licensing interests who had exercised their opt-out right; and the GMRO. Unless they had a direct deal in place, publishers would be paid through their chosen MRO. The GMRO would collect for works (or shares of works) not covered by a direct deal or represented by an MRO—including works with unknown owners—and attempt to locate and pay the relevant rightsholders. Licensees could thus achieve end-to-end coverage through the combination of MROs, direct licensors, and the GMRO.

As in the case of those seeking to withdraw specific performance uses from mandatory licensing, publishers who wished to opt out from one or more of the categories of mechanical licensing would need to identify the uses in question and provide this information (via their MRO if applicable) to the GMRO, along with identification of their works, licensing contact information, and other relevant data.[849] They would then be free to negotiate directly with, and be paid directly by, the licensee.[850] Absent provision of a notice that the publisher was exercising its right to opt out, that publisher's works would be licensed through its MRO.[851]

Cover Recordings

Section 115 permits digital services and others to reproduce and distribute copies of musical works embodied in existing recordings, provided that the user is also authorized to use the recording.[852] Another dimension of section 115 is that it can be used for permission to make new, "cover" recordings of songs, so long as the new version does not change the basic melody or "fundamental character" of the work.[853]

While the ability to make a cover recording has long been a feature of the law, it is not without controversy, especially among recording artists who write their own works. While some artist songwriters may view imitation as flattery, others do not appreciate that they are unable to prevent the re-recording of their songs by others. Many music creators seek more control over their works. As some artists see it, "[a]pproval is by far the most important right that an artist possesses."[854]

With respect to cover recordings, the Office recommends an approach whereby those who seek to re-record songs could still obtain a license to do so, including in physical formats. But the dissemination of such recordings for interactive new media uses, as well as in the form of downloads, would be subject to the publisher's ability to opt out of the compulsory regime. Thus, a publisher's choice to negotiate interactive streaming and DPD rights for its catalog of songs would include the ability to authorize the dissemination of cover recordings by those means. Or, put another way, where the publisher had opted out, someone who produced a cover recording would need to obtain a voluntary license to post the song on an interactive streaming or download service (just as would someone who wished to offer streams or downloads of the original recording of that work).

Audiovisual Uses

In their comments, the record companies explain that because consumers now access music on computers, phones and other devices with screens, they expect to see something when a song is playing—whether it is a video, album cover, or lyrics. The labels' observation corresponds to the fact that for music fans of today, YouTube—with a billion users a month—is "the largest service in terms of listening to music."[855]

The record companies urge that the licensing system for musical works needs to be updated to respond to the consumer desire for more—and more innovative— audiovisual content. To illustrate the point, the labels cite a recent record release— involving a variety of distinct consumer products—that necessitated over 1,400 individual licenses.[856]

The combination of music with visual content requires a synchronization license—and synch rights are not subject to government oversight. Section 115 is limited to audio- only uses of musical works. While not proposing a specific approach, the labels would like to see section 115 replaced with an updated blanket system that would extend to consumer audiovisual products.[857] In their view, such a change would facilitate many common synch transactions, such as the licensing of music videos to online services and incorporation of music in user-posted videos.

In the eyes of music publishers and songwriters, however, the labels' suggestion represents a dramatic and unacceptable expansion of the compulsory system. This reaction is perhaps not terribly surprising in light of the publishers' present desire to phase out mandatory audio-only licensing under section 115.[858]

The Office is sympathetic to the labels' concerns, but cannot at this time recommend that consumer synch uses be incorporated into a government-supervised licensing regime. As may be apparent from much of the foregoing discussion, once a compulsory license is implemented it becomes deeply embedded in industry practices and—even when its original rationale is lost in time—is difficult to undo. That alone should counsel caution in all but the most manifest instances of market failure.

Here, the Office does not observe such a failure and believes there is even some reason to be optimistic about private market solutions. First, in the case of new releases, the labels presumably have some ability (and leverage) to work through audiovisual licensing issues by virtue of their role with respect to the creation of music videos, album art, etc. Notably, in the RIAA's own example of "a single album project" requiring over a thousand licenses, it seems that licenses were obtained.[859]

Additionally, over the last decade, labels and publishers have entered into a series of NDMAs to facilitate the labels' licensing of music videos and other products from music publishers.[860] And in another significant development, YouTube, has developed a robust licensing program and entered into voluntary agreements that enable large and small labels and publishers to claim and monetize their content.[861] Taken together, these examples suggest that the market appears to be responding to the need for licensing of audiovisual uses by consumers and that there is probably no pressing need for government intervention.

b. Shift to Blanket Licensing

Regardless of its scope or whether it includes an opt-out right, the Office believes that section 115 should be updated to better meet the needs of the digital age. Congress attempted to do this in 2006 with the proposed SIRA legislation, which would have created a blanket mechanical license for digital uses. Although that bill got as far as passing the relevant House subcommittee,[862] it faced a degree of resistance from certain industry participants and ultimately foundered.

Based on stakeholders' sentiments, however—especially those of the digital services—the time seems ripe to revisit the concept of blanket mechanical licensing. Users have made a strong case in pointing out the inefficiencies of a system that requires multiple licensees to ascertain song-by-song licensing information and maintain it in redundant databases. At the same time, they have repeatedly expressed a willingness to pay royalties in cases where they are unable to track down licensing information for particular songs in order to mitigate their potential liability for unmatched works.[863]

But while considerably more user-friendly for licensees, blanket licensing cannot be viewed as a panacea. It does not cure the problem of bad or missing data, or the inability to match sound recordings with the musical works they embody. In any situation where a licensed transaction takes place, in order for a royalty to be paid to the rightsowner, there must be a link between the work used and the owner of that work. Especially in the case of lesser known works, it can be challenging to match a sound recording with the musical work it embodies, and that musical work to its owner.

Today, under section 115, the burden of identifying the song and its owners is on the licensee (or sometimes a third-party agent retained by the licensee); the link is made in the song-specific license that issues. Blanket licensing merely kicks this responsibility obligation down the road for another actor to address. Under a blanket system, the obligation to make the match between the exploited work and its owner falls on the licensing organization—for example, the PRO—which must identify the use and connect it to the owner.

Nonetheless, the Office believes that on the whole, the benefits of a blanket licensing approach clearly outweigh the conceded challenges of matching reported uses with copyright owners. Throughout this study, the Office has heard consistent praise for the efficiencies of blanket licensing by SoundExchange and the PROs, and widespread frustration with the song-by-song process required under section 115—including from publishers who find themselves burdened with deficient notices and accountings.

Ultimately, it is in the interest of music owners as well as licensees to improve the licensing process so it is not an obstacle for paying services. To further facilitate the rights clearance process and eliminate user concerns about liability to unknown rightsowners, the Office believes that mechanical licensing, like performance licensing, should be offered on a blanket basis by those that administer it. This would mean that a licensee would need only to file a single notice to obtain a repertoire-wide performance and mechanical license from a particular licensing entity. Song-by-song licensing is widely perceived as a daunting requirement for new services and an administrative drag on the licensing system as a whole.

The move to a blanket system would allow marketplace entrants to launch their services—and begin paying royalties—more quickly.

c. Ratesetting

As explained above, the Office supports integration of mechanical with performance rights administration to simplify the licensing process, especially where both rights are implicated, as in the case of interactive streaming.[864] Even if both rights are not implicated—as in the case of DPD licensing—it would still appear to make sense to combine licensing resources into unified MROs, especially in a world of declining mechanicals. In order to reap the rewards of a more unified licensing structure, the Office further recommends that the ratesetting procedures for mechanical and performance also be combined.

"As-Needed" Ratesetting

The CRB establishes mechanical rates for the various categories of use that fall under section 115.[865] The Office believes this responsibility should continue, though with an important modification: as is now the case with performance rights, rather than establish rates across the board every five years, the CRB should set rates for particular uses only on an as-needed basis when an MRO and licensee are unsuccessful in reaching agreement.

There are currently 17 distinct rate categories under the section 115 license,[866] each with its own specific rate. Under the current CRB regime, the parties are required to identify at the outset of the ratesetting proceeding every business model that may be relevant in the next five years so that a rate can be established for that use. As digital business models proliferate, so do the rates. The determination of government rates for a plethora of specific distribution models would seem to be an inefficient way to go about the ratesetting process. In the first place, new digital models spring up every day, so it is impossible to keep up with the changing marketplace prospectively. In addition, many of the rates required to be included in a global ratesetting process might be easily agreed by the parties without the need for government intervention—especially in the case of uses that are less economically significant.

Under the Office's approach, the CRB would be called upon to set a rate only in the case of an impasse between two parties. But to borrow from the existing CRB system, other interested parties (such as other MROs and other users) could choose to join the relevant proceeding, in which case those parties would be bound by the CRB-determined rate (except for publishers opting out of the MRO for the use in question.[867])

Use of Benchmarks

Throughout the study, there has been significant debate concerning the ratesetting standard that should be employed by the CRB—some supporting section 801(b)(1)'s four-factor test that applies to satellite radio and pre-existing subscription services under section 114, as well as mechanical uses under section 115, while others favor the willing buyer/willing seller standard that governs internet radio. As discussed above in connection with the issue of licensing parity, the Office believes that all music users should operate under a common standard, and that standard should aim to achieve market rates to the greatest extent possible.

But regardless of the rate standard invoked by the CRB (or for that matter, a rate court), a critical aspect of the ratesetting analysis is comparison of the requested rates with relevant market benchmarks, to the extent they exist. In the case of compulsory licensing, this is an elusive enterprise, since there are no freely negotiated licenses to inform the tribunal.

As noted above, the Office believes that all potentially informative benchmarks should be reviewed and evaluated in the ratesetting process. An advantage of the proposed opt-out system is that there would be a greater likelihood that actual market benchmarks would exist to inform the ratesetting tribunal. Even where rates remain subject to government oversight, the Office believes that copyright policy—and specifically the desire to fairly compensate creators—will be better served by a greater opportunity to establish rates with reference to real market transactions.[868]

Interim Rates

There is no current process for establishing an interim rate under the section 115 license. As with performance rights, the Office believes there should be a simple and expeditious procedure available to have the CRB establish a temporary mechanical rate for a new user pending final resolution of the applicable royalty by agreement of the parties or through a ratesetting proceeding.

d. Audit Right

Publishers and songwriters have long complained about the lack of an audit right under section 115.[869] In addition to monthly statements of use, the statute provides that each licensee must provide to the copyright owner a cumulative annual statement that is certified by a CPA.[870] But section 115 confers no express right for a copyright owner to audit a licensee's statements.[871]

Although section 114 does not include such an express audit right, it does provide that the CRB shall "establish requirements by which copyright owners may receive reasonable notice of the use of their sound recordings under [section 114], and under which records of such use shall be kept and made available by entities performing sound recordings."[872] Based on this authority, the CRB has promulgated regulations to permit audits of royalty payments of statutory licensees by SoundExchange.[873] Notably, there is parallel language in section 115, though it is limited to reporting in connection with the making of DPDs, and no equivalent royalty verification rules have been promulgated by the CRB under that provision.[874]

Regardless of any other potential adjustments to section 115, the Office believes that the mechanical licensing system should be amended to provide for an express audit right covering the full range of uses under section 115, with the particular logistics of the audit process to be implemented by regulation.[875]

The Office was not made aware during the study of any audit issue in relation to the PROs.[876] But the Office notes that in any updated system, it would be critical for copyright owners to be able to verify not just mechanical royalties but performance income as well (which could be combined under a bundled license). Audit activities could perhaps be coordinated through the GMRO; once an audit was noticed by one MRO, others could choose to participate in the audit process, sharing in its costs and any recovery.[877] This type of coordinated audit process has been implemented under the cable and satellite licenses as well as under the AHRA.[878]

e. Sunset of Existing Section 115 Licenses

PRO licenses typically have an initial term of up to five years.[879] A licensee may therefore need to renegotiate its license with one or more PROs every several years. For this reason, while specific details would undoubtedly need to be addressed, existing PRO licenses would not appear to present an obstacle to implementing the changes proposed here. A license granted under section 115, on the other hand, does not have an end date. A question therefore arises as to how the millions of existing section 115 licenses would be retired.

The Office believes there is an answer to this question—as, apparently, do the digital companies who have advocated for a new blanket system (as well as the publishers that have advocated for an end to section 115 altogether). Significantly, the rates and terms in a section 115 license do not continue in perpetuity but instead are adjusted every five years in accordance with the CRB's statutory schedule.[880] Thus, there can be no expectation on the part of a licensee that particular rates or terms will continue beyond the five-year statutory period.

In sunsetting the song-by-song licensing system, there would need to be a period of transition, of course, during which the user would apply for licenses from the several MROs. Assuming, however, that that period of transition were tied to the then-applicable rate period, the changeover should not harm any legitimate expectation concerning rates.

4. Section 112 and 114 Licenses

One of the few things that seems to be working reasonably well in our licensing system is the statutory license regime under sections 112 and 114, which permits qualifying digital services to engage in noninteractive streaming activities at a CRB-determined (or otherwise agreed) rate. The section 112 and 114 licenses—administered by SoundExchange, a nonprofit entity designated by the CRB—cover both internet and satellite radio providers and certain subscription music services. Although the differing ratesetting standards for these licenses—as well as some of the rates established under those standards—have been a source of controversy, from the record in this study, the licensing framework itself is generally well regarded.

Recording artists, as well as backup musicians and vocalists, appreciate the fact that they are paid their respective shares of royalties for digital performances under the statutory formula administered by SoundExchange.[881] SoundExchange deducts a modest administrative fee from distributed royalties—currently approximately 4.5%—to offset its costs of operations.[882]

SoundExchange engages in significant efforts to locate and register artists whose royalties it is holding. By regulation, unattributed royalties that remain unclaimed after a period of at least three years may be used to help defray SoundExchange's ongoing administrative expenses.[883] In recent years, the pool of unclaimed royalties that are three or more years old has ranged as high as $31 million dollars.[884] By comparison, however, SoundExchange's annual distributions totaled $773 million in 2014.[885]

a. Scope of Licenses

Notwithstanding the comparatively positive reviews of the section 112 and 114 licenses, there are a few ways in which some have suggested they should be tweaked.

Adjust to Include Terrestrial

In contrast to the general sentiments of musical work owners, some independent record labels and artists—who may be more challenged in negotiating with music services than their larger counterparts, and also like being paid through SoundExchange—have suggested that the section 112 and 114 compulsory licenses be expanded to cover interactive streaming in addition to noninteractive models.[886] Digital providers, too, would welcome such a change.[887]

While the Office understands these points of view, it seems unlikely as a political matter that the major record labels could be persuaded to give up their current ability to negotiate such rates in the open market. Moreover, the Office does not perceive that the voluntary market for licensing of sound recording rights is not functioning.

That said, assuming Congress broadens the sound recording performance right to include terrestrial broadcasts, in keeping with the principle that analogous uses should be treated alike, it would seem only logical that terrestrial uses should be included under the section 112 and 114 licenses. The CRB would be in the best position to establish equitable rates to apply to both over-the-air and internet radio.

Qualifying versus Nonqualifying Services

The section 112 and 114 licensing framework excludes interactive streaming and imposes additional technical requirements as well on those seeking a statutory licenses. While licensees complain about the constraints of section 114, on the other side of the coin, questions arise as to how much control a listener should be able to have over a customized radio playlist before the service is considered to be offering more of an on-demand than passive experience.

Section 114 defines an interactive service in relevant part as "one that enables a member of the public to receive a transmission of a program specially created for the recipient, or on request, a transmission of a particular sound recording, whether or not part of a program, which is selected by or on behalf of the recipient."[888] In 2009, the Second Circuit Court of Appeals held that the Launchcast music service—which did not offer on-demand streaming but customized its programming for recipients based on their individual ratings of songs—was not interactive within the meaning of this definition.[889] As a result of this precedent, internet radio services offering customized listening experiences are able to operate under the compulsory license regime.

Some question the Second Circuit's interpretation of the line between interactive and noninteractive streaming.[890] As articulated by the RIAA, "[t]he [*LaunchMedia*] decision has emboldened services to offer listeners an increasingly personalized listening experience under color of the statutory license, and all but extinguished voluntary licensing of personalized streaming services at a premium to the statutory rate."[891] The RIAA's chief concern appears to be that the rate for customized radio is the same as that for completely nonpersonalized offerings.

While the Office has some reservations about the interpretation of section 114 by the *Launch Media court*— which seems somewhat in tension with the statutory language— there appears to be no overwhelming entreaty to remove custom radio from the statutory regime.[892] Within that regime, however, it may be appropriate to distinguish between custom and noncustom radio, as the substitutional effect of personalized radio on potentially competing interactive streaming services may be greater than that of services offering a completely noncustomized experience. While the issue could be addressed legislatively, such an approach would not appear to require statutory change, as the CRB has the discretion to set different rate tiers today when the record supports such an outcome.[893]

For their part, internet providers have criticized the constraints that section 114 imposes on services that seek to operate under the compulsory license.[894] These include the "sound recording performance complement," a restriction that limits the frequency with which songs from the same album or by the same artist may be played by the service.[895] There is also a statutory prohibition against announcing upcoming songs—a practice that is common in the terrestrial world, and therefore presents problems for online simulcasters.[896] Congress included these limitations in the section 114 license to mitigate the potential substitutional impact of noninteractive streaming on sales or other revenue streams.[897]

In the Office's view, these sorts of requirements fall into a category of relative fine-tuning of the license. But for the fact that they are laid out in the statute itself, their particulars would seem to be more appropriately the province of regulation. As suggested below, the Office believes that in updating the music licensing system, Congress should commit more of its nuances to administrative oversight. The technical conditions for eligibility under the section 112 and 114 licenses would seem to fall into this category, as the effectiveness and impact of these provisions has likely changed, and will continue to change, over time.

Finally, some have suggested a modification of the provisions of section 112 and 114 that permit the making of server—or "ephemeral"—copies to facilitate licensed services. These parties seek to confirm that multiple server copies may be made and retained indefinitely by a licensed service.[898] Although the main provision at issue—17 U.S.C. § 112(e)—is less than a model of clarity,[899] the Office is not aware that the imprecision has resulted in any real-world disputes, and does not see this as an especially pressing issue.[900] Nonetheless, it would probably be worthwhile in any general update of section 112 and 114 to refine the statutory language with respect to the number and retention of server copies so as to eliminate any doubt as to the operation of the section 112 license.

b. Ratesetting

The embattled ratesetting standards for internet and satellite radio—section 801(b)(1) versus willing buyer/willing seller—are discussed at some length above in connection with overall questions of licensing parity. As explained there, the Office believes that government ratesetting processes for both sound recordings and music should be conducted under a single, market-oriented standard. Accordingly, in the Office's view, the section 112 and 114 rates currently set under the 801(b)(1) standard (i.e., those applicable to satellite radio and pre-existing subscription services) should be migrated to the willing buyer/willing seller standard or some alternative formulation aimed at establishing rates equivalent to those that would be negotiated in the free market.[901] The Office further recommends that ratesetting should occur on an "as-needed" basis, as described above.

c. Producer Payments

The Office notes the further concern of some that the section 112 and 114 royalty allocations do not recognize the contributions of sound recording producers, who in many instances not only supervise, but also have significant creative input into, finished recordings. Despite the fact that many producers are creators of sound recordings in their own right, they are not among the parties entitled by statute to direct payment by SoundExchange.[902]

Compensation of producers is contractually based. They may be paid an up-front fee for their efforts and/or receive a share of the artist's future royalties.[903] In some cases, an artist may provide a letter of direction requesting SoundExchange to pay the producer's share of the artist royalties collected by SoundExchange, which SoundExchange will honor.[904] NARAS has suggested that this informal practice—which is not contemplated by the statutory payment mechanism set forth in section 114—be recognized through a legislative amendment. In NARAS' words, this will provide producers "the same fair, direct-payment option available to performers."[905]

Because the producer's share comes out of the featured artist's statutory entitlement, such recognition would not require a change in the current statutory allocation, but would merely clarify the authority of SoundExchange to honor a letter of direction.

Though it would be beneficial to hear more from artists on this issue,[906] the Office agrees that NARAS' proposal to confirm the existing practice through a technical amendment of the statute merits consideration.

d. Termination Provision

Unlike section 115, sections 112 and 114 do not include a right to terminate a licensee that fails to account for and pay royalties. This not only severely undermines the ability of SoundExchange to police noncompliant licenses, but also allows such licensees to continue to exploit valuable sound recordings without payment to their owners. As SoundExchange explains it:

> "Noncompliance with statutory license requirements is commonplace. For 2013, approximately a quarter of royalty payments were not made on time; two-thirds of licensees required to deliver reports of the recordings they used have not delivered at least one required report; and at least one quarter of such licensees have not delivered any such reports at all."[907]

SoundExchange observes that it tries to work with problem licensees to improve their compliance. But when such efforts prove unsuccessful, SoundExchange—and the copyright owners it represents—should have a remedy. The Office does not see a justification for continued licensing of a user that is not meeting its obligations. The Office therefore agrees with SoundExchange that the section 112 and 114 statutory licenses should be amended to include a termination provision akin to that in section 115.[908]

5. *Public and Noncommercial Broadcasting*

Public broadcasters—including noncommercial educational broadcasters—lament the inefficiencies and limitations of the statutory provisions in sections 114 and 118 that govern their use of music content.[909] The Office concurs that these provisions are unwieldy and believes that they should be reviewed and updated to better reflect Congress' desire to accommodate public broadcasting activities.[910]

Especially in light of the relatively low royalty rates paid by public broadcasters, it makes little sense to require them to engage in a multitude of negotiations and ratesetting proceedings in different fora—before the CRB under sections 112 and 114 for digital sound recording performance rights, before the CRB under section 118 for over- the-air musical work performance and associated reproduction rights, under the consent decrees for digital musical works performance rights covered by ASCAP and BMI, and through private negotiations for musical work performance and reproduction rights falling outside of the foregoing categories.[911] Instead, the Office suggests that the ratesetting processes applicable to public broadcasters be consolidated within a unified license structure under section 118 under the auspices of the CRB.[912] By separating out all noncommercial uses for consideration under a single framework, the royalty rates for public broadcasters would likely be much more efficiently resolved.[913]

In reforming the section 118 license, Congress should ensure it appropriately facilitates digital transmissions by public broadcasters, including the streaming of archived programming.[914] But absent a significant change in congressional policy, the Office sees no need to expand the statutory license to include permanent uses such as downloads or physical products, as some noncommercial broadcasters have suggested.[915] The current statutory provisions for public broadcasting focus on performances in the course of over-the-air programming rather than the distribution of copyrighted works. Permanent uses by noncommercial entities—or even on-demand streaming of individual songs outside of the context of the original programming—could displace commercial sales, making it less clear that that special treatment is appropriate.

D. Licensing Efficiency and Transparency

There seems to be universal agreement among industry participants that accurate, comprehensive, and accessible licensing information, as well as transparent usage and payment data, are essential to a better functioning music licensing system.

1. Industry Data

a. Publicly Accessible Database

Some stakeholders have suggested that the government—for example, the Copyright Office—could undertake the task of creating and maintaining a comprehensive database of musical work and sound recording information, including a system of standard identifiers.[916] As appealing as such a vision may be, the Office believes that it would not be the best result for the twenty-first century marketplace to have the government start from scratch. The relevant universe of music data comprises tens of millions of musical works, sound recordings and information about them. Setting aside any legal impediments, as a practical matter, it would be extremely challenging for the government to gather, ingest, and standardize this ocean of information to be made available within a useful time frame. Any such database would be highly dynamic and require a constant flow of information from MROs, publishers and others concerning newly created works, transfers of ownership, and changes in licensing authority to be kept up to date. These are functions already performed in varying degrees by existing private organizations in collaboration with individual stakeholders.

In light of the above considerations, the Office believes that any solution to the music data problem should not compete with, but instead draw upon, existing industry resources. As a threshold matter, any centralized database should be closely tied to the interests of the copyright owners and licensees it serves. That said, the government should establish incentives through the statutory licensing regime to encourage private actors to coordinate their efforts and contribute to a publicly accessible and authoritative database. In other words, there is a role for both the government and private sector alike.[917]

b. Adoption of Data Standards

The lack of unique and universally employed identifiers for the millions of musical works and sound recordings in the marketplace has been a topic of discussion—and source of discouragement—among industry participants for many years. As a result, there have been some laudable efforts within the industry to address the data problem by persuading market participants to adopt standard identifiers and messaging formats, with some amount of success. The DDEX messaging system appears to have emerged as a leading industry standard for the formatting and delivery of metadata relating to transactions involving digital music.[918] A more recent example of collaboration is the MusicMark initiative, which would rationalize and reconcile sometimes conflicting PRO song data among the American and Canadian PROs ASCAP, BMI, and SOCAN.[919]

But despite these efforts, so far, no comprehensive solution to the data issue has emerged.[920] In part, this appears to be a problem of coordinating private actors, many of whom are invested in, and understandably rely upon, their own data systems and do not wish to undermine these important assets. It is also a legacy problem, in that much of the data used today originated in the pre-digital era, when standardization and interoperability were not critical concerns. For example, the industry did not implement standard conventions for the treatment of artist or songwriter names. Some actors may see little short-term gain to be realized from the substantial investment of resources it would take to clean up and harmonize older records.

Some stakeholders advocate for an entirely new approach to tracking creative works and usage, suggesting that we should look to new technologies to attach unique identifiers to each different version of a song, each different recording of that song, each individual's interest in that song, and each individual use of that song.[921] One interesting proposal would rely on audio fingerprinting rather than just metadata to identify songs.[922] The Office hopes that these or other technological innovations may someday be deployed to the benefit of the music marketplace.

For now, though, the Office believes it is important to focus on what might be reasonably achieved in the near term—again taking into consideration and capitalizing upon industry practices as they exist today. To this end, the Office solicited comments on the most commonly used and useful identifiers, and received helpful guidance from a number of parties.[923] Based on these comments, it appears that the most critical and widely (though not universally) used identifiers are, in the case of musical works, the ISWC, and in the case of sound recordings, the ISRC. The Office believes these two identifiers should, over a period of time (*e.g.*, five years) become required elements within the proposed GMRO-managed database, as described below.

A more recent standard is the ISNI, which can be used to identify songwriters and recording artists, and is gaining acceptance in the industry. There appears to be general agreement that, as new users and uses continue to proliferate, and individual writers and artists seek to participate in the marketplace, it is of critical importance to be able to identify creators unambiguously.[924] ASCAP and BMI have already begun implementing use of

ISNI.[925] This is another data standard that the Office believes should be encouraged and possibly made mandatory over a plausible time frame.

The ISWC standard and the ISRC standard are internationally recognized, as is the ISNI. The ISWC, developed by CISAC, is assigned by individual qualified regional or local numbering agencies; in the U.S. and Canada, ASCAP is the appointed ISWC administrator.[926] The ISRC, administered by IFPI, is allocated by appointed regional agencies in each country; the U.S. ISRC agency is the RIAA.[927] The ISNI standard, launched with CISAC's participation, is meant to replace existing, disparate identification standards for individual creators.[928] ISNIs are assigned to U.S. authors by one or more designated private registration agencies.[929]

The Office's focus on the above standards does not mean that others are unimportant or irrelevant.[930] Legacy standards remain useful for particular entities,[931] and new standards may come into play. The possibility of identifying sound recordings and musical works through audio-based sampling technologies is especially intriguing. Based on the current state of affairs, however, the Office believes that the most realistic strategy to address the data issues plaguing the music industry at present would be to strongly incentivize the universal adoption and dissemination of at least the three data standards described above. Beyond this, as discussed below, it would make sense to provide for regulatory authority to allow for the consideration and adoption of additional data standards over time as appropriate.

2. Fair Reporting and Payment

a. Writer and Artist Shares

Throughout the study, a paramount concern of songwriters and recording artists is transparency in reporting and payment. As digital licensing deals multiply and increase in complexity, it can become quite difficult to follow the money. Songwriters and artists want to ensure that they understand the royalty scheme, are able to track the use of their works, and are paid what they are owed.

In the case of performance royalties, such concerns are greatly diminished when the songwriter or artist is paid through a PRO or SoundExchange. PROs employ distribution rules that are generally known by their members,[932] while SoundExchange allocates royalties according to the statutory formula. In the case of a direct deal, however, the label or publisher is obligated only by the terms of the artist or songwriter agreement, which may not expressly address these issues.[933]

Of particular concern are the sometimes sizeable advances against future royalties that are paid by online services to major record labels and music publishers, and whether and how these are reported to and shared with artists and writers. Sometimes, if royalty obligations are less than anticipated, such an advance may not be fully recouped by the service during the licensing period, so there are leftover funds. In such a situation, there may be no clear understanding—or contractual provision—that addresses whether those funds should be paid out to the songwriter or artist, and if so, on what basis. A recent example of the advance issue cited by songwriters is a direct deal between the publisher Sony/ATV and DMX music service for public performance rights, in which Sony/ATV apparently received a large advance from the service—possibly in exchange for a lower royalty rate.[934] Songwriters worry that they are not able to monitor this type of arrangement to ensure that they receive their fair share of the total consideration paid for the use of their works.

Also concerning to music creators is the fact that labels and publishers are now known to take equity stakes in online services as part of their licensing arrangements. For example, the major labels together reportedly negotiated a nearly 18% stake in Spotify.[935] Questions arise as to how such equity deals are (or are not) reported to artists and songwriters, and whether the value received by the label or publisher impacts the royalties that are paid.[936] Again, the artist or songwriter contract may not address such issues.[937]

These concerns must be addressed as part of any updated licensing framework, especially one that allows publishers to opt out of the statutory licensing system and pursue direct deals. As mentioned above, under any such deal, songwriters should have the option of being paid their writer's share of performance royalties directly through their preferred MRO. That is, even if the music service is paying the publisher's royalties (including mechanicals) to the publisher directly, it would transmit a copy of its usage report and the writer's share of performance royalties to the MRO for the MRO to administer.[938] The Office trusts that such an approach could be acceptable to the publishers, since the major publishers who have been contemplating withdrawal from the PROs appear also to be considering the possibility of continuing administration of royalty distributions by the PROs under directly licensed deals.[939]

While there has been less focus on this issue in relation to SoundExchange—which is not facing a large-scale "withdrawal" problem[940]—the Office notes that the same principle should apply there. To the extent record companies enter into direct licensing relationships with digital providers, artists and musicians should have the option of continuing to receive their share of royalties through that organization.

b. Best Practices for Transparency

More generally, issues surrounding transparency in reporting and payment by music publishers and record labels under songwriter and artist agreements are concerns that might be productively addressed through the consideration and adoption of best practices to ease friction in this area. In 2009, for instance, record labels and music publishers agreed to a series of voluntary changes to improve licensing practices and the flow of royalties under section 115, which have been memorialized in a continuing memorandum of understanding.[941] A similar effort might be undertaken to establish best practices to ensure transparency in label and publisher reporting and payment to creators. The Office hopes that major labels and publishers will consider engaging with artists and publishers in a voluntary fashion to make progress on these issues in the private realm.

E. An Updated Music Licensing System

As noted above, nearly ten years ago, music publishers and digital media companies appealed to Congress to pass SIRA, legislation that would have created a new collective licensing system under section 115 for the digital use of musical works. While SIRA was more limited in scope than what would seem to be called for today, it nonetheless featured some concepts that the Office believes could help to inform a more general overhaul of our licensing system.

First, SIRA recognized that it could be appropriate to allow more than one entity (referred to as a "designated agent") to administer licenses, so long as each such entity represented at least a certain prescribed share of the publishing market. Second, SIRA would have offered licensees the opportunity to obtain licenses on a blanket, rather than song-by-song, basis by serving notice on the designated agents. Third, SIRA recognized that one such agent (the "general designated agent") should serve as a default licensing entity for publishers that had not selected a different agent. And finally, SIRA provided for each designated agent to maintain a database listing ownership information for the musical works it administers.[942] While there was disagreement about the details of SIRA, these basic organizing principles were appealing to many.[943] The Office's proposal for an updated licensing framework also draws upon these concepts.

But even though SIRA may represent a good starting point, it is only that. As digital models have proliferated, the drawbacks of our current system have become more pronounced. The intervening decade has produced a greater sense of urgency concerning the strains on the current system.

Stakeholders focus in particular on the lack of reliable licensing data, which leads to inefficiencies and failures in the licensing process. The Office agrees with commenting parties that much of what is ailing our system would be greatly ameliorated if all those who needed it had access to authoritative data concerning the ownership of musical works and sound recordings. In addition, because digital services typically receive only track-based information for sound recordings that is not tied to the underlying musical work, there needs to be an efficient mechanism for licensees to associate the sound recordings they use with the musical works they embody.

1. MROs

Under the Office's proposal, except to the extent they chose to opt out of the blanket statutory system, publishers and songwriters would be obligated to license their public performance and mechanical rights through their MROs.[944] As explained above, an MRO would have the ability to administer, and bundle, performance and mechanical rights on behalf of the publishers and songwriters it represented. It would also collect and distribute the royalties due under such licenses.[945]

An MRO could be any entity representing the musical works of publishers and songwriters with a market share in the mechanical and/or performance market above a certain minimum threshold, for example, 5%. Existing rights organizations, such as ASCAP, BMI, HFA and others, could thus qualify as MROs. Each MRO would enjoy an antitrust exemption to negotiate performance and mechanical licenses collectively on behalf of its members—as would licensee groups negotiating with the MROs—with the CRB available to establish a rate in case of a dispute.[946] But MROs could not coordinate with one another and, as discussed above, would be subject to at least routine antitrust oversight to guard against anticompetitive behavior. They would also be subject to potential CRB ratesetting for all uses of their members' works except for those that had been withdrawn.

Each MRO would be required to supply a complete list of the publishers, works, percentage shares and rights it represented, as well as the MRO's licensing contact information, to the GMRO, and would be obligated to keep that information current. The requirement to identify the titles and writers of represented works essentially tracks what is required today under the ASCAP consent decree and has long been voluntarily provided by the PROs and HFA through their public "lookup" databases.[947] The critical difference is that the publicly accessible data would be available in a more sophisticated database format that would facilitate automated matching functions, bulk licensing processes, and reconciliation of third-party databases.

MROs would also be responsible for notifying the GMRO of any members that had exercised opt-out rights by providing the relevant opt-out information, including where a direct license might be sought, for the central database so potential licensees would know where to go for license authority. Additionally, under requirements that would be phased in over time, MROs would need to supply the ISWC—and over time, the ISNI— identifiers for each of the works they represented. As everyone appears to agree, the move to unique identifiers as a primary means to recognize both musical works and sound recordings is essential to an efficient licensing system.

But MROs would not have to share all of their data for purposes of the public database. For example, there would be no need for an MRO to provide contact information for its members (other than those that opted out) since the MRO would be responsible for distributing royalties under the licenses it issued. Details about contractual arrangements between publishers and their songwriters that the MROs might need for their own distribution purposes would seem to be unnecessary to provide for public use. Under the Office's approach, MROs would only be required to furnish such information as would be necessary to facilitate accurate licensing transactions and usage reporting in a system of multiple MROs. As suggested below, the specific data to be supplied could be subject to regulatory oversight and adjusted over time.

2. The GMRO

Even though the preponderance of licensing activity would be carried out by the MROs and directly licensing publishers, the hub of the new licensing structure would be the GMRO. Similar to SoundExchange, the GMRO ("SongExchange"?) would be a non- profit entity designated, and regulated, by the government.[948] The GMRO would be overseen by a board that included representatives from both the music publishing and songwriter communities.

By virtue of maintaining authoritative and accessible ownership data, the GMRO would help to coordinate licensing and royalty payments across the MROs and individual publishers. But it would not serve as a centralized collection facility other than with respect to unidentified royalty recipients. The Office believes that adding an additional administrative layer to core royalty collection and distribution functions would add time and expense to these processes and should be avoided if possible.[949] At the same time, the GMRO would serve as the recipient for payments on behalf of unidentified owners.

a. Data-Related Responsibilities

The GMRO would ingest data from MROs and other authoritative sources to create its master database. The GMRO database would list the publishers, musical works, percentage shares and rights represented by the various MROs, along with prescribed identifiers such as ISWCs and ISNIs. In addition, the database would flag opt-out publishers, the specific rights and works that were opted out, and provide the publishers' licensing contact information.

In addition to musical work data, it seems that the GMRO could and should also incorporate sound recording data into the public database, including track titles, record labels, featured artists, play times and ISRCs. It is the Office's understanding that SoundExchange currently has identification and ownership information—including ISRCs—for approximately 14 million sound recordings.[950] The GMRO could absorb this data from SoundExchange.

Through SoundExchange's continuing administration of the section 112 and 114 licenses, an ISRC requirement for remaining tracks—as well as the ISNI standard—could be phased in under those licenses, with the ongoing results to be shared with the GMRO.[951]

Like SoundExchange, the GMRO would play an active role in gathering missing data, reconciling conflicting data, and correcting flawed data. It would need to establish a process to handle competing ownership claims as necessary.

But perhaps most important among the data-related responsibilities of the GMRO. would be to gather or generate "matches" of musical works with sound recordings. There is simply no easy means for licensees to acquire generalized data identifying the musical works embodied in individual sound recordings. Some private entities such as HFA have made substantial progress on this front through a combination of automated and manual matching protocols, but there is no comprehensive source for this information, and even HFA has yet to match millions of titles.[952]

A matching database would represent a huge advance in music licensing, as it would enable digital services efficiently to identify musical works and their owners based on the tracks they are using. Undoubtedly it is a significant undertaking, but given an appropriate level of resources it would seem to be achievable, at least with respect to the most frequently used songs. As HFA reports, 1-2 million sound recordings account for almost 95% of usage in a typical digital music service.[953] Happily (and not surprisingly), it is the most commercially valuable sound recordings and musical works that tend to be the easiest to identify and associate with one another.

On the licensee side of the equation, whenever an ISWC, IRSC or ISNI (or other prescribed identifier) appeared in the database, it would be a required element in a licensee's report under a section 114 or 115 license. The consistent use of these standards would undoubtedly facilitate the GMRO's efforts to match musical works to sound recordings and distribute royalties to their owners.

Finally, as noted above, the song data and licensing information collected by the GMRO would be publicly accessible—not only in the form of individual records through a "lookup"-style database, but also in bulk form and/or via APIs that would allow licensees the ability to use it to update their records or perform matching or other functions relating to their licensing needs.

b. Default Licensing and Payment

Notwithstanding the GMRO database and other available resources, there would still be works (and shares of works) for which the owners were not identified.[954] The GMRO would therefore also serve as the default licensing and collection agent for musical works (or shares of works) that licensees were unable to associate with an MRO or opt- out publisher. Services relying on blanket performance and/or mechanical licenses for musical works that had usage-based payment obligations would transmit records of use for unmatched works, along with associated payments, to the GMRO.[955] The GMRO would then attempt to identify the MRO or individual rightsowner itself and, if successful, pay the royalties out.[956] If unsuccessful in its research efforts, the GMRO would add the usage record to a public unclaimed royalties list and hold the funds for some period of time—*e.g.*, three years—to see if a claimant came forward. As is the case with SoundExchange, after that period, the GMRO could use any remaining unclaimed funds to help offset the costs of its operations. Such a default licensing and payment option would provide protection for licensees—by reporting unmatched works and paying the associated royalties to the GMRO, they could avoid liability for infringement for those uses.

But any such system would require appropriate incentives to ensure that both licensees and publishers were holding up their respective ends of the bargain. Setting aside any general funding obligations in relation to the GMRO, which are discussed below, the Office believes that licensees should be required to pay an administrative fee (perhaps assessed on a per-title basis) for any unmatched uses reported to the GMRO.[957] In addition to encouraging due diligence on the part of licensees to locate missing information before resorting to the default system, such fees would help underwrite the GMRO's efforts to locate and pay rightsholders.

At the same time, MROs and their members should also be encouraged to maintain complete and reliable data with the GMRO. The primary incentive to do so, of course, would be to facilitate prompt and accurate payments by licensees. In this regard, the Office believes it could be useful to establish phased-in compliance targets over a period of several years for the provision of the most critical publisher data, including missing ISWCs, to the GMRO.[958] If, after an appropriate review of the situation and an opportunity to rectify concerns, an MRO were found to fall short of the mark, any licensee required to pay the GMRO's administrative fee for unmatched works to that publisher would be entitled to recoup some portion of that fee (say half) from its royalty payments to that publisher pending correction of the problem.

c. Resources and Funding

A question that will inevitably arise in any discussion concerning an overhaul of our music licensing system is how the new system—more specifically, the startup costs and various activities of the GMRO—would be funded. The Office has some suggestions to offer on this point.

First, the Copyright Office believes that both copyright owners and users should bear the costs of the new system, as both groups will share in its benefits. Traditionally, publishers and songwriters have underwritten much of the cost of licensing performance and mechanical rights and distributing royalties through commissions paid to the PROs and HFA. But record labels and digital services have also borne significant administrative costs in gathering and compiling the data necessary to obtain and report under licenses.

As envisioned by the Office, the GMRO would build and maintain a public database of ownership and licensing information for musical works and sound recordings. As part of this obligation, it would be responsible for matching sound recording data to musical works. The GMRO would also be responsible for collecting and distributing royalties for unclaimed works. These are substantial undertakings. Some licensees have expressed willingness to help fund a more workable system.[959] The Office believes that publishers and songwriters will also need to contribute, although much of their contribution might be in the form of shared data.

As explained above, under the Office's proposal, every MRO, as well as SoundExchange, will be required to contribute key elements of data to create and maintain a centralized music database. MROs will be responsible for allocating and distributing the vast majority of royalties (and will charge commissions to publishers and songwriters for those services). In exchange for these contributions on the part of copyright owners, the Office believes that the primary financial support for the data-related and default licensing activities of the GMRO should come from fees charged to users of the section 112, 114, and 115 licenses.

Although music users would be paying royalties directly to MROs and individual publishers—and to SoundExchange as well—they would have a separate obligation to pay a licensing surcharge to the GMRO in recognition of the value it would be providing to the licensee community. The licensing surcharge might, for example, be assessed as a small percentage of royalties due from the licensee under its section 112, 114, and/or 115 statutory licenses, including any direct deals for equivalent rights. In order to fund startup costs, licensees could perhaps contribute a lump sum against future surcharge assessments, to be recouped over time.

The surcharge to be paid by statutory licensees could be determined by the CRB through a periodic administrative process based on the GMRO's costs, and would be offset by other sources of funding. For example, in addition to the generally applicable surcharge, as explained above, the Office believes that individual licensees should be charged an administrative fee in connection with reporting and paying unattributed uses to the GMRO.[960] Publishers not affiliated with an MRO who claimed works from the unmatched list would also be expected to pay a processing fee, as they would at an MRO. Nonstatutory licensees could be required to pay the GMRO's reasonable costs for the bulk provision of data. Such fees—which would help to offset the costs of the GMRO—could be considered by the CRB in establishing the surcharge.

An additional source of funding would be any royalties that remained unclaimed by publishers after the prescribed holding period (perhaps three years). Such unattributed monies—or "black box" funds—would also be available to offset the GMRO's administrative costs. As with the GMRO's other sources of income, these funds, too, could be considered by the CRB in establishing the licensing surcharge.[961]

3. The CRB

a. New Ratesetting Protocol

Under the Office's proposal, ratesetting by the CRB would shift from a five-year cycle to a system under which the CRB would step in only as necessary—that is, only when an MRO or SoundExchange and licensee could not agree on a rate.

The unfortunate reality is that the costs of ratesetting are very high, whether the proceeding occurs in federal court or before an administrative tribunal. The Office believes that the current approach under the section 112, 114, and 115 licenses—under which rates are required to be established for the full spectrum of uses for the upcoming five years—is probably not the most efficient use of resources. Such an approach presents the nontrivial problem of how to identify, evaluate and price still-nascent business models. Even if they are identified, some of these uses might be easily settled outside of the context of a CRB proceeding. In the case of existing models, the extant rates may be sufficiently satisfactory for both sides to continue in effect. Greater flexibility in the ratesetting process would allow the ratesetting body to address only those rates that were worthwhile to litigate.

In support of its proposal, the Office observes that ASCAP and BMI have operated under such an *adhoc* system in the federal rate courts, with only a relatively small number of their rates actually litigated. A likeminded CRB approach could yield more voluntary agreements and less litigation. Further, licensees would no longer have to shoehorn themselves into an existing rate category to take advantage of statutory licensing, because MRO licenses could be specifically tailored to address the nuances of the business model at hand.

Last but not least, it is difficult to see how an integrated licensing framework such as that proposed by the Office could function under two different ratesetting paradigms, as exist in their separate worlds today. In order to bundle performance and mechanical licensing—or, as discussed below, sound recording and musical work rights—in an efficient manner, there should be a unified ratesetting process. The CRB would face enormous administrative challenges if it had to administer both periodic and *adhoc* ratesetting proceedings simultaneously.[962]

b. All-In Rates for Noninteractive Streaming

During the study, various commenting parties floated the suggestion of all-in blanket licensing that would encompass both sound recording and musical work rights.[963] Our current framework presents seemingly insuperable hurdles to achieving what many view as a tantalizing goal. Even under the framework proposed by the Office—which notwithstanding publisher opt-out rights still contemplates ratesetting for musical works that has no equivalent on the sound recording side—it would be difficult to implement all-in rates on a broad basis.

In one area, however—the licensing of noninteractive streaming uses by internet services, satellite and terrestrial radio, and others—such a model might be achievable. Here the Office has suggested that government supervision of the public performance right be moved from the federal rate courts to the CRB. Accordingly, both sound recording owners and musical work owners would be subject to CRB ratesetting to the extent they were unable to negotiate agreements with digital providers. The Office believes that any such proceedings could potentially be combined.

Taking the suggestion of the RIAA, for example, record labels and music publishers could agree up front to a split of royalties as between them for the category of use to be litigated.[964] They could then participate jointly in the ratesetting proceeding vis-à-vis the licensee. The licensee's focus before the CRB would thus be on its total royalty obligation, rather than the particular amounts to be paid to labels or publishers. Even barring an up-front agreement between the labels and publishers, ratesetting for the service in question might still proceed on an all-in basis, with the CRB to establish the split between sound recordings and musical works in a separate phase of the proceeding that did not include the licensee.

c. GMRO Surcharge

As noted above, under the Office's proposal, the GMRO would be funded in part by a licensing surcharge to be paid directly by licensees to the GMRO. The Office believes that the CRB, with its in-house economic expertise, would be well equipped to determine the surcharge through a periodic review process. That process would be conducted separate and apart from any ratesetting activities. Indeed, an important element of such a proceeding would be to preclude any consideration of royalty rates in establishing the licensing surcharge (and vice versa). The surcharge would be set independently, based on licensee data and the GMRO's costs and capital needs.[965]

d. Procedural Improvements

In addition to the substance of the CRB's ratesetting determinations, a number of seasoned stakeholders addressed the procedural rules that currently govern the CRB's work. The CRB is constrained by procedural mandates set forth in section 803 of the Copyright Act, which govern the initiation and conduct of ratesetting proceedings, including such matters as filing rules for participants, the timing and content of direct cases, the handling of various evidentiary and discovery matters, and settlement negotiations.[966] This sort of procedural detail is unusual in a federal statutory scheme and is more typically left to regulation or the discretion of the tribunal.

Stakeholders complain that the current CRB system is unduly burdensome and expensive. Currently, ratesetting participants are required to put in their written direct statement before they conduct discovery—that is, they are required to construct and support their rate proposals to the CRB without the benefit of economic information from the other side.[967] This is completely counterintuitive to anyone familiar with ordinary litigation practice.

In keeping with this construct, ratesetting proceedings are divided into separate direct and rebuttal phases, with discovery conducted after each phase.[968] Parties may seek to amend their rate proposals in response to what they learn in discovery.[969] In practical effect, this means there are two trial proceedings, with overlapping arguments and evidence, instead of one. As might be expected, stakeholders would prefer to have the issues for trial fully joined and addressed in single proceeding. The Office is sympathetic to these concerns and believes the CRB process should be modified so it more closely resembles typical litigation. As has been suggested by some, this could include greater reliance on the Federal Rules of Civil Procedure and Federal Rules of Evidence, albeit with appropriate modifications (such as relaxation of hearsay rules).[970]

Multifactor ratesetting standards also contribute to the length and expense of proceedings, as parties feel compelled to furnish evidence and argument on each statutorily prescribed factor. A move to a simpler standard such as willing buyer/willing seller—perhaps unembellished by specific considerations (in contrast to the standard as currently embodied in section 114[971])—might also help to streamline the ratesetting process by permitting each side to focus on the most salient aspects of their case.

Many CRB participants complained that the existing process does not facilitate early settlement. In order for a settlement to be the basis for an industrywide rate, it must be adopted by the CRB.[972] The CRB does not appear always to be comfortable in adopting settlement agreements that settle less than the entire proceeding—for example, a settlement among fewer than all participants—while the rest of the proceeding remains pending.[973] And the record shows that participants feel obligated to continue litigating until a settlement is adopted.[974] This is not an efficient system. The Office agrees that this should be rectified by clarifying the statutory provisions governing the CRB to favor partial settlements at any stage of the proceeding when requested by the settling participants.[975]

Finally, while the Office believes that the high-level procedural concerns described should be addressed by legislative amendments, Congress may also wish to remove unnecessary procedural details in the statute that are better left to regulation. The CRB should have the latitude to develop specific procedural rules—and modify them as appropriate—within the basic parameters set forth in the statute.

4. Regulatory Implementation

Should Congress decide to restructure the music licensing system, the Office believes that it might be most productive for any resulting legislation to set out the essential elements of the updated system and leave the particulars to regulation. Such a construct would likely be more realistic to enact than an exhaustive statutory prescription— especially in the case of music licensing, where the particulars can be overwhelming. In addition to whatever legislative advantages it might confer, a more general approach would have added benefit of flexibility, since regulations can be adjusted over time to address new developments and unforeseen contingencies.

Logically, the Copyright Office should have primary regulatory responsibility for the many issues that would need to be addressed in implementing a new statutory framework. For example, the Office could establish rules for the provision of data to the GMRO, licensee reporting requirements, and collective audits. It could also promulgate technical requirements for the statutory licenses, with the power to update such specifications as necessary.

The CRB, too, would have regulatory responsibilities. In addition to its periodic review of the surcharge to be assessed by the GMRO, the CRB would enact rules that would govern the filing and conduct of the ratesetting proceedings it would oversee. Like the Copyright Office, the CRB should have the requisite regulatory authority to carry out its responsibilities.

5. Further Evaluation

Should Congress choose to embark upon a series of changes to our licensing system such as those described above, the Office recommends that the new system be evaluated by the Copyright Office after it has been operation for a period of several years. Assuming that the new licensing framework includes an opt-out mechanism as described above, the efficacy of that process would be of particular interest. If the opt- out system were found to be having adverse effects on the marketplace, Congress could consider narrowing those rights. If, on the other hand, the opt-out option were working well, Congress might wish to expand it to other categories.

APPENDIX A. FEDERAL REGISTER NOTICES

LIBRARY OF CONGRESS
Copyright Office
[Docket No. 2014–03]
Music Licensing Study: Notice and Request for Public Comment
AGENCY: Copyright Office, Library of Congress.
ACTION: Notice of Inquiry.

Summary

The United States Copyright Office announces the initiation of a study to evaluate the effectiveness of existing methods of licensing music. To aid this effort, the Office is seeking public input on this topic. The Office will use the information it gathers to report to Congress. Congress is currently conducting a review of the U.S. Copyright Act, 17 U.S.C. 101 *et seq.*, to evaluate potential revisions of the law in light of technological and other developments that impact the creation, dissemination, and use of copyrighted works.

Dates

Written comments are due on or before May 16, 2014. The Office will be announcing one or more public meetings to address music licensing issues, to take place after written comments are received, by separate notice in the future.

Addresses

All comments shall be submitted electronically. A comment page containing a comment form is posted on the Office Web site at http://www.copyright.gov/ docs/musiclicensingstudy. The Web site interface requires commenting parties to complete a form specifying their name and organization, as applicable, and to upload comments as an attachment via a browser button. To meet accessibility standards, commenting parties must upload comments in a single file not to exceed six megabytes (MB) in one of the following formats: The Portable Document File (PDF) format that contains searchable, accessible text (not an image); Microsoft Word; WordPerfect; Rich Text Format (RTF); or ASCII text file format (not a scanned document). The form and face of the comments must include both the name of the submitter and organization. The Office will post the comments publicly on the Office's Web site in the form that they are received, along with associated names and organizations. If electronic submission of comments is not feasible, please contact the Office at 202–707–8350 for special instructions.

For Further Information Contact

Jacqueline C. Charlesworth, General Counsel and Associate Register of Copyrights, by email at *jcharlesworth@loc.gov* or by telephone at 202–707–8350; or Sarang V. Damle, Special Advisor to the General Counsel, by email at *sdam@loc.gov* or by telephone at 202–707–8350.

Supplementary Information

I. Background

Congress is currently engaged in a comprehensive review of the U.S. Copyright Act, 17 U.S.C. 101 *et seq.,* to evaluate potential revisions to the law in light of technological and other developments that impact the creation, dissemination, and use of copyrighted works. The last general revision of the Copyright Act took place in 1976 ("Copyright Act" or "Act") following a lengthy and comprehensive review process carried out by Congress, the Copyright Office, and interested parties. In 1998, Congress significantly amended the Act with the passage of the Digital Millennium Copyright Act ("DMCA") to address emerging issues of the digital age. Public Law 105–304, 112 Stat. 2860 (1998). While the Copyright Act reflects many sound and enduring principles, and has enabled the internet to flourish, Congress could not have foreseen all of today's technologies and the myriad ways consumers and others engage with creative works in the digital environment. Perhaps nowhere has the landscape been as significantly altered as in the realm of music.

Music is more available now than it has ever been. Today, music is delivered to consumers not only in physical formats, such as compact discs and vinyl records, but is available on demand, both by download and streaming, as well as through smartphones, computers, and other devices. At the same time, the public continues to consume music through terrestrial and satellite radio, and more recently, internet-based radio. Music continues to enhance films, television, and advertising, and is a key component of many apps and video games.

Such uses of music require licenses from copyright owners. The mechanisms for obtaining such licenses are largely shaped by our copyright law, including the statutory licenses under Sections 112, 114, and 115 of the Copyright Act, which provide government-regulated licensing regimes for certain uses of sound recordings and musical works.

A musical recording encompasses two distinct works of authorship: The musical work, which is the underlying composition created by the songwriter or composer, along with any accompanying lyrics; and the sound recording, that is, the particular performance of the musical work that has been fixed in a recording medium such as CD or digital file. The methods for obtaining licenses differ with respect to these two types of works, which can be—and frequently are—owned or managed by different entities. Songwriters and composers often assign rights in their musical works to music publishers and, in addition, affiliate themselves with performing rights organizations ("PROs"). These intermediaries, in turn, assume responsibility for licensing the works. By contrast, the licensing of sound recordings is typically handled directly by record labels, except in the case of certain types of digital uses, as described below.

Musical Works—Reproduction and Distribution. Under the Copyright Act, the owner of a musical work has the exclusive right to make and distribute phonorecords of the work (i.e., copies in which the work is embodied, such as CDs or digital files), as well as the exclusive right to perform the work publicly. 17 U.S.C. 106(1), (3). The copyright owner can also authorize others to engage in these acts. *Id.* These rights, however, are typically licensed in different ways.

The right to make and distribute phonorecords of musical works (often referred to as the "mechanical" right) is subject to a compulsory statutory license under Section 115 of the Act. *See generally* 17 U.S.C. 115. That license—instituted by Congress over a century ago with the passage of the 1909 Copyright Act—provides that, once a phonorecord of a musical work has been distributed to the public in the United States under the authority of the copyright owner, any person can obtain a license to make and distribute phonorecords of that work by serving a statutorily compliant notice and paying the applicable royalties. *Id.*

In 1995, Congress confirmed that a copyright owner's exclusive right to reproduce and distribute phonorecords of a musical work, and the Section 115 license, extend to the making of "digital phonorecord deliveries" ("DPDs")—that is, the transmission of digital files embodying musical works. *See* Digital Performance Right in Sound Recordings Act of 1995 ("DPRSRA"), Public Law 104–39, sec. 4, 109 Stat. 336, 344–48; 17 U.S.C. 115(c)(3)(A).[976] The Copyright Office has thus interpreted the Section 115 license to cover music downloads (including ringtones), as well as the server and other reproductions necessary to engage in streaming activities. *See* In the Matter of Mechanical and Digital Phonorecord Delivery Rate

Adjustment Proceeding, Docket No. RF 2006–1 (Oct. 16, 2006), http://www.copyright.gov/docs/ ringtone-decision.pdf; Compulsory License for Making and Distributing Phonorecords, Including Digital Phonorecord Deliveries, 73 FR 66173 (Nov. 7, 2008).

Licenses under Section 115 are obtained on a song-by-song basis. Because a typical online music service needs to offer access to millions of songs to compete in the marketplace, obtaining the licenses on an individual basis can present administrative challenges.[977] Many music publishers have designated the Harry Fox Agency, Inc. as an agent to handle such song-by- song mechanical licensing on their behalf.

The royalty rates and terms for the Section 115 license are established by an administrative tribunal—the Copyright Royalty Board ("CRB")[978]— which applies a standard set forth in Section 801(b) of the Act that considers four different factors. These include: The availability of creative works to the public; economic return to the owners and users of musical works; the respective contributions of owners and users in making works available; and the industry impact of the rates.[979]

The Section 115 license applies to audio-only reproductions that are primarily made and distributed for private use. See 17 U.S.C. 101, 115. Reproductions and distribution of musical works that fall outside of the Section 115 license—including "synch" uses in audiovisual media like television, film, and videos; advertising and other types of commercial uses; and derivative uses such as "sampling"—are licensed directly from the copyright owner according to negotiated rates and terms.

Musical Works—Public Performance. The method for licensing public performances of musical works differs significantly from the statutory mechanical license provided under Section 115. Licensing fees for such performances are generally collected on behalf of music publishers, songwriters, and composers by the three major PROs: the American Society of Composers, Authors and Publishers ("ASCAP"), Broadcast Music, Inc. ("BMI"), and SESAC. Songwriters and composers, as well as their publishers, commonly affiliate with one of the three for purposes of receiving public performance income. Rather than song- by-song licenses, the PROs typically offer "blanket" licenses for the full range of music in their repertories. These licenses are available for a wide variety of uses, including terrestrial, satellite, and internet radio, on-demand music streaming services, Web site and television uses, and performance of music in bars, restaurants, and other commercial establishments. The PROs monitor the use of musical works by these various entities and apportion and distribute collected royalties to their publisher, songwriter, and composer members.

Unlike the mechanical right, the public performance of musical works is not subject to compulsory licensing under the Copyright Act. Since 1941, however, ASCAP and BMI's licensing practices have been subject to antitrust consent decrees overseen by the Department of Justice.[980] These consent decrees were designed to protect licensees from price discrimination or other anti-competitive behavior by the two PROs. Under the decrees, ASCAP and BMI administer the public performance right for their members' musical works on a non-exclusive basis. They are required to provide a license to any person who seeks to perform copyrighted musical works publicly, and must offer the same terms to similarly situated licensees. In addition, ASCAP's consent decree expressly bars it from offering mechanical licenses.[981] Since 1950, prospective licensees that are unable to agree to a royalty rate with ASCAP or BMI have been able to seek a determination of a reasonable license fee in the federal district court for the Southern District of New York.[982]

The two PRO consent decrees were last amended well before the proliferation of digital music: The BMI decree in 1994,[983] and the ASCAP decree in 2001.[984] The consent decrees have been the subject of much litigation over the years, including, most recently, suits over whether music publishers can withdraw digital licensing rights from the PROs and negotiate public performance licenses directly with digital music services.[985]

Sound Recordings—Reproduction and Distribution. Congress extended federal copyright protection to sound recordings in 1972. That law, however, did not provide retroactive protection for sound recordings fixed prior to February 15, 1972, and such works therefore have no federal copyright status.[986] They are, however, subject to the protection of applicable state laws until 2067. *See* 17 U.S.C. 301(c).[987]

The owner of a copyright in a sound recording fixed on or after February 15, 1972, like the owner of a musical work copyright, enjoys the exclusive right to reproduce and distribute phonorecords embodying the sound recording, including by means of digital transmission, and to authorize others to do the same. 17 U.S.C. 106(1), (3), 301(c). Except in the limited circumstances where statutory licensing applies, as described below, licenses to reproduce and distribute sound recordings—such as those necessary to make and distribute CDs, transmit DPDs, and operate online music services, as well as to use sound recordings in a television shows, films, video games, etc.—are negotiated directly between the licensee and sound recording owner (typically a record label). Thus, while in the case of musical works, the royalty rates and terms applicable to the making and distribution of CDs, DPDs, and the operation of interactive music services are subject to government oversight, with respect to sound recordings, licensing for those same uses takes place without government supervision.

Sound Recordings—Public Performance. Unlike musical works, a sound recording owner's public performance right does not extend to all manner of public performances. Traditionally, the public performance of sound recordings was not subject to protection at all under the Copyright Act. In 1995, however, Congress enacted the DPRSRA, which provided for a limited right when sound recordings are publicly performed "by means of a digital audio transmission." Public Law 104–39, 109 Stat. 336; 17 U.S.C. 106(6), 114(a). This right extends, for example, to satellite radio and internet-based music services.[988] Significantly, however, the public performance of sound recordings by broadcast radio stations remains exempt under the Act. 17 U.S.C. 114(d)(1).[989]

For certain uses, including those by satellite and internet radio, the digital public performance right for sound recordings is subject to statutory licensing in accordance with Sections 112 and 114 of the Act. Section 112 provides for a license to reproduce the phonorecords (sometimes referred to as "ephemeral recordings") necessary to facilitate a service's transmissions to subscribers, while Section 114 licenses the public performances of sound recordings resulting from those transmissions. This statutory licensing framework applies only to noninteractive (i.e., radio-style) services as defined under Section 114; interactive (or on-demand services) are not covered. *See* 17 U.S.C. 112(e); 17 U.S.C. 114(d)(2), (f). For interactive services, sound recording owners negotiate licenses directly with users.

The rates and terms applicable to the public performance of sound recordings under the Section 112 and 114 licenses are established by the CRB. *See* 17 U.S.C. 801 *et seq.* The royalties due under these licenses are paid to an entity designated by the CRB—currently

SoundExchange, Inc.—which collects, processes, and distributes payments on behalf of rights holders.[990]

Notably, under Section 114, the rate standard applicable to those satellite radio and music subscription services that existed as of July 31, 1998 (i.e., "preexisting" services[991]) differs from that for other services such as internet radio.[992] Royalty rates for pre-existing satellite radio and subscription services are governed by the four-factor standard in Section 801(b) of the Act—that is, the standard that applies to the Section 115 license for musical works.[993] By contrast, under the terms of Section 114, rates and terms for noninteractive public performances via internet radio and other newer digital music services are to be determined by the CRB based on what a "willing buyer" and "willing seller" would have agreed to in the marketplace.[994]

Subjects of Inquiry

The Copyright Office seeks public input on the effectiveness of the current methods for licensing musical works and sound recordings. Accordingly, the Office invites written comments on the specific subjects above. A party choosing to respond to this Notice of Inquiry need not address every subject, but the Office requests that responding parties clearly identify and separately address each subject for which a response is submitted.

Musical Works

1. Please assess the current need for and effectiveness of the Section 115 statutory license for the reproduction and distribution of musical works.
2. Please assess the effectiveness of the royalty ratesetting process and standards under Section 115.
3. Would the music marketplace benefit if the Section 115 license were updated to permit licensing of musical works on a blanket basis by one or more collective licensing entities, rather than on a song-by-song basis? If so, what would be the key elements of any such system?
4. For uses under the Section 115 statutory license that also require a public performance license, could the licensing process be facilitated by enabling the licensing of performance rights along with reproduction and distribution rights in a unified manner? How might such a unified process be effectuated?
5. Please assess the effectiveness of the current process for licensing the public performances of musical works.
6. Please assess the effectiveness of the royalty ratesetting process and standards applicable under the consent decrees governing ASCAP and BMI, as well as the impact, if any, of 17 U.S.C.114(i), which provides that "[l]icense fees payable for the public performance of sound recordings under Section 106(6) shall not be taken into account in any administrative, judicial, or other governmental proceeding to set or adjust the royalties payable to copyright owners of musical works for the public performance of their works."
7. Are the consent decrees serving their intended purpose? Are the concerns that motivated the entry of these decrees still present given modern market conditions and legal developments? Are there alternatives that might be adopted?

Sound Recordings

8. Please assess the current need for and effectiveness of the Section 112 and Section 114 statutory licensing process.
9. Please assess the effectiveness of the royalty ratesetting process and standards applicable to the various types of services subject to statutory licensing under Section 114.
10. Do any recent developments suggest that the music marketplace might benefit by extending federal copyright protection to pre-1972 sound recordings? Are there reasons to continue to withhold such protection? Should pre-1972 sound recordings be included within the Section 112 and 114 statutory licenses?
11. Is the distinction between interactive and noninteractive services adequately defined for purposes of eligibility for the Section 114 license?

Platform Parity

12. What is the impact of the varying ratesetting standards applicable to the Section 112, 114, and 115 statutory licenses, including across different music delivery platforms. Do these differences make sense?
13. How do differences in the applicability of the sound recording public performance right impact music licensing?

Changes in Music Licensing Practices

14. How prevalent is direct licensing by musical work owners in lieu of licensing through a common agent or PRO? How does direct licensing impact the music marketplace, including the major record labels and music publishers, smaller entities, individual creators, and licensees?
15. Could the government play a role in encouraging the development of alternative licensing models, such as micro-licensing platforms? If so, how and for what types of uses?
16. In general, what innovations have been or are being developed by copyright owners and users to make the process of music licensing more effective?
17. Would the music marketplace benefit from modifying the scope of the existing statutory licenses?

Revenues and Investment

18. How have developments in the music marketplace affected the income of songwriters, composers, and recording artists?
19. Are revenues attributable to the performance and sale of music fairly divided between creators and distributors of musical works and sound recordings?
20. In what ways are investment decisions by creators, music publishers, and record labels, including the investment in the development of new projects and talent, impacted by music licensing issues?

21. How do licensing concerns impact the ability to invest in new distribution models?

Data Standards

22. Are there ways the federal government could encourage the adoption of universal standards for the identification of musical works and sound recordings to facilitate the music licensing process?

Other Issues

23. Please supply or identify data or economic studies that measure or quantify the effect of technological or other developments on the music licensing marketplace, including the revenues attributable to the consumption of music in different formats and through different distribution channels, and the income earned by copyright owners.
24. Please identify any pertinent issues not referenced above that the Copyright Office should consider in conducting its study.

Dated: March 11, 2014.
Jacqueline C. Charlesworth,
General Counsel and Associate, Register of Copyrights.
[FR Doc. 2014–05711 Filed 3–14–14; 8:45 am]
BILLING CODE 1410–30–P

LIBRARY OF CONGRESS
U.S. Copyright Office
[Docket No. 2014–03]
Music Licensing Study
AGENCY: U.S. Copyright Office, Library of Congress.
ACTION: Notice of public roundtables.

Summary

The U.S. Copyright Office is undertaking a study to evaluate the effectiveness of current methods for licensing musical works and sound recordings. The study will assess whether and how existing methods serve the music marketplace, including new and emerging digital distribution platforms. In addition to soliciting written comments, the Office is conducting three two-day public roundtables on music licensing issues. A Notice of Inquiry soliciting written comments in response to a number of subjects was issued on March 17, 2014, and written comments are due on or before May 16, 2014. *See* 78 FR 14739 (Mar. 17, 2014). At this time, the Copyright Office announces three public roundtables to be held in June 2014 in Nashville, Los Angeles, and New York.

Dates

The two-day public roundtable in Nashville will be held on June 4 and 5, 2014, on both days from 9:00 a.m. to 5:00 p.m. The two-day public roundtable in Los Angeles will be held on June 16 and 17, 2014, on both days from 9:00 a.m. to 5:00 p.m. The two-day public roundtable in New York will be held on June 23 and 24, 2014, from 9:00 a.m. to 5:00 p.m. on June 23, and from 8:30 a.m. to 4:00 p.m. on June 24. Requests to participate in the roundtables must be received by the Copyright Office by May 20, 2014.

Addresses

The Nashville roundtable will take place at Belmont University's Mike Curb College of Entertainment and Music Business, 34 Music Square East, Nashville, Tennessee 37203. The Los Angeles roundtable will take place at the UCLA School of Law, 385 Charles E. Young Drive East, Los Angeles, California 90095. The New York roundtable will take place at the New York University School of Law, 40 Washington Square South, New York, New York 10012. Requests to participate in the roundtables should be submitted using the form available on the Office's Web site at http://www.copyright.gov/docs/musiclicensingstudy. If electronic submission is not feasible, please contact the Office at 202–707–8350 for special instructions.

For Further Information Contact

Jacqueline C. Charlesworth, General Counsel and Associate Register of Copyrights, by email at *jcharlesworth@ loc.gov* or by telephone at 202–707–8350; or Sarang V. Damle, Special Advisor to the General Counsel, by email at sdam@loc.gov or by telephone at 202–707–8350.

Supplementary Information

Congress is currently engaged in a comprehensive review of the U.S. Copyright Act, 17 U.S.C. 101 *et seq.*, to evaluate potential revisions to the law in light of technological and other developments that impact the creation, dissemination, and use of copyrighted works. In light of Congress's review and significant changes to the music industry in recent years, the U.S. Copyright Office is conducting a study to assess the effectiveness of current methods for licensing sound recordings and musical works. The Office published a Notice of Inquiry on March 17, 2014, seeking written comments on twenty-four subjects concerning the current environment in which music is licensed. *See* 78 FR 14739 (Mar. 17, 2014).

At this time, the Copyright Office is providing notice of its intention to seek further input for its study through three two-day public roundtables to be held in Nashville, Los Angeles, and New York. The public roundtables will offer an opportunity for interested parties to comment on pertinent music licensing issues. The roundtables will address topics set forth in the Notice of Inquiry, including: The current music licensing landscape; licensing of sound recordings, including under the Section 112 and 114 statutory licenses and the treatment of pre-1972 recordings; licensing of musical works, including under the Section 115 statutory license and through the performing rights organizations (''PROs''); fair royalty rates and platform parity; industry data standards; industry incentives and investment; and potential future developments in music licensing. Following discussion of the various agenda topics by roundtable participants, observers at the roundtables will be provided a limited opportunity to offer additional comments.

The roundtable hearing rooms will have a limited number of seats for participants and observers. Those who seek to participate should complete and submit the form available on the Office's Web site at http://www.copyright.gov/docs/musiclicensingstudy so it is received by the Office no later than May 20, 2014. For individuals who wish to observe a roundtable, the Office will provide public seating on a first-come, first-serve basis on the days of the roundtable.

Dated: April 30, 2014.

Jacqueline C. Charlesworth,
General Counsel and Associate Register of Copyrights.
[FR Doc. 2014–10242 Filed 5–2–14; 8:45 am]
BILLING CODE 1410–30–P

LIBRARY OF CONGRESS
Copyright Office
[Docket No. 2014–03]
Music Licensing Study: Second Request for Comments
AGENCY: U.S. Copyright Office, Library of Congress.
ACTION: Notice of inquiry.

Summary

The U.S. Copyright Office has undertaken a study to evaluate the effectiveness of current methods for licensing musical works and sound recordings. At this time, the Office seeks additional comments on whether and how existing music licensing methods serve the music marketplace, including new and emerging digital distribution platforms.

Dates

Written comments are due on or before August 22, 2014.

Addresses

All comments shall be submitted electronically. A comment page containing a comment form is posted on the Office Web site at http://www.copyright.gov/200B;docs/200B;

musiclicensingstudy. The Web site interface requires commenting parties to complete a form specifying their name and organization, as applicable, and to upload comments as an attachment via a browser button. To meet accessibility standards, commenting parties must upload comments in a single file not to exceed six megabytes (MB) in one of the following formats: The Portable All comments shall be submitted electronically. A comment page containing a comment form is posted on the Office Web site at http://www.copyright.gov/ 200B;docs/200B;musiclicensingstudy. The Web site interface requires commenting parties to complete a form specifying their name and organization, as applicable, and to upload comments as an attachment via a browser button. To meet accessibility standards, commenting parties must upload comments in a single file not to exceed six megabytes (MB) in one of the following formats: The Portable Document File (PDF) format that contains searchable, accessible text (not an image); Microsoft Word; WordPerfect; Rich Text Format (RTF); or ASCII text file format (not a scanned document). The form and face of the comments must include both the name of the submitter and organization. The Office will post the comments publicly on its Web site in the form that they are received, along with associated names and organizations. If electronic submission of comments is not feasible, please contact the Office at 202–707–8350 for special instructions.

For Further Information Contact

Jacqueline C. Charlesworth, General Counsel and Associate Register of Copyrights, by email at *jcharlesworth@ loc.gov* or by telephone at 202–707–8350; or Sarang V. Damle, Special Advisor to the General Counsel, by email at *sdam@loc.gov* or by telephone at 202–707–8350.

Supplementary Information

I. Background

The U.S. Copyright Office is conducting a study to assess the effectiveness of the current methods for licensing musical works and sound recordings. To aid with this study, the Office published an initial Notice of Inquiry on March 17, 2014 ("First Notice") seeking written comments on twenty-four subjects concerning the current environment in which music is licensed. 78 FR 14739 (Mar. 17, 2014). The eighty-five written submissions received in response to this initial notice can be found on the Copyright Office Web site at http://www.copyright.gov/docs/musiclicensing study/200B;comments/Docket2014_3/. In June 2014, the Office conducted three two-day public roundtables in Nashville, Los Angeles, and New York City. The three roundtables provided participants with the opportunity to share their views on the topics identified in the First Notice and other issues relating to music licensing. *See* 79 FR 25626 (May 5, 2014). Transcripts of the proceedings at each of the three roundtables will be made available on the Copyright Office Web site at http://www.copyright. gov/docs/200B;musiclicensingstudy/.

In the initial round of written comments and during the roundtable sessions, a number of significant issues were discussed that the Office believes merit additional consideration.

First, as explained in the First Notice, in 2013, the two federal district courts overseeing the antitrust consent decrees governing the largest performance rights organizations ("PROs"), American Society of Composers, Authors and Publishers ("ASCAP") and Broadcast Music, Inc. ("BMI"), held in separate opinions that under those decrees, music publishers could not withdraw selected rights—such as "new media" rights—to be directly licensed outside of the PROs; rather, a particular publisher's song catalog must either be "all in" or "all out."[995] Following these rulings, both in public statements and at the recent roundtables, certain major music publishers have indicated that, if the consent decrees remain in place without modification, they intend to withdraw their entire catalogs from the two PROs and directly license public performances.[996] Such a move would affect not only online services, but more traditional areas of public performance such as radio, television, restaurants, and bars.

Stakeholders at the roundtables expressed significant concerns regarding the impact of major publishers' complete withdrawal from the PROs. Notably, traditional songwriter contracts typically include provisions that assume that a songwriter's performance royalties will be collected by and paid directly to the songwriter through a PRO, without contemplating alternative arrangements. Songwriters and composers raised questions as to how withdrawing publishers would fulfill this responsibility in the future, including whether they would be in a position to track and provide adequate usage and payment data under a direct licensing system. Another concern is how such withdrawals would affect the PROs' cost structures and the commission rates for smaller entities and individual creators who continued to rely upon these organizations to license and administer their public performance rights. At the same time, some stakeholders questioned the existing distribution methodologies of the PROs, suggesting that the PROs should rely more on census-based reporting (as is typically supplied by digital services) and less on sampling or non-census-based approaches to allocate royalty fees among members.

Next, many stakeholders appear to be of the view that the Section 115 statutory license for the reproduction and distribution of musical works should either be eliminated or significantly modified to reflect the realities of the digital marketplace. While music owners and music users have expressed a range of views as to the particulars of how this might be accomplished, much of the commentary and discussion has centered on two possible approaches. The first would be to sunset the Section 115 license with the goal of enabling musical work owners to negotiate licenses directly with music users at unregulated, marketplace rates (as the synchronization market for musical works currently operates). Some stakeholders have acknowledged, however, that such a market-based system might still have to allow for the possibility of collective licensing to accommodate individuals and smaller copyright owners who might lack the capacity or leverage to negotiate directly with online service providers and others.

A second model, advocated by the record labels, would be to eliminate Section 115 and instead allow music publishers and sound recording owners collectively to negotiate an industrywide revenue-sharing arrangement as between them. For the uses falling under this approach, a fixed percentage of licensing fees for use of a recorded song would be allocated to the musical work and the remainder would go to the sound recording owner. Record labels would be permitted to bundle musical work licenses with their sound recording licenses, with third-party licensees to pay the overall license fees to publishers and labels according to the agreed industry percentages. While musical work owners would retain control over the first recordings of their works, such an arrangement would cover not only audio-only uses but would extend to certain audiovisual uses not currently covered by the Section 115 license, such as music videos and lyric display.

Another theme that emerged from the first round of written comments and the public roundtables relates to the Section 112 and 114 statutory licenses for the digital performance of sound recordings.[997] Although there appeared to be substantial agreement that these licenses are largely effective, there was also a general consensus that improvements could be made to the Copyright Royalty Judges' ("CRJs") statutorily mandated ratesetting procedures. For instance, under 17 U.S.C. 803(b)(6), parties in proceedings before the CRJs must submit written direct statements before any discovery is conducted. A number of commenters believed that the ratesetting process could be significantly streamlined by allowing for discovery before presentation of the parties' direct cases, as in ordinary civil litigation. Stakeholders were also of the view that it would be more efficient to combine what are now two separate direct and rebuttal phases of ratesetting hearings, as contemplated by 17 U.S.C. 803(b)(6)(C), into a single integrated trial—again as is more typical of civil litigation. There was also general agreement that more could be done to encourage settlement of rate disputes, such as adoption of settlements earlier in the process and allowing suchsettlements to be treated as non- precedential with respect to non-settling participants.

Finally, many commenting parties pointed to the lack of standardized and reliable data related to the identity and ownership of musical works and sound recordings as a significant obstacle to more efficient music licensing mechanisms. Stakeholders observed that digital music files are often distributed to online providers without identifiers such as the International Standard Recording Code ("ISRC") and/or International Standard Musical Work Code ("ISWC"), and that the lack of these identifiers (or other unique or universal identifiers) makes it difficult for licensees or others to link particular music files with the copyrighted works they embody. In addition to problems identifying the musical works and sound recordings themselves, commenters noted the difficulties of ascertaining ownership information, especially in the case of musical works, which frequently have multiple owners representing varying percentages of particular songs. These issues, in turn, relate to a more general "transparency" concern of music creators that usage and payment information—including information about advances and equity provided by licensees to publishers and labels—may not be fully and readily accessible to songwriters, composers and artists.

At this time, the Office is soliciting additional comments on these subjects, as set forth in the specific questions below. Parties may also take this opportunity to respond to the positions taken by others in the first round of comments and/or at the roundtables. Those who plan to submit additional comments should be aware that the Office has studied and will take into consideration the comments already received, so there is no need to restate previously submitted material. While a party choosing to respond to this Notice of Inquiry need not address every subject below, the Office requests that responding parties clearly identify and separately address each subject for which a response is submitted.

Subjects of Inquiry

Data and Transparency

1. Please address possible methods for ensuring the development and dissemination of comprehensive and authoritative public data related to the identity and ownership of musical works and sound recordings, including how best to incentivize private actors to gather, assimilate and share reliable data.
2. What are the most widely embraced identifiers used in connection with musical works, sound recordings, songwriters, composers, and artists? How and by whom are they issued and managed? How might the government incentivize more universal availability and adoption?
3. Please address possible methods for enhancing transparency in the reporting of usage, payment, and distribution data by licensees, record labels, music publishers, and collective licensing entities, including disclosure of non-usage-based forms of compensation (*e.g.*, advances against future royalty payments and equity shares).

Musical Works

4. Please provide your views on the logistics and consequences of potential publisher withdrawals from ASCAP and/or BMI, including how such withdrawals would be governed by the PROs; whether such withdrawals are compatible with existing publisher agreements with songwriters and composers; whether the PROs might still play a role in administering licenses issued directly by the publishers, and if so, how; the effect of any such withdrawals on PRO cost structures and commissions; licensees' access to definitive data concerning individual works subject to withdrawal; and related issues.
5. Are there ways in which the current PRO distribution methodologies could or should be improved?
6. In recent years, PROs have announced record-high revenues and distributions. At the same time, many songwriters report significant declines in income. What marketplace developments have led to this result, and what implications does it have for the music licensing system?
7. If the Section 115 license were to be eliminated, how would the transition work? In the absence of a statutory regime, how would digital service providers obtain licenses for the millions of songs they seem to believe are required to meet consumer expectations? What percentage of these works could be directly licensed without undue transaction costs and would some type of collective licensing remain necessary to facilitate licensing of the remainder? If so, would such collective(s) require government oversight? How might uses now outside of Section 115, such as music videos and lyric displays, be accommodated?

Sound Recordings

8. Are there ways in which Section 112 and 114 (or other) CRB ratesetting proceedings could be streamlined or otherwise improved from a procedural standpoint?

International Music Licensing Models

9. International licensing models for the reproduction, distribution, and public performance of musical works differ from the current regimes for licensing musical works in the United States. Are there international music licensing models the Office should look to as it continues to review the U.S. system?

Other Issues

10. Please identify any other pertinent issues that the Copyright Office may wish to consider in evaluating the music licensing landscape.

Dated: July 18, 2014.
Jacqueline C. Charlesworth,
General Counsel and Associate, Register of Copyrights.
[FR Doc. 2014–17354 Filed 7–22–14; 8:45 am]
BILLING CODE 1410–30–P

LIBRARY OF CONGRESS
Copyright Office
[Docket No. 2014–03]
Music Licensing Study
AGENCY: U.S. Copyright Office, Library of Congress.
ACTION: Notice of extension of comment period.

Summary

The United States Copyright Office is extending the deadline for public comments regarding the effectiveness of existing methods of licensing music that were solicited in a July 23, 2014 Notice of Inquiry. *See* 79 FR 42833 (July 23, 2014).

Dates

Written comments are now due on or before September 12, 2014.

Addresses

All comments shall be submitted electronically. A comment page containing a comment form is posted on the Office Web site at http://www.copyright.gov/docs/musiclicensingstudy. The Web site interface requires commenting parties to complete a form specifying their name and organization, as applicable, and to upload comments as an attachment via a browser button. To meet accessibility standards, commenting parties must upload comments in a single file not to exceed six megabytes (MB) in one of the following formats: The Portable Document File (PDF) format that contains searchable, accessible text (not an image); Microsoft Word; WordPerfect; Rich Text Format (RTF); or ASCII text file format (not a scanned document). The form and face of the comments must include both the name of the submitter and organization. The Office will post the comments publicly on the Office's Web site in the form that they are received, along with associated names and organizations. If electronic submission of comments is not feasible, please contact the Office at 202–707–8350 for special instructions.

For Further Information Contact

Jacqueline C. Charlesworth, General Counsel and Associate Register of Copyrights, by email at *jcharlesworth@ loc.gov* or by telephone at 202–707–8350; or Sarang V. Damle, Special Advisor to the General Counsel, by email at *sdam@loc.gov* or by telephone at 202–707–8350.

Supplementary Information

I. Background

The U.S. Copyright Office is conducting a study to assess the effectiveness of current methods for licensing sound recordings and musical works. The Office received written comments responding to an initial Notice of Inquiry, and held three public roundtables in Nashville, Los Angeles and New York. *See* 78 FR 13739 (Mar. 17, 2014); 79 FR 25626 (May 5, 2014).

On July 23, 2014, the Office published a second Notice of Inquiry, seeking additional written comments on ten subjects concerning the music licensing environment. 79 FR 42833. To ensure commenters have sufficient time to address the topics set forth in the July 2014 Notice of Inquiry, the Office is extending the time for filing written comments from August 22, 2014 to September 12, 2014.

Dated: July 28, 2014.
Maria A. Pallante,
Register of Copyrights.
[FR Doc. 2014–18096 Filed 7–31–14; 8:45 am]
BILLING CODE 1410–30–P

APPENDIX B. COMMENTING PARTIES AND ROUNDTABLE PARTICIPANTS

Parties Who Responded to First Notice of Inquiry

1. ABKCO Music & Records, Inc. (ABKCO)
2. American Association of Independent Music (A2IM)
3. American Society of Composers, Authors and Publishers (ASCAP)
4. Audiosocket
5. Barnett III, William
6. Brigham Young University Copyright Licensing Office
7. Broadcast Music, Inc. (BMI)
8. Camp, Ben
9. Center for Copyright Integrity
10. Castle, Christian L.
11. Cate, John
12. Consumer Federation of America (CFA) and Public Knowledge
13. Content Creators Coalition
14. Continental Entertainment Group
15. Copyright Alliance
16. Council of Music Creators
17. CTIA – The Wireless Association (CTIA)
18. Digital Data Exchange, LLC (DDEX)
19. Digital Media Association (DiMA)
20. DotMusic
21. Educational Media Foundation (EMF)
22. Ferrick, Melissa
23. Future of Music Coalition (FMC)
24. Gear Publishing Company and Lisa Thomas Music Services, LLC
25. Geo Music Group & George Johnson Music Publishing
26. Global Image Works
27. Greco, Melanie Holland
28. Harris, Jim
29. Hayes, Bonnie
30. Henderson, Linda S.
31. Herstand, Ari
32. Indiana University, Archives of African American Music and Culture
33. Interested Parties Advancing Copyright (IPAC)
34. Jessop, Paul
35. Kohn, Bob
36. LaPolt, Dina
37. Library of Congress
38. Lincoff, Bennett
39. Lowery, David
40. McAuliffe Esq., Emmett

41. Menell, Peter S.
42. Mitchell, John T.
43. Modern Works Music Publishing
44. Music Choice
45. Music Library Association
46. Music Reports, Inc. (MRI)
47. National Academy of Recording Arts & Sciences (NARAS)
48. National Association of Broadcasters (NAB)
49. National Music Publishers' Association (NMPA) and Harry Fox Agency, Inc. (HFA)
50. National Public Radio, Inc. (NPR)
51. National Religious Broadcasters Music License Committee (NRBMLC)
52. National Religious Broadcasters Noncommercial Music License Committee (NRBNMLC)
53. National Restaurant Association
54. Nauman, Vickie
55. Newman Esq., Deborah
56. Netflix, Inc.
57. Novak, Adam
58. Pagnani, Aidan
59. Pala Rez Radio
60. Pattison, Pat
61. Public Knowledge and Consumer Federation of America (CFA)
62. Public Television Coalition (PTC)
63. Radio Music License Committee, Inc. (RMLC)
64. Recording Industry Association of America, Inc. (RIAA)
65. Robin Green, Lynne
66. Rys, Jason
67. Schlieman, Derek S.
68. Screen Actors Guild – American Federation of Television and Radio Artists (SAG-AFTRA) and American Federation of Musicians of the United States and Canada (AFM)
69. SESAC, Inc. (SESAC)
70. Shocked, Michelle
71. Simpson, Jerrod
72. Sirius XM Radio Inc.
73. Society of Composers & Lyricists (SCL)
74. Songwriters Guild of America, Inc. (SGA)
75. SoundExchange, Inc.
76. Spotify USA Inc.
77. SRN Broadcasting
78. St. James, Charles
79. Television Music License Committee, LLC (TMLC)
80. Traugh, David
81. United States Marine Band
82. Willey, Robert
83. Wixen Music Publishing, Inc.

84. Yates, James M.

Participants in Nashville Hearings

1. Barker, John (ClearBox Rights and IPAC)
2. Buresh, Heather (Music Row Administrators Group)
3. Chertkof, Susan (RIAA)
4. Coleman, Dan (Modern Music Works Publishing)
5. Driskill, Marc (Sea Gayle Music and AIMP, Nashville Chapter)
6. Earls, Kent (UMPG)
7. Gervais, Daniel (Vanderbilt University Law School)
8. Gottlieb, Tony (Get Songs Direct, LLC)
9. Herbison, Barton (NSAI)
10. Johnson, George (Geo Music Group and George Johnson Music Publishing)
11. Kass, Fritz (Intercollegiate Broadcasting System, Inc.)
12. Kimes, Royal Wade (Wonderment Records)
13. Knife, Lee (DiMA)
14. Marks, Steven (RIAA)
15. McIntosh, Bruce (Codigo Music and Fania Records)
16. Meitus, Robert (Meitus Gelbert Rose LLP)
17. Mosenkis, Sam (ASCAP)
18. Oxenford, David (Wilkinson Barker Knauer LLP)
19. Schaffer, Brittany (NMPA and Loeb & Loeb LLP)
20. Sellwood, Scott (Google and YouTube)
21. Soled, Janice (My Music Screen)
22. Stollman, Marc (Stollman Law, PA)
23. Turley-Trejo, Ty (Brigham Young University Copyright Licensing Office)
24. Waltz, Reid Alan (SESAC)

Participants in Los Angeles Hearings

1. Anthony, Paul (Rumblefish)
2. Arrow, Ed (UMPG)
3. Barker, John (ClearBox Rights and IPAC)
4. Bernstein, Keith (Crunch Digital)
5. Blake, Lawrence J. (Concord Music Group, Inc.)
6. Bull, Eric D. (Create Law)
7. Cate, John (American Music Partners)
8. Cohan, Timothy A. (PeerMusic)
9. Goldberg, Ilene (IMG Consulting)
10. Greaves, Deborah (Label Law, Inc.)
11. Greenstein, Gary R. (Wilson Sonsini Goodrich & Rosati)
12. Harbeson, Eric (Music Library Association)
13. Hauth, Russell (Salem Communications and NRBMLC)

14. Irwin, Ashley (SCL)
15. Kokakis, David (UMPG)
16. Kossowicz, Tegan (UMG)
17. LaPolt, Dina (Dina LaPolt P.C.)
18. Lemone, Shawn (ASCAP)
19. Lipsztein, Leonardo (Google and YouTube)
20. Lord, Dennis (SESAC)
21. Marks, Steven (RIAA)
22. Menell, Peter (UC Berkeley School of Law)
23. Miller, Jennifer (Audiosocket)
24. Muddiman, Hélène (Hollywood Elite Composers)
25. Nauman, Vickie (CrossBorderWorks)
26. Prendergast, Brad (SoundExchange, Inc.)
27. Rudolph, John (Music Analytics)
28. Rys, Jason (Wixen Music Publishing, Inc.)
29. Sanders, Charles J. (SGA)
30. Schyman, Garry (SCL)
31. Watkins, Les (MRI)

Participants in New York Hearings

1. Albert, Eric (Stingray Digital Group)
2. Badavas, Christos P. (HFA)
3. Barker, John (ClearBox Rights and IPAC)
4. Barron, Gregg (BMG Rights Management)
5. Bengloff, Richard (A2IM)
6. Bennett, Jeffrey (SAG-AFTRA)
7. Besek, June (Columbia Law School, Kernochan Center for Law, Media and the Arts)
8. Carapella, Cathy (Global Image Works)
9. Carnes, Rick (SGA)
10. Coleman, Alisa (ABKCO)
11. Conyers III, Joe (Downtown Music Publishing)
12. DeFilippis, Matthew (ASCAP)
13. Diab, Waleed (Google and YouTube)
14. Donnelley, Patrick (Sirius XM Radio Inc.)
15. Duffett-Smith, James (Spotify USA Inc.)
16. Dupler, Todd (NARAS)
17. Fakler, Paul (NAB and Music Choice)
18. Finkelstein, Andrea (SME.)
19. Gibbs, Melvin (Content Creators Coalition)
20. Greer, Cynthia (Sirius XM Radio Inc.)
21. Griffin, Jodie (Public Knowledge)
22. Hoyt, Willard (TMLC)
23. Huey, Dick (Toolshed Inc.)
24. Kass, Fritz (Intercollegiate Broadcasting System, Inc.)

25. Knife, Lee (DiMA)
26. Kohn, Bob (Kohn on Music Licensing)
27. Lee, Bill (SESAC)
28. Lummel, Lynn (ASCAP)
29. Mahoney, Jim (A2IM)
30. Malone, William (Intercollegiate Broadcasting System, Inc.)
31. Marin, Aldo (Cutting Records, Inc.)
32. Marks, Steven (RIAA)
33. Merrill, Tommy (The Press House and #IRespectMusic)
34. Morgan, Blake (ECR Music Group and #IRespectMusic)
35. Potts, Cheryl (Crystal Clear Music & CleerKut)
36. Rae, Casey (FMC)
37. Raff, Andrew (Shutterstock, Inc.)
38. Raffel, Colin (Prometheus Radio Project)
39. Reimer, Richard (ASCAP)
40. Resnick, Perry (RZO, LLC)
41. Rich, Bruce (RMLC)
42. Rinkerman, Gary (Drinker, Biddle & Reath LLP)
43. Rosen, Stuart (BMI)
44. Rosenthal, Jay (NMPA)
45. Rushing, Colin (SoundExchange, Inc.)
46. Steinberg, Michael G. (BMI)
47. Wood, Doug (National Council of Music Creator Organizations)

Parties Who Responded to Second Notice of Inquiry

1. ABKCO Music & Records, Inc. (ABKCO)
2. American Association of Independent Music (A2IM)
3. American Society of Composers, Authors and Publishers (ASCAP)
4. Bean, David
5. Broadcast Music, Inc. (BMI)
6. Buckley, William Jr.
7. Carapetyan, Gregory
8. Castle, Christian L.
9. Columbia Law School, Kernochan Center for Law, Media and the Arts
10. Computer & Communications Industry Association (CCIA)
11. Concord Music Group, Inc.
12. Content Creators Coalition
13. Deutsch, L. Peter
14. Digital Media Association (DiMA)
15. Future of Music Coalition (FMC)
16. Geo Music Group & George Johnson Music Publishing
17. Guyon, Cindy
18. Guyon, Rich
19. Interested Parties Advancing Copyright (IPAC)

20. LaPolt, Dina
21. Modern Works Music Publishing
22. Music Choice
23. Music Managers' Forum (MMF) and Featured Artists' Coalition (FAC)
24. Music Reports, Inc. (MRI)
25. Nashville Songwriters Association International (NSAI)
26. National Academy of Recording Arts & Sciences (NARAS)
27. National Association of Broadcasters (NAB)
28. National Music Publishers' Association (NMPA) and Harry Fox Agency, Inc. (HFA)
29. National Public Radio, Inc. (NPR)
30. Office of the County Attorney, Montgomery County, Maryland
31. Pangasa, Maneesh
32. Parker, Brad
33. Pilot Music Business Services, LLC
34. Pipeline Project 2014, Belmont University's Mike Curb College of Music Business and Entertainment
35. Production Music Association (PMA)
36. Public Knowledge
37. Radio Music License Committee, Inc. (RMLC)
38. Recording Industry Association of America, Inc. (RIAA)
39. Resnick, Perry (RZO, LLC)
40. Righeimer, Carolyn
41. Rinkerman, Gary (Drinker, Biddle & Reath LLP)
42. Samuels, Jon M.
43. Screen Actors Guild – American Federation of Television and Radio Artists (SAG-AFTRA) and American Federation of Musicians of the United States and Canada (AFM)
44. Sirius XM Radio Inc.
45. Songwriters Guild of America, Inc. (SGA)
46. SoundExchange, Inc.
47. Stone, Bob
48. Szajner, Robert
49. Television Music License Committee, LLC (TMLC)
50. U.S. Chamber of Commerce, Global Intellectual Property Center (GIPC)
51. Wager, Gregg

APPENDIX C. ABBREVIATIONS

A2IM	American Association of Independent Musicians
ABKCO	ABKCO Music & Records, Inc.
AFM	American Federation of Musicians of the United States and Canada
AHRA	Audio Home Recording Act
AIMP	Association of Independent Music Publishers
ASCAP	American Society of Composers, Authors and Publishers

BMI	Broadcast Music, Inc.
BYU	Brigham Young University Copyright Licensing Office
CARP	Copyright Arbitration Royalty Panel
CCIA	Computer & Communications Industry Association
CFA	Consumer Federation of America
CISAC	International Confederation of Societies of Authors and Composers
CRB	Copyright Royalty Board
CRT	Copyright Royalty Tribunal
CTIA	CTIA—The Wireless Association
DDEX	Digital Data Exchange, LLC
DiMA	Digital Media Association
DMCA	Digital Millenium Copyright Act
DOJ	United States Department of Justice
DPD	Digital phonorecord delivery
DPRSRA	Digital Performance Right in Sound Recordings Act
EMF	Educational Media Foundation
EMI	EMI Music Publishing Ltd.
FAC	Featured Artists' Coalition
FMC	Future of Music Coalition
FTC	United States Federal Trade Commission
GMR	Global Music Rights
GMRO	General music rights organization
GIPC	U.S. Chamber of Commerce, Global Intellectual Property Cent
GRD	Global Repertoire Database
HFA	Harry Fox Agency, Inc.
IFPI	International Federation of the Phonographic Industry
IMR	International Music Registry
ISNI	International Standard Name Identifier
IPAC	Interested Parties Advancing Copyright
IPI	Interested Parties Information
ISO	International Organization for Standardization
ISRC	International Standard Recording Code
ISWC	International Standard Musical Work Code
MMF	Music Managers' Forum
MRI	Music Reports, Inc.
MRO	Music rights organization
Music Biz	Music Business Association
NAB	National Association of Broadcasters
NARAS	National Academy of Recording Arts & Sciences
NCTA	National Cable & Telecommunications Association
NDMA	New digital media agreement
NMPA	National Music Publishers' Association
NOI	Notice of Intent
NPR	National Public Radio, Inc.
NRBMLC	National Religious Broadcasters Music License Committee

NRBNMLC	National Religious Broadcasters Noncommercial Music License Committee
NSAI	Nashville Songwriters Association International
NTIA	National Telecommunications and Information Administration
PPL	Phonographic Performance Ltd.
PRO	Performing rights organization
PTC	Public Television Coalition
RESPECT Act	Respecting Senior Performers as Essential Cultural Treasures Act
RMLC	Radio Music License Committee, Inc.
RIAA	Recording Industry Association of America, Inc.
SAG-AFTRA	Screen Actors Guild-American Federation of Television and Radio Artists
SCL	Society of Composers & Lyricists
SEA	Songwriters Equity Act
SGA	Songwriters Guild of America, Inc.
SIRA	Section 115 Reform Act of 2006
SME	Sony Music Entertainment, Inc.
Sony/ATV	Sony/ATV Music Publishing LLC
SOCAN	Society of Composers, Authors and Music Publishers of Canada
TMLC	Television Music License Committee, LLC
UMG	Universal Music Group
UMPG	Universal Music Publishing Group
UPC	Universal Product Code
USPTO	U.S. Patent and Trademark Office
WIPO	World Intellectual Property Organization
WMG	Warner Music Group

APPENDIX D. LICENSING AND RATESETTING CHARTS

Copyright and the Music Marketplace:
Proposed Ratesetting Framework

Musical works
publishers/songwriters

Sound recordings
record labels/artists

- Reproduction and distribution (mechanical) and public performance rights (MRO- and GMRO- administered)
- Mechanical and public performance rights subject to withdrawal, synch rights, etc.
- Reproduction and distribution rights, public performance rights for digital interactive, synch rights, etc.
- Public performance rights for noninteractive (internet, satellite, and terrestrial (AM/FM) radio, etc.)

Rates negotiated in the free market

Market-oriented standard (*e.g.*, willing buyer/willing seller)

Copyright Royalty Board (as needed)

End Notes

[1] Press Release, H. Comm. on the Judiciary, Chairman Goodlatte Announces Comprehensive Review of Copyright Laws (Apr. 24, 2013), http://judiciary.house.gov/index.cfm/2013/4/chairmangoodlatteannounces comprehensivereviewofcopyrightlaw.

[2] Of the seventeen hearings that have been held so far as part of the congressional review, two were specifically dedicated to music licensing. *Music Licensing Under Title 17 (Part I & II): Hearing Before the Subcomm. on Courts, Intell. Prop., and the Internet of the H. Comm. on the Judiciary*, 113th Cong. (2014) ("*Music Licensing Hearings*"). Music industry representatives also participated in a number of other hearings. *See, e.g., Moral Rights, Termination Rights, Resale Royalty, and Copyright Term: Hearing Before the Subcomm. on Courts, Intell. Prop. and the Internet of the H. Comm. on the Judiciary*, 113th Cong. (2014); *Section 512 of Title 17: Hearing Before the Subcomm. on Courts, Intell. Prop. and the Internet of the H. Comm. on the Judiciary*, 113th Cong. (2014); *The Scope of Fair Use: Hearing Before the Subcomm. on Courts, Intell. Prop. and the Internet of the H. Comm. on the Judiciary*, 113th Cong. (2014).

[3] Music Licensing Study: Notice and Request for Public Comment, 78 Fed. Reg. 14,739 (Mar. 17, 2014). This Notice of Inquiry, along with the Office's second Notice of Inquiry and Notice of Public Roundtables, are attached as Appendix A. A list of the parties who responded to the Office's Notices of Inquiry, along with a list of participants in the Office's public roundtables, is attached as Appendix B.

[4] The comments received in response to the First Notice are available on the Copyright Office website at http://copyright.gov/docs/musiclicensingstudy/comments/Docket2014_3/index.html. References to these comments in this document are by party name (abbreviated where appropriate) followed by "First Notice Comments" (*e.g.*, "DiMA First Notice Comments").

[5] *See* Music Licensing Study, 79 Fed. Reg. 25,626 (May 5, 2014). Transcripts of the proceedings at each of the three roundtables are available on the Copyright Office website at http://copyright. gov/docs/musiclicensingstudy/transcripts/.

[6] Music Licensing Study: Second Request for Comments, 79 Fed. Reg. 42,833 (July 23, 2014).

[7] The comments received in response to the Second Notice are available on the Copyright Office website at http://copyright.gov/docs/musiclicensingstudy/comments/Docket2014_3/ extension_comments/. References to these comments in this document are by party name (abbreviated where appropriate) followed by "Second Notice Comments" (*e.g.*, "RIAA Second Notice Comments").

[8] As noted above, the Office has included charts in Appendix D of this report that provide a bird's-eye view of the licensing and ratesetting systems for music. The charts are intended as high-level references and do not capture every nuance or quirk of the system. A list of abbreviations used in the report is included as Appendix C.

[9] Act of May 31, 1790, ch. 15, 1 Stat. 124.

[10] *See Clayton v. Stone*, 5 F. Cas. 999, 1000 (C.C.S.D.N.Y. 1829) (No. 2872); I. Trotter Hardy, *Copyright and New Use Technologies*, 23 NOVA L. REV. 659, 664 (1999).

[11] Act of Feb. 3, 1831, ch. 16, 4 Stat. 436.

[12] *See* Maria A. Pallante, ASCAP at 100, 61 J. COPYRIGHT SOC'Y 545, 545-46 (2014).

[13] Act of Mar. 3, 1897, ch. 392, 29 Stat. 694; *see also* Zvi S. Rosen, *The Twilight of the Opera Pirates: A Prehistory of the Exclusive Right of Public Performance for Musical Compositions*, 24 CARDOZO ARTS & ENT. L.J. 1157, 1158-59 (2007).

[14] This report uses both the term "compulsory" and the term "statutory" when describing the section 112, 114, and 115 licenses.

[15] Digital Performance Right in Sound Recordings Act of 1995 ("DPRSRA"), Pub. L. No. 104-39, § 4, 109 Stat. 336, 344-48; *see also* 17 U.S.C. § 115(c)(3)(A).

[16] *See* U.S. COPYRIGHT OFFICE, FEDERAL COPYRIGHT PROTECTION FOR PRE-1972 SOUND RECORDINGS 7, 11 (2011) ("PRE-1972 SOUND RECORDINGS REPORT"); Michael Erlinger, Jr., *An Analog Solution in a Digital World: Providing Federal Copyright Protection for Pre-1972 Sound Recordings*, 16 UCLA ENT. L. REV. 45, 57-58 (2009).

[17] Pub. L. No. 92-140, 85 Stat. 391 (1971) ("Sound Recording Act of 1971"); *see generally* PRE-1972 SOUND RECORDINGS REPORT at 7-12.

[18] *See* PRE-1972 SOUND RECORDINGS REPORT at 12-14.

[19] DPRSRA §§ 2, 3. The digital performance right is also subject to a number of exceptions, including for transmissions to or within a business for use in the ordinary course of its business, for nonsubscription broadcast transmissions, and for certain geographically limited retransmissions of nonsubscription broadcast transmissions. 17 U.S.C. § 114(d)(1)(A), (B), (C)(ii), (C)(iv).

[20] The Copyright Act sometimes draws a distinction between "dramatic" musical works—that is, musical works that are part of a dramatic show such as an opera, ballet, or musical—and "nondramatic" musical works. For example, the compulsory license under section 115 for the making and distributing of phonorecords applies only to nondramatic works. *See* 17 U.S.C. § 115. In practice, however, the distinction drawn in section 115 does not appear especially consequential except when a licensee is seeking to use the work in the context of

the dramatic production; for instance, a show tune that is recorded for release as an individual song is understood to be licensable under section 115.

[21] For ease of reference, this report will collectively refer to these creators of musical works as "songwriters."

[22] DONALD S. PASSMAN, ALL YOU NEED TO KNOW ABOUT THE MUSIC BUSINESS 220 (8th ed. 2013) ("PASSMAN").

[23] See generally AL KOHN & BOB KOHN, KOHN ON MUSIC LICENSING 329-44 (4th ed. 2010) ("KOHN").

[24] See Ed Christman, *First-Quarter Music Publishing Rankings: SONGS Surges Again*, BILLBOARD (May 12, 2014), http://www.billboard.com/biz/articles/news/publishing/6084783/first-quartermusic-publishing-rankings-songs-surges-again.

[25] NMPA & HFA First Notice Comments at 1.

[26] Nate Rau, *New Nashville Group to Push for Copyright Reform*, THE TENNESSEAN (May 25, 2014), http://www.tennessean.com/story/money/industries/music/2014/05/25/nashville-copyrightgroup-emerges/9513731.

[27] See Ben Sisario, *Pandora Suit May Upend Century-Old Royalty Plan*, N.Y. TIMES (Feb. 13, 2014), http://www.nytimes.com/2014/02/14/business/media/pandora-suit-may-upend-century-oldroyalty-plan.html.

[28] *About Us*, SESAC, http://www.sesac.com/about/about.aspx (last visited Jan. 26, 2014).

[29] See Chris Versace, *The Future of Streaming Music Rests With Congress*, FOX BUSINESS (June 23, 2014), http://www.foxbusiness.com/technology/2014/06/23/future-streaming-music-rests-withcongress (SESAC "controls approximately 5% of the market"); In re Pandora Media, Inc. ("Pandora Ratesetting"), 6 F. Supp. 3d 317, 351 & n.55 (S.D.N.Y. 2014) (noting that during license negotiations SESAC had used a 10% figure to describe its market share, but that the actual figure "is impossible to know with certainty").

[30] See GMR, http://www.globalmusicrights.com (last visited Jan. 30, 2015); see also Ed Christman, Gail Mitchell, and Andrew Hampp, *Pharrell to Leave ASCAP for Irving and Grimmet's Global Music Rights*, BILLBOARD (July 25, 2014), www.billboard.com/articles/business/6188942/pharrell-toleave-ascap-for-irving- and-grimmets-global-music-rights; Ben Sisario, *New Venture Seeks Higher Royalties for Songwriters*, N.Y. TIMES (Oct. 29, 2014), http://www.nytimes.com/2014/10/30/ business/media/new- venture-seeks- higher-royalties-for-songwriters.html.

[31] ASCAP must admit anyone who has published a single musical work or is actively engaged in the music publishing business; BMI similarly accepts anyone who has written at least one musical work that is likely to be "performed soon." See United States v. ASCAP, No. 41-1395, 2001 WL 1589999, 2001-02 Trade Cas. (CCH) ¶ 73,474, § XI (S.D.N.Y. June 11, 2001) ("ASCAP Consent Decree"); United States v. BMI, No. 64-civ-3787, 1966 U.S. Dist. LEXIS 10449, 1966 Trade Cas. (CCH) ¶ 71,941, § V (S.D.N.Y. 1966), as amended by, 1994 U.S. Dist. LEXIS 21476, 1996-1 Trade Cas. (CCH) ¶ 71,378 (S.D.N.Y. 1994). The most readable version of the current BMI consent decree is the version provided on the Department of Justice's ("DOJ's") website, and is the version cited throughout this report. See United States v. BMI, No. 64-civ-3787 (S.D.N.Y. Nov. 18, 1994) (final judgment) ("BMI Consent Decree"), available at http://www.justice.gov/ atr/cases/ f307400/307413.pdf.

[32] *Radio Music License Comm., Inc. v. SESAC*, 29 F. Supp. 3d 487, 498 (E.D. Pa. 2014); Pandora Ratesetting, 6 F. Supp. 3d at 351; GMR, http://www.globalmusicrights.com (last visited Jan. 30, 2015).

[33] KOHN at 771-72, 808-10.

[34] HARRY FOX AGENCY, http://www.harryfox.com (last visited Jan. 9, 2015).

[35] KOHN at 803-806. For example, HFA licenses allow licensees to account for royalties on a quarterly basis, as opposed to the monthly reporting required under section 115. *Become an HFA Licensee*, HARRY FOX AGENCY, http://www.harryfox.com/license_music/become_hfa_ licensee.html (last visited Jan. 25, 2015).

[36] See MRI First Notice Comments at 1-3.

[37] See 17 U.S.C. § 114(g) (dividing statutory royalty proceeds among these groups).

[38] See *Sound Recordings at a Glance*, SAG-AFTRA, http://www.sagaftra.org/files/sag/ documents/soundrecordings_ataglance_2014.pdf (last visited Jan. 25, 2014).

[39] See Dan Daley, *Points of Survival: Producers Adapt to a New Economic Landscape in the Music Industry*, GRAMMY.COM (Sept. 1, 2010), http://www.grammy.com/news/points-of-survival; NARAS First Notice Comments at 5-6.

[40] Unlike royalties paid under section 114, royalties under the 112 license are not distributed directly to featured and nonfeatured artists, but instead are paid to the sound recording owner. See 17 U.S.C. § 114(g)(2); see also 17 U.S.C. § 112(e).

[41] NARAS First Notice Comments at 1.

[42] *About Us*, FUTURE OF MUSIC COALITION, https://www.futureofmusic.org/about (last visited Jan. 25, 2015).

[43] SAG-AFTRA & AFM First Notice Comments at 1-2.

[44] KOHN at 1454.

[45] PASSMAN at 63. Labels may also secure mechanical rights to musical works embodied in sound recordings.

[46] A2IM, the U.S. trade association that represents the interests of independent record labels, objects to the term "major label." According to A2IM, independent labels, collectively, represent 34.6% of the U.S. music market, making them "the largest music label industry segment." A2IM First Notice Comments at 1, 3.

[47] The three major labels all own and operate smaller labels. For example Atlantic Records and Rhino Entertainment Company are both owned by WMG.

[48] A2IM First Notice Comments at 1, 3.

[49] Sebastian Torrelio, *Jody Gerson Appointed Chairman and CEO of Universal Music Publishing Group*, VARIETY (Aug. 1, 2014), http://variety.com/2014/biz/news/jody-gerson-appointed-chairman-andceo-of-universal-music-publishing-group-1201273829; *Profile: Sony Corp*, REUTERS, http://www.reuters.com/finance/stocks/companyProfile?symbol=SNE.N; *About Us*, WARNER/CHAPPELL MUSIC, http://www.warnerchappell.com/about (last visited Jan. 25, 2015).

[50] IFPI, http://www.ifpi.org (last visited Jan. 15, 2015).

[51] Glenn Peoples, *SoundExchange Distributes Record $153 Million in Q3, Celebrates 10-Year Anniversary*, BILLBOARD (Oct. 4, 2014), http://www.billboard.com/biz/articles/news/5748060/ soundexchange- distributes-record-153-million-in-q3-celebrates-10-year.

[52] NAB First Notice Comments at 1.

[53] RMLC First Notice Comments at 1.

[54] TMLC First Notice Comments at 1.

[55] NRBMLC First Notice Comments at 2-3; NRBNMLC First Notice Comments at 1-2. The National Cable & Telecommunications Association ("NCTA"), which represents cable operators, has its own music license committee to negotiate PRO licenses for public performances of music in cable operators' local programming. *See* NCTA, Comments Submitted in Response to the DOJ's Antitrust Consent Decree Review at 1 (Aug. 6, 2014), *available at* http://www.justice.gov/atr/ cases/ascapbmi/comments/307982.pdf.

[56] DiMA First Notice Comments at 1.

[57] CTIA First Notice Comments at 2-4.

[58] CCIA Second Notice Comments at 1.

[59] *About*, MUSIC BUSINESS ASSOCIATION, http://musicbiz.org/about (last visited Jan. 25, 2015).

[60] CFA & Public Knowledge First Notice Comments at 1; *About Us*, PUBLIC KNOWLEDGE, https://www.publicknowledge.org/about-us (last visited Jan. 25, 2015).

[61] 17 U.S.C. § 106(1), (3).

[62] 17 U.S.C. § 106(2).

[63] 17 U.S.C. § 106(5).

[64] 17 U.S.C. § 106(4).

[65] *See Buffalo Broad. Co., Inc., v. ASCAP*, 744 F.2d 917, 920 (2d Cir. 1984) ("The 'synch' right is a form of the reproduction right also created by statute as one of the exclusive rights enjoyed by the copyright owner." (citing 17 U.S.C. § 106(1))); *Agee v. Paramount Commc'ns, Inc.*, 59 F.3d 317, 321 (2d Cir. 1995) (observing that a defendant "might have infringed [plaintiff's] exclusive right to prepare derivative works" by synchronizing music to an audiovisual work, but the court "need not resolve that question" as copying (and a defense to this right) were already proven).

[66] *See* KOHN at 674. By 1919, a single department store chain—Woolworth's—was selling over 200 million copies of sheet music. *Id.* at 6.

[67] Sheet music was generally sold for 10 cents per copy. *Id.* at 6.

[68] *Id.* at 6-7.

[69] *White-Smith Music Publ'g Co. v. Apollo Co.*, 209 U.S. 1, 8-9, 17-18 (1908).

[70] H.R. REP.NO. 60-2222, at 6-8 (1909); *see also Miller v. Goody*, 139 F. Supp. 176, 182 (S.D.N.Y. 1956).

[71] H.R. REP.NO. 59-7083, pt. 2, at 5 (1907); RUSSELL SANJEK UPDATED BY DAVID SANJEK, PENNIES FROMHEAVEN 22-23 (1996).

[72] H.R. REP.NO. 60-2222, at 7-8; Copyright Act of 1909, Pub. L. No. 60-349, §1(e), 35 Stat. 1075, 1075-76. Adjusted for inflation, the 2 cent rate would be more than 50 cents today. *Music Licensing Hearings* (statement of David M. Israelite, President and Chief Executive Officer, NMPA).

[73] Copyright Act of 1909 § 1(e).

[74] H.R. REP.NO. 94-1476, at 111 (1976), *reprinted in* 1976 U.S.C.C.A.N. 5659, 5726. Notably, the Register of Copyrights had proposed elimination of the compulsory license in the process leading up to the adoption of the 1976 Copyright Act, but music publishers and composers ultimately chose to oppose such a change, opting instead for the three-quarter cent rate increase. *See* U.S. COPYRIGHT OFFICE, 88TH CONG., REP. OF THE REGISTER OF COPYRIGHTS ON THE GENERAL REVISION OF THE U.S. COPYRIGHT LAW 33, 36 (Comm. Print 1961) ("GENERAL REVISION OF COPYRIGHT REPORT"); S. REP.NO. 94-473, at 91-92 (1975); *see also Music Licensing Reform: Hearing Before the Subcomm. on Intell. Prop. of the S. Comm. on the Judiciary*, 109th Cong. (2005) ("*Music Licensing Reform Hearing*") (statement of Marybeth Peters, Register of Copyrights), *available at* http://copyright.gov/docs/regstat071205.html (stating that publishers and songwriters were concerned that elimination of the statutory license would cause "unnecessary disruptions in the music industry").

[75] Copyright Act of 1976, Pub. L. No. 94-553, §§ 801-802, 90 Stat. 2541, 2594-96.

[76] Copyright Royalty Tribunal Reform Act of 1993, Pub. No. 103-198, § 802, 107 Stat. 2304, 2305 (1993).

[77] 17 U.S.C. §§ 801-805; Copyright Royalty and Distribution Reform Act of 2004, Pub. L. No. 108 419, 118 Stat. 2341. The statute calls the ratesetting body the "Copyright Royalty Judges." *See* 17 U.S.C. § 801. But it is more commonly referred to as the "Copyright Royalty Board," including in the regulations, and this report uses that convention. *See* 37 C.F.R. § 301.1 ("The Copyright Royalty Board is the institutional entity in the Library of Congress that will house the Copyright Royalty Judges . . . .").

[78] *See* S. REP. NO. 104-128, at 10 (1995), *reprinted in* 1995 U.S.C.C.A.N. 356, 357 ("The purpose of [this Act] is to ensure that performing artists, record companies and others whose livelihood depends upon effective copyright protection for sound recordings, will be protected as new technologies affect the ways in which their creative works are used. . . . In addition, the bill clarifies the application of the existing reproduction and distribution rights of musical work and sound recording copyright owners in the context of certain digital transmissions."); *see also* 17 U.S.C. § 115(c)(3)(A).

[79] 17 U.S.C. § 115(c)(3)(A).

[80] Compulsory License for Making and Distributing Phonorecords, Including Digital Phonorecord Deliveries, 73 Fed. Reg. 40,802, 40,804-05 (July 18, 2008).

[81] Compulsory License for Making and Distributing Phonorecords, Including Digital Phonorecord Deliveries, 73 Fed. Reg. 66,173, 66,174 (Nov. 7, 2008) ("The interim regulation clarifies that (1) whenever there is a transmission that results in a DPD, all reproductions made for the purpose of making the DPD are also included as part of the DPD, and (2) limited downloads qualify as DPDs.").

[82] Mechanical and Digital Phonorecord Delivery Rate Determination Proceeding, 74 Fed. Reg. 4510, 4514-15 (Jan. 26, 2009); 37 C.F.R. §§ 385.1-385.5, 385.10-385.17.

[83] 17 U.S.C. § 115(b)(1).

[84] 17 U.S.C. § 115(c)(5).

[85] 17 U.S.C. § 115(b)(1).

[86] *See* 17 U.S.C. § 115(c)(1); 37 C.F.R. § 201.18(f)(3).

[87] KOHN at 792-93; *see* 17 U.S.C. § 115(a)(1).

[88] 17 U.S.C. § 115(a)(2).

[89] KOHN at 742; 17 U.S.C. § 804(b)(4).

[90] 17 U.S.C. § 801(b)(1).

[91] Adjustment of Determination of Compulsory License Rates for Mechanical and Digital Phonorecords, 78 Fed. Reg. 67,938, 67,939 (Nov. 12, 2013).

[92] For songs over five minutes, the rate is higher—1.75 cents per minute or fraction thereof. 37 C.F.R. § 385.3(a).

[93] 37 C.F.R. § 385.3(b).

[94] 37 C.F.R. §§ 385.12-385.14, 385.23.

[95] Mechanical and Digital Phonorecord Delivery Rate Adjustment Proceeding, 71 Fed. Reg. 64,303, 64,308-09 (Nov. 1, 2006) (discussing "voluntary license agreements granting the labels the right to create ringtones at specified mutually-negotiated royalty rates").

[96] *Id.* at 64,303.

[97] Mechanical and Digital Phonorecord Delivery Rate Determination Proceeding, 74 Fed. Reg. at 4517-18; *id.* at 4522 (explaining that those licenses constitute "valuable rate evidence from the marketplace for" ringtones but not for "other products at issue in this proceeding (i.e., CDs and permanent downloads)").

[98] 17 U.S.C. § 115(c)(3)(E)(i).

[99] W. Jonathan Cardi, *Über-Middleman: Reshaping the Broken Landscape of Music Copyright*, 92 IOWA L. REV. 835, 841-42 (2007).

[100] KOHN at 771.

[101] *Id.* at 771-72.

[102] SIRA, H.R. 5553, 109th Cong. (2006). SIRA was later incorporated into the Copyright Modernization Act of 2006, H.R. 6052, 109th Cong. (2006).

[103] *See generally* Copyright Modernization Act of 2006, H.R. 6052; Skyla Mitchell, *Reforming Section 115: Escape from the Byzantine World of Mechanical Licensing*, 24 CARDOZO ARTS & ENT. L.J. 1239, 1271 (2007).

[104] Mitchell, *Reforming Section 115: Escape from the Byzantine World of Mechanical Licensing* at 1277. Groups such as Public Knowledge and the Electronic Frontier Foundation opposed SIRA because of its provisions regarding temporary copies and recognition that interactive streaming involves the making of DPDs. *Id.* at 1277-81.

[105] *See Reforming Section 115 of the Copyright Act for the Digital Age: Hearing Before the Subcomm. on Courts, the Internet, and Intell. Prop. of the H. Comm. on the Judiciary*, 110th Cong. 4 (2007) ("*Reforming Section 115 Hearing*") (statement of Rep. Howard Coble).

[106] *See generally Copyright Office Views on Music Licensing Reform: Hearing Before the Subcomm. on Courts, the Internet, and Intell. Prop. of the H. Comm. on the Judiciary*, 109th Cong. 21-36 (2005) ("*Copyright Office Views on Music Licensing Reform Hearing*") (statement of Marybeth Peters, Register of Copyrights).

[107] *Id.* at 56-57 (letter from Jonathan Potter, Executive Director, DiMA); *id.* at 59-60 (letter from Steven M. Marks, RIAA); *id.* at 99 (comments of ASCAP); *id.* at 62-64 (comments of NMPA).

[108] See Steve Wilf, *The Making of the Post-War Paradigm in American Intellectual Property Law*, 31 COLUM. J.L. & ARTS 139, 176 (2008); Noel L. Hillman, *Intractable Consent: A Legislative Solution to the Problem of Aging Consent Decrees in United States v. ASCAP and United States v. BMI*, 8 FORDHAM INTELL. PROP.MEDIA& ENT. L.J. 733, 737 (1998).

[109] *BMI v. CBS*, 441 U.S. 1, 4-5 (1979); *see also Alden-Rochelle, Inc. v. ASCAP*, 80 F. Supp. 888, 891 (S.D.N.Y. 1948).

[110] *BMI v. CBS*, 441 U.S. at 4-5; *see also Alden-Rochelle*, 80 F. Supp. at 891.

[111] *Meredith Corp.*, 1 F. Supp. 3d at 190; *BMI v. CBS*, 441 U.S. at 5.

[112] See KOHN at 1263, 1275-80. The Copyright Act exempts many small commercial establishments from the need to obtain a public performance license. *See* 17 U.S.C. § 110(5).

[113] David Oxenford, *What is the RMLC, And Why Should a Radio Station Pay Their Bill?*, BROAD. L. BLOG (Aug. 24, 2012), http://www.broadcastlawblog.com/2012/08/articles/what-is-the-rmlc-andwhy-should-a- radio-station-pay-their-bill.

[114] *Meredith Corp.*, 1 F. Supp. 3d at 189-90.

[115] See generally Lauren M. Bilasz, *Note: Copyrights, Campaigns, and the Collective Administration of Performance Rights: A Call to End Blanket Licensing of Political Events*, 32 CARDOZO L.REV. 305, 323 & nn.111-112 (2010) (descriptions of each license).

[116] *See, e.g.*, KOHN at 1266 (discussing per-program licenses).

[117] This prohibition was a result of antitrust litigation brought by movie theater owners in the 1940s. *Alden-Rochelle*, 80 F. Supp. 888; see *also* Christian Seyfert, *Copyright and Anti-Trust Law: Public Performance Rights Licensing of Musical Works into Audiovisual Media* 6, 20 (Sept. 1, 2005) (unpublished LL.M. thesis, Golden Gate University School of Law), *available at* http:// digitalcommons.law.ggu.edu/theses/13 at 19.

[118] *See id.* at 19.

[119] *Id.*; *see also* Netflix First Notice Comments at 1-2; *ASCAP Reports Increased Revenues in 2011*, ASCAP (Mar. 8, 2012), http://www.ascap.com/press/2012/0308_ascap-reports.aspx (reflecting blanket licenses with Netflix and Hulu). Licensing of performance rights from SESAC and GMR occurs without direct antitrust oversight, and those smaller PROs may refuse to license their repertoires to potential licensees.

[120] 15 U.S.C. § 1.

[121] *Arizona v. Maricopa Cnty. Med. Soc'y*, 457 U.S. 332, 342-43 (1982).

[122] *Associated Press v. United States*, 326 U.S. 1, 27 (1945).

[123] *Arizona*, 457 U.S. at 343-44.

[124] *Id.* at 344-45.

[125] *N. Pac Ry. Co. v. United States*, 356 U.S. 1, 5 (1958).

[126] *Eastman Kodak Co. v. Image Technical Servs., Inc.*, 504 U.S. 451, 4662 (1992).

[127] *Tying the Sale of Two Products*, FTC, http://www.ftc.gov/tips-advice/competition-guidance/ guide-antitrust-laws/single-firm-conduct/tying-sale-two-products (last visited Jan. 26, 2015).

[128] *Id.*

[129] *See generally United States v. BMI*, 275 F.3d 168, 171-72 (2d Cir. 2001) (describing the history); *see also Antitrust Consent Decree Review*, U.S. DOJ, http://www.justice.gov/atr/cases/ascap-bmi-decreereview.html (last visited Jan. 26, 2015).

[130] Christian Seyfert, *Copyright and Anti-Trust Law: Public Performance Rights Licensing of Musical Works into Audiovisual Media* at 6, 20; *see also* Wilf at 177.

[131] Seyfert, *Copyright and Anti-Trust Law: Public Performance Rights Licensing of Musical Works into Audiovisual Media* at 20-21.

[132] *BMI v. CBS*, 441 U.S. at 10.

[133] Seyfert, *Copyright and Anti-Trust Law: Public Performance Rights Licensing of Musical Works into Audiovisual Media* at 20-21.

[134] *BMI v. CBS*, 441 U.S. at 11.

[135] *BMI v. CBS*, 441 U.S. at 12 n.20.

[136] Seyfert, *Copyright and Anti-Trust Law: Public Performance Rights Licensing of Musical Works into Audiovisual Media* at 22; *see also* BMI Consent Decree.

[137] ASCAP Consent Decree §§ IV.B-C, VI, VIII, XI; BMI Consent Decree §§ IV.A, V, VIII.

[138] ASCAP Consent Decree § V; BMI Consent Decree § IX.

[139] ASCAP Consent Decree §§ II.J-K, VII; BMI Consent Decree § VIII.B. Note that under the ASCAP consent decree, the per-segment license has a number of conditions that must be met before it can be used. ASCAP Consent Decree § VII.

[140] ASCAP Consent Decree § IV.A.

[141] *See* BMI, Comments on Department of Commerce Green Paper at 4-5 (Nov. 13, 2013), *available at* http://www.ntia.doc.gov/files/ntia/bmi_comments.pdf.

[142] ASCAP Consent Decree § IX; BMI Consent Decree § XIV.

[143] *Antitrust Consent Decree Review*, U.S. DOJ, http://www.justice.gov/atr/cases/ascap-bmi-decreereview.html (last visited Jan. 26, 2015).

[144] ASCAP, Comments Submitted in Response to the DOJ's Antitrust Consent Decree Review at 18, 22, 31 (Aug. 6, 2014), *available at* http://www.justice.gov/atr/cases/ascapbmi/comments/307803.pdf ("ASCAP Antitrust Consent Decree Review Comments"); BMI, Comments Submitted in Response to the DOJ's Antitrust Consent Decree Review at 2 (Aug. 6, 2014), *available at* http://www.justice.gov/atr/cases/ascapbmi/comments/307859.pdf ("BMI Antitrust Consent Decree Review Comments").

[145] *Antitrust Consent Decree Review*, U.S. DOJ, http://www.justice.gov/atr/cases/ascap-bmi-decreereview.html (last visited Jan. 26, 2015).

[146] Ed Christman, *Dept. of Justice Sends Doc Requests, Investigating UMPG, Sony/ATV, BMI and ASCAP Over Possible "Coordination,"* BILLBOARD (July 13, 2014), http://www.billboard.com/biz/ articles/news/publishing/6157513/dept-of-justice-sends-doc-requests-investigating-umpgsonyatv. Members of the DOJ Antitrust Division attended and observed the Office's roundtables for this study in Nashville and New York.

[147] *BMI v. CBS*, 441 U.S. at 6.

[148] *Id.* at 24.

[149] *CBS v. ASCAP*, 620 F.2d 930, 938-39 (2d Cir. 1980).

[150] *Buffalo Broad. v. ASCAP*, 744 F.2d at 926-32; *see also id.* at 934 (Winter, J., concurring) ("[S]o long as composers or [publishers] have no horizontal agreement among themselves to refrain from source or direct licensing and there is no other artificial barrier, such as a statute, to their use, a non-exclusive blanket license cannot restrain competition.").

[151] *Nat'l Cable Television Ass'n, Inc. v. BMI*, 772 F. Supp. 614, 628 (D.D.C. 1991).

[152] *BMI v. DMX*, 683 F.3d at 35, 43.

[153] *Id.* at 38.

[154] *Id.*

[155] *Id.* at 47-49.

[156] *In re Pandora Media, Inc.*, Nos. 12-cv-8035, 41-cv-1395, 2013 WL 5211927, at *2 (S.D.N.Y. Sept. 17, 2013); *BMI v. Pandora Media, Inc.*, Nos. 13-cv-4037, 64-cv-3787, 2013 WL 6697788, at *2-3 (S.D.N.Y. Dec. 19, 2013).

[157] Not long afterward, EMI's music catalog was bought by Sony/ATV. *In re Pandora*, 2013 WL 5211927, at *3.

[158] *In re Pandora*, 2013 WL 5211927, at *5-7; *BMI, v. Pandora*, 2013 WL 6697788, at *3-4.

[159] *Pandora Ratesetting*, 6 F. Supp. 3d at 321-22.

[160] *Id.* at 354.

[161] *Id.* at 357-61.

[162] *Meredith Corp.*, 1 F. Supp. 3d at 192-93; *RMLC v. SESAC*, 29 F. Supp. 3d at 492-94.

[163] Memorandum of Law in Support of Plaintiffs' Unopposed Motion for Preliminary Approval of Settlement at 1-2, 5, *Meredith Corp.*, 1 F. Supp. 3d 180 (No. 09-cv-9177). TMLC, which was not a party to the litigation, was also a signatory to the settlement. *Id.* at 1 n.2.

[164] ASCAP Consent Decree § VI; BMI Consent Decree § IV.A.

[165] ASCAP Consent Decree § IX.F; BMI Consent Decree § XIV.A.

[166] ASCAP Consent Decree § IX.E; BMI Consent Decree § XIV.A.

[167] ASCAP Consent Decree § IX.A; BMI Consent Decree § XIV.A.

[168] Paul Fakler, *Music Copyright Royalty Rate-Setting Litigation: Practice Before the Copyright Royalty Board and How It Differs from ASCAP and BMI Rate Court Litigation*, 33 THE LICENSING J. 1, 5 (2013), *available* at http://www.arentfox.com/sites/default/files/FaklerLicensingJournalArticle.pdf.

[169] ASCAP Consent Decree § IX.B-D; BMI Consent Decree § XIV.A.

[170] *Pandora Ratesetting*, 6 F. Supp. 3d at 353 (citation omitted).

[171] *BMI v. DMX*, 683 F.3d at 45 (internal quotation marks, citations, and alterations omitted).

[172] The interim fee proceedings are to be completed within 90 days in ASCAP's case and 120 days in BMI's case. *See* ASCAP Consent Decree § IX(F); BMI Consent Decree § XIV.B.

[173] *See* ASCAP Consent Decree § IX(F); BMI Consent Decree § XIV.B.

[174] *See* ASCAP Consent Decree § IX(F); BMI Consent Decree § XIV.B.

[175] 17 U.S.C. § 114(i).

[176] DPRSRA § 3.

[177] BMI First Notice Comments at 11.

[178] 17 U.S.C. § 118(c).

[179] 17 U.S.C. § 118(c)(1), (f) (limiting performance license to "noncommercial educational broadcast station[s]" as defined in 47 U.S.C. § 397); 47 U.S.C. § 397 (defining "noncommercial educational broadcast station" as a "television or radio broadcast station"); *see also* NRBMLC First Notice Comments at 14 (describing section 118 license as being "confined to over-the-air transmissions").

[180] *See id.* at 14-15 (explaining that for "digital transmission of musical works . . . noncommercial broadcasters are required to negotiate with ASCAP, BMI, and SESAC").

[181] 17 U.S.C. § 114(b)

[182] NPR First Notice Comments at 4-5. Section 114(b) extends to "educational television and radio programs." 17 U.S.C. § 114(b). (Note that section 114(b) defines "educational television and radio programs" by referencing 47 U.S.C. § 397, but Congress deleted that definition from section 397 in 1978 without changing section 114(b). See 47 U.S.C. § 397 note. At the time of § 114(b)'s enactment in 1976, the term was defined in section 397 as "programs which are primarily designed for educational or cultural purposes.").

[183] NRBMLC First Notice Comments at 2-3; NPR First Notice Comments at 3-4.

[184] 17 U.S.C. § 106(1), (3).

[185] 17 U.S.C. § 106(2).

[186] 17 U.S.C. § 106(6).

[187] 17 U.S.C. § 114(d)(1).

[188] See DiMA First Notice Comments at 8.

[189] See generally DPRSRA.

[190] Digital Millennium Copyright Act ("DMCA"), Pub. L. No. 105-304, § 405(a), 112 Stat. 2860, 2890-2899 (1998).

[191] Id. §§ 402, 405(b).

[192] See 17 U.S.C. § 114(d)(1).

[193] See S. REP. NO. 104-128, at 14-15 ("It is the Committee's intent to provide copyright holders of sound recordings with the ability to control the distribution of their product by digital transmissions, without hampering the arrival of new technologies, and without imposing new and unreasonable burdens on radio and television broadcasters, which often promote, and appear to pose no threat to, the distribution of sound recordings.").

[194] Id.

[195] See U.S. GOV'T ACCOUNTABILITY OFFICE, GAO-10-862, TELECOMMUNICATIONS: THE PROPOSED PERFORMANCE RIGHTS ACT WOULD RESULT IN ADDITIONAL COSTS FOR BROADCAST RADIO STATIONS AND ADDITIONAL REVENUE FOR RECORD COMPANIES, MUSICIANS, AND PERFORMERS 13-21 (2010), available at http://www.gao.gov/assets/310/308569.pdf ("GAO REPORT").

[196] Zach O'Malley, Truth in Numbers: Six Music Industry Takeaways From Year-End Data, FORBES (Jan. 22, 2015), available at http://www.forbes.com/sites/zackomalleygreenburg/2015/01/22/truth in-numbers-six-music-industry-takeaways-from-year-end-data/ (noting live music comprises 26% and satellite radio subscription 10%).

[197] Only a handful of countries countries—including Iran and North Korea—lack such a right, in addition to the United States. See, e.g, A2IM First Notice Comments at 8; SoundExchange First Notice Comments at 17.

[198] GAO REPORT at 30 (estimates based on language of the Performance Rights Act, S. 379, 111th Cong. (2009)). The NAB disputes these figures. NAB First Notice comments at 29-30 & n.15.

[199] See Ed Christman, Here's Why Warner Music's Deal with Clear Channel Could be Groundbreaking for the Future of the U.S. Music Biz (Analysis), BILLBOARD (Sept. 12, 2013), http:// www.billboard.com/biz/articles/news/5694973/heres-why-warner-musics-deal-with-clearchannel-could-be-groundbreaking.

[200] Id.

[201] Id.; see also Ben Sisario, Clear Channel-Warner Music Deal Rewrites the Rules on Royalties, N.Y. TIMES (Sept. 12, 2013), http://www.nytimes.com/2013/09/13/business/media/clear-channelwarner-music-deal- rewrites-the-rules-on-royalties.html.

[202] See, e.g., Performance Rights Act, H.R. 848, S. 379, 111th Cong. (2009); Performance Rights Act, H.R. 4789, S. 2500, 110th Cong. (2010); Free Market Royalty Act, H.R. 3219, 113th Cong. (2013).

[203] See, e.g., Internet Streaming of Radio Broadcasts: Balancing the Interests of Sound Recording Copyright Owners with Those of Broadcasters: Hearing Before the Subcomm. on Courts, the Internet, and Intell. Prop. of the H. Comm. on the Judiciary, 108th Cong. (2004) ("Internet Streaming of Radio Hearing"); Music Licensing Hearings

[204] See, e.g., The Performance Rights Act and Parity Among Music Delivery Platforms: Hearing Before the S. Comm. on the Judiciary, 111th Cong. 117-18 (2009) ("Performance Rights Act Hearing") (statement of Marybeth Peters, Register of Copyrights); Ensuring Artists Fair Compensation: Updating the Performance Right and Platform Parity for the 21st Century: Hearing Before the Subcomm. on Courts, the Internet, & Intellectual Prop. of the H. Comm. on the Judiciary, 111th Cong. 13-30 (2007) ("Ensuring Artists Fair Compensation Hearing") (statement of Marybeth Peters, Register of Copyrights); Internet Streaming of Radio Hearing at 8-22 (statement of David O. Carson, General Counsel, U.S. Copyright Office); U.S. COPYRIGHT OFFICE, PERFORMANCE RIGHTS IN SOUND RECORDINGS (Comm. Print 1978), available at http://copyright.gov/reports/performance-rights-sound-recordings.pdf ("PERFORMANCE RIGHTS REPORT").

[205] Free noninteractive internet radio services not exempt under 17 U.S.C. § 114(d)(1) qualify as "eligible nonsubscription services" and paid noninteractive internet radio services qualify as "new subscription services" in the parlance of section 112 and 114. See 17 U.S.C. § 114(j)(6), (8).

[206] A preexisting satellite digital audio radio service is a subscription satellite audio radio service provided pursuant to a satellite digital audio radio service license issued by the FCC on or before July 31, 1998. 17 U.S.C. § 114(j)(10). Currently, there is only one satellite service, Sirius XM. See Determination of Rates and Terms for

Preexisting Subscription Services and Satellite Digital Audio Radio Services, 78 Fed. Reg. 23,054, 23,055 (Apr. 17, 2013) ("PSS/Satellite II").

[207] A preexisting subscription service is a noninteractive audio-only service that was in existence on or before July 31, 1998. U.S.C. § 114(j)(11). Music Choice—which transmits music via cable and satellite television and the internet—is an example of a pre-existing subscription service. PSS/Satellite II, 78 Fed. Reg. at 23,055 n.5.

[208] 17 U.S.C. § 114(d)(2).

[209] DMCA § 402; 17 U.S.C. § 112(e)(1); H.R. REP. NO. 105-796, at 89 (1998) (Conf. Rep.)

[210] See 17 U.S.C. § 114(d)(2)(B)-(C).

[211] 17 U.S.C. § 114(d)(2)(B)(i), (d)(2)(C)(i), (j)(13).

[212] 37 C.F.R. § 380.11 ("*Collective* is the collection and distribution organization that is designated by the Copyright Royalty Judges. For the 2011-2015 license period, the Collective is SoundExchange, Inc."); *see also Intercollegiate Broad. Sys., Inc. v. Copyright Royalty Bd.*, 571 F.3d 69, 91 (D.C. Cir. 2009).

[213] *Technology Briefing: Internet; Online Royalty Pool Created*, N.Y. TIMES, Nov. 29, 2000, at C4; *Global Business Briefs*, WALL ST. J., Oct. 2, 2003, at B5.

[214] 17 U.S.C. § 114(g)(2); *see About Digital Royalties*, SOUNDEXCHANGE, http://www.soundexchange.com/artist-copyright-owner/digital-royalties/ (last visited Jan. 26, 2015). Royalties collected pursuant to section 112 are not distributed according to this split, and instead are paid entirely to the record labels. Review of Copyright Royalty Judges Determination, 73 Fed. Reg. 9143, 9146 (Feb. 19, 2008).

[215] 17 U.S.C. § 112(e); *see also* Review of Copyright Royalty Judges Determination, 73 Fed. Reg. 9143, 9146 (Feb. 19, 2008) (explaining that "[r]oyalties collected under section 114 are paid to the performers and the copyright owners of the sound recordings . . . whereas, the royalties collected pursuant to the section 112 license are not paid to performers").

[216] 17 U.S.C. § 114(g)(3).

[217] *See* 17 U.S.C. 114(g)(2); *About Digital Royalties*, SOUNDEXCHANGE, http://www.soundexchange.com/artist-copyright-owner/digital-royalties/ (last visited Jan. 26, 2015); *see also Music Licensing Hearings* at 14 (statement of Neil Portnow, President/CEO of The Recording Academy).

[218] NARAS First Notice Comments at 5.

[219] *Our Work*, SOUNDEXCHANGE, http://www.soundexchange.com/about/our-work/ (last visited Jan. 26, 2015).

[220] *SoundExchange Outreach Efforts*, SOUNDEXCHANGE, http://www.soundexchange.com/wpcontent/uploads/2014/11/Outreach-Fact-Sheet_11.5.14.pdf (last visited Jan. 26, 2015).

[221] *See* Glenn Peoples, *SoundExchange Financials Show Fewer Unclaimed Royalties, Persistent Data Problems*, BILLBOARD (Dec. 24, 2014), http://www.billboard.com/articles/business/6415147/ soundexchange- fewer-unclaimed-royalties-data-problems.

[222] *Id.*

[223] *See, e.g.*, 37 C.F.R. §§ 380.8, 380.17, 380.27.

[224] *See* 17 U.S.C. §§ 112(e), 114(d)(2)-(3), (f). The distinction between interactive and noninteractive services has been the matter of some debate, and is addressed *infra*.

[225] 17 U.S.C. § 114(j)(7).

[226] *Launch Media*, 578 F.3d 148, 161, 163-64 (2d Cir. 2009).

[227] 17 U.S.C. § 114(j)(10), (11); *see* PSS/Satellite II, 78 Fed. Reg. at 23,055.

[228] *See* 17 U.S.C. §§ 114(f)(1), 115(c)(3), 801(b)(1).

[229] *See* 17 U.S.C. §§ 114(f)(1), 801(b)(1); PSS/Satellite II, 78 Fed. Reg. at 23,055 & n.5.

[230] 17 U.S.C. § 114(f)(2)(B). The provision further requires the CRB to consider "whether use of the service may substitute for or may promote the sales of phonorecords or otherwise may interfere with or may enhance the sound recording copyright owner's other streams of revenue from its sound recordings," and "the relative roles of the copyright owner and the transmitting entity in the copyrighted work and the service made available to the public with respect to relative creative contribution, technological contribution, capital investment, cost, and risk." *Id.*

[231] 17 U.S.C. § 801(b)(1).

[232] 17 U.S.C. § 804(b).

[233] 17 U.S.C. § 802(a).

[234] 17 U.S.C. § 802(a).

[235] H.R. REP. NO. 108-408, at 26 (2004) *reprinted in* 2004 U.S.C.C.A.N. 2,332, 2,341; 17 U.S.C. § 802(f)(1).

[236] 17 U.S.C. § 803(d)(1).

[237] H.R. REP. NO. 108-408, at 24.

[238] 17 U.S.C. §§ 112(e)(2), 114(e)(1), 115(c)(3)(B) (These antitrust exemptions are limited to negotiations addressing rights within the scope of the statutory licenses in sections 112, 114, and 115).

[239] *See* 17 U.S.C. § 803(b)(1)-(3).

[240] 17 U.S.C. § 801(b)(7).

[241] *See* SoundExchange First Notice Comments at 8-9; *see also* Digital Performance Right in Sound Recordings and Ephemeral Recordings, 76 Fed. Reg. 13,026, 13,027 (Mar. 9, 2011) (adopting partial settlement entered into in June 2009 as basis for final rates and terms for commercial webcasters).

[242] *See* 17 U.S.C. § 803(b)(6).

[243] 17 U.S.C. § 803(b)(6).

[244] 17 U.S.C. § 803(b)(6)(C).

[245] *See, e.g.,* 37 C.F.R. § 380.3(a)(1); *see also* Determination of Reasonable Rates and Terms for the Digital Performance of Sound Recordings and Ephemeral Recordings, 67 Fed. Reg. 45,240, 45,272 (July 8, 2002). Section 112 rates have been a relatively insignificant part of the CRB's ratesetting proceedings, and have been established as a modest percentage of the 114 rate. *See e.g.,* 37 C.F.R. § 385.3(c) (establishing ephemeral recording rate to be 5% of the total royalties paid under the section 112 and 114 licenses).

[246] *See* Webcaster Settlement Act of 2008, Pub. L. No. 110-435, 122 Stat. 4974. Congress later extended the timeframe for negotiations. *See* Webcaster Settlement Act of 2009, Pub. L. No. 11136, 123 Stat. 1926; *see also* Terry Hart, *A Brief History of Webcaster Royalties*, COPYHYPE (Nov. 29, 2012), http://www.copyhype.com/2012/11/a-brief-history-of-webcaster-royalties.

[247] Small Webcaster Settlement Act of 2002, Pub. L. No. 107-321, 116 Stat. 2780.

[248] Notification of Agreements Under the Webcaster Settlement Act of 2009, 74 Fed. Reg. 34,796, 34,797 (July 17, 2009); Brian T. Yeh, *Statutory Royalty Rates for Digital Performance of Sound Recordings: Decision of the Copyright Royalty Board*, *in* MUSIC LICENSING RIGHTS AND ROYALTY ISSUES 35, 49 (Thomas O. Tremblay ed., 2011).

[249] Notification of Agreements Under the Webcaster Settlement Act of 2009, 74 Fed. Reg. at 34,799 800; KOHN at 1498.

[250] 17 U.S.C. § 114(d)(3)(C).

[251] A2IM Second Notice Comments at 5-6; Resnick Second Notice Comments at 2-3; *see also* Hannah Karp, *Artists Press for Their Share*,WALL ST. J. (July 21, 2014), http://online.wsj.com/news/articles/SB20001424052702303833804580023700490515416 (reporting that Warner Music Group received an advance from Google of over $400 million).

[252] *See* Helienne Lindvall, *Behind the Music: The Real Reason Why the Major Labels Love Spotify*, GUARDIAN (Aug. 17, 2009), http://www.theguardian.com/music/musicblog/2009/aug/17/majorlabels-spotify.

[253] Sound Recording Act of 1971, 85 Stat. at 392.

[254] The Copyright Act expressly permits states to continue state law protection for pre-1972 sound recordings until February 15, 2067, at which time all state protection will be preempted by federal law and pre-1972 sound recordings will enter the public domain. 17 U.S.C. § 301(c). There is, however, a significant class of pre-1972 sound recordings that do enjoy federal copyright protection—sound recordings of foreign origin for which copyright protection was "restored" as part of the Uruguay Round Agreements Act in 1994. *See* PRE-1972 SOUND RECORDINGS REPORT at 17-20.

[255] *See* PRE-1972 SOUND RECORDINGS REPORT at 64-70.

[256] *See generally id.*

[257] *Id.* at 48.

[258] *Id.* at 86-87.

[259] In a 1977 report on public performance rights in sound recordings, the Copyright Office recognized that Congress had left the decision whether or not to recognize a performance right for pre-1972 sound recordings to the states. PERFORMANCE RIGHTS REPORT at 18.

[260] Tr. at 161:18-21 (June 5, 2014) (Scott Sellwood, Google/YouTube); Tr. at 152:04-09 (June 5, 2014) (Steven Marks, RIAA).

[261] Music Choice First Notice Comments at 15; Tr. at 190:08-18 (June 24, 2014) (Paul Fakler, Music Choice).

[262] PRE-1972 SOUND RECORDINGS REPORT at 45 n.196; *but see* PSS/Satellite II, 78 Fed. Reg. at 23,073 (indicating pre-1972 sound recordings are not covered by section 112 and 114 licenses).

[263] *See* Hannah Karp, *Turtles and Sirius XM: Not Happy Together*, WALL ST. J. (Aug. 3, 2013), http://blogs.wsj.com/speakeasy/2013/08/03/turtles-and-sirius-xm-not-happy-together. Previously, Sirius XM did include pre-1972 recordings in its royalty accounting logs to SoundExchange, which were non-itemized, but stopped in 2011 after SoundExchange asked Sirius XM to start reporting exactly what it was paying for. *See* Hannah Karp, *Sirius Is Sued Over Music Royalties for Pre-1972 Recordings*, WALL ST. J. (Aug. 26, 2013), http://www.wsj.com/articles/ SB10001424127887324591204579037260890310376.

[264] *See Flo & Eddie Inc. v. Sirius XM* ("*Flo & Eddie v. Sirius XM CA*"), No. 13-cv-5693, 2014 U.S. Dist. LEXIS 139053, at *22-23 (C.D. Cal. Sept. 22, 2014).

[265] *Capitol Records, LLC v. Sirius XM*, No. BC520981 (Cal. Super. Ct. Oct. 14, 2014) (order regarding jury instructions), *available at* http://www.project-72.org/documents/Sirius-XM-Order-GrantingJury-Mot.pdf.

[266] *See Flo & Eddie Inc. v. Sirius XM* ("*Flo & Eddie v. Sirius XM NY*"), No. 13-cv-5784, 2014 U.S. Dist. LEXIS 166492, at *40-44, *50-52 (S.D.N.Y. Nov. 14, 2014) (denying Sirius XM's motion for summary judgment, and asking Sirius XM to show cause why judgment should not be entered on behalf of plaintiffs), *reconsideration denied*, 2014 U.S. Dist. LEXIS 174907 (Dec. 12, 2014).

[267] *See Flo & Eddie, Inc. v. Pandora Media, Inc.*, No. 14-cv-07648 (C.D. Cal. Oct. 2, 2014); Complaint, *Capitol Records, LLC v. Pandora Media, Inc.*, No. 651195/2014 (N.Y. Sup. Ct. Apr. 17, 2014); *see also* Eriq Gardner,

Sony, Google, Apple Hit With Lawsuits Over Pre-1972 Music, HOLLYWOOD REPORTER (Jan. 23, 2015), http://www.hollywoodreporter.com/thr-esq/sony-google-apple-hit-lawsuits766187.

[268] *See* 17 U.S.C. § 512(a)-(d).

[269] 17 U.S.C. § 512(c).

[270] 17 U.S.C. § 301(c).

[271] PRE-1972 SOUND RECORDINGS REPORT AT 130-32.

[272] *Capitol Records, Inc. v. MP3tunes, LLC*, 821 F. Supp. 2d 627, 640–42 (S.D.N.Y. 2011). *But see Capitol Records, Inc. v. MP3tunes, LLC*, No. 07-cv-9931, 2012 WL 242827, at *1–*2 (S.D.N.Y. Jan. 9, 2012) (citing Copyright Office report and acknowledging that its earlier decision "may involve a 'substantial ground for difference of opinion'").

[273] *Capitol Records, LLC v. Vimeo, LLC*, 972 F. Supp. 2d 500, 536-37 (S.D.N.Y. 2013); *see also Capitol Records, LLC v. Vimeo, LLC*, 972 F. Supp. 2d 537, 552 (S.D.N.Y. 2013) (denying motion for reconsideration); *Capitol Records, Inc. v. Naxos of America, Inc.*, 830 N.E.2d 250 (N.Y. 2005).

[274] *See Steele v. Turner Broad. Sys., Inc.* 646 F. Supp. 2d 185, 193 (D. Mass. 2009).

[275] *See, e.g., Buffalo Broad. v. ASCAP*, 744 F.2d at 920; *Agee*, 59 F.3d at 321.

[276] *See* NMPA & HFA First Notice Comments at 16; Tr. at 60:20-22 (June 4, 2014) (Brittany Schaffer, NMPA/Loeb & Loeb LLP) ("synchronization licenses are generally divided in terms of income 50/50 between sound recording and the musical composition."). While parity may be commonplace for individually negotiated deals, the same does not seem to hold true for broader licenses with consumer-facing video services such as YouTube. Under an HFA-administered YouTube license, publishers are paid 15% of YouTube's net revenue from videos uploaded by non-record label users that incorporate HFA-controlled publishing rights and embody a commercially released or distributed sound recording (i.e., a lip sync video), and 50% of revenue from videos that incorporate HFA-controlled publishing rights but a user-created recording (i.e., a cover recording). NMPA/HFA/YOUTUBE LICENSING OFFER, *Licensing Offer Overview*, http://www.youtubelicenseoffer.com/docs/notice.pdf (last visited Jan. 29, 2015). By comparison, YouTube's standard contract for independent record labels reportedly allocates 45% of YouTube subscription music video revenue to labels, as compared to 10% to publishers. Ed Christman, *Inside YouTube's Controversial Contract with Indies*, BILLBOARD June 20, 2014, http:// www. billboard.com/biz/articles/news/digital-and-mobile/6128540/analysis-youtube-indie-labels-contract-subscription-service?mobile_redirection=false.

[277] NMPA & HFA Second Notice Comments at 10-13.

[278] *Id.* at 14-15.

[279] *See* PASSMAN at 177-78 (reflecting the decline of the traditional market for music video on platforms such as the MTV television network); KOHN at 1119 (noting that promotional music videos have synchronization fees that are "quite nominal, set at an amount intended merely to cover the administrative costs of preparing the paperwork for the license grant. This is because the copyright owner stands to substantially benefit from . . . performance royalties resulting from the exhibition of the music video.").

[280] RIAA Second Notice Comments at 14.

[281] Vevo is a joint venture between UMG, SME, the Abu-Dhabi Media Company, and YouTube. *See* Alex Pham, *YouTube Confirms Vevo Deal*, BILLBOARD (July 2, 2013), http://www.billboard.com /biz/articles/news/digital-and-mobile/1568816/youtube-confirms-vevo-deal; *see also* PASSMAN at 259 (for record company-produced videos streamed, "the record labels get about 70% of ad revenues and/or subscription monies," and generally pay publishers "in the range of 10% of the ad revenues (a little under 15% of the 70% that the company gets)").

[282] *See* RIAA First Notice Comments at 14 n.28; NMPA Second Notice Comments at 33.

[283] *See id.* at 33; Susan Butler, *UMG/NMPA Broker Model License Agreement*, MUSIC CONFIDENTIAL, June 21, 2012; Ed Christman, *NMPA Inks Deal With Universal Music Group Over VEVO, YouTube Videos*, BILLBOARD (June 19, 2012), http://www.billboard.com/biz/articles/news/publishing/ 1093134/nmpa- inks-deal-with-universal-music-group-over-vevo-youtube. The licensing arrangement excludes rights for synch uses in motion pictures, television, advertising, video games and other products that are typically individually negotiated by publishers. *Id.*

[284] *See YouTube Licensing Offer Overview*, YOUTUBE LICENSING OFFER, http://www.youtubelicenseoffer.com/notice (last visited Jan. 26, 2015).

[285] *See The Football Ass'n Premier League Ltd. v. YouTube, Inc.*, 633 F. Supp. 2d 159 (S.D.N.Y. 2009).

[286] *YouTube License Agreement*, YOUTUBE LICENSING OFFER, http://www.youtubelicenseoffer.com/docs/license.pdf (last visited Jan. 26, 2015); *see also* Susan Butler, *Anatomy of a Trade Group License*, MUSIC CONFIDENTIAL, Sept. 9, 2011.

[287] *See YouTube Licensing Offer Overview*, YOUTUBE LICENSING OFFER, http://www.youtubelicenseoffer.com/notice (last visited Jan. 26, 2015).

[288] Susan Butler, *U.S. Music Licensing: The Rights Holders (Part Two, Conclusion)*, MUSIC CONFIDENTIAL, June 5, 2014.

[289] Ed Christman, *RIAA & NMPA Eyeing Simplified Music Licensing System, Could Unlock 'Millions' in New Revenue*, BILLBOARD (June 13, 2013), http://www.billboard.com/biz/articles/news/recordlabels/1566550/riaa-nmpa-eyeing-simplified-music-licensing-system-could.

[290] *See* RIAA First Notice Comments at 8 ("To be competitive, today's streaming, cloud and subscription music services require licenses to the full catalog of songs (and shares thereof) owned by virtually every music publisher."); DiMA Second Notice Comments at 16 ("Digital service providers and record companies do, in fact, need to obtain licenses for millions of songs in order to meet consumer expectations and be commercially viable."). Notably, the recently launched streaming service "The Overflow" offers a limited catalog of "Christian music" and related genres. Glenn Peoples, *David Beside Goliath: New Christian Music Streaming Service The Overflow Points to a New Strategy*, BILLBOARD (Jan. 05, 2015) http://www.billboard.com/articles/ business/6429451/overflow-christian-subscription-streaming-music-service; THE OVERFLOW, http://theoverflow.com (last visited Jan. 20, 2015) (reporting on recently launched streaming service The Overflow, which offers a limited catalog of Christian music and related genres).

[291] DAVID TOUVE, MUSIC BUSINESS ASSOCIATION, THE INNOVATION PARADOX: HOW LICENSING AND COPYRIGHT IMPACTS DIGITAL MUSIC STARTUPS 6-7 (2012) ("TOUVE"); *see also* John Seabrook, *Revenue Streams: Is Spotify the Music Industry's Friend or Its Foe?*, NEW YORKER (Nov. 24, 2014), *available at* http://www.newyorker.com/magazine/2014/11/24/revenue-streams (reporting that Spotify's U.S. licensing efforts took two years).

[292] TOUVE at 5.

[293] *See* Jessop First Notice Comments at 4.

[294] *What is an ISWC*, ISWC INTERNATIONAL AGENCY, http://www.iswc.org/en/iswc.html (last visited Jan. 9, 2015).

[295] Tr. at 334:13-337:20 (June 23, 2014) (Andrea Finkelstein, SME; Jacqueline Charlesworth & Sarang Damle, U.S. Copyright Office); Tr. at 343:2-344:16, 346:17-21 (June 23, 2014) (Lynn Lummel, ASCAP).

[296] ASCAP Second Notice Comments at 11 ("It should be underscored that each work will have two identifiers—the ISWC as well as the PRO's own internal Work ID number.").

[297] *Obtaining Code*, USISRC, http://www.usisrc.org/about/obtaining_code.html (last visited Jan. 25, 2015). RIAA also authorizes "ISRC managers" to assign ISRCs to sound recordings produced by artists and labels that do not wish to manage their own ISRC assignments. *Id.*; *see also Registration Fees*, USISRC, http://www.usisrc.org/faqs/registration_fees.html (last visited Jan. 25, 2015).

[298] Pipeline Project 2014, Belmont University's Mike Curb College of Music Business and Entertainment ("Pipeline Project") Second Notice Comments at 7; *see also Types*, USISRC, https://www.usisrc.org/applications/types.html (last visited Jan. 25, 2015).

[299] SoundExchange Second Notice Comments at 4-5.

[300] Pipeline Project Second Notice Comments at 7.

[301] *The IPI System*, IPISYSTEM.ORG, http://www.ipisystem.org/SUISASITES/IPI/ipipublic.nsf/ pages/index1 (last visited Jan. 9, 2015).

[302] *See* Jennifer Gatenby & Andrew MacEwan, *ISNI: A New System For Name Identification*, INFORMATION STANDARDS QUARTERLY, Summer 2011, at 4-5, *available at* http://www.niso.org/ publications/isq/2011/v23no3/gatenby; Jennifer Gatenby & Joep Kil, *ISNI From Development to Operations*, ISNI, www.isni.org/filedepot_download/58/95.

[303] *See* Gatenby & MacEwan, *ISNI: A New System For Name Identification* at 4-5.

[304] ISNI, http://www.isni.org (last visited Jan. 9, 2015).

[305] Pipeline Project Second Notice Comments at 5. Bowker, an affiliate of ProQuest, assigns ISNIs and tracks the assignment and usage of them. *See Bowker Becomes First ISNI Registration Agency in the U.S.*, BOWKER (June 21, 2012), http://www.bowker.com/en-US/aboutus/press_room/2012/ pr_06212012a.shtml; Bowker, *Use of ISNI Is Growing Fast Among Authors, Says New Bowker Analysis*, YAHOO FINANCE (May 7, 2014), http://finance.yahoo.com/news/isni-growing-fastamong-authors-144800650.html.

[306] *How to Get UPC Barcodes for Your Products*, WALL ST. J., http://guides.wsj.com/smallbusiness/starting-a-business/how-to-get-upc-codes-for-your-products-2 (last visited Jan. 9, 2014); Kristin Thomson, *Metadata for Musicians*, FUTURE OF MUSIC COALITION (Nov. 4, 2014), https://futureofmusic. org/article/article/metadata-musicians.

[307] Michael Brown, *White Paper: Audio Fingerprinting*, MAXIMUM PC (Apr. 3, 2009), http:// www.maximumpc.com/article/features/white_paper_audio_fingerprinting.

[308] *See* Ciumac Sergiu, *Duplicate Songs Detector Via Audio Fingerprinting*, CODE PROJECT (June 20, 2013), http://www.codeproject.com/Articles/206507/Duplicates-detector-via-audio-fingerprinting.

[309] ROBERT BRAUNEIS, ABRAHAM L. KAMINSTEIN SCHOLAR IN RESIDENCE, U.S. COPYRIGHT OFFICE, TRANSFORMING RECORDATION AND REENGINEERING AT THE UNITED STATES COPYRIGHT OFFICE 127-129 (2015) ("BRAUNEIS"), *available at* http://www.copyright.gov/docs/recordation/.

[310] Technological Upgrades to Registration and Recordation Functions, 78 Fed. Reg. 17,722 (Mar. 22, 2013); BRAUNEIS at 120-121.

[311] As of March 2013, for example, ISRCs were associated with only 5,510 (0.03%) of registration records in the Copyright Office Catalog. *Id.* at 121.

[312] *Id.* at 110-111.

[313] *Id.* The Office has recently embarked upon public processes to consider possible upgrades to its systems that could improve the searchability and usability of its records. Such changes might include, for example, a more robust registration database and a shift to a more user-friendly and accessible electronic recordation system. See Strategic Plan for Recordation of Documents, 79 Fed. Reg. 2696 (Jan. 15, 2014); Technological Upgrades to Registration and Recordation Functions, 78 Fed. Reg. 17,722 (Mar. 22, 2013).

[314] SoundExchange Second Notice Comments at 5.

[315] SONGFILE, http://www.songfile.com (last visited Jan. 25, 2015).

[316] ASCAP's database is called ACE, and BMI's database is called the BMI Repertoire. *See Ace Title Search*, ASCAP, https://www.ascap.com/Home/ace-title-search/index.aspx (last visited Jan. 29, 2015); *BMI Repertoire*, BMI, http://repertoire.bmi.com/startpage.asp (last visited Jan. 29, 2015). SESAC also has a database called SESAC Repertory. *SESAC Repertory*, SESAC, http://www.sesac.com/Repertory/RepertorySearch.aspx?x=39&y=19 (last visited Jan. 29, 2015).

[317] MUSICMARK, http://www.musicmark.com (last visited Jan. 9, 2015).

[318] *See* SONGFILE, http://www.songfile.com (last visited Jan. 25, 2015); *Ace Title Search*, ASCAP, https://www.ascap.com/ Home/ace-title-search/index.aspx (last visited Jan. 29, 2015); *BMI Repertoire*, BMI, http://repertoire.bmi.com/startpage.asp (last visited Jan. 29, 2015); *SESAC Repertory*, SESAC, http://www.sesac.com/Repertory/RepertorySearch.aspx?x=39&y=19 (last visited Jan. 29, 2015).

[319] *Terms of Use Agreement*, ASCAP, http://www.ascap.com/about/legal-terms/terms-of-use.aspx (last visited Jan. 16, 2015); *Terms and Conditions of Use*, BMI, http://www.bmi.com/legal/entry/ terms_and_conditions_of_use (last visited Jan. 25, 2015); *SESAC Repertory Terms and Conditions*, SESAC, http://www.sesac.com/Repertory/Terms.aspx (last visited Jan. 25, 2015); *Songfile Terms of Use*, SONGFILE, http://www.songfile.com/termsofuse.html (last visited Jan. 25, 2015).

[320] Notably, in the wake of the *Pandora* decision—which criticized UMPG's and Sony/ATV's failure to provide catalog data to Pandora—these publishers have recently posted their U.S. catalogs online. *See* Press Release, UMPG, Universal Music Publishing Group To Offer Expanded Access To Song Catalog Data Through Company's Website (June 27, 2014), *available at* http://www.umusicpub.com/#contentRequest=newsdetail&contentLocation=sub& contentOptions=%26articleID%3D6437%26from%3Dpressreleases; *Sony/ATV Makes Entire Catalogue Available Online*, MUSIC BUSINESSWORLDWIDE (JULY 16, 2014), http://www.musicbusinessworldwide.com/sonyatv-makes-entire-catalogue-available-online/.

[321] *PRS 'disappointed' at Global Repertoire Database collapse*, MUSIC ALLY (June 11, 2014), http://musically.com/2014/07/11/prs-disappointed-at-global-repertoire-database-collapse; Paul Resnikoff, *Repertoire Database Declared a Global Failure. . .*, DIGITAL MUSIC NEWS (July 10, 2014), http://www.digitalmusicnews.com/permalink/2014/07/10/global-repertoire-database-declaredglobal-failure.

[322] RICHARD HOOPER & ROS LYNCH, COPYRIGHT WORKS: STREAMLINING COPYRIGHT LICENSING FOR THE DIGITAL AGE 3 (2012), *available at* http://www.copyrighthub.co.uk/Documents/dcereport-phase2.aspx.

[323] THE COPYRIGHT HUB, http://www.copyrighthub.co.uk (last visited Jan. 25, 2015).

[324] *Id.*

[325] *Id.*; Tom Cox, *Copyright Hub Pilot Introduced in the UK*, INTELLECTUAL PROPERTY BLAWG (Aug. 8, 2013), http://www.intellectualpropertyblawg.com/copyright-law/copyright-hub-pilotintroduced-in-the-uk; *Welcome to the Copyright Hub*, WORLD INTELLECTUAL PROPERTY REVIEW (Jan. 9, 2013), http://www.worldipreview.com/article/welcome-to-the-copyright-hub.

[326] *See* DDEX First Notice Comments at 1.

[327] *See, e.g.,* MUSIC BUSINESS ASSOCIATION, MUSIC METADATA STYLE GUIDE V2, at 35-38, *available at* http://musicbiz.org/wp-content/uploads/2014/08/MusicMetadataStyleGuide-MusicBiz-FINAL.pdf (last modified Aug. 14, 2014).

[328] Press Release, RightsFlow, PRS For Music And Rightsflow Partner On DDEX Standardized Reporting Initiative (Dec. 13, 2010), http://mi2n.com/print.php3?id=136849.

[329] *See* DDEX First Notice Comments at 1-2.

[330] *What Copyright Infrastructure is needed to facilitate the Licensing of Copyrighted Works in the Digital Age: the International Music Registry?*, WIPO, http://www.wipo.int/edocs/mdocs/mdocs/en/ wipo_ip_aut_ge_11/wipo_ip_aut_ge_11_t12.doc; *The International Music Registry*, WIPO, http://www.wipo.int/imr/en (last visited Jan. 27, 2015).

[331] *See, e.g.*, Copyright Alliance First Notice Comments at 6 ("We believe all authors and creators are entitled to fair compensation for their creative work."); DiMA First Notice Comments at 1 ("DiMA members share the belief that rights owners should be appropriately compensated for the use of copyrighted works."); NMPA & HFA First Notice Comments at 31 (noting that "[f]or music publishers and songwriters, music licensing is only effective if it provides a fair market royalty for the use of their songs"); SGA First Notice Comments at 3 (identifying "fair market value compensation for the use of musical works" as an "indispensable need").

[332] *See, e.g.*, Public Knowledge & CFA First Notice Comments at 5 ("Copyright law's music licensing provisions can help alleviate . . . bottlenecks and make music licensing more efficient and fair for all."); NMPA & HFA First Notice Comments ("Music publishers and songwriters seek an efficient digital music marketplace. . . .");

RIAA Second Notice Comments at 13 ("Commenters desire a more efficient licensing process, and focused on blanket licensing as one way to achieve such efficiency."); NARAS First Notice Comments at 2 ("The Recording Academy supports a structure that is fair, simple and efficient for both the licensor and licensee."); GIPC Second Notice Comments at 7 (urging the Office to "keep in mind issues of efficiency in the marketplace so as to facilitate new, licensed services").

[333] *See, e.g.,* Modern Works Music Publishing First Notice Comments at 10 ("Congress should encourage cooperation among licensors to create technologies that enable licensees to easily search rights databases."); Pilot Music Business Services Second Notice Comments at 3 ("[O]ne centralized database is needed"); Pipeline Project Second Notice Comments at 18 ("It seems to us that the statutory license was the twenty-century's solution to efficiency; however, as we progress further into the digital age, and as data becomes more useful, we no longer see a great need for a compulsory license."); Tr. 381:04-11 (June 23, 2014) (Waleed Diab, Google/YouTube) ("[T]he ability to match the information on the sound recording side and the composition side is absolutely necessary. . . . I think what you are hearing is, there is absolutely a need for a centralized, standardized, data base, somewhere that services can go and pull that information.").

[334] *See, e.g.,* NSAI Second Notice Comments at 2-3 (expressing concern about advances and bonuses that "are never paid to the songwriter or composer" and proposing requiring that "such payments be disclosed by record labels and music publishers"); SGA First Notice Comments at 3 (calling for "complete transparency throughout the licensing, use and payment process"); Kohn First Notice Comments at 11 (proposing that service providers "be required to provide transparent access to transaction data in real-time to an independent validation service"); RIAA Second Notice Comments at 19 ("The major record companies . . . support the idea that where there is direct licensing, publishers/writers should have a direct audit right with respect to third parties that use their works.").

[335] *Harper & Row Publishers, Inc. v. Nation Enters.*, 471 U.S. 539, 545-46 (1985).

[336] *See* RIAA Second Notice Comments at 8 ("[N]obody seems to question the basic premise that royalty rates *should* reflect fair market value.").

[337] *See, e.g.,* SGA First Notice Comments at 10 ("[T]he income of the music and recording industries (and especially of individual music creators and recording artists) have been diminished, according to reliable estimates, by as much as two-thirds."); A2IM First Notice Comments at 10 (noting that "the decline in sound recording revenues" has "had a dramatic effect on the income of both music labels . . . and their recording artists"); *see also* Nate Rau, *Nashville's musical middle class collapses*, THE TENNESSEAN (Jan. 13, 2015), http://www.tennessean.com/story/entertainment/music/2015/01/04/nashville-musical-middle-classcollapses-new-dylans/21236245 (observing that industry trends have led to "the collapse of Nashville's music middle class").

[338] Under so-called "360" record deals, artists may be required to share a portion of these additional revenues with their label. *See* Doug Bouton, Note, *The Music Industry in Flux: Are 360 Record Deals the Saving Grace or the Coup de Grace?*, 9 VA. SPORTS & ENT. L.J. 312, 318 (2010).

[339] *See, e.g.,* IPAC First Notice Comments at 13 (observing that "the decline in revenue from physical album sales, to downloads, and ultimately streaming, has drastically reduced the income opportunities for songwriters and composers"); RIAA Second Notice Comments at 38 ("Songwriters and recording artists have become more dependent on performance revenue, but that revenue is not sufficient on its own to sustain a livelihood.").

[340] *See* RIAA, *A Fruitful Anniversary for iTunes*, MUSIC NOTES BLOG (Apr. 25, 2013), http://www.riaa.com/blog.php?content_selector=riaa-news-blog&blog_selector=A-FruitfulAnniversary-&blog_type=&news_month_filter=4&news_year_filter=2013 (providing 2004 chart); RIAA First Notice Comments at 51 (providing 2013 chart). Charts reproduced with the permission of RIAA.

[341] RIAA First Notice Comments at 50. Chart reproduced with the permission of RIAA.

[342] NMPA Second Notice Comments at 8 (citing sources).

[343] Ed Christman, *NMPA's David Israelite to Congress: A More Efficient Mechanical Licensing System*, Billboard (June 13, 2012), http://www.billboard.com/biz/articles/news/publishing/1093490/ nmpasdavid-israelite- to-congress-a-more-efficient-mechanical.

[344] Press Release, NMPA, U.S. Music Publishing Industry Valued at $2.2 Billion (June 11, 2014), *available at* https://www.nmpa.org/media/showrelease.asp?id=233.

[345] NIELSEN, 2014 NIELSEN MUSIC U.S. REPORT, http://www.nielsen.com/content/dam/corporate/ us/en/public%20 factsheets/Soundscan/2014-year-end-music-report.pdf.

[346] *Id.*; *see also* BMI Second Notice Comments at 16 ("[T]he instant availability to the public of the widest possible choice of recorded music by means of streaming technology has come at the expense of an accelerating drop-off in the sale of recordings (hard copies and downloads).").

[347] NSAI Second Notice Comments at 6.

[348] *See* IFPI, DIGITALMUSIC REPORT 2014, at 5, http://www.ifpi.org/downloads/Digital-MusicReport-2014.pdf ("It is now clear that music streaming and subscription is a mainstream model for our business."); ASCAP First Notice Comments at 5-6 (stating that "digital music streaming services account for an increasingly large portion of music revenues in the U.S."); SoundExchange First Notice Comments at 22 ("The music marketplace changed rapidly from one long dominated by the sale of physical products, to one in which digital

downloads are the primary means of acquiring ownership of copies. Now, it is changing again, and obtaining access to music through streaming services is ascendant.").

[349] See Michael DeGusta, *The REAL Death of the Music Industry*, BUSINESS INSIDER (Feb. 18, 2011), http://www.businessinsider.com/these-charts-explain-the-real-death-of-the-music-industry-2011 2.

[350] RIAA Second Notice Comments at 38.

[351] *How is Spotify contributing to the music business?*, SPOTIFY, http://www.spotifyartists.com/spotify-explained/#how-is-spotify-contributing-to-the-music-business (last visited Jan. 30, 2015) (citing global data).

[352] NAB First Notice Comments at 9-10.

[353] LaPolt Second Notice Comments at 3 ("[W]hile synchronization licenses are more plentiful than ever, these licenses are paying lower and lower rates per individual agreement for the average songwriter."); NMPA & HFA Second Notice Comments at 8 (noting that "increased competition has driven down synch fees"); NSAI Second Notice Comments at 6 ("With hundreds of television networks and online content providers compared to just a few years ago, more synch licenses are issued, but for a much lower amount per use.").

[354] See CFA & Public Knowledge First Notice Comments at 60-62 ("The leading edge of the shift was driven by unbundling of albums and the sale of singles. Consumers were no longer forced to buy songs they did not want in order to get the ones they desired."); Tr. at 274:01-12 (June 23, 2014) (Paul Fakler, NAB/Music Choice) ("Consumers no longer are forced to buy a bundled album containing recordings that they don't want to buy. So there are a lot of factors that have gone into declines of record sales.").

[355] IPAC Second Notice Comments at 8; *see also* NSAI Second Notice Comments at 6 ("One major reason is dramatically less income from album cuts not released as singles. A few years ago a non-single cut on an album with high sales volume produced greater income for many songwriters. Today album cuts, with a few rare exceptions, produce very little income.").

[356] IPAC Second Notice Comments at 8-9.

[357] DiMA First Notice Comments at 45 ("The substantial royalties paid by digital music services constitute new revenue streams that were unimagined just a few decades ago.").

[358] *Id.*

[359] RIAA First Notice Comments Ex. A at 1 ("In 2013, strong growth in streaming revenues contributed to a US music industry that was stable overall at $7 billion for the fourth consecutive year."); *see also* IFPI, DIGITALMUSIC REPORT 2014 at 5 ("The US music market continued to stabilize, growing slightly in trade revenue terms, helped by rising consumer demand for music streaming services.").

[360] Ben Sisario, *Collectors of Royalties for Music Publishers May See Better Results*, N.Y. TIMES (Sept. 23, 2013), http://www.nytimes.com/2013/09/23/business/media/collectors-of-royalties-for-musicpublishers-may-see-better-results.html; Press Release, *ASCAP Reports Strong Revenues in 2013*, ASCAP (Feb. 12, 2014), http://www.ascap.com/press/2014/0213-2013-financials.aspx.

[361] ABKCO First Notice Comments at 5; *see also, e.g.*, NMPA Second Notice Comments at 7 (noting that "performance royalties are increasing in importance while mechanical income has diminished. Almost all musical work owners are in agreement that this is the most challenging aspect of the new digital marketplace"); RIAA Second Notice Comments at 38; ASCAP Second Notice Comments at 23 (finding that "overall songwriter income has declined because mechanical right income has dropped by a large margin.").

[362] *How is Spotify contributing to the music business?*, SPOTIFY, http://www.spotifyartists.com/spotify-explained/#how-is-spotify-contributing-to-the-music-business (last visited Jan. 30, 2015). Spotify states, however, that its subscription service "aims to regenerate this lost value by converting music fans from these poorly monetized formats to our paid streaming format, which produces far more value per listener." *Id.*

[363] ASCAP First Notice Comments at 39.

[364] Seabrook, *Revenue Streams: Is Spotify the Music Industry's Friend or Its Foe?*; Stuart Dredge, *Thom Yorke Explains Why He Hates Spotify*, BUSINESS INSIDER (Oct. 7, 2013), http://www.businessinsider.com/thom-yorke-explains-why-he-hates-spotify-2013-10; Sasha Bogursky, *Taylor Swift, Garth Brooks and other artists lead the fight against Spotify*, FOX NEWS (Nov. 19, 2014), http://www.foxnews.com/entertainment/2014/11/19/taylor-swift-garth-brooks-artists-lead-fightagainst-spotify/.

[365] Jack Dickey, *Taylor Swift on 1989, Spotify, Her Next Tour and Female Role Models*, TIME (Nov. 13, 2014), http://time.com/3578249/taylor-swift-interview. In a similar move, GMR recently demanded that YouTube remove videos from its service containing approximately 20,000 songs that GMR represents, including the Eagles and PharrellWilliams. Eriq Gardner, *Pharrell Williams' Lawyer to YouTube: Remove Our Songs or Face $1 Billion Lawsuit*, HOLLYWOOD REPORTER (Dec. 22, 2014), http://www.hollywoodreporter.com/thr-esq/pharrell-williams-lawyer-youtube-remove759877.

[366] See, e.g., Maya Kosoff, *Pharell Made Only $2,700 In Songwriter Royalties From 43 Million Plays of 'Happy' On Pandora*, BUSINESS INSIDER (Dec. 23, 2014), http://www.businessinsider.com/pharrellmade-only-2700-in-songwriter-royalties-from-43-million-plays-of-happy-on-pandora-2014-12; David Lowery, *My Song Got Played On Pandora 1 Million Times and All I Got Was $16.89, Less Than What I Make From a Single T-Shirt Sale!*, THE TRICHORDIST (June 24, 2013), http://thetrichordist.com/2013/06/24; Doug Gross, *Songwriters: Spotify doesn't pay off . . . unless you're a Taylor Swift*, CNN (Nov. 13, 2014), http://www.cnn.com/

2014/11/12/tech/web/spotify-pay-musicians (noting that the songwriters of the Bon Jovi hit "Livin' on a Prayer" split $110 in royalties from Pandora for 6.5 million plays of that song).

[367] Aloe Blacc, *Streaming Services Need to Pay Songwriters Fairly*, WIRED (Nov. 5, 2014), http://www.wired.com/2014/11/aloe-blacc-pay-songwriters.

[368] DiMA First Notice Comments at 46.

[369] Andy Gensler, *Bette Midler Disparages Pandora, Spotify Over Artist Compensation*, BILLBOARD (Apr. 6, 2014), http://www.billboard.com/biz/articles/news/digital-and-mobile/6039697/bettemidler-disparages-pandora-spotify-over-artist; Alison Kosik, *The puzzling and 'antiquated' world of music royalties*, CNN MONEY (Nov. 17, 2014), http://money.cnn.com/2014/11/17/media/aloe-blaccmusic-royalties.

[370] DiMA First Notice Comments at 46; *see also* Glenn Peoples, *Pandora Revenue Up 40 Percent, Listening Growth Softens*, BILLBOARD (Oct. 23, 2014), http://www.billboard.com/biz/articles/news/ digital-and-mobile/6296383/pandora-revenue-up-40-percent-listening-growth-softens (noting Pandora pays 46.5% of its revenues in royalties to copyright owners).

[371] *See* DiMA First Notice Comments at 11 ("[M]uch of the current debate over rates stems from disagreement among the labels, publishers and PROs about how to allocate the *content owners' fixed share of the pie*, rather than from a notion that service providers are not paying enough, in the aggregate, for content.").

[372] *See* Tr. at 193:13-18 (June 4, 2014) (Scott Sellwood, Google/YouTube) ("[I]f there could be some agreement between publishers and labels as to total content cost, we don't—we're very agnostic, we don't care whether it's a performance or a reproduction, tell us how much it costs."); *accord* Tr. at 112:02-113:08 (June 17, 2014) (Vickie Nauman, CrossBorderWorks) ("[Third-party technology developers'] incentives are not to solve the problems between the publishers and the labels and the PROs . . . [T]hey want to know that they can come to a simple source and pay for the rights.").

[373] DiMA First Notice Comments at 47.

[374] *Id.*; *see also* NAB First Notice Comments at 10-12 ("To the extent recording artists have not been adequately sharing in the new revenue streams from on-demand streaming services . . . it is likely due to these same creative accounting schemes that the record companies have employed for decades to underpay artists.").

[375] SAG-AFTRA & AFM Second Notice Comments at 2.

[376] Rau, *Nashville's musical middle class collapses*.

[377] NSAI Second Notice Comments at 6.

[378] Rau, *Nashville's musical middle class collapses*.

[379] *Id.*

[380] CFA & Public Knowledge First Notice Comments at 70 ("In today's music market, the claim that piracy is still a problem is contradicted by a great deal of evidence on actual consumer behavior.").

[381] David Kravets, *Copyright Lawsuits Plummet in Aftermath of RIAA Campaign*, WIRED (May 18, 2010), http://www.wired.com/2010/05/riaa-bump/.

[382] Tr. at 98:02-04 (June 24, 2014) (Susan Chertkoff, RIAA); *see also* RIAA Second Notice Comments at 6 ("It remains a problem that the legitimate market for licensed musical works must operate in an environment in which there is also a huge amount of infringing use.").

[383] Tr. at 111:09-11 (June 24, 2014) (Lee Knife, DiMA).

[384] Tr. at 122:01-04 (June 24, 2014) (James Duffett-Smith, Spotify).

[385] 17 U.S.C. § 512(c); DMCA § 202(a).

[386] In a separate public process, the Department of Commerce's Internet Policy Task Force—led by the U.S. Patent and Trademark Office ("USPTO") and the National Telecommunications and Information Administration ("NTIA")—has, in keeping with its July 2013 Green Paper, established a "multi-stakeholder" dialogue on "improving the operation of the notice and takedown system for removing infringing content from the Internet under the DMCA." *See* Request for Comments on Department of Commerce Green Paper, Copyright Policy, Creativity, and Innovation in the Digital Economy, 78 Fed. Reg. 61,337, 61,338 (Oct. 3, 2013); *see also* DEPARTMENT OF COMMERCE INTERNET POLICY TASK FORCE, COPYRIGHT POLICY, CREATIVITY, AND INNOVATION IN THE DIGITAL ECONOMY 54 (2013) ("GREEN PAPER"), *available at* http://www.uspto.gov/news/publications/copyrightgreenpaper.pdf. The Office will be interested to see the results of that process.

[387] *See* Lincoff First Notice Comments at 9.

[388] Tr. at 136:10-139:05 (June 17, 2014) (Hélène Muddiman, Hollywood Elite Composers); *see also* Zoë Keating, *What should I do about Youtube?*, ZOEKEATING.TUMBLER.COM (Jan. 22, 2015) http://zoekeating.tumblr.com/post/108898194009/what-should-i-do-about-youtube (describing YouTube's negotiating tactics for licenses covering its new subscription service, which include excluding artists from YouTube's revenue-sharing program if the artist declines to license their works for the subscription service).

[389] Tr at 228:08-10 (June 16, 2014)(Jason Rys, Wixen Music Publishing); *see* Tr at 119:10-21 (June 24, 2014) (Dick Huey, Toolshed Inc.) (the DMCA is "a defense that's used by the largest tech companies in some cases to avoid direct licensing").

[390] Audiosocket First Notice Comments at 1; Buckley Second Notice Comments at 4; DotMusic First Notice Comments at 8.

[391] BMI First Notice Comments at 28-29 ("Another explanation [for reduced songwriter, composer and recording artist income] is the depressive effect of the [DMCA] safe harbors, which shield Internet service providers ... from liability for certain user activities."). To cite a recent example, Irving Azoff of GMR recently threatened litigation against YouTube for the unauthorized performances of his clients' music notwithstanding the safe harbors, explaining that "they are the ones that have been least cooperative and the company our clients feel are the worst offenders." Gardner, *Pharrell Williams' Lawyer to YouTube: Remove Our Songs or Face $1 Billion Lawsuit*. GMR's apparent position is that if YouTube is able to identify music for the purpose of monetizing it through its Content ID system, it should also be able to take it down without the service of individual takedown notices. *Id.*

[392] Joe Mullin, *Google Handled 345 Million Copyright Takedowns in 2014*, ARSTECHNICA (Jan. 6, 2015), http://arstechnica.com/tech-policy/2015/01/google-handled-345-million-copyrighttakedowns-in-2014; *Section 512 of Title 17: Hearing Before the Subcomm. On Courts, Intell. Prop., and the Internet of the H. Comm. on the Judiciary*, 113th Cong. 47 (2014) (Statement of Katherine Oyama, Sr. Policy Counsel, Google Inc.)

[393] 17 U.S.C. § 801(b)(1).

[394] ASCAP First Notice Comments at 25 (quoting *United States v. BMI (Music Choice II)*, 316 F.3d 189, 194 (2d Cir. 2003)); *ASCAP v. MobiTV, Inc.*, 681 F.3d 76, 82 (2d Cir. 2012) (stating that "the rate-setting court must take into account the fact that ASCAP, as a monopolist, exercises market-distorting power in negotiations for the use of its music").

[395] *See* 17 U.S.C. §§ 114(f)(1), 801(b)(1).

[396] *See* 17 U.S.C. §§ 112(e)(4), 114(f)(2)(B).

[397] *See, e.g.,* SoundExchange First Notice Comments at 6-8, 14-16; DiMA First Notice Comments at 40; RIAA First Notice Comments at 30-32; Public Knowledge & CFA First Notice Comments at 23-26; Sirius XM First Notice Comments at 3; NARAS First Notice Comments at 8-9.

[398] DiMA First Notice Comments at 40.

[399] Public Knowledge & CFA First Notice Comments at 24-25.

[400] Sirius XM First Notice Comments at 13.

[401] *Id.* at 14-15.

[402] DiMA First Notice Comments at 36 (emphasis in original).

[403] Spotify First Notice Comments at 7.

[404] *See, e.g.,* NMPA & HFA First Notice Comments at 8, 15-16; Wixen First Notice Comments at 2; BMI First Notice Comments at 3; IPAC First Notice Comments at 6; NARAS First Notice Comments at 1; Tr. at 292:17-20 (June 24, 2014) (Peter Brodsky, Sony/ATV).

[405] BMI First Notice Comments at 3.

[406] Tr. at 291:04-07 (June 24, 2014) (Peter Brodsky, Sony/ATV).

[407] SEA, H.R. 4079, 113th Cong. (2014); *see also Songwriter Equity Act Gains Support in Congress*, BMI, http://www.bmi.com/news/entry/songwriter_equity_act_gains_support_in_congress (last visited Jan. 30, 2015). The SEA would also eliminate the current prohibition in section 114(i) that prohibits the PRO rate courts from considering sound recording performance rates in establishing the performance royalties due for musical works.

[408] *BMI v. DMX*, 683 F.3d at 49.

[409] Indeed, as noted, Congress provided copyright owners and users with an antitrust exemption to allow those groups to engage in collective negotiation of rates under the statutory licenses. *See* 17 U.S.C. §§ 112(e)(2); 114(e)(1), 115(c)(3)(B).

[410] H.R. REP.NO. 108-408, at 25; *see generally* 17 U.S.C. § 802(a).

[411] Tr. at 237:08-21 (June 16, 2014) (Gary R. Greenstein, Wilson Sonsini Goodrich & Rosati).

[412] Kohn First Notice Comments at 12.

[413] Tr. at 194:05-18 (June 4, 2014) (Scott Sellwood, Google/YouTube) ("[T]he main concern for us that comes from fragmentation is an incremental creep in total content cost from which we can't really sustain the business."). RIAA, however, likened this concern to "saying if Dunkin' Donuts finds out that the price of coffee is going up that now they are going to tell their flour supplier that they are going to pay less." Tr. at 98:12-19 (June 24, 2014) (Susan Chertkoff, RIAA).

[414] Tr. at 258:01-14 (June 23, 2014) (James Duffett-Smith, Spotify).

[415] *See* NMPA & HFA First Notice Comments at 21-22; BMI First Notice Comments at 12; SESAC First Notice Comments at 3-5; NARAS First Notice Comments at 4; CTIA First Notice Comments at 11-12; Tr. at 268:11-269:14 (June 16, 2014) (Timothy A. Cohan, PeerMusic).

[416] *See* FMC First Notice Comments at 4 (suggesting that "it may be more useful to have arbitration and dispute resolution mechanisms take place under the same court, perhaps the Copyright Royalty Board"); Lincoff First Notice Comments at 4-11 (proposing a unified "digital transmission right" encompassing rights of musical works and sound recording owners with rates set by the CRB).

[417] The decisions came down shortly after the close of the record in this study, so it is possible that stakeholders' positions as to how our licensing system should handle pre-1972 recordings have evolved somewhat from their earlier expressed views.

[418] *See, e.g.*, DiMA First Notice Comments at 39; Music Choice First Notice Comments at 13-16.
[419] *See* PRE-1972 SOUND RECORDINGS REPORT at ix.
[420] *Id.*
[421] *See, e.g.*, Kernochan Center Second Notice Comments at *passim*; Brigham Young University Copyright Licensing Office ("BYU") First Notice Comments at 3; FMC First Notice Comments at 8-10; Kohn First Notice Comments at 14-15; Library of Congress First Notice Comments at 2-4; Public Knowledge Second Notice Comments at 3-5; Tr. at 164:22-165:02 (June 17, 2014) (Eric Harbeson, Music Library Association).
[422] NARAS First Notice Comments at 6.
[423] *See, e.g., id.* at 7-8; Tr. at 154:11-154:21 (June 5, 2014) (Robert Meitus, Meitus Gelbert Rose LLP). *But see* PRE-1972 SOUND RECORDINGS REPORT at 148-49 (recommending against federal termination rights to existing grants, but supporting such rights for grants made after effective date of federalization legislation). With respect to older recordings that fall within the scope of federal protection, one participant suggested providing authors of sound recordings with the opportunity to recapture their creations if the record labels stop exploiting the works commercially. Rinkerman Second Notice Comments at 2. According to the proposal, these rights would incentivize the continued availability of works and prevent works from languishing in limbo based on perceptions of marketability. *Id.* RIAA responded that, since digital music platforms make it easier to re-issue obscure recordings without the costs associated with physical distribution, owners do not need additional incentive to exploit commercially viable works under their control. Tr. at 211:16-212:09 (June 24, 2014) (Susan Chertkof, RIAA).
[424] Library of Congress First Notice Comments at 2-3.
[425] DiMA First Notice Comments at 39; BYU First Notice Comments at 3. Though DiMA "takes no view" on the federalization issue, it claims that, to the extent Congress considers incorporating pre-1972 sound recordings into federal copyright law, such a change should be "absolute and full." Tr. at 157:05-18 (June 5, 2014) (Lee Knife, DiMA).
[426] *See, e.g.*, A2IM First Notice Comments at 7-8; ABKCO First Notice Comments at 3; RIAA First Notice Comments at 32-33; *see also* NARAS First Notice Comments at 6-8 (supporting partial federalization as a "stop gap").
[427] SoundExchange First Notice Comments at 11-13.
[428] *Id.* at 11-12.
[429] Tr. at 180:11-14 (June 24, 2014) (Casey Rae, FMC).
[430] *See* LaPolt First Notice Comments at 10 ("Recording artists with pre-1972 recordings were denied an estimated $60 million in royalties in 2013 alone.").
[431] RESPECT Act, H.R. 4772, 113th Cong. (2014).
[432] 17 U.S.C. §§ 106(4), 106(6), 114(a).
[433] *See* SoundExchange First Notice Comments at 16 ("The rationale for requiring terrestrial radio services to pay royalties to artists and copyright owners is the same as for all other platforms."); *see also, e.g.*, A2IM First Notice Comments at 8; RIAA First Notice Comments at 30-31; SAGAFTRA & AFM First Notice Comments at 6.
[434] *See, e.g.*, SAG-AFTRA & AFM First Notice Comments at 6; SoundExchange First Notice Comments at 16.
[435] *See* A2IM First Notice Comments at 8 ("AM/FM broadcasters make billions selling ads to folks who tune in for our music while our sound recording creators get nothing."); NARAS First Notice Comments at 9 ("Broadcast radio is the only industry in America that bases its business on using the intellectual property of another without permission or compensation."); SAG-AFTRA & AFM First Notice Comments at 6 ("Radio has built a $15 billion industry based primarily on the exploitation of the creative work of Artists, and should finally be required to fairly compensate those Artists.").
[436] SoundExchange First Notice Comments at 16; LaPolt First Notice Comments at 6.
[437] DiMA First Notice Comments at 40-41; FMC First Notice Comments at 15; RIAA First Notice Comments at 30-31; Sirius XM First Notice Comments at 2-4; *see also* Copyright Alliance First Notice Comments at 2.
[438] Sirius XM First Notice Comments at 3-4; *see also* DiMA First Notice Comments at 40-41 (noting that "platform distinctions do not make sense in the digital environment where the very same consumer electronics devices—such as automobile in-dash receivers—are capable of receiving digital and/or analog transmissions of the same sound recording").
[439] Geo Music Group & George Johnson Music Publ'g at 13.
[440] *See* NAB First Notice Comments at 29.
[441] *Id.* at 28 (citing research indicating the promotional benefit provided to the recording industry from free radio airplay ranges from $1.5 to $2.4 billion annually).
[442] *Id.*; *see also* GAO REPORT at 50 (explaining that it is common for record companies to employ independent promoters to encourage the broadcast industry to perform their songs).
[443] *See* Tr. at 287:11-17 (June 23, 2014) (Blake Morgan, ECR Music Group and #IRespectMusic); *The Register's Call for Updates to U.S. Copyright Law: Hearing Before the Subcomm. on Courts, Intell. Prop. and the Internet of the H. Comm. on the Judiciary,* 113th Cong. 3 (2013) ("*The Register's Call for Updates Hearing*") (statement of Rep. Melvin L.Watt) ("I think it is time, and the time is long overdue, for Congress to recognize

a performance right in sound recordings .... To not do so just prolongs this longstanding inequity and keeps us out of pace with the international community."); SoundExchange First Notice Comments at 16-17 ("The free ride given to terrestrial radio also makes the U.S. an outlier internationally. At least 75 nations recognize some form of performance right for terrestrial radio, and the U.S. is the only western industrialized nation that does not.").

[444] *See, e.g.,* RIAA First Notice Comments at 30-31; FMC First Notice Comments at 14-15; SoundExchange First Notice Comments at 17.

[445] *See* GAO REPORT at 30; *see also* Mary LaFrance, *From Whether to How: The Challenge of Implementing a Full Public Performance Right in Sound Recordings*, 2 Harv. J. of Sports & Ent. L 221, 226 (2011).

[446] NAB claims that proponents of reconciling international performance right laws have "failed to substantiate the actual amount of revenue at issue." NAB Second Notice Comments at 3. It further asserts that, even if substantiated, "[t]he estimated ... $70 million dollars in foreign performance tariffs essentially constitute a rounding error to the major record companies." NAB First Notice Comments at 29 n.15.

[447] NAB Second Notice Comments at 3 ("[Proponents] also ignore the fact that many of these foreign regimes are distinctly less generous to sound recordings in other respects. If the U.S. is to adopt their regimes in one respect, presumably it should do so in others such as a much shorter term of protection, no protections against anti-circumvention devices, and cultural and other playlist quotas.").

[448] NAB alleges that "the U.K. adheres to 'simultaneous publication rules,' which grant U.S. sound recordings the same rights as U.K. sound recordings when they are released in both countries simultaneously," though no evidence documenting that point was submitted during the course of this study. NAB Second Notice Comments at 3-4; *see also* LaFrance, *From Whether to How: The Challenge of Implementing a Full Public Performance Right in Sound Recordings* at 225 (explaining that "[i]n practice, many foreign collecting societies ... have been willing to reciprocate even before being legally required to do so," but noting that laws and collecting society practices are not identical and reciprocal arrangements are generally negotiated on a caseby-case basis).

[449] SGA First Notice Comments at 4; *see also* BMI First Notice Comments at 3 (noting that "the decrees must be reviewed with an eye towards modernization"); LaPolt Second Notice Comments at 15 (explaining that the consent decrees are "restrictive and outdated"); NSAI Second Notice Comments at 6 ("Non-performing songwriters are threatened with extinction under ... the outdated ASCAP and BMI Consent Decree models."); Wixen First Notice Comments at 3 (ASCAP and BMI "cannot sufficiently represent songwriters' interests while operating under the outdated consent decrees.").

[450] ASCAP First Notice Comments at 3.

[451] NMPA, Comments Submitted in Response to the DOJ's Antitrust Consent Decree Review at 5 (Aug. 6, 2014), *available at* http://www.justice.gov/atr/cases/ascapbmi/comments/307900.pdf.

[452] *See, e.g.,* CFA & Public Knowledge First Notice Comments at 6 ("[T]he court's ruling in [*In re Petition of Pandora Media*] should put an end to the claims that these antitrust decrees are 'obsolete' or 'outdated.'"); CTIA First Notice Comments at 6 ("[T]he decrees remain essential to foster competitive market pricing for music performance rights."); DiMA Second Notice Comments at 16 ("[The PRO] collectives require government oversight .... [T]he natural behavior for collectives and monopolies is to instinctively leverage their position and attempt to extract supra-competitive rates and terms."); FMC First Notice Comments at 6 (Even if the consent decrees are examined regarding changes in the marketplace, "there would be no compelling reason to completely eliminate the consent decrees and the important limitations they place on PROs and publishers from engaging in anticompetitive behavior."); RMLC First Notice Comments at 5 ("[T]he pattern of price corrections and other decree enforcement measures implemented by the federal judiciary following vigorously contested trials and appeals is testimony to the continuing need for judicial supervision of ASCAP and BMI."); TMLC First Notice Comments at 5 ("[The] status quo requires, at the very least, maintaining constraints protecting music users such as those provided for in the ASCAP and BMI consent decrees.").

[453] *See, e.g.,* CTIA First Notice Comments at 6 ("Due to the nature of the markets, SESAC and the major publishers also exercise substantial supra-competitive market power. That market power should also be controlled.").

[454] *Antitrust Consent Decree Review*, U.S. DOJ, http://www.justice.gov/atr/cases/ascap-bmi-decreereview.html (last visited Jan. 30, 2015).

[455] DiMA First Notice Comments at 30.

[456] CTIA First Notice Comments at 6.

[457] ASCAP First Notice Comments at 26 (Royalty rates are "set at rates below what the evidence indicates are market levels."); LaPolt First Notice Comments at 11 ("The compulsory rates set by the rate courts for licenses are severely lower than their true market value."); NARAS Second Notice Comments at 2 (explaining that "recent rate court decisions made pursuant to the Consent Decrees have resulted in royalty rates for digital music services that are below fair market value").

[458] BMI First Notice Comments at 9.

[459] Council of Music Creators First Notice Comments at 5.

[460] SCL First Notice Comments at 12.

[461] ASCAP First Notice Comments at 29 n.45, 44 ("This almost 12-to-1 disparity in SoundExchange and PRO payments is unprecedented in the global music marketplace." ASCAP elsewhere notes the ratio may be higher, citing a rate of "12 to 14 times greater.") (citation omitted); BMI First Notice Comments at 2 (finding that "recording artists are paid as much as . . . twelve times [what songwriters and publishers are paid] for the public performance right."); Music Managers' Forum ("MMF") & Featured Artists' Coalition ("FAC") Second Notice Comments at 10 (noting "the price for musical compositions is disadvantaged by a factor of 10 or 12 to 1"); SESAC First Notice Comments at 4 (referencing a ratio of 13:1); Tr. at 58:19-21 (June 17, 2014) (Gary R. Greenstein, Wilson Sonsini Goodrich & Rosati) (referencing "14-to-1 fees to the sound recording copyright owner versus the musical work copyright owner").

[462] ASCAP First Notice Comments at 24; *see also* SESAC First Notice Comments at 6 ("The consent decrees . . . offer no definition or guidelines as to what constitutes 'reasonable.'").

[463] *See* BMI First Notice Comments at 10 ("We believe that the prohibition against the PRO rate courts considering the rates set for sound recordings provides in part an explanation for this unintended disparity."); *see also* ABKCO First Notice Comments at 2; ASCAP First Notice Comments at 29-30.

[464] ASCAP First Notice Comments at 25.

[465] *Id.* at 3 ("Rate court proceedings have become extremely time and labor-intensive, costing the parties millions in litigation expenses."); BMI First Notice Comments at 8-9 ("Federal rate court litigation is an exceptionally slow process to set prices to keep up with the rapidly-evolving digital marketplace, and it is exceedingly expensive for all participants . . . ."); SESAC First Notice Comments at 7 ("[T]he consent decrees . . . hold[] songwriters and music publisher royalties' hostage to systematically protracted rate negotiations and expensive, time-consuming rate court proceedings.").

[466] Netflix First Notice Comments at 6.

[467] Music Choice First Notice Comments at 5.

[468] ASCAP First Notice Comments at 23.

[469] Castle First Notice Comments at 8.

[470] *See* U. S. COPYRIGHT OFFICE, COPYRIGHT SMALL CLAIMS 24-26 (2013) *available at* http://copyright.gov/docs/smallclaims/usco-smallcopyrightclaims.pdf.

[471] BMI First Notice Comments at 9.

[472] ASCAP First Notice Comments at 22.

[473] LaPolt Second Notice Comments at app. 4.

[474] ASCAP First Notice Comment at 15; BMI First Notice Comment at 16.

[475] BMI First Notice Comments at 3; *see also* LaPolt Second Notice Comments at app. 4 (noting that "some licensees employ the rate court as a dilatory tactic to use performance licenses for a time without having to compensate the PROs.").

[476] BMI First Notice Comments at 16.

[477] ASCAP First Notice Comments at 16 & n.22.

[478] BMI First Notice Comments at 17; *see also* ASCAP First Notice Comments at 15-16.

[479] SCL First Notice Comments at 12 ("Commercial entities like SESAC, startups like Azoff MSG Entertainment [GMR] and a variety of foreign PROs are all competing for the opportunity to the collect revenues of the music creators but unlike ASCAP and BMI, are not constrained by antiquated regulations in their efforts to do so."); Sarah Skates, *Global Music Rights Has Growing Roster, Negotiating Power*, MUSIC ROW (Oct. 30, 2014), http://www.musicrow.com/2014/10/globalmusic-rights-has-growing-roster-negotiating-power/ (opining that GMR "would likely have more power than other PROs ASCAP and BMI when negotiating licenses on behalf of its members, due to the fact that it would not be subject to the same regulatory agreements that govern the more established organizations").

[480] Music Choice First Notice Comments at 10 ("Given the current state of SESAC's repertory, the same facts supporting the continued need for rate court regulation of ASCAP and BMI apply equally to SESAC, and SESAC should be subject to the same regulation and rate court supervision as the other PROs.").

[481] *See RMLC v. SESAC*, 29 F. Supp. 3d 487; *Meredith Corp.*, 1 F. Supp. 3d 180.

[482] RMLC First Notice Comments at 2.

[483] TMLC First Notice Comments at 14; *see also* Sirius XM First Notice Comments at 6 ("[SESAC's] combination of concentrated ownership and either an unwillingness or inability to be transparent as to what works are actually in the repertory creates a completely untenable situation.").

[484] *RMLC v. SESAC*, 29 F. Supp. 3d at 500-03 (dismissing price fixing allegation, but allowing monopoly claim to proceed); *Meredith Corp. v. SESAC LLC*, No. 09-cv-9177, 2011 WL 856266, at *1 (S.D.N.Y. Mar. 9, 2011) (denying motion to dismiss).

[485] Memorandum of Law in Support of Plaintiffs' Unopposed Motion for Preliminary Approval of Settlement at 1-2, 5, *Meredith Corp.*, 1 F. Supp. 3d 180 (No. 09-cv-9177). TMLC, which was not a party to the litigation, was also a signatory to the settlement. *Id.* at 1 n.2.

[486] Tr. at 61:04-11 (June 5, 2014) (Reid Alan Waltz, SESAC); *see also* Tr. at 58:20-59:03 (June 23, 2014) (Bill Lee, SESAC) ("Although SESAC is not under a rate court, many rate court decisions do have a negative impact on

[487] Production Music Association Second Notice Comments at 5.

[488] *See generally* RICHARD A. EPSTEIN, ANTITRUST CONSENT DECREES: IN THEORY AND PRACTICE 30-39 (2007) ("EPSTEIN") (describing differences between the decrees and concluding that the consent decrees "did not keep ASCAP and BMI in parity at all times, so that differential regulations governed key portions of their business").

[489] *See* BMI, Comments on Department of Commerce Green Paper at 4-5.

[490] LaPolt First Notice Comments at 12.

[491] BMI First Notice Comments at 9 ("[M]any knowledgeable publishers . . . have lost confidence in the efficacy of the rate court process to yield fair market-value. That loss of confidence is driving publishers to move away from the PROs to avoid this perceived inadequacy.").

[492] *See, e.g.*, Tr. at 23:17-20 (June 17, 2014) (Timothy Cohan, PeerMusic) ("[T]here seems to be consensus that there would be universal havoc—I think that's an apt term—if total withdrawals were to happen."); Tr. at 30:05-06 (June 17, 2014) (Ashley Irwin, SCL) (stating that publisher withdrawals would result in "total havoc").

[493] BMI Second Notice Comments at 12.

[494] Sisario, *Pandora Suit May Upend Century-Old Royalty Plan*.

[495] A2IM First Notice Comments at 6.

[496] *See, e.g.*, ASCAP Second Notice Comments at 3-4 (predicting that "withdrawing publishers will result in a loss of revenue but without an attendant drop in expenses, which will have to be unfairly borne by the remaining ASCAP members"); *see also* LaPolt First Notice Comments at 12 13; NARAS Second Notice Comments at 2.

[497] Tr. at 9:09-15 (June 5, 2014) (Sam Mosenkis, ASCAP) ("[I]f the revenues . . . decrease[] by 60 percent, clearly operating ratios are going to increase, possibly to a point where we can't operate efficiently enough and the whole concept of efficient licensing really drops down the drain."); *see also* NSAI Second Notice Comments at 3 ("If major music publishers directly license and collect the digital performance royalties easiest to accomplish, it is unlikely that ASCAP and BMI could continue to exist on what is left, at least with the same efficiency and cost.").

[498] *See, e.g.*, RIAA First Notice Comments at 39 ("[O]utright withdrawal is a possibility that imperils the whole musical work performance licensing system, and creates a risk that there will be no practical way to access works, and shares of works, owned by smaller publishers.").

[499] *See* ASCAP First Notice Comments at 36; Tr. at 37:02-39:08 (June 17, 2014) (David Kokakis, UMPG); *see also* Ed Christman, *Sony/ATV's Martin Bandier Repeats Warning to ASCAP, BMI*, BILLBOARD (July 11, 2014), http://www.billboard.com/biz/articles/news/publishing /6157469/sonyatvs-martin-bandier-repeats-warning-to-ascap-bmi (reporting the details of a letter sent by Sony/ATV chairman and CEO, Martin Bandier, to Sony/ATV songwriters explaining that Sony/ATV "may have no alternative but to take all of our rights out of ASCAP and BMI"). Warner/Chappell did not participate in the study, but previously announced "their intentions to withdraw their New Media licensing rights from ASCAP" along with other large publishers, following completion of the June 2012 deal between Pandora and Sony/EMI. *In re Pandora*, 2013 WL 5211927, at *3.

[500] Tr. at 34:18-35:09 (June 17, 2014) (David Kokakis, UMPG).

[501] *See, e.g.*, ASCAP First Notice Comments at 34-35.

[502] DiMA First Notice Comments at 32 ("[I]f the antitrust consent decrees were to be modified by the Department of Justice to accommodate 'limited' withdrawals . . . the marketplace for musical work public performance rights would be significantly compromised.").

[503] Music Choice First Notice Comments at 6.

[504] Public Knowledge & CFA First Notice Comments at 5 ("When ASCAP allowed the largest music publishers to remove their digital rights from the existing contracts, [the publishers] immediately returned to the abusive practices that had made the consent decree necessary in the first place."); Tr. at 52:07-20 (June 24, 2014) (Paul Fakler, Music Choice) ("[After publishers did partially withdraw] there was evidence from the record, of collusion, strong arm tactics to inflate the rates, sharing confidential information about negotiations.").

[505] Tr. at 12:07-09 (June 17, 2014) (Garry Schyman, SCL) ("We only receive the writer's share, and that's contractual."); Tr. at 24:13-16 (June 17, 2014) (Timothy Cohan, PeerMusic) ("Contracts have mentioned the writer's share for a long, long time. They are not consistent. It is often negotiated from contract to contract.").

[506] Tr. at 12:10-14 (June 17, 2014) (Garry Schyman, SCL) ("[V]ery often the contracts do not specify what would happen if the music is withdrawn from a PRO. It merely says if money is collected through your society, that you are entitled to receive your share.").

[507] NARAS Second Notice Comments at 2 (noting that "the rest of the music ecosystem would lose the efficiency, transparency and stability provided by the PROs."); Public Knowledge & CFA First Notice Comments at 18; Tr. at 33:22-34:06 (June 24, 2014) (Rick Carnes, SGA).

[508] FMC First Notice Comments at 6-7.

[509] Tr. at 31:16-32:04 (June 17, 2014) (Ashley Irwin, SCL) ("[M]y deal with [a foreign PRO] does not allow a sub-publisher to pull out of an American society. It contravenes my agreement with my local society. So I don't know if anybody has considered what the foreign societies will do if the publishers pull out here that are representing, once again, a reciprocity thing.").

[510] Tr. at 34:11-13, 43:09-10 (June 17, 2014) (David Kokakis, UPMG).

[511] *Id.* at 43:17-19.

[512] *Id.* at 38:06-08; BMI Second Notice Comments at 14; *see also* Tr. at 45:05-10 (June 16, 2014) (Ashley Irwin, SCL) (proposing bifurcation of public performance right between publishers and songwriters, so that songwriters could continue to utilize the PROs).

[513] ASCAP Second Notice Comment at 6.

[514] NSAI Second Notice Comments at 3; *see also* NMPA & HFA First Notice Comments at 20 ("[Withdrawal] presents a Hobson's choice for music publishers—either pull out of ASCAP completely (and take on the difficult burdens of general licensing, *e.g.*, licensing to small music users such as bars and clubs), or forfeit the right to negotiate agreements at market rates with digital service providers.").

[515] BMI First Notice Comments at 20; ASCAP First Notice Comments at 4.

[516] *Id.* at 37-38.

[517] *Id.* at 38; *see also* BMI First Notice Comments at 13 ("In 1979, the [DOJ] determined that entering into perpetual consent decrees was not in the public interest.").

[518] ASCAP First Notice Comments at 38.

[519] BMI First Notice Comments at 25.

[520] *See, e.g.*, Music Choice First Notice Comments at 8.

[521] *See, e.g.*, DiMA First Notice Comments at 15 ("The processes and protections assured by these consent decrees serve several important roles that are critical to an efficient, properly functioning marketplace for these rights . . . .").

[522] Netflix First Notice Comments at 7.

[523] *See, e.g.*, Tr. at 44:22-45:05 (June 5, 2014) (Lee Knife, DiMA) ("I think whenever you have that type of concentration of market power, that kind of demands some type of oversight, again, whether or not that's in the form of a compulsory license, a statutory license, a consent decree, or something like that."); Tr. at 52:07-20 (June 24, 2014) (Paul Fakler, Music Choice).

[524] ASCAP First Notice Comments at 23-24 (explaining that arbitration would offer a more definite timeline and would discourage applicants from relying on the license application or interim licenses); *Music Licensing Hearings* at 52 (statement of Michael O'Neill, CEO, BMI) ("We believe that replacing the current rate court with arbitration in New York under the American Arbitration Association rules would be a faster, less expensive, and a more market-responsive mechanism for all parties to obtain fair, market-value rate decisions."); Content Creators Coalition Second Notice Comments at 2-3.

[525] IPAC First Notice Comments at 9.

[526] NAB Second Notice Comments at 2; *see also* Music Choice Second Notice Comments at 8; Tr. at 55:14-16 (June 24, 2014) (Willard Hoyt, TMLC) ("It has been our experience that arbitration is not, necessarily, less expensive than the rate court.").

[527] Tr. at 88:21-89:05 (June 23, 2014) (Casey Rae, FMC).

[528] Music Choice First Notice Comments at 29.

[529] Netflix First Notice Comments at 7-8 (emphasis in original); *see also* Sirius XM First Notice Comments at 4 ("In our experience, the ASCAP and BMI consent decrees and the licensing process that they mandate work relatively well."); Spotify First Notice Comments at 10 (explaining that "the current system where the PROs are subject to regulation via the consent decrees is working well").

[530] MMF & FAC Second Notice Comments at 10.

[531] BMI First Notice Comments at 17.

[532] *See* ASCAP First Notice Comments at 30; DiMA First Notice Comments at 25 ("A mechanism should be put in place that enables the collective administration of an 'all-in,' combined mechanical and performance royalty."); IPAC First Notice Comments at 8 ("A unified licensing scheme for uses that require both public performance and mechanical licenses could benefit both licensees and copyright owners."); RIAA First Notice Comments at 6 ("[T]he marketplace needs bundles of rights."); Public Knowledge & CFA First Notice Comments at 28; SCL First Notice Comments at 12.

[533] NSAI Second Notice Comments at 8.

[534] NMPA & HFA First Notice Comments at 18; Tr. at 239:15-18 (June 24, 2014) (Jay Rosenthal, NMPA).

[535] ASCAP First Notice Comments at 30-34; BMI First Notice Comments at 15-16; Tr. at 273:13-15 (June 24, 2014) (Richard Reimer, ASCAP); Tr. at 38:03-04 (June 24, 2014) (Stuart Rosen, BMI).

[536] BMI First Notice Comments at 6; Tr. at 32:20-33:01 (June 4, 2014) (Dan Coleman, Modern Music Works Publishing); Tr. at 273:07-12 (June 24, 2014) (Richard Reimer, ASCAP).

[537] SEA, H.R. 4079 § 2.

[538] *See, e.g.,* NMPA & HFA First Notice Comments at 21-22; BMI First Notice Comments at 18-19; SESAC First Notice Comments at 3-4; NARAS First Notice Comments at 4; Geo Music Group & George Johnson Music

Publ'g First Notice Comments at 16; Tr. at 198:09-17 (June 5, 2014) (Daniel Gervais, Vanderbilt University Law School) (noting "when you read in the Copyright Royalty Board determination that the value of a sound recording is unrelated to the value of the song . . . [t]o me, that complete disconnect is not warranted").

[539] *See, e.g.,* BMI First Notice Comments at 18; ASCAP First Notice Comments at 27-30; SESAC First Notice Comments at 5; NMPA & HFA First Notice Comments at 26-28; NARAS First Notice Comments at 4; LaPolt First Notice Comments at 12.

[540] *See e.g.,* CTIA First Notice Comments at 12 (noting that "publishers want it both ways—they want the higher sound recording fees to be relevant in setting their fees, but they want to protect their affiliate record companies and ensure that sound recording fees are not dragged down by much lower musical works fees"); Music Choice First Notice Comments at 34 ("The simple fact is that the disparity in rates between the Section 114 license and the PRO licenses does not prove that the PRO rates are too low; it proves that the Section 114 rates are too high.").

[541] CTIA First Notice Comments at 11-12.; Tr. at 254:06-19 (June 16, 2014) (Russell Hauth, NRBMLC) ("Now that the sound recording industry has got a great rate, the musical works want the same, and they want to not be separated any longer. You know, I've got to say that's fairly hypocritical.").

[542] *See, e.g.,* NRBMLC First Notice Comments at 11-12; Tr. at 254:06-19 (June 16, 2014) (Russell Hauth, NRBMLC); Tr. at 76:22-79:07 (June 24, 2014) (Bruce Rich, RMLC); Tr. at 85:13-86:07 (June 24, 2014) (Paul Fakler, NAB).

[543] *See* ABKCO First Notice Comments at 1; BMI First Notice Comments at 5; Gear Publ'g Co. & Lisa Thomas Music Servs., LLC First Notice Comments at 4; IPAC First Notice Comments at 7; *see also* Tr. at 119:01-09 (June 17, 2014) (John Rudolph, Music Analytics); Tr. at 33:20-34:02 (June 23, 2014) (Jay Rosenthal, NMPA).

[544] *See* Carapetyan Second Notice Comments at 1 ("The reality is it is rarely used in standard industry practice, serving only as a framework for negotiating terms of direct licenses, but acting as a *de facto* ceiling for royalty rates nonetheless."); Geo Music Group & George Johnson Music Publ'g First Notice Comments at 10 (opining that "the *statutory rate is still a cap* and *as non-effective as it gets*.") (emphasis in original); NSAI Second Notice Comments at 7.

[545] *See* LaPolt Second Notice Comments at 9; MMF & FAC Second Notice Comments at 6; Modern Works Music Publishing First Notice Comments at 4-5; *see also* Tr. at 250:15-21 (June 4, 2014) (Brittany Schaffer, NMPA/Loeb & Loeb LLP).

[546] NMPA & HFA First Notice Comments at 16; Tr. at 266:14-267:05 (June 16, 2014) (Ilene Goldberg); *see also* Kohn First Notice Comments at 19-20.

[547] LaPolt First Notice Comments at 14; NMPA & HFA First Notice Comments at 16; *see also* Tr. at 60:20-22 (June 4, 2014) (Brittany Schaffer, NMPA/Loeb & Loeb LLP).

[548] *See* DiMA First Notice Comments at 23 ("The Section 801(b) standard has been time-tested to provide fair rates (i.e., 'reasonable fees') that have been accepted for more than half a century in many different contexts, including ratesetting proceedings under Sections 114(f)(1)(B), 115, and 116."); DiMA Second Notice Comments at 21; Sirius XM First Notice Comments at 13-14; *see also* Tr. at 310:01-09 (June 23, 2014) (Lee Knife, DiMA).

[549] DiMA First Notice Comments at 19.

[550] DiMA Second Notice Comments at 20; *see also* Music Choice First Notice Comments at 37.

[551] DiMA Second Notice Comments at 20-21; *see also* Tr. at 278:21-279:02 (June 23, 2014) (Paul Fakler, NAB/Music Choice); Tr. at 294:02-10 (June 23, 2014) (Cynthia Greer, Sirius XM).

[552] RIAA First Notice Comments at 25.

[553] *Id.*

[554] *See, e.g.,* BMI First Notice Comments at 5; DiMA First Notice Comments at 20; Spotify First Notice Comments at 3-5; RIAA First Notice Comments at 10-11.

[555] *See id.* at 40 (describing the previously high volume of mechanical licenses issued through HFA and the increasing practice of direct licensing for new songs and new albums).

[556] *See* DiMA First Notice Comments at 20 (noting that "the costs [in filing NOIs with the Copyright Office] can be overwhelming given the volume of works at issue"); Tr. at 172:06-13 (June 16, 2014) (Lawrence J. Blake, Concord Music).

[557] RIAA First Notice Comments at 23 n.36.

[558] DiMA First Notice Comments at 20.

[559] *Id.* at 20-21.

[560] CTIA First Notice Comments at 13 (explaining that "virtually all participants in the market have recognized that the licensing regime for the reproduction and distribution rights, which requires specific monthly reporting and payment, is complex and burdensome"); LaPolt Second Notice Comments at 10; Tr. at 234:21-235:01 (June 23, 2014) (Cheryl Potts, Crystal Clear Music & CleerKut).

[561] DiMA First Notice Comments at 22 (emphasis in original). *See* 17 U.S.C. § 115(c)(5).

[562] Gear Publ'g Co. & Lisa Thomas Music Servs., LLC First Notice Comments at 5-6; Geo Music Group & George Johnson Music Publ'g First Notice Comments at 9.

[563] Music Choice First Notice Comments at 21 ("Although many cases are filed by songwriters and recording artists for underpayment of royalties, far more cases go unlitigated. This is because, among other reasons, (1) the audit provisions in the authors' contracts are often very restrictive; (2) it is very expensive for an author to hire forensic accountants to conduct an audit; (3) once an audit begins, the record company or publisher uses various tactics, including accounting records that seem designed to obfuscate royalty revenues received and royalties due, to impede the audit; and (4) even after underpayments are established, authors often must accept pennies on the dollar for their claims because the cost of litigation against the record companies and publishers is so high.").

[564] NMPA & HFA First Notice Comments at 14.

[565] Castle First Notice Comments at 2. As discussed above, in lieu of requiring certifications, the mechanical licensing agent HFA instead conducts audits of licensees—a substantial benefit for its publisher members. *See* Michael Simon, *The Basics of Mechanical Licensing from Harry Fox*, ARTISTS HOUSEMUSIC (July 12, 2007), http://www.artistshousemusic.org/articles/the+basics+of+ mechanical+licensing+from+harry+fox (noting HFA's audits of licensees). But the section 115 license does not require this.

[566] IPAC First Notice Comments at 3-4 ("If the digital music service pays all royalties for the use of a musical work to only one co-owner, then that co-owner is obligated to pay the other co-owners of the musical work their respective share of the monies received. This practice effectively shifts to the copyright owner the accounting and payment obligations of the user. This example also puts co-owners of the musical work who have not received the Notice at a disadvantage—these co-owners will likely be unaware that their musical works are being used, be unaware that royalties are due, and be in a difficult position in terms of that co-owner's rights to audit the digital music service.").

[567] Rys First Notice Comments at 2.

[568] Tr. at 209:17-20 (June 16, 2014) (Keith Bernstein, Crunch Digital).

[569] Lowery First Notice Comments at 1; *see also* IPAC First Notice Comments at 3-4.

[570] Castle First Notice Comments at 3.

[571] RIAA Second Notice Comments at 19 (noting that major record companies "support the idea that where there is direct licensing, publishers/writers should have a direct audit right with respect to third parties that use their works").

[572] *See* DiMA First Notice Comments at 19-20.

[573] *Id.* at 21 ("For digital music services that rely on licenses under Section 115 as well as separate licenses for the public performance of musical works, it is often impossible to determine the appropriate deduction for musical work public performance royalties at the time that accountings under the Section 115 licenses are due. This is because the calculation of 'mechanical' royalty rates under Section 115 requires that public performance royalties be deducted; and public performance rates are often not determined—whether by 'interim agreement,' 'final agreement' or ratesetting proceeding—until long after the close of the month during which Section 115 royalties are due.").

[574] NMPA & HFA First Notice Comments at 9-10; *see also* Kohn First Notice Comments at 11.

[575] Lowery First Notice Comments at 3-4.

[576] *See, e.g., id.* 1-4.

[577] Carapetyan Second Notice Comments at 1 (noting that there is "a bevy of legally deficient 'Notices of Intention' that force publishers into the involuntary role of teaching the fundamentals of copyright to the masses—which is neither practical nor fair—and often in the end the cost in effort and man-hours far exceeds the minuscule royalties for the use").

[578] Lowery First Notice Comments at 2.

[579] *Id.* at 2-3; *see also* NMPA & HFA First Notice Comments at 15.

[580] *See, e.g.,* Castle Second Notice Comments at 3 ("[A] defaulter under the statutory license can lawfully continue sending NOIs for future licenses even if they have never paid a dime on past licenses—the only recourse a songwriter has in this case is termination and if that too is ignored, extraordinarily expensive federal copyright litigation.").

[581] IPAC First Notice Comment at 3; *see also* Rys First Notice Comments at 2.

[582] *See* DiMA First Notice Comments at 22 (observing differences between the royalty rate structures for some current rate categories).

[583] *Id.* at 21.

[584] *See, e.g.*, NMPA & HFA First Notice Comments at 8; NSAI Second Notice Comments at 7; IPAC First Notice Comments at 4.

[585] *See* ABKCO First Notice Comments at 1 ("The free market is stifled under Section 115 licensing requirements with government controlling rates which thereby limits and inhibits sector growth and innovation."); MMF & FAC Second Notice Comments at 14-15; RIAA Second Notice Comments at 4-5; Pipeline Project Second Notice Comments at 16.

[586] NMPA & HFA First Notice Comments at 7; *see also* IPAC First Notice Comments at 6.

[587] DiMA First Notice Comments at 19 (emphasis in original).

[588] Modern Works Music Publishing Second Notice Comments at 3 (explaining that section 115 is "an *antitrust provision* that accelerates the entry of musical works into the public sphere, while ensuring that copyright holders are paid.") (emphasis in original).

[589] Spotify First Notice Comments at 3.

[590] *See, e.g.,* NARAS First Notice Comments at 3-4; DiMA First Notice Comments at 16-17; IPAC First Notice Comments at 6-7; BMI First Notice Comments at 5; ASCAP First Notice Comments at 30-31. In 2006, the House Subcommittee on Courts, the Internet, and Intellectual Property considered SIRA, legislation that would have created a blanket license for digital uses under section 115. While SIRA enjoyed support from some key stakeholders and was approved by the subcommittee, it was not passed out of the full committee. *See Reforming Section 115 Hearing* at 4 (statement of Rep. Howard Coble) (detailing legislative history); Mitchell, *Reforming Section 115: Escape from the Byzantine World of Mechanical Licensing* at 1277 (describing support for SIRA).

[591] RIAA Second Notice Comments at 13.

[592] ABKCO First Notice Comments at 1-2.

[593] IPAC First Notice Comments at 6-7.

[594] Tr. 25:11-16 (June 4, 2014) (Steven Marks, RIAA).

[595] *Id.* at 25:16-18.

[596] *Id.* at 24:04-26:18.

[597] RIAA First Notice Comments at 15-17.

[598] *Id.* at 16. RIAA made clear that its proposed blanket license would not cover other uses of musical works, like synch rights for movie, television, and advertising, performances within live venue, stand-alone lyrics, and sheet music. *Id.* at 17.

[599] *Id.* at 15-18.

[600] *Id.* at 18-22.

[601] NMPA Second Notice Comments at 32-33; *see also* Tr. at 245:12-20 (June 24, 2014) (Peter Brodsky, Sony/ATV).

[602] LaPolt Second Notice Comments at 14; NMPA Second Notice Comments at 32-35; NSAI Second Notice Comments at 8; *see also* Tr. at 214:14-20 (June 16, 2014) (John Barker, IPAC); Tr. at 246:21-247:09 (June 24, 2014) (Peter Brodsky, Sony/ATV).

[603] NMPA Second Notice Comments at 32.

[604] RIAA First Notice Comments at 32 ("All services operating under the statutory licenses should pay fair market royalties set under the willing buyer/willing seller standard."). In contrast, RIAA criticized the "below-market royalty rates" set under the section 801(b)(1) standard for grandfathered services. *Id.* at 31.

[605] A2IM First Notice Comments at 3.

[606] CFA & Public Knowledge First Notice Comments at 8. Pandora did report a modest profit in Q3, 2013, but its current strategy is focused on expansion. Romain Dillet, *Pandora Beats, Q3 2013 Revenue Up 60% to $120M, Net Income of $2.1M; Q4 Forecast Much Lower Than Expected*, TECHCRUNCH (Dec. 4, 2012), http://techcrunch.com/2012/12/04/pandoras-q3-2013/; PANDORA MEDIA, INC., QUARTERLY REPORT (FORM 10-Q) 21 (Oct. 28, 2014), http://investor.pandora.com/ phoenix.zhtml?c=227956&p=irol-sec (click on Oct. 28, 2014 filing) ("[W]e expect to incur annual net losses on a U.S. GAAP basis in the near term because our current strategy is to leverage any improvements in gross profit by investing in broadening distribution channels, developing innovative and scalable advertising products, increasing utilization of advertising inventory and building our sales force.").

[607] DiMA First Notice Comments at 33 n.76.

[608] *Id.* at 36.

[609] *Id.* at 37; Educational Media Foundation ("EMF") First Notice Comments at 7-8; Sirius XM First Notice Comments at 14; Spotify First Notice Comments at 12.

[610] *See* 17 U.S.C. § 114(d)(2)(A)(i); *Launch Media*, 578 F.3d 148.

[611] ASCAP First Notice Comments at 44; *see also* BMI First Notice Comments at 22.

[612] RIAA First Notice Comments at 34.

[613] *See id.* ("[A]t this juncture, we do not necessarily advocate excluding from the statutory license services that have been generally accepted as operating within the statutory license based on the *Launch* decision.").

[614] ABKCO First Notice Comments at 3; *see also* RIAA First Notice Comments at 34.

[615] Sirius XM First Notice Comments at 20-21.

[616] A2IM First Notice Comments at 5.

[617] SAG-AFTRA & AFM First Notice Comments at 6 (note however, that SAG-AFTRA & AFM also support increased rates if a service has increased functionality).

[618] 17 U.S.C. § 114(d)(1)(C)(iv), (d)(2)(B)-(C), (j)(13).

[619] NAB First Notice Comments at 4-5; NPR First Notice Comments at 5; SRN Broadcasting First Notice Comments at 1.

[620] NAB First Notice Comments at 4.

[621] *Id.* at 5.

[622] NPR First Notice Comments at 5.
[623] "Ephemeral recordings are copies that are made and used by a transmitting organization to facilitate its transmitting activities." U.S. COPYRIGHT OFFICE, DMCA SECTION 104 REPORT 144 (2001), *available at* http://www.copyright.gov/reports/studies/dmca/sec-104-report-vol-1.pdf.
[624] CTIA First Notice Comments at 16-18; DiMA First Notice Comments at 35; DiMA Second Notice Comments at 18.
[625] NAB First Notice Comments at 7; Music Choice First Notice Comments at 13.
[626] DiMA Second Notice Comments at 18.
[627] *See, e.g.*, NAB First Notice Comments at 2; Sirius XM First Notice Comments at 9-10.
[628] RIAA Second Notice Comments at 31-32.
[629] *Id.* at 32.
[630] SoundExchange First Notice Comments at 2, 5.
[631] *Id.* at 5; *see also* 17 U.S.C. § 115(c)(6) (termination provision under section 115).
[632] *See* Music Choice First Notice Comments at 13; Resnick Second Notice Comments at 1.
[633] Music Choice First Notice Comments at 13; *see also* Resnick Second Notice Comments at 1.
[634] *See* NARAS First Notice Comments at 5.
[635] *2013 Letter of Direction*, SOUNDEXCHANGE (Apr. 14, 2013), https://www.soundexchange.com/wp-content/uploads/2013/05/Letter-of-Direction-04-14-13.pdf ("*2013 SoundExchange Letter of Direction*").
[636] *See* NARAS First Notice Comments at 5-6.
[637] NRBNMLC First Notice Comments at 14-15.
[638] EMF First Notice Comments at 8-9 (noting reasons noncommercial broadcasters are unlikely to settle in section 114 proceedings).
[639] NPR First Notice Comments at 7.
[640] NRBNMLC First Notice Comments at 15.
[641] NPR First Notice Comments at 7; *see also* Public Television Coalition ("PTC") First Notice Comments at 11.
[642] *See* NRBNMLC First Notice Comments at 16. While the 801(b)(1) "reasonable terms and rates" standard currently applies under section 118, sound recording uses under section 114(d) are subject to the willing buyer/willing seller standard. 17 U.S.C. §§ 114(d), 801(b)(1); Noncommercial Educational Broadcasting Compulsory License, 63 Fed. Reg. 49,823, 49,824 (Sept. 18, 1998) (noting the rate standard for section 118 is "reasonable terms and rates" with no further statutory criteria, but the legislative history of section 118 indicated that "the rate should reflect the fair value of the copyrighted material").
[643] *See* 17 U.S.C. § 801 *et seq.*
[644] *See, e.g.*, ASCAP First Notice Comments at 24 n.31; Music Choice First Notice Comments at 2931; RIAA First Notice Comments at 36; Sirius XM First Notice Comments at 17.
[645] *See, e.g.*, RIAA First Notice Comments at 36; SoundExchange First Notice Comments at 6-8.
[646] SoundExchange Second Notice Comments at 10; *see also* RIAA Second Notice Comments at 43 (noting a single-factor rate standard as a possible streamlining measure).
[647] 17 U.S.C. § 803(b)(6)(C).
[648] NAB First Notice Comments at 19 & n.11; Sirius XM First Notice Comments at 17.
[649] Music Choice First Notice Comments at 30; *see* Sirius XM First Notice Comments at 17 (same).
[650] NAB First Notice Comments at 20.
[651] *See* BMI First Notice Comments at 27; DiMA First Notice Comments at 23; RIAA First Notice Comments at 45; Tr. at 256:02-06 (June 16, 2014) (Jason Rys, Wixen Music Publishing).
[652] Kohn First Notice Comments at 14 (referencing the "unnecessarily complex set of individual rate regimes for the various uses contemplated by Section 114 by various kinds of defined transmitters").
[653] RIAA First Notice Comments at 24; *see also id.* at 11-12 (further noting frustrations with mechanical royalty ratesetting).
[654] *See, e.g.*, Tr. at 141:16-21 (June 16, 2014) (Tegan Kossowicz, UMG) ("With respect to an earlier mention of the implementation of CRB settlements, they should be expedited when possible, and that doesn't just pertain to both these sections, but as well as other proceedings that we may have in the future on licensing.").
[655] Tr. at 99:16-100:03 (June 16, 2014) (Brad Prendergast, SoundExchange); Tr. at 129:17-130:03 (June 23, 2014) (Steven Marks, RIAA).
[656] SoundExchange First Notice Comments at 9 n.12; Tr. at 122:15-22 (June 23, 2014) (Colin Rushing, SoundExchange).
[657] RIAA First Notice Comments at 24-25.
[658] Music Choice First Notice Comments at 30.
[659] SoundExchange First Notice Comments at 9-10.
[660] *Id.* at 9.
[661] *Id.* at 10.
[662] DiMA First Notice Comments at 38.
[663] *See id.* at 38-39; Music Choice First Notice Comments at 29-30; Sirius XM First Notice Comments at 15-16; Tr. at 104:10-105:12 (June 16, 2014) (Gary R. Greenstein, Wilson Sonsini Goodrich & Rosati).

[664] 17 U.S.C. § 803(b)(6)(C)(v).
[665] Music Choice First Notice Comments at 29; Sirius XM First Notice Comments at 16.
[666] *See* 17 U.S.C. § 803(b)(6).
[667] Music Choice First Notice Comments at 29; Tr. at 208:19-209:07 (June 4, 2014) (Lee Knife, DiMA).
[668] DiMA First Notice Comments at 38; *see also* NAB First Notice Comments at 20 (supporting longer discovery periods); Sirius XM First Notice Comments at 16-17 (same).
[669] DiMA First Notice Comments at 38-39; *see also* Music Choice First Notice Comments at 30 ("[G]iven the number of witnesses and the number of participants in most proceedings, the Copyright Act's limitation on depositions to ten per side (spread between direct and rebuttal discovery) is clearly insufficient.").
[670] NAB First Notice Comments at 3; Music Choice First Notice Comments at 31 ("The cost of participation in rate proceedings should not include the risk that confidential business information may be publicly disclosed. A standardized blanket protective order, similar to that employed by the Trademark Trial and Appeals Board, would be helpful.").
[671] NAB First Notice Comments at 21.
[672] SoundExchange Second Notice Comments at 10.
[673] Tr. at 115:20-116:07 (June 4, 2014) (Steven Marks, RIAA); *see* SoundExchange Second Notice Comments at 10.
[674] Tr. at 107:19-108:22 (June 4, 2014) (Steven Marks, RIAA); *see* RIAA Second Notice Comments at 43 (favoring "earlier disclosure of a focused set of critical information").
[675] *See, e.g.*, RIAA First Notice Comments at 17, 20, 22; NMPA & HFA First Notice Comments at 10-12; Peter Menell First Notice Comments at 2; Public Knowledge & CFA First Notice Comments at 28; RMLC First Notice Comments at 7-9; TMLC First Notice Comments at 16; Spotify First Notice Comments at 11; IPAC Second Notice Comments at 2; *Music Licensing Hearings* at 71-72 (statement of Jim Griffin, OneHouse LLC).
[676] RIAA First Notice Comments at 46.
[677] *See* Spotify First Notice Comments at 4.
[678] DiMA Second Notice Comments at 6 ("Neither ISRC Codes nor ISWC Codes are applied to all works, nor are they applied uniformly or correctly, even when they are attached to work."); *but compare* Tr. at 382:20-22 (June 23, 2014) (Andrea Finkelstein, SME) ("I would say for the majors, everything that is in digital release has an ISRC associated."), *with* MMF & FAC Second Notice Comments at 29 ("Contrary to oral testimony to the New York Roundtable in June, the [ISRC] has not, in our experience, achieved the penetration that is seen with ISWC.").
[679] *See* Tr. at 336:17-19 (June 23, 2014) (Andrea Finkelstein, SME) ("No, we don't have ISWCs, and we certainly don't have them at that point [when a sound recording is sent to a digital service provider].").
[680] CCIA Second Notice Comments at 2 ("[A]lthough Industry Standard Recording Codes (ISRCs) have existed for more than two decades, there is still not a recorded database of them."); Tr. at 345:05-06 (June 23, 2014) (Andrea Finkelstein, SME) ("There is [an ISRC database] cooking at SoundExchange.").
[681] Tr. at 53:09-17 (June 23, 2014) (Waleed Diab, Google/YouTube).
[682] *See* Pipeline Project Second Notice Comments at 5; Tr. at 516:02-09 (June 23, 2014) (Bob Kohn, Kohn on Music Licensing); Tr. at 558:11-14 (June 23, 2014) (Lynn Lummel, ASCAP); *see also* ISNI, http://www.isni.org (last visited Jan. 30, 2015).
[683] RIAA Second Notice Comments at 32; *see also* NMPA & HFA First Notice Comments at 10-11.
[684] Menell First Notice Comments at 2.
[685] DiMA First Notice Comments at 17, 29.
[686] *Pandora Ratesetting*, 6 F. Supp. 3d at 358-60.
[687] Spotify First Notice Comments at 11.
[688] RIAA First Notice Comments at 46; *Music Licensing Hearings* at 74-75 (statement of Jim Griffin, OneHouse LLC).
[689] SoundExchange First Notice Comments at 25.
[690] *Id.*
[691] RIAA Second Notice Comments at 17; *see also Music Licensing Hearings* at 75 (statement of Jim Griffin, OneHouse LLC) ("[A]bsent the use of [global universal identifiers] money disappears along its path to its intended receiver. Where does that money go? To pools of unattributed income, divided through market share formulas at the organizations that collect the money.").
[692] Tr. 38:05-08 (June 4, 2014) (Brittany Schaffer, NMPA/Loeb & Loeb).
[693] A2IM Second Notice Comments at 2.
[694] DiMA Second Notice Comments at 3-4, 7; Tr. at 381:08-11(June 23, 2014) (Waleed Diab, Google/YouTube).
[695] DiMA Second Notice Comments at 5; *see* Sirius XM First Notice Comments at 6-7; SoundExchange Second Notice Comments at 6; A2IM Second Notice Comments at 2; *see also* CCIA Second Notice Comments at 3.
[696] FMC First Notice Comments at 22; *see* Public Knowledge & CFA First Notice Comments at 28.
[697] NAB Second Notice Comments at 2; CTIA First Notice Comments at 7; DiMA Second Notice Comments at 6-7.
[698] *Music Licensing Hearings* at 72 (statement of Jim Griffin, OneHouse LLC).
[699] NMPA & HFA Second Notice Comments at 3.

[700] ASCAP Second Notice Comments at 12-13 (citing "ASCAP's searchable database, named ASCAP Clearance Express or ACE, at http://www.ascap.com/ace"); BMI Second Notice Comments at 9 (citing BMI's extensive searchable repertoire database at http//www.bmi.com).

[701] *Id.* at 5; ASCAP Second Notice Comments at 7-8.

[702] *See, e.g.,* RIAA Second Notice Comments at 35-36; Tr. at 346:01-349:13 (June 23, 2014) (Lynn Lummel, ASCAP; Andrea Finkelstein, SME; Jacqueline Charlesworth & Sarang Damle, U.S. Copyright Office) (discussing assignment of ISRC in relation to ISWC).

[703] *See, e.g.,* Pipeline Project Second Notice Comments at 9; DiMA Second Notice Comments at 6-8; RIAA Second Notice Comments at 35-36.

[704] *Id.* at 33; SoundExchange Second Notice Comments at 4.

[705] RIAA Second Notice Comments at 33.

[706] SoundExchange Second Notice Comments at 4; RIAA Second Notice Comments at 33; Tr. at 336:02-12 (June 23, 2014) (Andrea Finkelstein, SME; Sarang Damle, U.S. Copyright Office) (describing metadata delivered by record companies).

[707] RIAA Second Notice Comments at 33.

[708] SoundExchange Second Notice Comments at 4-5.

[709] *Id.* at 5.

[710] *Id.*; RIAA Second Notice Comments at 35.

[711] SoundExchange Second Notice Comments at 5.

[712] *Id.*; RIAA Second Notice Comments at 35. These parties noted that the CRB is currently considering updates to the relevant notice and recordkeeping regulations.

[713] Tr. at 86:01-03 (June 4, 2014) (Brittany Schaffer, NMPA/Loeb & Loeb LLP) (explaining that "there's a lack of trust between the record companies and the publishers"); Tr. at 77:15-17 (June 16, 2014) (Eric D. Bull, Create Law) (noting that "there's such distrust because of the amount of the money that is going to be exchanged"); Tr. at 14:03-05 (June 17, 2014) (Garry Schyman, SCL) ("[W]e really don't trust a publisher who is not in a position to tell us what we are entitled to.").

[714] Resnick Second Notice Comments at 2 ("Spotify alone is reported to have paid hundreds of millions in dollars in upfront and non-recoupable payments for the privilege of licensing major label catalogues.").

[715] SAG-AFTRA & AFM First Notice Comments at 7; SAG-AFTRA & AFM Second Notice Comments at 2 ("Whatever the individual royalty artist's share, it will not be paid directly, it will be subject to recoupment, and it will only be verifiable (if at all) through a complex and expensive individual audit under the royalty contract.").

[716] *See* A2IM Second Notice Comments at 5-6 (defining breakage as "excess revenue that cannot be attributed to specific recordings or performances and, therefore, is not required to be shared with artists, songwriters or the actual sound recording copyright owner"); Resnick Second Notice Comments at 2 ("[E]xcess payments are not shared with recording artists.").

[717] Karp, *Artists Press for Their Share*.

[718] For example, Martin Bandier of Sony/ATV has stated that his company does not share extra advance money because "there [isn't] much to share." Karp, *Artists Press for Their Share*.

[719] A2IM Second Notice Comments at 6; Tr. at 143:08-11 (June 23, 2014) (Richard Bengloff, A2IM).

[720] Tr. at 109:13-110:03 (June 5, 2014) (Robert Meitus, Meitus Gelbert Rose LLP).

[721] SGA Second Notice Comments at 14-15 (Sony/ATV was also paid $300,000 for administrative expenses).

[722] *See* Lindvall, *Behind the Music: The Real Reason Why the Major Labels Love Spotify*.

[723] Resnick Second Notice Comments at 2.

[724] Karp, *Artists Press for Their Share*.

[725] According to one source, "[m]ost performance data is drawn from broadcast sources, under the assumption that the music being performed over radio and television is roughly the same as the music being performed in cafes, hotels, sports arenas, . . . restaurants, and nightclubs." KOHN at 1281.

[726] *See* NMPA & HFA First Notice Comments at 9. For instance, SoundExchange pays almost entirely on a census basis, and does not generally use sampling. *See* SoundExchange Second Notice Comments at 7.

[727] *ASCAP Payment System: Keeping Track of Performances*, ASCAP, http://www.ascap.com/members/payment/keepingtrack.aspx (last visited Jan. 30, 2014).

[728] *Payment System: The ASCAP Surveys*, ASCAP, http://www.ascap.com/members/payment/surveys.aspx (last visited Jan. 30, 2014).

[729] *Royalty Policy Manual*, BMI, http://www.bmi.com/creators/royalty_print/detail (last visited Jan. 16, 2015).

[730] *ASCAP's Survey and Distribution System: Rules & Policies*, ASCAP (June 2014), http://www.ascap.com/~/media/files/pdf/members/payment/drd.pdf; *Royalty Policy Manual*, BMI, http://www.bmi.com/creators/royalty_print/detail (last visited Jan. 16, 2015).

[731] Tr. at 261:20-262:03 (June 5, 2014) (Phil Perkins, Music Services).

[732] Tr. at 22:14-25:19 (June 5, 2014) (Royal Wade Kimes, Wonderment Records); *see* Simpson First Notice Comments at 2.

[733] Tr. at 28:17-29:02 (June 5, 2014) (Sam Mosenkis, ASCAP).

[734] Modern Works Music Publishing Second Notice Comments at 6-7.
[735] ASCAP Second Notice Comments at 17.
[736] BMI Second Notice Comments at 15.
[737] Council of Music Creators First Notice Comments at 2-3.
[738] SCL First Notice Comments at 11.
[739] Music Choice First Notice Comments at 20.
[740] SGA First Notice Comments at 7.
[741] NSAI Second Notice Comments at 4.
[742] ASCAP and BMI also express displeasure with the analogous "through-to-the-audience" licenses required under the ASCAP and BMI consent decrees, where a party that procures a license from the PRO is able to authorize transmissions by additional distributors. *See* ASCAP Consent Decree § V; BMI Consent Decree § IX. Originally conceived to allow networks to obtain licenses that extend to downstream broadcasts by affiliates, the concept has been extended to online services such as YouTube that allow their video content to be shared and embedded on third-party websites that may be generating revenue through advertisements or otherwise. ASCAP First Notice Comments at 19. Per ASCAP, "a through-to-the-audience license request can give unfettered permission to a huge number of users without the benefit of full remuneration to music creators." *Id.* at 20.
[743] SGA First Notice Comments at 6-7. In recently promulgated regulations, the Copyright Office added a new requirement for section 115 licensees that requires them to break down royalty statements to indicate usage by third-party services, so copyright owners can at least see what is being reported to the section 115 licensee. 37 C.F.R. §§ 210.16-210.17.
[744] LaPolt Second Notice Comments at 11; *see also* NMPA &HFA First Notice Comments at 12 ("To the extent compulsory licensees pass through mechanical rights to a third-party digital music distributor and do not report who the third-party distributor is, songwriters and music publishers do not even know how their compositions are being used and cannot evaluate the accuracy of the compulsory licensees reporting."); Kohn First Notice Comments at 9 ("Passthrough licenses, at least insofar as they apply to digital transmission, should be eliminated.").
[745] RIAA Second Notice Comments at 19.
[746] *See, e.g.*, Daryl P. Friedman, *MusicBus Gaining Speed as Members of Congress Climb On*, GRAMMYNEWS (June 18, 2014), http://www.grammy.com/blogs/musicbus-gaining-speed-asmembers-of-congress-climb-on (noting support for omnibus legislation by Rep. Jerrold Nadler, Rep. Kevin McCarthy and Rep. Nancy Pelosi]).
[747] During the course of the study, the Office and others employed the term "platform parity" in referencing the concern that existing licensing policies have a disparate impact on different distribution platforms. The Office now adopts the broader term "licensing parity" in recognition of the fact that the current licensing framework also disparately impacts different classes of copyright owners and creators.
[748] NSAI, http://www.nashvillesongwriters.com (last visited Jan. 18, 2014).
[749] While synch uses by consumer video sites such as YouTube are not subject to compulsory licensing, the degree of copyright owner control with respect to sites featuring user-posted content is complicated by the safe harbor provisions of section 512, which limit such sites' liability for hosting the content.
[750] While the same argument can of course be made with respect to physical formats such as CDs and vinyl records—where labels also have the freedom to negotiate and publishers do not—in pursuing issues of fair compensation, stakeholders appear overwhelmingly to be concerned with digital, rather than physical, uses. Likely this is because they are looking to the future, and the future is digital. In addition, even though section 115 applies to both digital and physical uses, the licensing situation for physical goods is somewhat distinguishable. Most physical goods are in album format, and thus generate significantly higher mechanical revenues by virtue of their inclusion of multiple songs. Additionally, because the first use of a musical work is not subject to compulsory licensing, publishers have the right to demand a higher than statutory rate when licensing the original recording—at least in theory; for reasons that are not entirely clear, it appears that publishers almost never exercise this option. *See* RIAA First Notice Comments at 16 n.31 (stating that "the system should recognize the reality that songwriters and publishers have always chosen to license first uses at the same royalty rates as other recordings and allow that to happen by means of the same business processes."); *see also* Tr. at 251:07-252:04 (June 4, 2014) (Brittany Schaffer, NMPA/Loeb & Loeb LLP) (explaining that standard record agreement provisions, such as controlled composition clauses, often prevent publishers and songwriters from negotiating first use rates higher than the compulsory rate). Unlike in the digital realm, once the original recording is released by the record company, it is not nearly as common for third parties to seek a mechanical license to reproduce and distribute that same recording in a physical format. For these reasons—as well as the scant record before the Office concerning physical product—the Office believes that the question of whether the proposed opt-out right should extend to physical uses is perhaps best left for future consideration.
[751] Both digital music services and record companies have urged the Office to consider such an approach. DiMA First Notice Comments at 25 (noting that "[i]n an ideal world, services that require a combination of musical

work public performance rights, as well as reproduction and distribution rights under Section 115, would be able to acquire such rights from a single licensing source under a single statutory license and pay a single royalty to a common agent"); Spotify First Notice Comments at 10 (stating that "[a] licensing regime in which public performance rights and mechanical reproduction rights could be obtained from a single source or pursuant to a single license is an interesting idea and could in theory lead to efficiencies."); RIAA First Notice Comments at 16-17 (supporting single blanket license covering all rights in a song).

[752] If such an approach were adopted, some thought would need to be given as to whether and how a separate settlement would be accommodated on the part of the sound recording owners or musical work owners once the ratesetting aspect of the proceeding was underway.

[753] According to figures from the Radio Advertising Bureau, radio revenues have increased each year since 2009, when revenues were $16,029,000,000, to 2013, when revenues totaled $17,649,000,000—an increase of nearly 10%. *RAB Revenue Releases*, RADIO ADVERTISING BUREAU, http://www.rab.com/ public/pr/revpr.cfm?search=2013 &section=press (click on "Annual Radio Revenue Trends") (last visited Jan. 22, 2015).

[754] Although the Copyright Act exempts terrestrial performances of sound recordings, following recent judicial decisions in California and New York—which interpreted those states' laws as supporting a right of public performance to sound recording owners—it is not clear that over-the-air broadcasters enjoy a complete exemption under state law. *See Flo & Eddie v. Sirius XM CA*, 2014 U.S. Dist. LEXIS 139053; *Capitol Records, LLC v. Sirius XM Radio Inc.*, No. BC520981 (order regarding jury instruction); *Flo & Eddie v. Sirius XM NY*, 2014 U.S. Dist. LEXIS 166492. Although those cases were brought against digital providers, the courts' reasoning does not appear to be limited to digital performance rights.

[755] *See, e.g.*, *Performance Rights Act Hearing* (statement of Marybeth Peters, Register of Copyrights); *Ensuring Artists Fair Compensation Hearing* (statement of Marybeth Peters, Register of Copyrights); *Internet Streaming of Radio Hearing* at 8-22 (statement of David O. Carson, General Counsel, U.S. Copyright Office); PERFORMANCE RIGHTS REPORT.

[756] *See Public Performance Right for Sound Recordings*, FUTURE OF MUSIC COALITION (Nov. 5, 2013) https://www.futureofmusic.org/article/fact-sheet/public-performance-right-sound-recordings; A2IM First Notice Comments at 8; Modern Works Music Publishing First Notice Comments at 7; SoundExchange First Notice Comments at 16-17. Supporters of a more complete terrestrial sound recording performance right point out that the U.S. position on this is "in contrast to nearly every developed nation on the planet [with] notable exceptions includ[ing] Iran and North Korea." FMC First Notice Comments at 14; *see also The Register's Call for Updates Hearing* at 3 (statement of Rep. Melvin L. Watt).

[757] *The Register's Call for Updates Hearing* at 7 (statement of Maria A. Pallante, Register of Copyrights and Director, U.S. Copyright Office); Maria A. Pallante, *The Next Great Copyright Act*, 36 COLUM. J. L. & ARTS 315, 320-21 (2013).

[758] *The Register's Call for Updates Hearing* at 63 (statement of Maria A. Pallante, Register of Copyrights and Director, U.S. Copyright Office).

[759] NAB First Notice Comments at 29.

[760] Although the practice of "payola"—whereby record companies pay radio stations to play certain recordings—has been banned, labels still devote resources to encouraging broadcasters to perform their songs. *See* GAO REPORT at 50 (explaining that although "payola" has been formally outlawed unless the station announces any arrangements to play songs in exchange for consideration, it is common industry practice for record companies to employ independent promoters).

[761] Interestingly, despite the lack of legal recognition for such a right, there has been forward movement on this issue in the private marketplace. Media conglomerate iHeartMedia (formerly Clear Channel)—which offers both terrestrial and streamed radio—has entered into voluntary license agreements with WMG and a number of smaller record labels that cover both digital and terrestrial performance rights (with the digital rates apparently more favorable to iHeartMedia than those established by the CRB). *See* Christman, *Here's Why Warner Music's Deal with Clear Channel Could be Groundbreaking for the Future of the U.S. Music Biz (Analysis)*; Sisario, *Clear Channel-Warner Music Deal Rewrites the Rules on Royalties*. Reportedly, iHeartMedia was motivated to do this by it desire to have a more predictable cost structure to grow the digital side of its business. *Id.* Such a step may point to the potential for broader industry compromise on this issue.

[762] Tr. at 183:07-18 (June 24, 2014) (Jim Mahoney, A2IM) ("One only need to turn on Sirius XM and see the many stations that programmed fully with pre-1972 copyright songs, recordings and conclude that they still have value to listeners. They still want to hear those songs a lot. To programmers who program multiple stations there's a 40's station, a 50's station, a 60's station. There's classic rock, all the pre-1972 sound recordings. So, the public still values them, corporations still value them. They should still maintain a value for the recording artists.").

[763] Specifically, Congress directed the Office to discuss: "(1) the effect that federal protection would have with respect to the preservation of pre-1972 sound recordings; (2) the effect that federal protection would have with respect to providing public access to the recordings; and (3) the impact that federal protection would have on the economic interests of right holders of the recordings" and to provide appropriate recommendations. PRE-1972 SOUND RECORDINGS REPORT at vii.

[764] *Id.* at viii.

[765] *Id.* at ix-x.

[766] *See Flo & Eddie v. Sirius XM CA*, 2014 U.S. Dist. LEXIS 139053; *Capitol Records, LLC v. Sirius XM Radio Inc.*, No. BC520981 (order regarding jury instructions); *Flo & Eddie v. Sirius XM NY*, 2014 U.S. Dist. LEXIS 166492, *reconsideration denied*, 2014 U.S. Dist. LEXIS 174907.

[767] Paul Resnikoff, *What the pre-1972 Decision Really Means for the Future of Radio . . . .*, DIGITAL MUSICNEWS (Oct. 13, 2014), http://www.digitalmusicnews.com/permalink/2014/10/13/pre-1972 decision-really- means-future-radio-2 (noting pending litigation by Flo & Eddie (of the band The Turtles) against Sirius XM in Florida, in addition to suits in California and New York).

[768] RESPECT Act, H.R. 4772 § 2.

[769] *See* "Existing Ratesetting Framework" chart, Appendix D., for a depiction of the current ratesetting standards and bodies.

[770] 17 U.S.C. § 801(b)(1)(D).

[771] *See* SEA, H.R. 4079.

[772] *See* EMF First Notice Comments at 6, 8 n.14 (noting negotiated agreements are rare for webcasters, but noncommercial rates were successfully negotiated before a final decision in Digital Performance Right in Sound Recordings and Ephemeral Recordings, 76 Fed. Reg. 13,026 (Mar. 9, 2011)).

[773] Small Webcaster Settlement Act of 2002, Pub. L. No. 107-321, 116 Stat. 2780 (2002) (codified as amended at 17 U.S.C. § 114(f) (2010)); Webcaster Settlement Act of 2008, Pub. L. No. 110-435, 122 Stat. 4974 (2008) (codified as amended at 17 U.S.C. § 114(f) (2010)).

[774] 17 U.S.C. § 114(f)(3)(B).

[775] *Pandora Ratesetting*, 6 F. Supp. 3d at 353-54; *see also BMI v. DMX, Inc.*, 726 F. Supp. 2d 355, 356 (S.D.N.Y. 2010) (citing "well-established" reasonable fee approach to determine fair market value).

[776] *BMI v. DMX*, 683 F.3d at 45 n.14 (noting in both the ASCAP and BMI consent decree, the burden of proof is on the PRO to establish the reasonableness of the fee it seeks).

[777] *United States v. BMI*, 316 F. 3d 189, 194 (2d Cir. 2003) ("This determination [of whether a rate is reasonable] is often facilitated by the use of a benchmark—that is, reasoning by analogy to an agreement reached after arms' length negotiation between similarly situated parties."); *see ASCAP v. MobiTV*, 681 F. 3d at 82 ("In [setting a rate], the rate-setting court must take into account the fact that ASCAP, as a monopolist, exercises market-distorting power in negotiations for the use of its music.").

[778] Determination of Rates and Terms for Preexisting Subscription Services and Satellite Digital Audio Radio Services, 73 Fed. Reg. 4080, 4097 (Jan. 24, 2008).

[779] *See, e.g.*, DiMA First Notice Comments at 33-34 (noting relatively higher rates under the willing buyer/willing seller standard); NMPA & HFA First Notice Comments at 27 ("Pandora . . . paid 48% of its revenue to artists and labels using the willing buyer willing seller standard and only 4% of its revenue to publishers and songwriters using rates set by the rate court."); Spotify First Notice Comments at 7.

[780] *But see* Digital Performance Right in Sound Recordings and Ephemeral Recordings, 72 Fed. Reg. 24,084, 24,094-95 (May 1, 2007) (musical work benchmark rejected as being "flawed" for sound recordings because the sellers are different and selling different rights, use of the benchmark would ignore the different investments and incentives of the each seller, and the record contained ample empirical evidence that the markets are not necessarily equivalent); *Pandora Ratesetting*, 6 F. Supp. 3d at 333, 366-67 (court declined to use royalty rates for sound recordings as a benchmark, explaining, "[t]he disparity between rates for the public performance of compositions versus sound recordings does not exist for most of ASCAP's revenue streams since . . . the need to acquire sound recording licenses only applies to services who conduct digital audio transmissions[,]" for those digital audio transmissions, whose rates are set by the CRB, there is a "statutory prohibition on considering sound recording rates in setting a rate for a license for public performance of a musical work" and otherwise "the record is devoid of any principled explanation given . . . why the rate for sound recording rights should dictate any change in the rate for composition rights.").

[781] As expressed in section 114, the willing buyer/willing seller standard includes consideration of several specific factors, including these. *See* 17 U.S.C. § 114(f)(2)(B).

[782] Notably, in the deliberations leading to the adoption of the 1976 Act, then Register of Copyrights Abraham L. Kaminstein recommended elimination of the section 115 compulsory license, concluding that the underlying concerns about a publisher monopoly were no longer relevant. *See* GENERAL REVISION OF COPYRIGHT REPORT at 36. Publishers did not ultimately pursue that opportunity, however, instead agreeing to maintain the compulsory license in exchange for a statutory rate hike from 2 to 2.75 cents per use. *See Music Licensing Reform Hearing* (statement of Marybeth Peters, Register of Copyrights); S. REP.NO. 94-473, at 88-92.

[783] Outside of the copyright context, rare instances of government price-fixing involve commodities, not differentiated goods. The Federal Energy Regulatory Commission conducts a ratesetting process for interstate transmission of electricity and natural gas, *see* 16 U.S.C. §§ 824d, 824e, 15 U.S.C. §§ 717c, 717d, and the United States Department of Agriculture issues federal milk marketing orders that set minimum (not maximum) prices for the sale of milk in most regions of the United States, *see* 7 U.S.C. § 608c(5).

[784] 17 U.S.C. §§ 111, 119, 122; *see also* U.S. COPYRIGHT OFFICE, SATELLITE TELEVISION EXTENSION AND LOCALISM ACT: § 302 REPORT 129-40 (2011), *available at* http://www.copyright.gov/reports/ section302-report.pdf ("STELA REPORT") (recommending ways in which the cable and satellite compulsory retransmission licenses might be phased out).

[785] *See* 47 U.S.C. § 325.

[786] *BMI v. CBS*, 441 U.S. at 23-25 (holding that the blanket license should be subject to rule of reason analysis and remanding to lower courts to apply that analysis); *CBS v. ASCAP*, 620 F.2d at 932 (on remand from Supreme Court, sustaining blanket license under rule of reason analysis because CBS had failed to prove the non-availability of alternatives to the blanket license); *Buffalo Broad. v. ASCAP*, 744 F.2d at 926-32 (sustaining blanket license under rule of reason analysis in context of local television stations*)*.

[787] U.S. DOJ, ANTITRUST DIV., ANTITRUST DIV.MANUAL III 146-47 (5th ed. 2014), *available at* http:// www.justice.gov/atr/public/divisionmanual/atrdivman.pdf.

[788] *Id.* (explaining that the DOJ's adoption of a policy that favors sunset provisions was "based on a judgment that perpetual decrees were not in the public interest"). In addition to policy concerns, there may be some interesting due process questions concerning the length of the consent decrees.

[789] Press Release, U.S. DOJ, Antitrust Div., Antitrust Division Announces New Streamlined Procedure for Parties Seeking to Modify or Terminate Old Settlements and Litigated Judgments (Mar. 28, 2014), *available at* http://www.justice.gov/atr/public/press_releases/2014/304744.pdf (noting that "[s]ince 1980, there have been significant changes in markets and technology and substantial changes in antitrust law").

[790] *Id.*

[791] Interestingly, the Office heard considerably less about the market power of large technology companies or other dominant distributors of music and whether that poses similar concerns. *But see, e.g.*, MMF & FAC Second Notice Comments at 21-22 (noting the "market power of a few tech giants").

[792] *See* U.S. DOJ & FTC, ANTITRUST ENFORCEMENT AND INTELLECTUAL PROPERTY RIGHTS: PROMOTING INNOVATION AND COMPETITION 110 (2007), *available at* http://www.justice.gov/atr/ public/hearings/ip/222655.pdf ("ANTITRUST ENFORCEMENT AND IP RIGHTS REPORT") ("Whether the legal analysis applied to intellectual property bundling is some form of the per se rule or the more searching rule of reason, a plaintiff will have to establish that a defendant has market power in the tying product."); *cf. Illinois Tool Works Inc. v. Indep. Ink, Inc.*, 547 U.S. 28, 42-43 (2006) (explaining the following about tying arrangement involving patented products: "While some such arrangements are still unlawful, such as those that are the product of a true monopoly or a market wide conspiracy, . . . that conclusion must be supported by proof of power in the relevant market rather than by a mere presumption thereof."); *see also* HERBERT HOVENKAMP, FEDERAL ANTITRUST POLICY: THE LAW OF COMPETITION AND ITS PRACTICE 2 (4th ed. 2011) ("An important goal of antitrust law-arguably its only goal—is to ensure that markets are competitive.").

[793] *See, e.g.*, Farrell Malone & J. Gregory Sidak, *Should Antitrust Consent Decrees Regulate Post-Merger Pricing?*, 3 J. COMPETITION L. & ECON. 471, 477 (2007) (explaining that, in expressing its preference for structural remedies over conduct remedies in situations involving anticompetitive merger, the DOJ "explicitly criticizes price agreements as a component of consent decrees" and that the "[DOJ] disfavors using consent decrees to fix a price or an allowable range of prices for the post-merger firm"); *see also* HERBERTHOVENKAMP,MARK D. JANIS,MARK A. LEMLEY & CHRISTOPHER R. LESLIE, IP AND ANTITRUST: AN ANALYSIS OF ANTITRUST PRINCIPLES APPLIED TO INTELLECTUAL PROPERTY LAW 22-62 (2d ed. Supp. 2013) ("As a general matter, antitrust should not favor solutions that turn the federal courts into price control agencies.").

[794] Dickey, *Taylor Swift on 1989, Spotify, Her Next Tour and Female Role Model* (quoting Taylor Swift: "I think that people should feel that there is a value to what musicians have created, and that's that.") *see* Mitchell Peters, *Big Machine's Scott Borchetta Explains Why Taylor Swift Was Removed From Spotify*, BILLBOARD (Nov. 8, 2014), http://www.billboard.com/articles/news/6312143/bigmachine-scott-borchetta-explains- taylor-swift-1989-removal-from-spotify-nikki-sixx (quoting Big Machine Label Group CEO Scott Borchetta: "We determined that her fan base is so in on her, let's pull everything off of Spotify, and any other service that doesn't offer a premium service . . . Now if you are a premium subscriber to Beats or Rdio or any of the other services that don't offer just a free-only, then you will find her catalogue."); Bogursky, *Taylor Swift, Garth Brooks and other artists lead the fight against Spotify*.

[795] Gardner, *Pharrell Williams' Lawyer to YouTube: Remove Our Songs or Face $1 Billion Lawsuit*.

[796] Notably, Swift's sound recordings are not subject to compulsory licensing when used for interactive services, and GMR's clients—who are not represented by ACSCAP or BMI—have asserted rights not covered by the consent decrees.

[797] RIAA First Notice Comments at 30 n.43; *see also Find a Music Service*, WHYMUSICMATTERS.COM, http://whymusicmatters.com/find-music (last visited Feb. 2, 2015) (listing licensed music services).

[798] For example, in a 2011 study conducted by the Copyright Office, cable and satellite operators operating under the section 111, 119 and 122 compulsory licenses expressed strong opposition to the possibility of phasing them out. STELA REPORT at 8.

[799] ANTITRUST ENFORCEMENT AND IP RIGHTS REPORT at 2.

[800] *In re Pandora*, 2013 WL 5211927, at *11; *BMI v. Pandora*, 2013 WL 6697788, at *5.

[801] "New media" services are those available by means of the internet, a wireless mobile telecommunications network, and/or a computer network. *In re Pandora*, 2013 WL 5211927, at *2; *BMI v. Pandora*, 2013 WL 6697788, at *2.

[802] To some degree, the move to withdraw was also likely spurred by technological evolution. Unlike traditional media such as broadcast radio stations, digital providers are equipped to track and report each use of a musical work (for example, each time a song is streamed to an individual subscriber) and thus provide full census reporting to a copyright owner. When such census reporting is available, there is no need for an intermediary organization such as a PRO to survey or sample the service to allocate royalty payments among songwriters; a publisher has the means to allocate the royalties itself. Thus, it is more feasible for the publisher to self-administer a directly negotiated license.

[803] *Pandora Ratesetting*, 6 F. Supp. 3d at 330, 339-40, 355.

[804] *In re Pandora*, 2013 WL 5211927, at *11; *BMI v. Pandora*, 2013 WL 6697788, at *5.

[805] Christman, *First-Quarter Music Publishing Rankings: SONGS Surges Again*.

[806] *See id.*

[807] *See* Sisario, *Pandora Suit May Upend Century-Old Royalty Plan*.

[808] *See Meredith Corp.*, 1 F. Supp. 3d 180; *RMLC v. SESAC*, 29 F. Supp. 3d 487.

[809] *See* Memorandum of Law in Support of Plaintiffs' Unopposed Motion for Preliminary Approval of Settlement 1-2, *Meredith Corp. v. SESAC, LLC*, 1 F. Supp. 3d 180 (S.D.N.Y. 2014) (No. 09-cv-9177); *Meredith Corp. v. SESAC, LLC*, No. 09-cv-9177 (S.D.N.Y. Oct. 31, 2014) (order granting preliminary approval of settlement).

[810] *See, e.g.*, SGA First Notice Comments at 8-9.

[811] MMF & FAC Second Notice Comments at 46 (reproducing the "MMF Public response to the Sony/ATV Statement").

[812] *Pandora Ratesetting*, 6 F. Supp. 3d at 353-54, 372.

[813] *Id.* at 333, 366.

[814] 17 U.S.C. § 114(i) provides that "[l]icense fees payable for the public performance of sound recordings . . . shall not be taken into account in any . . . proceeding to set or adjust the royalties payable to copyright owners of musical works for the public performance of their works."

[815] *Pandora Ratesetting*, 6 F. Supp. 3d at 360-61

[816] *Id.* at 345-46, 361.

[817] *Id.* at 357-58.

[818] *Id.* at 347.

[819] *Id.* at 369.

[820] *See* Ed Christman, *Sony/ATV Makes Organized Catalog Available Online*, BILLBOARD (July 16, 2014), http://www.billboard.com/biz/articles/news/publishing/6157855/sonyatv-makesorganized-catalog-available-online; Ed Christman, *UMPG to Make Entire Database Easier for Licensees*, BILLBOARD (June 27, 2014), http://www.billboard.com/biz/articles/news/publishing/ 6140985/umpg-to-make- entire-database-easier-for-licensees.

[821] *See* EPSTEIN at 36 (concluding that "there is no comparative advantage in using a judicial body as opposed to some administrative agency" for ratesetting).

[822] ASCAP and BMI also seek to have rate disputes decided outside of federal court. Both have recommended some sort of system of (apparently private) arbitration without providing much detail. ASCAP First Notice Comments at 4, 23-24 (recommending "expedited private arbitration"); Music Licensing Hearings at 52(statement of Michael O'Neill, CEO, BMI) ("We believe that replacing the current rate court with arbitration in New York under the American Arbitration Association rules would be a faster, less expensive, and a more market-responsive mechanism for all parties to obtain fair, market-value rate decisions."). For the reasons discussed above, the Office believes the CRB is the logical venue to determine public performance rates. As an added benefit, the CRB does not depend upon the payment of private arbitration fees (a significant factor in the demise of the CARPs that preceded the CRB). *See* H.R. REP. NO. 108-408, at 21, 99-100. At the same time, based on stakeholders' input, the Office is recommending certain changes to the CRB system, which are outlined below.

[823] SEA, H.R. 4079; SEA, S. 2321, 113th Cong. (2014).

[824] *Pandora Ratesetting*, 6 F. Supp. 3d at 366-67.

[825] The Office does not believe that the fact that the limitation was originally proposed by musical work owners, even if ill-conceived, is a sufficient basis to determine it should continue in effect.

[826] *See* ASCAP Consent Decree § IX.E; BMI Consent Decree § XIV.A.

[827] ASCAP First Notice Comments at 15-16; BMI First Notice Comments at 16-17.

[828] *See also, e.g.*, MMF & FAC Second Notice Comments at 10 ("As far as we know most of the societies in the EU require potential licensees to provide important financial and operational data (and in the case of a startup, their business projections, and projected user numbers) when making their application. To us this seems sound common sense and, coupled with an ability by societies to require an interim payment, would rebalance the negotiating process more fairly.").

[829] See BMI Antitrust Consent Decree Review Comments at 20-21. The ASCAP consent decree requires that the court set an interim rate within 90 days of a request. See ASCAP Antitrust Consent Decree Review Comments at 12.

[830] See ASCAP Antitrust Consent Decree Review Comments at 14 n.20; BMI Antitrust Consent Decree Review Comments at 21.

[831] The proposed opt-out right would be by publisher, not by individual work.

[832] As discussed above, the concept of MROs was proposed by former Register Marybeth Peters in testimony before Congress in 2005. *Copyright Office Views on Music Licensing Reform Hearing* at 2136 (statement of Marybeth Peters, Register of Copyrights).

[833] This option could also help to alleviate concerns about the status of non-U.S. writers affiliated with foreign PROs if the U.S. publisher of their works chooses to pursue partial withdrawal.

[834] *See* Mechanical and Digital Phonorecord Delivery Rate Determination Proceeding, 74 Fed. Reg. at 4531-32 (setting forth the CRB's proposed regulations that established the rates and terms for the use of musical works in limited downloads, interactive streaming and incidental digital phonorecord deliveries); *see also* Compulsory License for Making and Distributing Phonorecords, Including Digital Phonorecord Deliveries, 73 Fed. Reg. 66,173, 66,180 (adopting rule that permitted server and other copies necessary to certain streaming processes to be licensed under section 115).

[835] *See Copyright Office Views on Music Licensing Reform Hearing* at 6 (statement of Marybeth Peters, Register of Copyrights).

[836] *See, e.g., id.* at 62 (statement of NMPA) ("[W]e believe the Copyright Office proposal is fatally flawed and would be harmful to songwriters and music publishers.").

[837] Such a unified licensing model has been in effect for 17 years in the United Kingdom. *Our History*, PRSFORMUSIC, http://www.prsformusic.com/aboutus/ourorganisation/ourhistory/Pages/ default.aspx (last visited Jan. 22, 2015).

[838] The U.K.'s unified licensing system may provide a helpful model in this regard. PRS for Music was created by joining together the U.K. Performing Right Society ("PRS") and the Mechanical Copyright Protection Society ("MCPS"). For royalties received under its unified licenses, the PRS for Music distribution committee determines various splits between PRS and MCPS depending upon the type of use, which allocations are subject to ratification by the PRS and MCPS boards. *PRS Distribution Policy Rules*, PRSFORMUSIC, http://www.prsformusic.com/creators/memberresources/Documents/Distribution %20policy/Distribution%20 Policy%20Rules%20as% 20at%20November%202014.pdf (last visited Jan. 22, 2015). Out of those splits, 100% of mechanical royalties are paid to the publisher, while performance royalties are split 50/50 between writer and publisher unless an alternate division of royalties is specified. *Music Registration Policy*, PRSFORMUSIC, http://www.prsformusic.com/creators/memberresources/how_it_works/musicregpolicy/ Pages/musicregpolicy.aspx (last visited Jan. 22, 2015).

[839] *See* ASCAP Second Notice Comments at 23.

[840] Ed Christman, *NMPA Puts U.S. Publishing Revenues at $2.2 Billion Annually*, BILLBOARD (June 11, 2014), http://www.billboard.com/biz/articles/news/publishing/6114215/nmpa-puts-uspublishing-revenues -at-22-billion-annually.

[841] Although three record companies dominate, independent record labels enhance the market with a rich variety of content, including well-known hit recordings. A2IM First Notice Comments at 1 ("Billboard Magazine, using Nielsen SoundScan data, identified the Independent music label sector as 34.6 percent of the music industry's U.S. recorded music sales market in 2013."). Many independent labels are represented by organizations that aggregate repertoire for collective licensing, such as the U.K.-based Merlin, which issues licenses to digital services such as YouTube and Spotify on a global basis. *Merlin Strikes Licensing Deal with YouTube*, MERLIN (Oct. 19, 2011), http://www.merlinnetwork.org/news/post/ merlin-strikes-licensing-deal-with-youtube.

[842] In recent years, as with recorded music, there has been significant consolidation in the music publishing industry, such that the three major publishers now represent some 63% of the market—approaching the record company figure of 65%. *See* Christman, *First-Quarter Music Publishing Rankings: SONGS Surges Again*; Bruce Houghton, *Indie Labels Now Control 34.6% Of U.S. Market*, HypeBot (Jan. 16, 2014), http://www.hypebot .com/hypebot/2014/01/indie-labels-nowcontrol-346-of-us-market.html.

[843] *See, e.g*, PASSMAN at 304-05 (explaining that "[t]rue co-administration" deals, in which all parties retain the right to administer their own share of a composition, are among the most common arrangements for songs co-owned by publishers of approximately equal status).

[844] *Information*, SPOTIFY, https://press.spotify.com/us/information/ (last visited Jan. 22, 2015).

[845] IPAC First Notice Comments at 6 ("Owners of musical works are sympathetic to those entities that need an efficient process by which to obtain licenses for musical works. In that regard, IPAC supports the creation of one or more licensing agencies to negotiate fair market license rates and grant licenses on behalf of the copyright owners of the musical works on a blanket license or individual song basis."); NMPA First Notice Comments at 18 ("Compulsory licensing is not needed to achieve the efficiency of bundled licenses . . . the only thing stopping performance rights organizations such as ASCAP and BMI from offering a bundle of

reproduction, performance, and distribution rights from songwriters/publishers willing to appoint them as their agents for such rights are outdated consent decrees.").

[846] The category of downloads includes both permanent downloads and limited downloads. While permanent downloads are available to the purchaser indefinitely, limited downloads can be accessed for only a limited period of time or limited number of plays. 37 C.F.R. § 385.11. Download uses also include ringtones, for which a separate rate has been established under section 115. 37 C.F.R. § 385.3; *see also* Mechanical and Digital Phonorecord Delivery Rate Adjustment Proceeding, 71 Fed. Reg. at 64,316 (setting forth the Copyright Office's 2006 Memorandum Opinion concluding ringtones qualify as DPDs).

[847] *See United States v. ASCAP*, 627 F.3d 64, 68 (2d. Cir. 2010) (holding that downloading a digital music file over the internet does not constitute a public performance of the work embodied in that file); *In re Cellco Partnership*, 663 F. Supp. 2d 363, 374 (S.D.N.Y. 2009) (holding that downloading a ringtone to a cellular phone does not in and of itself constitute a public performance of a musical work). Also note that musical work owners do not collect mechanical royalties for noninteractive streaming uses subject to section 112 and 114 statutory licensing. *See* NMPA First Notice Comments at 24; Mechanical and Digital Phonorecord Delivery Rate Determination Proceeding, 74 Fed. Reg. at 4513.

[848] Although physical products, such as CDs and vinyl records, also fall into this category, stakeholder concerns have focused far less on the physical marketplace, which (despite a recent increase in the niche market of vinyl records) continues to decline. As noted above, the Office believes that the question of opt-out rights for physical product could be deferred for future consideration.

[849] As noted above, at least for the time being, the Office believes that opt-out rights for publishers should be by publisher, not by individual work. Thus, opt-out publishers would be responsible for their entire catalog.

[850] In contrast to performance rights, songwriter agreements do not assume that the writer's share of mechanical royalties will flow through a PRO. Accordingly, while it may be a matter worthy of further discussion, the Office is not now suggesting that songwriters should have the right to redirect their mechanical shares through a chosen MRO.

[851] Some publishers could opt out only to find that the licensee declined to pursue individual negotiations with them. For this reason, it seems it would be useful to have some sort of mechanism for such a rightsowner to reverse its opt-out and return to the collective system if it wished.

[852] 17 U.S.C. § 115(a)(1).

[853] *Id.* § 115(a)(2).

[854] *See, e.g.*, Dina LaPolt and Steven Tyler, Comments Submitted to the Department of Commerce's Green Paper on Copyright Policy, Creativity, and Innovation in the Digital Economy, at 2 (Feb. 10, 2014), *available at* http://www.uspto.gov/ip/global/copyrights/lapolt_and_ tyler_comment_paper_02-10-14.pdf (objecting to a compulsory remix license). This perspective was voiced by a number of prominent artists in response to a suggestion to consider a new licensing framework for remixes that has been put forth by USPTO and NTIA as part of the "Green Paper" process of the Internet Policy Task Force. *See* GREEN PAPER; Steve Knopper, *Don Henley, Steven Tyler Condemn Potential Copyright Law Change*, ROLLING STONE (Feb. 13, 2014), http://www.rollingstone.com/music/news/don-henley-steven-tyler-condemn-potential-copyrightlaw-change-20140213. The Green Paper suggestion—motivated by a desire to facilitate the reuse of creative works—would extend to music. *See* GREEN PAPER at 28-29 (citing concerns about music sampling). Various commenters addressed the Green Paper suggestion in their comments to the Copyright Office. Because it is not a Copyright Office initiative, this report does not address the remix issue other than to note that, based on the comments submitted to the Office, it appears to have drawn opposition within the music community. *See, e.g.*, CCC Second Notice Comments at 3; LaPolt First Notice Comments at 15; NMPA & HFA Second Notice Comments at 37-38. *But see* Menell First Notice Comments at 3 (advocating for the creation of a compulsory license for remixes). The Office hopes that this report will prove useful to the USPTO and NTIA in their evaluation of the remix issue as it relates to music.

[855] Tr. at 155:16-17 (June 4, 2014) (Steven Marks, RIAA); *see also* Glenn Chapman, *YouTube debuts subscription music service*, YAHOONEWS (Nov. 12, 2014) http://news.yahoo.com/youtube-debutssubscription- music-video-190223540.html ("YouTube is the world's biggest online source of free streaming music and the site has about a billion users a month.").

[856] RIAA First Notice Comments at 10 ("The record company responsible for one current, successful release obtained 1481 licenses for the project.").

[857] The labels are not proposing to extend any synch licensing solution to uses in "third-party created product[s]," such as in advertisements and television, which have always required individualized negotiations with both labels and publishers. *See id.* at 17.

[858] *See* NMPA Second Notice Comments at 32-33 ("The RIAA rationalizes this approach by claiming a total abdication of approval rights by musical work owners combined with expanding the scope of formats authorized under Sec. 115 would promote greater efficiency and would simplify the music licensing process. With an Orwellian spin, they promote the idea that musical work owners would be enriched if they are, ultimately, disempowered in the digital music marketplace."); NSAI Second Notice Comments at 8 ("While the concept of a more efficient licensing system is something everyone agrees on, the RIAA proposal would

basically eliminate the ability of music publishers or self-published songwriters and composers to initiate or directly negotiate their own agreements."). Interestingly, just a few years ago, the publishers were of a somewhat different mindset, with NMPA advocating for a blanket-style license to cover synch uses by YouTube and similar services: "If we don't . . . figure out a way to do mass synchronizations, we are going to miss out on many business opportunities that could provide solutions to the declining fortunes of the whole music industry." David Israelite, *David Israelite, NMPA President's Guest Post: Why Music Publishers Must Adopt Blanket Licensing*, BILLBOARD (June 24, 2011), http://www.billboard.com/biz/articles/news/publishing/1177339/david-israelite-nmpapresidents-guest-post-why-music-publishers.

[859] RIAA First Notice Comments at 6, 10.

[860] For example, in 2012 NMPA negotiated a licensing framework with UMG to permit independent publishers to grant UMG the synch rights necessary to stream videos containing their works on VEVO and YouTube. *See* NMPA Second Notice Comments at 33; Butler, *UMG/NMPA Broker Model License Agreement*; Christman, *NMPA Inks Deal With Universal Music Group Over VEVO, YouTube Videos*.

[861] In this regard, however, it is worth noting that independent publishers had to pursue an infringement action against YouTube before YouTube presented them with a licensing offer under a settlement negotiated by NMPA. *See Football Ass'n Premier League v. YouTube*, 633 F. Supp. 2d 159.

[862] *See* SIRA, H.R. 5553. In 2006, the House Judiciary Committee's Subcommittee on Courts, the Internet, and Intellectual Property forwarded SIRA to the full Judiciary Committee by unanimous voice vote. *See H.R. 5553*, CONGRESS.GOV (June 8, 2006), https://www.congress.gov/bill/109thcongress/house-bill/5553.

[863] Notably, section 115 has, since its inception, provided a mechanism to file a notice of intent to use a musical work with the Copyright Office if the owner of the work cannot be found in Copyright Office records. *See* 17 U.S.C. § 115(b)(1). Under section 115, no royalties are required to be collected by the Office in connection with these filings. *See id.* It is the Office's understanding, however, that this provision does little to ameliorate concerns of digital services in light of the filing fees that the Office must charge to administer such song-by-song notices, which may number in the thousands or perhaps even the millions for a large service. *See* DiMA First Notice Comments at 20 ("[T]o the extent that a service chooses to file statutory license notices with the Copyright Office for the many musical works for which the relevant rightsowners cannot be identified, the costs can be overwhelming given the volume of works at issue."). Under its current fee schedule, the Office charges a fee of $75 for a notice of intention covering a single title, and for notices incorporating additional titles, a fee of $20 per 10 additional titles submitted on paper, and $10 per 100 additional titles submitted electronically. 37 C.F.R. § 201.3(e). Moreover, due to IT constraints within the Library of Congress, the Office is still not able to accept such submissions in bulk electronic form.

[864] Although publishers traditionally have not sought royalties for the server and other reproductions necessary to facilitate noninteractive streaming, it would probably be helpful to clarify the law to provide that any necessary mechanical rights were covered as part of a bundled license. *Cf.* Compulsory License for Making and Distributing Phonorecords, Including Digital Phonorecord Deliveries, 73 Fed. Reg. at 66,180-81 ("[I]f phonorecords are delivered by a transmission service, then under the last sentence of 115(d) it is irrelevant whether the transmission that created the phonorecords is interactive or non-interactive.").

[865] A section 115 license is only available after phonorecords of the work in question have first been distributed to the public in the United States under the authority of the copyright owner. 17 U.S.C. § 115(a)(1). The Office is not recommending any change to this aspect of the statutory system, which permits musical work owners to control the so-called "first use" (or initial recording) of their works.

[866] These categories include: physical phonorecords and permanent digital downloads (*see* 37 C.F.R. § 385.3(a)); ringtones (*see* 37 C.F.R. § 385.3(b)); five compensation models for services offering interactive streams and limited downloads (*see* 37 C.F.R. § 385.13(a)); three types of promotional activities involving interactive streams and limited downloads (*see* 37 C.F.R. § 385.14(b)-(d)); mixed service bundles, music bundles, limited offerings, paid locker services, and purchased content locker services (*see* 37 C.F.R. § 385.23(a)); and free trial periods for certain service offerings (*see* 37 C.F.R. § 385.24).

[867] Section 115 already recognizes that a voluntary agreement can supersede the statutory rate. 17 U.S.C. § 115(c)(3)(E)(i). As a practical matter, however, while voluntary rates for uses subject to mandatory licensing may be lower, they will not exceed the statutorily fixed rate because the user may always resort to the compulsory process.

[868] Of course, this was the concept pursued by the publishers who withdrew from ASCAP and BMI to negotiate separate rates with Pandora. There, as explained above, the court rejected two of the proffered benchmarks due to what it viewed as coercive conduct on the part of the publishers in the negotiation process. The CRB, too, is free to reject benchmarks that it perceives to be unreasonable or otherwise without merit. *Music Choice v. Copyright Royalty Board*, Nos. 131174, 13-1183, 2014 WL 7234800, at *7 (D.C. Cir. Dec. 19, 2014) ("The [CRJs] were within their broad discretion to discount [SoundExchange's proposed] benchmarks and look elsewhere for guidance," as the CRJs' "mandate to issue determinations . . . does not hamstring the Judges when neither party proposes reasonable or comparable benchmarks."). Copyright owners would of course need to ensure that they proceeded carefully and independently in their dealings with licensees so as not to undermine the value of their agreements for ratesetting purposes.

[869] *See, e.g.*, Castle First Notice Comments at 2-3; NMPA & HFA First Notice Comments at 14-15.

[870] In a notable departure from the terms of section 115, HFA, which licenses mechanical rights on behalf of numerous publishers, does not rely upon the submission of certified annual statements but instead conducts royalty examinations of significant licensees to verify their payments.

[871] By contrast, the section 111 and 119 cable and satellite compulsory licenses, as well as the Audio Home Recording Act ("AHRA"), provide for a royalty verification process for the benefit of copyright owners. *See* 17 U.S.C. §§ 111(d)(6) (cable licensees); 119(b)(2) (satellite licensees); 1003(c)(2) (manufacturers of digital audio recording devices and media).

[872] 17 U.S.C. § 114(f)(4)(A).

[873] 37 C.F.R. §§ 380.6, 380.15, 380.25.

[874] 17 U.S.C. § 115(c)(3)(D).

[875] In light of the Office's primary responsibility under the existing section 115 framework for determining the requirements for statements of account, it may be sensible to assign rulemaking responsibility for audits of these statements to the Office rather than the CRB. *See* 17 U.S.C. § 115(c)(5); 17 U.S.C. § 803(c)(3) (CRBs may specify recordkeeping requirements as part of a ratesetting determination); *see also* Division of Authority Between the Copyright Royalty Judges and the Register of Copyrights under the Section 115 Statutory License, 73 Fed. Reg. 48,396 (Aug. 19, 2008) (explaining responsibilities of the Office versus the CRB in this area).

[876] It appears that currently, PROs do not have any significant audit rights, compelling them to accept "payments at best-effort levels and face value, but not necessarily accurate." Derek Crownover, *Small Music Publishers Face Uphill Battle*, THE TENNESSEAN (Aug. 14, 2014), http://www.tennessean.com/story/money/industries/music/2014/08/15/small-music-publishersface-uphill-battle/14075783/. In fact, the ASCAP consent decree merely suggests that ASCAP "may require its . . . licensees to provide ASCAP with all information reasonably necessary to administer the per-program or per-segment license," while the BMI consent decree has no such requirement. ASCAP Consent Decree § VIII.C; BMI Consent Decree.

[877] Publishers who had negotiated direct licenses with digital providers would be responsible for managing their own audits in keeping with their individual contracts.

[878] *See* 37 C.F.R. § 201.30 (setting forth the procedure for verification of statements of account submitted by cable operators and satellite carriers).

[879] *See* ASCAP Consent Decree § IV.D (ASCAP is prohibited from "[g]ranting any license to any music user for rights of public performance in excess of five years' duration."). This restriction is not found in the BMI Consent Decree, although the Office understands that BMI's licensing practices tend to track ASCAP's in this regard, perhaps due to the fact that "the DOJ often takes the view that BMI and ASCAP should operate under similar rules." BMI First Notice Comments at 16. It is the Office's further understanding that such licenses may be subject to automatic extensions unless terminated by either the PRO or licensee.

[880] Notably, because HFA licenses incorporate the key aspects of section 115, they too are subject to the periodic statutory rate adjustments.

[881] Section 114 provides that 45% of royalties are to be paid to the featured artist, 2.5% to the union that represents nonfeatured musicians, and 2.5% to the union for nonfeatured vocalists, with the remaining 50% paid to the owner of the sound recording, typically a record label. 17 U.S.C. § 114(g)(2).

[882] SoundExchange First Notice Comments at 4.

[883] 37 C.F.R. § 380.8.

[884] Press Release, SoundExchange, SoundExchange Releases List of Recording Artists and Record Labels with Unclaimed Digital Performance Royalties (Aug. 15, 2012), http://www.soundexchange.com/pr/soundexchange-releases-list-of-recording-artists-and-record-labels-withunclaimed-digital-performance-royalties/. SoundExchange recently reallocated $9.3 million from its unclaimed royalty pool to its administrative fund. Glenn Peoples, *SoundExchange Finally Releases Old, Unclaimed Royalties*, BILLBOARD (Jan. 31, 2014), http://www.billboard.com/biz/ articles/news/ 5893782/soundexchange-finally-releases-old-unclaimed-royalties.

[885] *See* Glenn Peoples, *SoundExchange Paid Out a Whopping $773 Million in 2014*, BILLBOARD (Jan. 29, 2015), http://www.billboard.com/articles/business/6457827/soundexchange-digitalperformance-royalty-distributions-2014.

[886] *See* FMC First Notice Comments at 11-12; Kohn First Notice Comments at 13-14; SAG-AFTRA & AFM First Notice Comments at 6; *see also* A2IM First Notice Comments at 5 (supporting a narrower definition of "interactive").

[887] *See* Tr. at 138:19-139:09 (June 4, 2014) (Lee Knife, DiMA) ("The idea that we [DiMA services] have to go to all of these different people, depending on whether you're interactive, you're noninteractive, whether you're downloading, whether you're streaming it and the download is available to be heard while it's downloading . . . most of my services want to or do engage in all of those different activities at once. We'd love to be able to just get a license for music and simply report what the type of use was and pay for it.").

[888] 17 U.S.C. § 114(j)(7).

[889] *Launch Media*, 578 F.3d at 164.

[890] *See* RIAA First Notice Comments at 33-34; SAG-AFTRA & AFM First Notice Comments at 5-6; *see also* NARAS First Notice Comments at 5; NAB First Notice Comments at 4; NRBMLC First Notice Comments at 24; NPR First Notice Comments at 5; SRN Broadcasting First Notice Comments at 1.

[891] RIAA First Notice Comments at 34.

[892] *See, e.g., id.* ("While, at this juncture, we do not necessarily advocate excluding from the statutory license services that have been generally accepted as operating within the statutory license based on the [*Launch Media*] decision, we do think it is important, at a minimum, that services offering more functionality, such as personalization features, should pay higher rates.").

[893] *See* 17 U.S.C. § 114(f)(1)(A)-(2)(A) (rates and terms "shall distinguish among different types of . . . services in operation"); *id.* § 803(c)(3) (CRB's determination to be supported by written record).

[894] *See* NAB First Notice Comments at 4; NRBMLC First Notice Comments at 24; NPR First Notice Comments at 5; SRN Broadcasting First Notice Comments at 1.

[895] 17 U.S.C. § 114(j)(13).

[896] 17 U.S.C. § 114 (d)(2)(C)(ii). *See, e.g.,* NAB First Notice Comments at 4-5; NRBMLC First Notice Comments at 24; NPR First Notice Comments at 5; SRN Broadcasting First Notice Comments at 1.

[897] *See* H.R. REP. No. 104-274, at 13-15, 20-21.

[898] CTIA First Notice Comments at 16-18; NAB First Notice Comments at 2, 7; Music Choice First Notice Comments at 11-13; DiMA Second Notice Comments at 18.

[899] Section 112(e) somewhat cryptically indicates that only a single phonorecord (i.e., server copy) can be made "unless the terms and conditions of the statutory license allow for more." 17 U.S.C. § 112(e).

[900] A larger question may be whether the provisions of the section 112 license pertaining to the copies made to support section 114 services should be folded into section 114 to create a truly unified license covering both performances and necessary reproduction rights. As it currently stands, the CRB is obligated in the relevant ratesetting proceedings to set a separate (and in practice, essentially nominal) rate for the ephemeral uses. *See* 17 U.S.C. § 112(e)(3); *SoundExchange, Inc. v. Librarian of Congress*, 571 F.3d 1220, 1225-26 (D.C. Cir. 2009) (remanding to the CRB to specify a royalty for the use of the ephemeral recordings); Determination of Rates and Terms for Preexisting Subscription Services and Satellite Digital Audio Radio Services, 75 Fed. Reg. 5513 (Feb. 3, 2010) (setting a separate rate for the 112(e) license). The proportion of royalties payable under section 112 is of some economic consequence, however, as unlike section 114 royalties—which are paid directly to performing artists and musicians as well as to record labels—section 112 royalties are paid only to sound recording owners. *See* Review of Copyright Royalty Judges Determination, 73 Fed. Reg. at 9146. Because it was not a focus of discussion during the study, the Office has not formed an opinion on this.

[901] Section 114 provides for an interim ratesetting process for new services. *See* 17 U.S.C. § 114(f)(2)(C) (allowing copyright owners or new services to initiate out-of-cycle proceeding). It does not provide for expedited proceedings, however. The Office did not hear much about the use or efficacy of this process in the course of its study, perhaps because it is rarely invoked. As discussed in connection with musical work performance and mechanical licenses, however, the Office believes it is important to have a cost-effective and expeditious interim ratesetting procedure, which could be implemented for the section 112 and 114 licenses as well under the Office's proposed system.

[902] These include sound recording owners, featured artists, and unions representing nonfeatured musicians and vocalists. 17 U.S.C. § 114(g)(2).

[903] PASSMAN at 121-126.

[904] *2013 SoundExchange Letter of Direction*.

[905] *See* NARAS First Notice Comments at 5-6.

[906] Recording artists did not comment on this proposal in the course of the study.

[907] SoundExchange First Notice Comments at 5.

[908] Section 115 provides that:
If the copyright owner does not receive the monthly payment and the monthly and annual statements of account when due, the owner may give written notice to the licensee that, unless the default is remedied within thirty days from the date of the notice, the compulsory license will be automatically terminated. Such termination renders either the making or the distribution, or both, of all phonorecords for which the royalty has not been paid, actionable as acts of infringement under section 501 and fully subject to the remedies provided by sections 502 through 506.
17 U S.C. § 115(c)(6).

[909] *See* EMF First Notice Comments at 5-15; NPR First Notice Comments at 4-7; NRBNMLC First Notice Comments at 14-22; PTCat3-12.

[910] *See, e.g.*, H.R. REP.NO. 94-1476, at 117 (noting "that encouragement and support of noncommercial broadcasting is in the public interest" and "that the nature of public broadcasting does warrant special treatment in certain areas").

[911] *See generally* NRBNMLC First Notice Comments at 14-15.

[912] *See* EMF First Notice Comments at 14-15. In so amending the section 118 license to cover both sound recording and public performance rights, it may be appropriate to expand the antitrust exemption currently contained in

section 118 to facilitate collective negotiation of rights between noncommercial users and copyright owners for uses outside the statutory license as well. *See* PTC First Notice Comments at 11.

[913] *Compare* NRBNMLC First Notice Comments at 14 (noting that "[f]or the last several license terms, religious broadcasters . . . have been able to agree upon rates and terms with ASCAP, BMI, and SESAC without the need for a rate-setting proceeding"), *with* EMF First Notice Comments at 8-9 (noting that the section 114 rulemaking joins both commercial and noncommercial entities, and that noncommercial entities "are rarely able to negotiated a pre-litigation settlement—forcing their participation in the CRB litigation process").
In establishing a unified license for public broadcast activities, the Office sees no need to depart from its view that, as with other statutory uses, the CRB should consider such rates under a generally applicable, market-based standard. Experience with the section 112 and 114 ratesetting process for noncommercial entities has shown, for example, that the willing buyer/willing seller standard can adequately account for the limited financial resources of, and other factors particular to, noncommercial users. *See* NRBNMLC First Notice Comments at 11-13 (noting that the CARP and CRB have consistently set lower rates for noncommercial broadcasters).

[914] NRBNMLC First Notice Comments at 14.

[915] *See* NPR First Notice Comments at 7.

[916] ABKCO First Notice Comments at 4; DiMA Second Notice Comments at 5.

[917] This does not mean that the Copyright Office should not itself seek to maintain more robust music data. To the extent it has the resources to modernize its systems to accommodate more comprehensive data, it should. For example, the copyright registration database could be modified to incorporate identifiers such as ISRCs and ISWCs. The Office's paper-based recordation system should be reengineered to become an electronic process so it is easier to record and research transfers of ownership. Both of these changes would help would-be licensees locate music owners. The Office has been reviewing these and other technology and data-driven questions in separate public processes. *See, e.g.*, BRAUNEIS; *see also* Maria Pallante, *Next Generation Copyright Office: What it Means and Why it Matters*, 61 J. Copyright Soc'y U.S.A. 213 (2014).

[918] *About DDEX*, DDEX, http://www.ddex.net/about-ddex (last visited Jan. 9. 2015).

[919] Tr. at 263:21-264:03 (June 24, 2014) (Stuart Rosen, BMI); *see also ASCAP, BMI and SOCAN Collaborate on MusicMark*, ASCAP (Apr. 2, 2014), http://www.ascap.com/playback/2014/04/action/ascap-bmi-socan-musicmark-collaboration.aspx.

[920] *PRS 'disappointed' at Global Repertoire Database collapse*, MUSIC ALLY.

[921] *Music Licensing Hearings* at 71-72 (statement of Jim Griffin, OneHouse).

[922] Tr. at 243:13-18 (June 17, 2014) (Helene Muddiman, CEO, Hollywood Elite Composers); *see also How Content ID Works*, GOOGLE, https://support.google.com/youtube/answer/2797370?hl=en (last visited Jan. 23, 2015).

[923] Of particular assistance was the student submission from the Pipeline Project 2014, Belmont University's Mike Curb College of Music Business and Entertainment, which provided an insightful summary and analysis of relevant data standards based on a series of interviews the students conducted with music industry professionals. *See* Pipeline Project Second Notice Comments.

[924] Kristin Thomson, *Metadata for Musicians*.

[925] ASCAP Second Notice Comments at 8; *see also* Pipeline Project Second Notice Comments at 4 5.

[926] *Frequently Asked Questions*, ISWC INTERNATIONAL AGENCY, http://www.iswc.org/en/faq.html (last visited Jan. 23, 2015); Pipeline Project Second Notice Comments at 5.

[927] *Obtaining Code*, USISRC.ORG, http://www.usisrc.org/about/obtaining_code.html (last visited Jan. 23, 2015); Pipeline Project Second Notice Comments at 6.

[928] *See* Gatenby & MacEwan at 5-6.

[929] The first U.S. registration agency is Bowker, an affiliate of the research and technology company ProQuest. *See id.*; *Bowker Becomes First ISNI Registration Agency in the U.S.*, BOWKER (June 21, 2012), http://www.bowker.com/en-US/aboutus/press_room/2012/pr_06212012a.shtml; Bowker, *Use of ISNI Is Growing Fast Among Authors, Says New Bowker Analysis*, YAHOO FINANCE (May 7, 2014), http://finance.yahoo.com/news/isni-growing-fast-among-authors-144800650.html.

[930] As suggested below, additional standards that might be useful in either the short or longer term could be evaluated and potentially adopted by regulation.

[931] For example, if IPIs and UPCs (discussed above) continue to be relevant in some contexts, and might be considered as potential additional data elements to be collected in the GMRO database.

[932] *ASCAP's Survey and Distribution System: Rules & Policies*, ASCAP (June 2014), http://www.ascap.com/~/media/files/pdf/members/payment/drd.pdf; *Royalty Policy Manual*, BMI, http://www.bmi.com/creators/royalty_print (last visited Jan. 16, 2015). Although songwriters appear generally to have confidence that the PROs are reporting to them accurately, there are some writers who take issue with the distribution rules themselves. For example, ASCAP and BMI pay substantial bonuses for current hits, which reduce the royalty pool for "evergreen" titles. In addition, PROs rely on sampling techniques rather than census data to calculate royalties in many contexts, which some complain may cause less popular songs to be overlooked. Tr. at 22:11-27:01 (June 5, 2014) (Royal Wade Kimes, Wonderment Records) ("We do need a collective, ASCAP, BMI, somebody to collect the stuff, but we also need it to be distributed rightly.").

[933] Indeed, at least until recently, songwriter agreements with publishers simply assumed payment of the writer's share of performance royalties by a PRO. *See, e.g.*, Tr. at 71:13-72:03 (June 5, 2014) (Brittany Schaffer, NMPA/Loeb & Loeb LLP).

[934] MMF & FAC Second Notice Comments at 16-17, 47 n.70; SGA Second Notice Comments at 1415, Exhibit 2 n.7.

[935] *See* Lindvall, *Behind the Music: The Real Reason Why the Major Labels Love Spotify.*

[936] *See* A2IM Second Notice Comments at 5-7 (explaining that some of the largest digital music services have entered into direct licensing deals with record labels or publishers that include compensation in the form of advances or equity, but that such compensation is not necessarily shared with creators); SGA Second Notice Comments at 14-15.

[937] Notably, however, music publishers have addressed this issue in their negotiated streaming settlement under section 115, since adopted as regulation. 37 C.F.R. § 385. The definition of revenue to which the percentage royalty rate is applied in the streaming regulations requires record companies to account for "anything of value given for the identified rights to undertake the licensed activity, including, without limitation, ownership equity, monetary advances, barter or any other monetary and/or nonmonetary consideration . . ." *Id.* § 385.11, 385.21 (definition of "applicable consideration").

[938] To ensure the transparency of such a hybrid arrangement, the withdrawing publishers should make the material financial terms of their direct deals—the royalty rates, advances, and any other consideration from the licensee attributable to the use of the songwriter's work—available to their songwriters.

[939] *See Pandora Ratesetting*, 6 F. Supp. 3d at 337; *see also* Tr. at 38:06-08 (June 17, 2014) (David Kokakis, UMPG); BMI Second Notice Comments at 14 ("In the context of partial rights withdrawal, BMI can still assist publishers in providing certain royalty administration services for their direct licenses covering the withdrawn rights, with administration terms and fees as agreed to by the parties. BMI would continue to provide its customary licensing and distribution services to the publishers and songwriters with regard to all other aspects of the public performing right.").

[940] In this regard, however, it should be noted that there has recently been some direct licensing of noninteractive digital performance rights outside of SoundExchange. As mentioned above iHeartMedia has entered into licensing agreements with WMG and some independent labels for deals covering both terrestrial and internet radio. Christman, *Here's Why Warner Music's Deal with Clear Channel Could be Groundbreaking for the Future of the U.S. Music Biz (Analysis)*. Pandora recently struck a direct deal with Merlin, an entity that negotiates on behalf of independent record labels; under this arrangement, though, Pandora agreed to continue to pay artist royalties through SoundExchange. Glenn Peoples, *Pandora Signs First Direct Label Deal with Merlin*, BILLBOARD (Aug. 6, 2014), http://www.billboard.com/articles/business/6207058/pandora-labeldeal-merlin.

[941] *See NMPA Late Fee Program*, NMPA LATE FEE SETTLEMENT.COM, http://www. nmpalatefeesettlement.com/index (last visited Jan. 22, 2015) (explaining the terms of the MOU in which record labels and music publishers (represented by RIAA and NMPA/HFA respectively) agreed to improve mechanical licensing practices and encourage prompt resolution of disputes); *see also Memorandum of Understanding (MOU 2)*, NMPA LATE FEE SETTLEMENT.COM, http://www.nmpalatefeesettlement.com/docs/mou2.pdf (last visited Jan. 22, 2015) (in which the record labels and music publishers extended the 2009 MOU through 2017).

[942] SIRA, H.R. 5553.

[943] *See* HFA, *Legislative News: Section 115 Reform Act of 2006 (SIRA) Introduced*, SOUNDCHECK, June 2006, at 1, *available at* https://secure.harryfox.com/public/userfiles/file/Soundcheck/ viewSoundCheck606.pdf ("While [DiMA, the NMPA, and the RIAA] have not reached complete agreement on all aspects of this legislation, we are optimistic that in the coming weeks we will work together with Chairman Smith and Representative Berman to ultimately pass historic legislation that will promote greater innovation and competition among digital music providers, deliver fair compensation to music creators and most importantly, greatly expand music choice and enjoyment for music fans.").

[944] Regardless of opt-out status, however, just as is the case today, a willing publisher could agree to a voluntary license with a willing licensee outside of the statutory regime. But in order to *require* the licensee to negotiate outside of the statutory process, the publisher would need to assert its opt-out right. Additionally, to effectuate such a voluntary arrangement, the publisher would need to notify the MRO of the agreement, so that the MRO could make appropriate adjustments to its collection and distribution processes.

[945] Under the new MRO-based system, record labels would no longer engage in "pass-though" licensing of musical works as they are entitled to do today under section 115. Third-party services would instead seek blanket licenses from the MROs, or directly from any publishers who had opted out. Apart from long-time concerns by publishers and songwriters about their inability to receive direct payment from digital services under the pass-through regime, the possibility of varying rates under the updated licensing framework being proposed would seemingly render pass-through licensing inefficient at best. In their comments, record labels indicated a willingness to eliminate this aspect of section 115. *See* RIAA Second Notice Comments at 19 ("The major record companies generally support in principle the elimination of pass-through licensing.").

[946] The section 112, 114, and 115 licenses contain antitrust exemptions to allow copyright owners and users to negotiate collectively, and the PROs are permitted to do so under the consent decrees. *See* 17 U.S.C. §§ 112(e)(2), 114(e)(1), 115(c)(3)(B).

[947] *See* ASCAP Consent Decree § X; *Ace Title Search*, ASCAP, https://www.ascap.com/Home/acetitle-search/index.aspx (last visited Jan. 29, 2015); *BMI Repertoire*, BMI, http://repertoire.bmi.com/ startpage.asp (last visited Jan. 29, 2015); HFA, *Songfile Search*, SONGFILE, https://secure. harryfox.com/songfile/public/publicsearch.jsp (last visited Jan. 16, 2015).

[948] SoundExchange is regulated by the Copyright Royalty Board as the designated collective. *See, e.g.* 37 C.F.R. §§ 380.2(c), 380.4.

[949] SIRA took a similar approach by providing for direct payment to the individual designated agents. SIRA, H.R. 5553.

[950] SoundExchange Second Notice Comments at 4-5.

[951] SoundExchange is currently exploring making its data available to others. *See id.* at 5 ("SoundExchange is actively exploring means by which it might provide interested services a means of accessing [its sound recording] data for use in identifying to SoundExchange with greater precision the recordings they use under the statutory licenses.").

[952] Tr. at 217:02-218:16 (June 23, 2014) (Christos P. Badavas, HFA).

[953] NMPA & HFA First Notice Comments at 13.

[954] This is a particular concern with respect to new releases, as publisher and songwriter disagreements over their respective ownership shares in songs often delay the finalization of mechanical licenses for months or even years after the record is released. Tr. at 340:05-341:14 (June 23, 2014) (Andrea Finkelstein, SME).

[955] Since royalty obligations might vary among MROs and publishers, the default payments would need to be made in an amount sufficient to cover the highest potential rate payable to any entity with which the licensee had a licensing arrangement. In some cases, a blanket license might require payment of a set amount for the reporting period in question regardless of usage (for example, a fixed percentage of the service's revenues, as in the case of ASCAP's license with Pandora), with the royalty pool to be allocated by the collecting agent. In such a case, there would be no need to pay into the GMRO, and any reporting issues would need to be addressed by the MRO.

[956] Any difference between the royalties paid to the GMRO and the actual rate of a subsequently identified publisher could be contributed to the GMRO to offset costs. In the case of a publisher not affiliated with an MRO and hence not subject to any rate agreement, the publisher should receive the lowest potential rate that the licensee might pay for that use and the GMRO could also deduct a reasonable administrative fee not greater than any fee currently charged by any of the MROs. This latter rule would incentivize publishers to affiliate with an MRO of their choice rather than rely on the much less efficient GMRO claims procedure.

[957] A somewhat analogous fee is currently required for the filing of an NOI with the Office under section 115 in lieu of serving it on a licensee when the licensee cannot be found in the Office's records (though no royalty payment is required). *See* 37 C.F.R. § 201.3(e)(1). As noted above, large-scale licensees appear to be reluctant to avail themselves of this process due to the filing fees (which reflect the costs incurred by the Office in administering these notices, as per 17 U.S.C. § 708(a)). The level of the administrative fee that would be assessed by the GMRO—which would receive more general funding from users, as discussed below—would need to be carefully assessed in relation to its purpose.

[958] By way of illustration, in year one, 20% of works listed by an MRO might be required to include the ISWC; in year two, 40%; and so on up to near-total compliance.

[959] *See, e.g.*, DiMA Second Notice Comments at 5 (suggesting that the government "designate a small portion of license fees" paid by licensees to cover costs); RIAA First Notice Comment at 22 ("Record companies are prepared to contribute information concerning new works, and potentially a share of start-up costs.").

[960] As noted above, an MRO that failed to contribute adequate data to the GMRO could be required to absorb some portion of such administrative fees.

[961] If the black box funds were ever to exceed the GMRO's costs, the excess could be distributed to publishers by the GMRO based on a market-share-based allocation process.

[962] In this regard, Congress might also wish to amend the statutory framework for the CRB to allow for greater flexibility in staffing. Currently, the statute is highly specific, in that it provides for three full-time staff members: one to be paid no more than the basic rate for level 10 of GS-15 of the General Schedule; one to be paid between the basic rate for GS-13 and level 10 of GS-14; and one to be paid between the basic rate for GS-8 and level 10 of GS-11. 17 U.S.C. § 802(b), (e)(2). Especially if its duties were expanded to include additional licensing activities and fee-setting responsibilities, the CRB would seemingly be better served with a statute that provided more discretion with respect to the number and seniority of the legal staff that assist the three Judges.

[963] *See, e.g.*, RIAA First Notice Comments at 14-17 (proposing a blanket licensing solution for all rights implicated when using musical works); Tr. at 194:05-18 (June 4, 2014) (Scott Sellwood, Google/YouTube) ("I certainly like the idea of an all-in valuation of the music copyright.").

[964] RIAA First Notice Comments at 15-17. Any such agreement concerning the royalty split would presumably need to address the parties' obligations to each other in relation to a settlement rather than a litigated outcome.

[965] As it does in CRB proceedings today, in considering appropriate fees, the CRB could impose safeguards to protect against public dissemination of confidential business information.

[966] *See generally* 17 U.S.C. § 803.

[967] *Id.* § 803(b)(6)(C)(ii).

[968] *Id.* § 803(b)(6)(C)(i)-(ii).

[969] *Id.* § 803(b)(6)(C)(i).

[970] *See id.* § 803(b)(6)(C)(iii) (allowing hearsay to be admitted upon CRB discretion).

[971] *Id.* § 114(f)(2)(B).

[972] *Id.* § 801(b)(7).

[973] The CRB has occasionally adopted settlements resolving some but not all rate concerns. *See, e.g.*, Adjustment of Rates and Terms for Preexisting Subscription and Satellite Digital Audio Radio Services, 72 Fed. Reg. 71,795 (Dec. 19, 2007); Determination of Rates and Terms for Preexisting Subscription Services and Satellite Digital Audio Radio Services, 73 Fed. Reg. 4080. But adoption of partial settlements is not the norm.

[974] *See, e.g.*, Tr. at 122:15-22 (June 23, 2014) (Colin Rushing, SoundExchange) ("But it was this group, College Webcasters, Inc. We entered into a settlement with them. We also did a settlement with NAB. Neither of these settlements were actually adopted by the CRB until the very end of the proceeding. And so we found ourselves unsure of what, you know, whether the settlements were, actually, going to be adopted."); Tr. at 99:16-100:03 (June 16, 2014) (Brad Prendergast, SoundExchange) (the current system "leaves a lot of parties still in the litigation proceeding, when they'd rather not be"); Tr. at 129:17-130:03 (June 23, 2014) (Steven Marks, RIAA) ("I also think that the CRB, it would be nice to have, maybe, some set times for the CRB to rule on settlements that are proposed. We had, our last mechanical settlement that was offered, a delay of almost a year.").

[975] Notably, this problem would also likely be ameliorated by a move to an "as-needed" ratesetting system as recommended by the Office, where rate determinations would bind only the participants to the proceeding (notwithstanding their potential influence on other market actors). Such proceedings would focus on narrower disputes and should therefore be easier to resolve than proceedings covering a multitude of rates and stakeholders.

[976] Under the terms of Section 115, a record company or other entity that obtains a statutory license for a musical work can, in turn, authorize third parties to make DPDs of that work. *See* 17 U.S.C. 115(c)(3). In such a "pass-through" situation, the statutory licensee is then responsible for reporting and paying royalties for such third-party uses to the musical work owner.

[977] Concerns about the efficiency of the Section 115 licensing process are not new. For instance, in 2005, then-Register of Copyrights Marybeth Peters testified before Congress that Section 115 had become "outdated," and made several proposals to reform the license. *See Copyright Office Views on Music Licensing Reform: Hearing Before the Subcomm. on Courts, the Internet, and Intellectual Property of the H. Comm. on the Judiciary*, 109th Cong. 4–9 (2005). In 2006, the House Judiciary Committee's Subcommittee on Courts, the Internet, and Intellectual Property forwarded the Section 115 Reform Act ("SIRA") to the full Judiciary Committee by unanimous voice vote. *See* H.R. 5553, 109th Cong. (2006). This bill would have updated Section 115 to create a blanket-style license. The proposed legislation was not reported out by the full Judiciary Committee, however.

[978] The Copyright Royalty Board ("CRB") is the latest in a series of administrative bodies Congress has created to adjust the rates and terms for the statutory licenses. The first, the Copyright Royalty Tribunal ("CRT"), was created in 1976. *See* Public Law 94–553, sec. 801, 90 Stat. 2541, 2594–96 (1976). In 1993, Congress replaced the CRT with a system of ad-hoc copyright arbitration royalty panels ("CARPs"). *See* Copyright Royalty Tribunal Reform Act of 1993, Public Law 103–198, sec. 2, 107 Stat. 2304, 2304–2308. Congress replaced the CARP system with the CRB in 2004. *See* Copyright Royalty and Distribution Reform Act of 2004, Public Law 108–419, 118 Stat. 2341.

[979] *See* 17 U.S.C. 801(b)(1).

[980] *See generally United States v. Broadcast Music, Inc.*, 275 F.3d 168, 171–72 (2d Cir. 2001) (describing the history). SESAC, a smaller performing rights organization created in 1930 to serve European publishers, is not subject to a similar consent decree, although it has been involved recently in private antitrust litigation. *See Meredith Corp. v. SESAC LLC*, No. 09–cv–9177, 2014 WL 812795 (S.D.N.Y. Mar. 3, 2014).

[981] *United States v. ASCAP*, No. 41–cv–1395, 2001– 2 Trade Cas. (CCH) ¶ 73,474, 2001 WL 1589999, *3 (S.D.N.Y. June 11, 2001). Although BMI has taken the position that a strict reading of its consent decree does not bar it from offering mechanical licenses, it generally has not done so. *See* Broadcast Music, Inc., Comments on Department of Commerce Green Paper 4–5 (Nov. 13, 2013), available at http://www.ntia.doc.gov/files/ntia/bmi_comments.pdf.

[982] Significantly, musical work owners are precluded from offering evidence concerning the licensing fees paid for digital performances of sound recordings as a point of comparison in the district court ratesetting proceedings. Section 114 of the Copyright Act provides that license fees payable for the public performance of sound

recordings may not be taken into account "in any administrative, judicial, or other governmental proceeding to set or adjust the rates payable to" musical work copyright owners. 17 U.S.C. 114(i).

[983] *United States v. Broadcast Music, Inc.*, No. 64– cv–3787, 1966 Trade Cas. (CCH) ¶ 71,941 (S.D.N.Y. 1966), *as amended*, 1996 Trade Cases (CCH) ¶ 71,378, 1994 WL 901652 (S.D.N.Y. Nov. 18, 1994).

[984] *United States v. ASCAP*, No. 41–cv–1395, 2001– 2 Trade Cas. (CCH) ¶ 73,474, 2001 WL 1589999 (S.D.N.Y. June 11, 2001).

[985] *See In re Pandora Media, Inc.*, Nos. 12–cv– 8035, 41–cv–1395, 2013 WL 5211927 (S.D.N.Y. Sept. 17, 2013); *Broadcast Music, Inc.* v. *Pandora Media, Inc.*, Nos. 13–cv–4037, 64–cv–3787, 2013 WL 6697788 (S.D.N.Y. Dec. 19, 2013).

[986] In 2009, Congress asked the Copyright Office to study the "desirability and means" of extending federal copyright protection to pre-February 15, 1972 sound recordings. Public Law 111–8, 123 Stat. 524 (2010) (explanatory statement). In 2011, the Office completed that study, issuing a report recommending that federal copyright protection be so extended. United States Copyright Office, *Federal Copyright Protection for Pre-1972 Sound Recordings* (2011), *available at* http:// www.copyright.gov/docs/sound/pre-72-report.pdf.

[987] Thus, a person wishing to digitally perform a pre-1972 sound recording cannot rely on the Section 112 and 114 statutory licenses and must instead obtain a license directly from the owner of the sound recording copyright. *See* Determination of Rates and Terms for Preexisting Subscription Services and Satellite Digital Audio Radio Services, 78 FR 23054, 23073 (Apr. 17, 2013) (determination of the CRB finding that "[t]he performance right granted by the copyright laws for sound recordings applies only to those recordings created on or after February 15, 1972" and adopting provisions allowing exclusion of performances of pre-1972 sound recordings from certain statutory royalties).

[988] In 1998, as part of the DMCA, Congress amended Sections 112 and 114 of the Copyright Act to clarify that the digital sound recording performance right applies to services like webcasting. *See* Public Law 105–304, secs. 402, 405, 112 Stat. 2860, 2888, 2890.

[989] The Copyright Office has long supported the extension of the public performance right in sound recordings to broadcast radio. *See Internet Streaming of Radio Broadcasts: Balancing the Interests of Sound Recording Copyright Owners With Those of Broadcasters: Hearing Before the Subcomm. on Courts, the Internet, and Intellectual Property of the H. Comm. on the Judiciary*, 108th Cong. 6–7 (2004) (statement of David Carson, General Counsel, U.S. Copyright Office), *available at* http://www.copyright.gov/docs/carson071504.pdf. Only a handful of countries lack such a right; in addition to the United States, the list includes China, North Korea, and Iran. This gap in copyright protection has the effect of depriving American performers and labels of foreign royalties to which they would otherwise be entitled, because even countries that recognize a public performance right in sound recordings impose a reciprocity requirement. According to one estimate, U.S. rights holders lose approximately $70 million each year in royalties for performances in foreign broadcasts. *See generally* Mary LaFrance, *From Whether to How: The Challenge of Implementing a Full Public Performance Right in Sound Recordings*, 2 Harv. J. of Sports & Ent. L 221, 226 (2011).

[990] The Act requires that receipts under the Section 114 statutory license be divided in the following manner: 50 percent to the owner of the digital public performance right in the sound recording, $2^{1/2}$ percent to nonfeatured musicians, $2^{1/2}$ percent to nonfeatured vocalists, and 45 percent to the featured recording artists. 17 U.S.C. 114(g)(2).

[991] 17 U.S.C. 114(j)(10), (11). Today, Sirius/XM is the only preexisting satellite service that seeks statutory licenses under Section 114. *See* Determination of Rates and Terms for Preexisting Subscription Services and Satellite Digital Audio Radio Services, 78 FR 23054, 23055 (Apr. 17, 2013). There are two preexisting subscription services, Music Choice and Muzak. *Id.*

[992]

[993] *See* 17 U.S.C. 114(f)(1), 801(b)(1).

[994] 17 U.S.C. 114(f)(2)(B) instructs the CRB to "establish rates and terms that most clearly represent the rates and terms that would have been negotiated in the marketplace between a willing buyer and willing seller." The provision further requires the CRB to consider "whether use of the service may substitute for or may promote the sales of phonorecords or otherwise may interfere with or may enhance the sound recording copyright owner's other streams of revenue from its sound recordings," and "the relative roles of the copyright owner and the transmitting entity in the copyrighted work and the service made available to the public with respect to relative creative contribution, technological contribution, capital investment, cost, and risk." *Id.*
For all types of services eligible for a Section 114 statutory license, the rates for the phonorecords (ephemeral recordings) used to operate the service are to be established by the CRB under Section 112 according to a "willing buyer/willing seller" standard. 17 U.S.C. 112(e). In general, the Section 112 rates have been a relatively insignificant part of the CRB's ratesetting proceedings, and have been established as a subset of the 114 rate. *See, e.g.,* Determination of Rates and Terms for Preexisting Subscription Services and Satellite Digital Audio Radio Services, 78 FR 23054, 23055–56 (Apr. 17, 2013).

[995] *In re Pandora Media, Inc.*, Nos. 12–cv–8035, 41– cv–1395, 2013 WL 5211927 (S.D.N.Y. Sept. 17, 2013); *Broadcast Music, Inc.,* v. *Pandora Media, Inc.*, Nos. 12–cv–4037, 64–cv–3787, 2013 WL 6697788 (S.D.N.Y. Dec. 19, 2013).

[996] *See* Ed Christman, *Universal Music Publishing Plots Exit From ASCAP, BMI,* Billboard (Feb. 1, 2013), http://www.billboard.com/biz/articles/news/publishing/1537554/universal-music-publishing-plots-exit-from-ascap-bmi; *see also* Ed Christman, *Sony/ATV's Martin Bandier Repeats Warning to ASCAP, BMI, Billboard* (July 11, 2014), http:// www.billboard.com/biz/articles/news/publishing/6157469/sonyatvs-martin-bandier-repeats-warning-to-ascap-bmi.

[997] Based upon written comments and discussion at the roundtables, it appears that certain language in the First Notice concerning the lack of availability of licenses for pre-1972 recordings under Sections 112 and 114 may have been misinterpreted by some. In a footnote, the First Notice observed that "a person wishing to digitally perform a pre-1972 sound recording cannot rely on the Section 112 and 114 statutory licenses and must instead obtain a license directly from the owner of the sound recording copyright." 78 FR 14739, 14741 n.12. In making this statement, the Office was not opining on the necessity of obtaining such a license under state law, but merely observing that licenses for the digital performance of pre-1972 sound recordings, and for the reproductions to enable such performances, are not available under Section 112 or 114. A licensee seeking such a license would thus need to obtain it directly from the sound recording owner (as the Office understands to be the current practice of some licensees with respect to performances of pre-1972 recordings). On the other side of the coin, it appears that others have misread the Office's observation in its report on pre-1972 sound recordings that "[i]n general, state law does not appear to recognize a performance right in sound recordings" as an official statement that no such protection is (or should be) available under state law. *See U.S. Copyright Office, Federal Copyright Protection for Pre-1972 Sound Recordings* 44 (2011). This, too, is a misinterpretation. While, as a factual matter, a state may not have affirmatively acknowledged a public performance right in pre-1972 recordings as of the Office's 2011 report, the language in the report should not be read to suggest that a state could not properly interpret its law to recognize such a right. As the Office explained, "common law protection is amorphous, and courts often perceive themselves to have broad discretion." *Id.* at 48.

Chapter 2

TESTIMONY OF LEE THOMAS MILLER, PRESIDENT, NASHVILLE SONGWRITERS ASSOCIATION INTERNATIONAL. HEARING ON "MUSIC LICENSING UNDER TITLE 17 PART ONE"[*]

My name is Lee Thomas Miller. I grew up on a small tobacco farm in Jessamine County, Kentucky. I started playing piano by ear when I was 11. By age 15 I was writing bad songs and playing them with my even worse band. But we were kids, so the people cheered, if only out of pity.

I went to college to study Music Theory and Composition and graduated with a Bachelors degree from Eastern Kentucky University. That just meant I was overqualified to play in the honkytonks where I'd been singing. I was formally educated in classical music composition while writing country songs on the side. These are two very different things. Just ask my professors! My parents were thrilled when I finished college and mortified when I saved $1000 and immediately moved to Nashville.

For years I wrote songs -- hundreds of songs. I played in bands and took temporary jobs to pay the bills if needed. I studied songs I heard on the radio and began meeting and learning from the songwriters who wrote them. On September 1st, 1996, I became a fulltime songwriter. Then the real work started. Eleven years. From the day I moved to Nashville it took 11 years to have a hit song on that radio.

Since then I have been lucky and blessed. I have had hits and continue to earn a living by walking into a room where there is nothing and making something up out of thin air -- something that is real and tangible -- something that creates commerce. My craft fuels the entire music business. My songs generate thousands of jobs and shapes the very culture we live in because let's face it- nearly everybody loves music. But I am one of the remaining few. Since I started, nine out of ten of my colleagues don't write songs as a profession anymore, because their royalties cannot feed their families.

The current system is unjust and must be changed. Rules established in 1909, largely to prevent one player piano roll company from becoming a monopoly, require me to grant a compulsory license paying 9.1 cents for the sale of a song, which I split with my co-writers

---

[*] This is an edited, reformatted and augmented version of testimony presented June 10, 2014 before the House Judiciary Committee, Subcommittee on Courts, Intellectual Property and the Internet.

and our music publishers, regardless of what the marketplace might say my song is worth. That's not much of a pay raise from the original two cents paid in 1909.

Royalties from my song performed on an internet radio station are set under consent decrees from World War II. The judges who determine those rates are forbidden from considering what the marketplace says my song is worth. Consequently, I only receive thousandths of a penny for those performances.

I appreciate the luxury of the internet as much as you do and I suppose I am as much of a slave to my smart phone as anyone. But the current system has devalued the musical composition to the point where songwriters are being crushed. It is bad enough that it is so easy to steal music today. But a legal framework that allows songs to be streamed for nearly free will destroy the livelihood of the American songwriter if it is allowed to continue.

An important piece of legislation called the "Songwriter Equity Act" has been introduced that would allow my copyright's value, in the modern marketplace, to be considered in rate-setting proceedings. I want to thank introducing sponsors Congressmen Doug Collins and Hakeem Jeffries and all of the co-sponsors of this legislation.

While it is a great start, even bolder revisions to the current copyright law and music licensing rules are necessary to establish true equity for today's songwriters and composers. It is time for Congress to eliminate the compulsory license. It is time for Congress to eliminate or drastically alter World War II era consent decrees.

In the future songwriters should be represented on the governing bodies of music licensing and collection entities and dispute resolution committees. Future licensing and collection agencies should be able to compete with those with large market shares. There should be true transparency throughout the entire collection and payment process.

I am America's smallest small business. I sit down and make stuff up. I do not succeed if my songs are not recorded, sold and played and when I do get paid I pay self-employment income tax. With the money that remains I raise babies. I buy bread, gasoline, anniversary flowers, cough medicine, braces, and guitar strings.

I can make you laugh *or* cry. I can make you do both inside the same 3-minute story. That's the power of music, and it all begins with a song. Congress, I ask you on behalf of my family and the families of American songwriters to change the archaic government regulations that prohibit us from pursuing a fair market opportunity for the songs we create.

Thank you Mr. Chairman, Ranking Member Nadler and Members of the Committee.

In: Copyright and the Music Marketplace
Editor: Keith Turner

ISBN: 978-1-63482-869-7
© 2015 Nova Science Publishers, Inc.

Chapter 3

STATEMENT OF NEIL PORTNOW, PRESIDENT AND CEO, THE RECORDING ACADEMY. HEARING ON "MUSIC LICENSING UNDER TITLE 17 PART ONE"[*]

Chairman Goodlatte, Chairman Coble, Ranking Members Conyers and Nadler, and Members of the Subcommittee: My name is Neil Portnow and I am President and CEO of The Recording Academy. Known internationally for our GRAMMY Awards, The Academy is the trade association that represents music's creators: songwriters and composers, vocalists and musicians, and record producers and engineers. I thank you for the opportunity to address the Subcommittee this morning.

THE FRAMERS' VISION: PROTECTING MUSIC'S AUTHORS

Perhaps a good place to begin my testimony is literally at the beginning – with the copyright clause of the Constitution. In Article I, Section 8, the Framers gave authors the exclusive right to their works, for a time, in order to promote the progress of science and useful arts.

As today's hearing is focused on music licensing, we should, at the outset, remember who the "authors" of music are. They are the songwriters and composers who create the very DNA of music. They are the featured and background performers who bring those songs to life. They are the producers and engineers who create the overall sound of the recordings we love.

Over the next two hearings, you will hear from many interests in the music space. But I urge you to keep foremost in your mind music's creators, the authors our founders expressly protected.

---

[*] This is an edited, reformatted and augmented version of a statement presented June 10, 2014 before the House Judiciary Committee, Subcommittee on Courts, Intellectual Property and the Internet.

Copyright Law No Longer Serves as an Adequate Incentive to Create

Of course, the Framers intended copyright to be an incentive to create. And for the next two centuries, Congress passed bills that mostly accomplished that vision. But today, we have a patchwork of laws that do not address the challenges of the digital marketplace and often create a *dis*incentive to make music as a career. Low streaming rates prevent creators from making a living. Performers and composers must police the entire internet to take down infringing works. And traditional radio continues to use artists' recordings without compensation, while leveraging this unfair advantage as they move into the digital world.

Recently, one of our elected Board leaders of The Academy's New York Chapter testified before Congress regarding Section 512 of Title 17, the so-called notice and takedown provision. The multiple-GRAMMY-winning composer Maria Schneider noted the extensive amount of time required to take down all of her recordings from online sites, stating:

> "The *majority* of my time is now spent on activities that allow me some chance of protecting my work online. Only a fraction of my time is now available for the creation of music. So instead of the Copyright Act providing an *incentive* to create, it provides a *disincentive*."

But even on sites with legally acquired content, it is important to note how large technology businesses are being built upon the aggregation of recordings, and how little of that revenue returns to creators. As streaming becomes the dominant consumption model, these services must provide meaningful and fair compensation or few will be able to make a living as an artist, writer or producer.

The Corporate Radio Loophole Must Be Closed

There are many serious discussions about music royalty rates today: which are too low, which are too high, and what is fair. Yet AM/FM terrestrial radio broadcasters continue to deny musicians *any* right whatsoever to performance royalties for the use of their music, which radio giants use to make billions in annual advertising revenue.

Terrestrial radio is the only industry in America that's built on using another's intellectual property without permission or compensation. Broadcasters in every other developed country in the world compensate performers. The result is that the U.S., which should be the standard bearer for intellectual property rights, is among such countries as China, North Korea and Iran which do not recognize these fundamental rights.

The National Association of Broadcasters (NAB) has spent a lot of money lobbying to maintain their free ride. During each session of Congress, they spread myths that never stand up to any reasonable assessment of the facts. For example:

NAB Myth: A performance right is a money grab from record labels.

Fact: Artists would be the main beneficiaries of a performance right. Artists would receive 50 percent of royalties for their creative contributions, and an increasing number of artists are also copyright owners and would, therefore, get the other 50 percent too. When the performance right campaign launched, hundreds of artists signed on to join. This quest is about them.

NAB Myth: The campaign started because piracy hurt the record business, so record labels needed to look elsewhere for revenue.

Fact: Artists have been fighting for this basic right for nearly 90 years. Legends such as Bing Crosby and Frank Sinatra have spoken on the issue. The renewed focus on the issue is a result of "new" radio (Internet and Satellite) paying this royalty, exposing the hypocrisy of exempting "old" radio from paying their fair share.

NAB Myth: Promotional support by radio creates a "symbiotic relationship" with artists.

Fact: Even by the NAB's own (dubious) study, the benefit to radio outpaces the benefit to artists by 10 to 1. And any promotional effect would be taken into account by the rate-setting body. Internet and Satellite radio also provide promotion, but pay a royalty. Further, a GAO study found "no consistent pattern between the cumulative broadcast radio airplay and the cumulative number of digital single sales." Even Clear Channel CEO Bob Pittman admitted that, "clearly [promotion] is not enough, or there wouldn't be a decades-long battle over [performance royalties]."

NAB Myth: The royalty would put small stations out of business.

Fact: The last legislation introduced on this subject exempted every small radio station and even medium sized ones, requiring 75 percent of stations to pay as little as a few dollars a day for music.

NAB Myth: The free market is addressing the issue with private deals.

Fact: There is no "free" market when one side of the transaction does not have a right to its property. Without a performance right, there can be no "free" negotiations. And when a bill was introduced to create a free market where musicians would have a chance to negotiate for fair compensation (the Free Market Royalty Act), the broadcast lobby opposed it.

NAB Myth: A performance royalty is a tax.

Fact: In Civics 101, everyone learns that taxes go to the government. Paychecks go to people who provide goods or services for money. Performance royalties would not go to the government, but rather to those who created the sound recordings. Therefore, they are not a tax. This obvious point was made clearly in a letter signed by seven free-market organizations, including Americans for Tax Reform: "A performance royalty is not a tax.... Paying a private citizen or business for the use of their property is clearly not a tax."

The NAB has run out of arguments and out of time. The White House, the Copyright Office, and political groups ranging from the AFL-CIO and the NAACP to Americans for Tax Reform and Tea Party Nation all agree with us. And while radio touts a nonsensical – and nonbinding – resolution, Congressional leaders from both parties are working on *real* legislation to resolve this issue. Any copyright reform simply must include a radio performance right.

SONGWRITERS SUFFER UNDER RATES SET BELOW MARKET

The Recording Academy believes the current mechanical rate as set by the CRB under Sections 115(c)(3)(D) and 801(b)(1) is substandard. These provisions direct the CRB to apply a standard that does not reflect fair market value, but rather a standard based on a collection of vague objectives. The application of these antiquated standards has resulted in depressed mechanical license rates relative to other non-compulsory royalty streams, which have increased at greater rates over the same period of time. The CRB needs to have the authority to recognize and apply fair market standards.

The Songwriter Equity Act ("SEA"), H.R. 4079/S. 2321, is an important step toward modernizing the music licensing system. In particular, SEA would amend Sections 115 and 801 by directing the Copyright Royalty Judges to apply the following standard with respect to compulsory mechanical license rate-setting:

> The Copyright Royalty Judges shall establish rates and terms that most clearly represent the rates and terms that would have been negotiated in the marketplace between a willing buyer and a willing seller. In establishing such rates and terms, the Copyright Royalty Judges shall base their decision on marketplace, economic, and use information presented by the participants. In establishing such rates and terms, the Copyright Royalty Judges may consider the rates and terms for comparable uses and comparable circumstances under voluntary license agreements. Further, The Recording Academy believes that the current implementation of 17 U.S.C. 114(i) creates an unacceptable, uneven playing field which results in songwriters and composers receiving royalties that are substantially less than fair market value.

In addition, SEA would amend Section 114(i) to allow federal rate courts to consider all relevant evidence, including sound recording royalty rates, when establishing royalty rates for songwriters. How the rate court would apply the evidence is left to the discretion of the court.

Accordingly, The Recording Academy supports SEA. Like other property owners, songwriters and composers deserve to be paid the fair market value for their intellectual property. The enactment of the Songwriter Equity Act would ensure that songwriters and composers are appropriately compensated for the use of their musical compositions without impacting artist royalties.

RECORD PRODUCER PAYMENTS MUST BE STREAMLINED AND CONSISTENTLY APPLIED

It must be noted that the third, equally important author in the sound recording process (along with the artist and songwriter) is not mentioned at all in statute. Record producers provide the overall creative direction for a recording project (similar to the role of a film director on a motion picture) as well as the overall sound of the recording. Not represented in Washington in 1995, producers were not granted a statutory share of the royalty in the Digital Performance Right in Sound Recordings Act of that year ("DPRA"). Without a statutory share established in the DPRA, producers (and royalty-earning engineers) earn royalties based on contract (usually with the featured artist).

To provide the same fair, direct-payment option of performance royalties available to artists, the agency SoundExchange currently offers a still developing service for producers whereby SoundExchange, upon direction by the featured artist, will process the share owed to producers by contract with the featured artist. The Recording Academy appreciates SoundExchange's ongoing efforts to develop an efficient system for direct pay for producers.

However, producers should be assured that this process will be consistent and permanent, applied by SoundExchange and any successor or competing agency in the future.

The Recording Academy is continuing productive dialogue with SoundExchange and others on this matter and looks forward to resolving this issue with all relevant stakeholders.

MUSIC ISSUES SHOULD BE RESOLVED IN ONE MUSIC OMNIBUS BILL

To resolve some of the above issues, several thoughtful bills have been introduced this Congress. The Songwriter Equity Act as noted, would allow songwriters to be paid the equivalent of fair market value for their work. The Protecting the Rights of Musicians Act would insist that if broadcasters value their *own* content, they must value the content of others. The RESPECT Act would remove a legal loophole that denies royalties to older artists.

But now it is time for a unified, holistic approach to music licensing. It's time for a Music Omnibus Bill, or MusicBus, for short. With copyright review underway, we need our industry and Congress to be visionary and create a unified approach for the future of our business. For all the complexities of the MusicBus concept, its goal is actually simple: Fair market pay, for all music creators, across all platforms. And as as a united music community, we can more effectively work with other stakeholders in the music ecosystem – who connect the music maker to the music fan – and create a licensing regime that works for all.

A music omnibus bill need not wait for the entire copyright act to be revised. As Congress' own advisor on copyrights – Register Maria Pallante – noted, "Congress already has had more than a decade of debate on the public performance right for sound recordings, and has given serious consideration to improving the way in which musical works are licensed in the marketplace. These issues are ripe for resolution."

The Recording Academy strongly urges Congress to pass music omnibus legislation that treats all authors fairly.

Mr. Chairman, a legal framework that includes compulsory licenses, government rate courts and consent decrees already diminishes the Framers' vision of exclusive rights. If music makers must be subject to these restrictions, let's at least assure them that the result will represent what a free market would have provided. We are not asking for special treatment. We are simply asking for what is fair. Fair market pay, for all music creators, across all platforms. A simple concept. A single bill. A just framework for music licensing. Thank you.

Chapter 4

TESTIMONY OF DAVID M. ISRAELITE, PRESIDENT AND CHIEF EXECUTIVE OFFICER, NATIONAL MUSIC PUBLISHERS' ASSOCIATION. HEARING ON "MUSIC LICENSING UNDER TITLE 17 PART ONE"[*]

Good morning Mr. Chairman, Ranking Member Nadler and Members of the Subcommittee. I appreciate the opportunity to appear before you today to discuss the impact of current copyright law on music publishers and their songwriter partners and to support legislation that would begin to remedy the pay inequity that today's law creates.

I serve as President and CEO of the National Music Publishers' Association (NMPA), the principal trade association of music publishers and their songwriter partners in the United States. The NMPA's mandate is to protect and advance the interests of music publishers and songwriters in matters relating to the domestic and global protection of music copyrights.

I urge the Subcommittee to consider several important points as you review the music licensing landscape.

First, copyright law today contains antiquated regulations that unfairly distort the value of creators' work. Provisions of the law – some of which were enacted more than a century ago – are in dire need of reevaluation to determine whether they are still necessary in the digital age. The copyright in a song is a property right, and should not be regulated by the government unless there is a compelling reason to do so. There should be a presumption that a property right should be valued in a free market.

Second, if any part of a songwriter's creative process must be regulated by government, then at a minimum creators deserve to be paid a fair market value. Congress should look first and foremost at ways to eliminate government regulation in the songwriting business. But in the absence of a free market, the processes that determine what creators are paid must be improved to attempt to reflect fair market compensation.

Third, Congress should reject any attempt to expand compulsory licenses, which would further erode the ability of creators to negotiate the terms under which their works are used. The music industry operates in a dynamic marketplace and Congress should exercise restraint when it comes to any additional regulation that could have long-term consequences for

---

[*] This is an edited, reformatted and augmented version of testimony presented June 10, 2014 before the House Judiciary Committee, Subcommittee on Courts, Intellectual Property and the Internet.

creators. Instead, Congress should allow private negotiations to dictate the terms of existing and future music offerings. There will be a great deal of debate about what would make it easier for a licensee who wants to use the works created by a songwriter. Those interests should be subservient to the property rights of those who create the works.

Finally, I thank Representatives Doug Collins and Hakeem Jeffries as well as the members of the subcommittee – including Chairman Coble – for supporting H.R. 4079, the "Songwriter Equity Act" (SEA). The introduction of this bill marks an important step to ensure that the interests of songwriters and publishers – which are too often overlooked – are at the fore of the discussion on music licensing. I will discuss the details of the legislation later in my testimony.

TWO SEPARATE COPYRIGHTS

As you know, there are two separate and distinct copyrights involved in music.

- The first copyright is for the underlying musical composition created by one or more songwriter, and often owned or represented by a music publisher. I am here representing that half of the music industry;
- The second copyright is for any recording of that song – commonly known as the sound recording copyright – and often represented by a record label.

It is crucial to appreciate that these two different copyrights are controlled and represented by different interests, and are often treated very differently under the law and through government regulation.

As the Subcommittee continues to review the Copyright Act, I trust you will recognize and address the inherent unfairness of today's status quo on songwriters and publishers. That gross unfairness is reflected in two simple yet striking data points:

- Seventy-five percent of the income for songwriters and publishers is regulated by outdated laws and antiquated government oversight, which has for too long resulted in devalued intellectual property rights and undervalued royalty rates;
- We estimate that songwriter and publisher revenues are significantly below what they would be if fair rate standards and free market negotiations were used to determine such royalties.

It is long overdue for Congress to consider seriously why the price for other forms of intellectual property such as movies, books, video games, magazines, television shows and recorded music are all properly negotiated in the free market, while songwriters remain uniquely singled-out and subject to heavy regulation. If this does not change, the ultimate outcome will be fewer professional songwriters and fewer songs, as many established songwriters will simply stop writing. Others will never start.

THE ROLE OF MUSIC PUBLISHERS

A music publisher is a company or individual that represents the interests of songwriters by promoting and licensing the use of their songs. Music publishers are often involved at the very beginning of a songwriter's career. After signing a writer to a publishing deal, a publisher will do everything from helping the writer find co-writers to securing artists to record the writer's songs. Frequently, when a songwriter enters into a relationship with a publisher, the publisher will advance desperately needed money to the writer to help pay living expenses so the writer can focus on what he or she does best: write music.

Songwriters and music publishers attempt to earn a living through three primary means of utilizing their separate copyright – mechanical reproductions, public performances, and audio-visual synchronizations. The ratio of how much each contributes to the bottom line has been in flux in recent years as listeners move away from ownership models such as CDs and downloads toward streaming and video as their preferred mode of music consumption.

It is important to note that songwriters and publishers depend on royalties for their livelihood. Unlike recording artists, most songwriters cannot supplement their income through touring, merchandise sales, or endorsements.

MECHANICAL REPRODUCTIONS – SECTION 115

The mechanical reproduction right affords songwriters and publishers a royalty when a musical composition is embodied in a physical format such as a record, CD or – more commonly in the digital age – when a consumer downloads a song from iTunes or streams music through an interactive service like Spotify.

The mechanical reproduction right is regulated by Section 115 of the Copyright Act, which imposes a compulsory license system that dates back to 1909. At that time, Congress chose to regulate the mechanical reproduction of musical compositions embodied on player piano rolls to prevent exclusive deals between music publishers and player piano makers that might lead to a monopoly in the player piano roll market. While player piano rolls disappeared long ago, this outdated regulation continues to undermine the exclusive rights of music publishers and songwriters. As a result of this Congressional decision that pre-dates World War I, songwriters and music publishers have been denied the ability to negotiate the value of their intellectual property in a free market.

Instead, this statutory mechanism allows anyone who wants to use a musical work to obtain a license to reproduce and distribute copies of the work, in exchange for paying a royalty set by the government. In 1909, the rate for mechanical licenses was set directly by Congress at 2 cents per song. Today, rates are set by a three-judge panel called the Copyright Royalty Board (CRB). Based on the initial price set in 1909, today's mechanical rate would be more than 50 cents if adjusted for inflation. Remarkably more than 100 years later, the current statutory rate stands at only 9.1 cents.

This paltry increase is due to the fact that the law directs the CRB to apply an antiquated, below-market standard when setting mechanical rates. This standard – known as an 801(b) standard – requires the CRB to ensure "[the] copyright *user* a fair income under existing economic conditions," and to "minimize any disruptive impact on the structure of the industries involved...." In other words, the law not only dictates that songwriters and publishers must license their songs to everyone, but also imposes the price they will receive based on what the CRB thinks potential licensees can pay without any disruption to their businesses. Without question, the law's emphasis on the interests of users depresses the rate that music publishers and songwriters might otherwise be able to negotiate in a free market.

On the other side of the music business, the recorded music industry has been able to thrive in the marketplace and negotiate freely without suffering under the burden of a compulsory license regime. When it comes to the use of master recordings to make and distribute CDs or digital downloads, there is no compulsory license or obligation to license whatsoever. As a result of exercising their unfettered right to license master rights for reproduction and distribution, a record label receives approximately 81 cents of the $1.29 charged by Apple for the typical iTunes download. This is approximately nine times as much as the 9.1 cents that a songwriter and publisher must split when the very same song – the song that they wrote – is downloaded.

It is fundamentally unfair for the law to continue to subject songwriters and music publishers to *BOTH* a compulsory license and a below-market rate standard. This review presents the perfect opportunity for Congress to consider getting rid of the section 115 compulsory license. As former Register of Copyrights Mary Beth Peters so eloquently argued during her tenure:

> A fundamental principle of copyright law is that the author should have the exclusive right to exploit the market for his work, except where doing so would conflict with the public interest. While the Section 115 statutory license may have served the public interest well with respect to a nascent music reproduction industry after the turn of the century and for much of the 1900's, it is no longer necessary and unjustifiably abrogates copyright owners' rights today.

If Congress does not eliminate section 115, it should at the very least require that the CRB apply a fair market rate standard when determining the statutory rate.

PUBLIC PERFORMANCE RIGHT

Songwriters and publishers also receive royalties for the public performance of their works. Examples include when their music is publicly performed on the radio, via streaming services, and in many public venues, including restaurants and bars. Because of the large number of entities that use music, obviously it would be a challenge for songwriters and publishers to negotiate individual licenses directly and effectively monitor all public performances of their music. Instead, songwriters and publishers generally affiliate with a performing rights organization (PRO) – ASCAP, BMI or SESAC – which negotiates blanket licenses, collects royalties, and enforces rights on their behalf.

While the performance right is not explicitly regulated by law, the onerous Department of Justice consent decrees that have governed ASCAP and BMI since 1941 result in songwriters and publishers also receiving below-market compensation for performance of their music.

Under these World War II-era consent decrees, songwriters and music publishers do not get to negotiate the value of their intellectual property in a free market. Additionally, the consent decrees allow for a period of free-rate licensing during which the property of songwriters and music publishers is utilized without compensation for vast lengths of time as the parties attempt to negotiate a license. If an agreement cannot be reached voluntarily by the parties, a federal judge decides the terms of the license.

As streaming continues to cannibalize the mechanical royalties traditionally received from CD sales and downloads, compensation from the public performance right has become an increasingly larger portion of a songwriter's income. Unfortunately, the current royalties paid by digital webcasters cannot sustain songwriters who are trying to pay their rent and put food on the table for their families. To provide some perspective regarding how little songwriters and publishers are compensated by Internet radio, NMPA hosted an event on Capitol Hill in conjunction with the Subcommittee's last hearing on music licensing issues. The event featured five songwriters whose five well-known songs had been streamed on Pandora more than 33 million times in the first quarter of 2012. In return for the use of their works those writers and their publishers collectively received $2,033.

This week the Department of Justice announced it is undertaking a review to examine the operation and effectiveness of the consent decrees. It is our hope that the DOJ will act quickly to lift or significantly modify the consent decrees to ensure that publishers can continue to affiliate with ASCAP and BMI without having to sacrifice fair market compensation. Arguably, collective licensing benefits licensees as much – if not more – as the licensors, so all parties have an interest in finding a new model that works for everyone.

In addition to the Justice Department amending the consent decrees, Congress can also help by amending section 114(i) of the law, which currently prevents the federal rate courts from considering the rates paid to SoundExchange for digital performances of sound recordings as evidence when setting rates. NMPA believes that those rates, which can be more than 12 times greater than what songwriters and publishers receive, would help the federal rate courts to determine more accurately fair rates for the performance of musical compositions.

SYNCHRONIZATION (SYNC) RIGHTS

The use of music synchronized with video is the third significant source of revenue for songwriters and publishers. Traditionally this has included the use of music in movies, television, and commercials. Newer forms of this right include music videos and the use of music in user-generated content such as on YouTube.

For songwriters and music publishers, this is a free market right not regulated by law. Because the sync market is unregulated, NMPA believes it is a useful barometer for assessing the fair market value for mechanical reproductions and performances of musical compositions. If an automobile company wants to use a popular song in a commercial for its new car, it must negotiate with the music publisher and the record company for the use of their respective copyrights. Not surprisingly, given that both copyrights are then negotiated in a free market, the common industry practice is to pay both copyright owners under the same terms. This free market benchmark suggests that the 9:1 split that record companies receive for downloads and the 12:1

split they receive for webcasting are simply a product of the regulation that publishers are subject to in those areas.

Some have called for compulsory licenses to include sync rights. This is the wrong approach and would only discourage investment in songwriting. The sync licensing market is operating efficiently without government regulation and currently compensates songwriters fairly for their creativity and publishers for their investment. In addition, for those who would use scare tactics regarding what would happen if regulation were lifted in other areas, the efficiency and smooth operation of the synchronization market provides a perfect illustration of how the music industry can thrive in the absence of unnecessary regulation.

The Songwriter Equity Act (SEA)

The SEA addresses two significant inequities under current copyright law that prevent songwriters and music publisher from receiving compensation that reflects the fair market value of their intellectual property.

The SEA would ensure that the government applies a market-based rate standard when setting licensing rates for the mechanical reproduction of musical compositions - the same rate standard enjoyed by artists and record labels for non-exempt businesses in the digital sound recording performance right. The SEA would also allow the federal courts that set rates for the public performance of musical compositions to look at relevant evidence, which they are currently prohibited by law from considering.

These modest changes to the law will help level the playing field in the rate setting proceedings that are currently undeniably stacked against songwriters and publishers.

Proposals to Devalue the Rights of Songwriters/Publishers

The RIAA's recent submission to the Copyright Office regarding music licensing issues suggests that licensing would be more efficient if songwriters and publishers simply allowed record labels to administer our copyrights for us. This is not a realistic or constructive proposal.

Songwriters and publishers value the ability to determine how their works are used and to negotiate the terms for their use. Having a direct relationship with licensees is also frequently an important component of understanding and advancing mutual interests. While NMPA believes strongly in a more efficient and effective licensing system, the answer is not to subjugate the rights of songwriters and music publishers to record labels.

The elimination or, at the very least, modification of the government-mandated compulsory license and consent decrees in favor of a licensing structure that more closely resembles free market negotiations favors not only music publishers and songwriters, but music services, consumers and the music market generally. The CRB proceedings that set the Section 115 compulsory license rates and categories for mechanical rights occur once every five years, far slower than the development of new technology for digital music distribution.

The government-enforced consent decrees that govern the licensing of public performance rights restrict the ability of both the PROs and music publishers to bundle the multiple, global rights that new digital music services now require to operate and compete on a world-wide scale. These restrictive and antiquated regulations result in a slow and reactive market for the licensing of songs, and do not provide the necessary flexibility to license rights properly and proactively in an ever-evolving, dynamic online music world. Only in the free market—or in a system that closely approximates free market conditions—can new music services obtain all of the rights needed as that technology develops, allowing those music services to enter the market and the ears of music-loving consumers more quickly.

CONCLUSION

As our global digital marketplace rapidly evolves, songwriters and music publishers will continue to embrace new delivery models and technology, but much of the copyright framework is outdated. A copyright update should build upon a foundation of intellectual property rights that enable a vibrant, legal music marketplace. Not just for songwriters, but for all creators. Congress should review the law with a presumption against regulations that severely limit creators' property rights.

Most importantly, we must ensure that future business models fairly compensate songwriters. Licensing new business models efficiently does no good if such new business models do not allow a songwriter to earn a living. Without updates to the law songwriting as a profession will give to way songwriting as a hobby and an important American treasure will be in jeopardy.

NMPA looks forward to participating in discussions on how to work together to improve our copyright law.

In: Copyright and the Music Marketplace
Editor: Keith Turner

ISBN: 978-1-63482-869-7
© 2015 Nova Science Publishers, Inc.

Chapter 5

STATEMENT OF MICHAEL O'NEILL, CHIEF EXECUTIVE OFFICER, BMI. HEARING ON "MUSIC LICENSING UNDER TITLE 17 PART ONE"[*]

Mr. Chairman, thank you for the opportunity to present testimony before the Subcommittee on Courts, Intellectual Property, and the Internet (the "Subcommittee") of the U.S. House of Representatives Committee on the Judiciary (the "Committee") on the important subject of music licensing. I would also like to thank the Ranking Minority Member and the other members of the Subcommittee.[1]

My name is Michael O'Neill. I am Chief Executive Officer of Broadcast Music, Inc. ("BMI"), one of the world's leading music performing right organizations ("PROs"). Mr. Chairman, America's copyright laws provide a firm legal foundation to support a vibrant community of creative songwriters, composers and music publishers whose works fuel a robust and vibrant entertainment industry. After giving some brief background information about BMI's mission and the benefits of collective licensing, my testimony will address three areas of music licensing in the current digital environment: (1) modernizing the BMI consent decree to enable BMI to meet the needs of the digital marketplace; (2) the need for the Songwriter Equity Act to achieve fair market value royalties for performances and mechanical licenses; and (3) updating the public performing right for the digital age, including confirming the applicability of the "making available" right recognized in the WIPO Copyright Treaty ("WCT") (to which the United States is a signatory).

I. BMI AND COLLECTIVE LICENSING

BMI is celebrating its 75th anniversary this year. Since its incorporation in 1939, BMI's traditional role has been to license on a non-exclusive basis one of the six exclusive copyright rights identified by Congress in the U.S. Copyright Act: the right to publicly perform musical works. Public performances of musical works occur on radio, television, cable, satellite and

---

[*] This is an edited, reformatted and augmented version of a statement presented June 10, 2014 before the House Judiciary Committee, Subcommittee on Courts, Intellectual Property and the Internet.

the Internet as well as at concert halls, sports arenas, restaurants, hotels, retail stores and universities, to name a few of the many categories of BMI licensees. BMI licenses its music repertoire literally wherever music is performed or communicated to the public. BMI operates on a non-profit-making basis, distributing all income (less overhead and reasonable reserves) to its affiliated songwriters and publishers.

BMI is proud to represent the public performing rights to more than 8.5 million musical works, and over 600,000 songwriters, composers and publishers, more than any other PRO. BMI also represents the works of thousands of foreign composers and songwriters when their works are publicly performed in the United States. BMI's repertoire includes works from outstanding creators in every style and genre of musical composition. BMI provides benefits to music creators and users alike. BMI also provides viable competition and choice for America's songwriters in the licensing of the public performing right in their musical works.

For its licensed music users, BMI offers an easy and friction-free solution for clearing the public performing rights to its works through the mechanism of a blanket license for one modest annual license fee. BMI's core competency is as a trusted third party in licensing the public performing right of musical creators to a broad range of entities that incorporate music into their products or services. To be successful in this mission, we have developed an understanding of and appreciation for the business models and programming needs of the hundreds of thousands of businesses across the nation that provide our creators' music to the public. BMI's blanket licensing has been endorsed over the decades by virtually all parties across the copyright licensing spectrum and, over the past four decades, has been embraced by Congress as a model for statutory licensing and applauded by the Registers of Copyright in several reports presented to Congress and this Committee.

BMI also plays an extremely active role in the international copyright arena, serving on many committees and in leadership capacities in CISAC, the International Confederation of Societies of Authors and Composers. BMI has over 90 reciprocal licensing agreements with foreign PROs that give users outside the United States access to perform the BMI catalog and give users within the United States instant access to a global catalog of music. In an increasingly international economy fueled by the rapid expansion of the Internet, BMI's structure and long history of cooperation with international content owners is all the more relevant and compelling.

Since the dawn of the Internet, BMI has seen opportunity both for the digital businesses using BMI-represented music as part of their offerings, and for the songwriters, composers and music publishers we represent. In many ways, digital media has democratized the entertainment industry – knocking down economic and technological barriers and creating opportunity for more creators. We believe that technology and artistic creativity are symbiotic, not antagonistic. Today, we can each walk around with access to literally millions of songs from all genres through a device that fits neatly in our shirt or coat pockets. Tomorrow, as the market continues to innovate, it will become even easier for consumers to take greater control of their content – what they see or listen to, as well as how and where and when they do it.

For 75 years, BMI has served as a bridge between the business and creative communities as new opportunities to build commercial enterprises and generate revenue from music content have emerged. BMI's roster of licensees is a "who's who" of the global digital media. From Rhapsody to Spotify, Netflix to Hulu, and YouTube to Apple, we have a strong track record of crafting commercial relationships that work for business and our writers and publishers.

Through these innovative licenses, we have successfully addressed new business and content models, from ad-supported to subscription services, long-form programming to on-demand and crowd-sourced playlists. We respect the exciting innovations that our digital licensees are bringing to market. We ask in return that the services recognize the value of music and creativity in the marketplace when standards and rules are established and when royalty fees are negotiated.

Despite our impressive track record of growth, BMI, like any organization, must continue to evolve to address the needs of its customers and the marketplace. What follows are achievable suggestions of what is needed for BMI to continue to fulfill its mission of serving its affiliates and promoting the growth of music.

II. THE BMI CONSENT DECREE MUST BE MODERNIZED TO MEET THE MARKETPLACE NEEDS OF THE DIGITAL AGE

BMI's business operations are governed by a nearly 50-year-old consent decree that was written at a time when television was an adolescent industry, analog broadcasting was the norm, and most popular music was on AM radio stations and could only be purchased by fans in small mom-and-pop record stores. Needless to say, the world is a vastly different place in the early 21st century. The BMI decree is in dire need of important repair and modernizing in order for BMI to continue to bridge the needs of music users and owners.

BMI has been in discussions with the United States Department of Justice ("DOJ"), as well as music users and the music publishing industry, about ways to modernize its decree to meet the needs of the current and future marketplace. We see the need to loosen or eliminate archaic restrictions that keep necessary, in-demand products from the marketplace, or that result in fees that are not market-based, or that create an obstacle course that jeopardizes the ability of small, independent publishers (and the songwriters who have contracted with these publishers) to continue to compete with their larger publisher competitors, thereby injuring the public. I will address four areas of proposed decree reform.

A. Digital Rights Withdrawal Should Be Permitted under the BMI Decree

Concerned that the PROs were being paid license fees that were not market-based for many digital music services, several larger publishers decided in the last few years to withdraw from BMI and the American Society of Authors, Composers and Publishers ("ASCAP") the right to license their catalogs for certain defined digital uses and instead to license those uses directly in the unregulated marketplace. Unlike many traditional media music users, it appears that there are a small number of very large digital music services that those publishers believe they can license themselves without the intermediary of BMI. Those publishers apparently believe that, if their digital rights are negotiated away from the confines of the consent decrees' compulsory license regime, they can achieve rates that more accurately reflect fair market value.

BMI believes that its consent decree permits partial withdrawal of rights (*i.e.*, permitting publishers to designate BMI to license some license categories but not others).[2] However, in separate decisions in 2013, both the BMI and ASCAP rate courts determined that the PROs' consent decrees do not allow their publishers to choose to have their works licensed by BMI (or ASCAP) for certain uses while retaining their rights to license PRO customers for other uses. The BMI rate court held that a publisher must use BMI for *all* public performing rights purposes or *none*, thus putting publishers in the position of having to leave PROs entirely if they wish to retain any licensing right exclusively for themselves.

These decisions present publishers with a dilemma: "all in" or "all out." If forced into an all-or-nothing choice, publishers could be compelled to turn their backs on the efficiencies and value that BMI brings to wide swaths of the music licensing market in order to explore market opportunities for digital music rights.[3] This threatens the entire licensing ecosystem that BMI services, including the songwriters, the hundreds of thousands of music users who depend on blanket licenses to comply with the copyright law, and the international web of reciprocal license agreements. Thus, in our discussions with the DOJ we are seeking to clarify our consent decree with the DOJ to provide for partial withdrawal of rights under some reasonable structural guidelines.

B. BMI Should Be Able to License Multiple Rights

In today's world, multiple rights – for example, performing rights, mechanical rights, lyric display, publication and reproduction rights, and synchronization rights – are often necessary in order to disseminate music. Currently, users must negotiate these complementary rights with multiple parties in circumstances where the ability to negotiate all of them with a single party would be more efficient. As the Commerce Department Internet Policy Task Force recently noted, the current disaggregated system is inefficient, and bundled licensing could spur innovation.

While the BMI consent decree does not prohibit the licensing of multiple rights, ASCAP's consent decree does. However, in Europe, where collective music rights organizations handle both performance and mechanical rights, it is a common practice for PROs to offer "one-stop shop" licensing for multiple rights in musical works. Yet despite the demands of the marketplace for bundled rights solutions, BMI and ASCAP do not generally license mechanical rights or synchronization rights, either separately or as a complement to their blanket licensing of public performing rights for digital music services.[4]

For over 10 years, digital music services have complained about the difficulty of licensing mechanical rights under Section 115. The Section 115 compulsory license is a work-specific license, whereas digital music services need access to a large volume of works to launch competitive music offerings online. These services have called for a blanket license under Section 115 as well as the ability to bundle the various music publishing rights they need through "one-stop shops." PROs ought to have no restrictions on the product lines they can offer to users who need all rights.

This clarification of the BMI decree is especially critical if some publishers elect to withdraw their digital rights from BMI. If partial rights withdrawal were permitted under the BMI consent decrees, we expect that some larger publishers would take the opportunity to license – and bundle – rights to certain music users outside of BMI's licensing mechanism. However, most publishers – including especially smaller and independent publishers – would likely opt to remain with BMI, as they may lack the resources necessary to explore such licensing opportunities or may simply prefer to avail themselves of the value provided by BMI.

It is therefore critical that the BMI consent decree make clear that these smaller and independent publishers – through BMI – are able to bundle digital rights in the same way as their larger competitors do. In this way, smaller publishers will be able to offer the same licensing products as large publishers, and digital music services will have access to all the rights they need from BMI affiliates on a one-stop basis.

In addition, under changes to the copyright law enacted effective in 1978 and just now becoming operational, songwriters who gave their rights to publishers in or after 1978 can recapture their copyrights after 35 years. This will create an ever-growing universe of songwriters who will become, essentially, their own publishers, and, just like the small and independent publishers, will need the resources of the PROs to fully exploit their works and compete with the larger publishers who offer bundled rights products outside of the PROs.

Maintaining BMI's role as a trusted digital licensing representative for independent music publishers and songwriters also would ensure the continued diversity and competition in the music publishing sector, which has seen consolidation in recent years. PROs should be explicitly authorized to handle reproduction and distribution rights required by digital services, either separately or as a part of bundled rights offerings. Such capabilities will also bring the United States into greater harmony with global PROs.

C. The BMI Rate Court Should Be Replaced or Streamlined

Under the BMI consent decree, a licensee has an automatic right to a blanket license to use any, some, or all of BMI's music upon written request for a license. If BMI and the licensee cannot reach an agreement on reasonable fees through negotiations, either party can petition the designated judge in the United States District Court for the Southern District of New York to determine those fees (referred to as the BMI "rate court"). When a fee dispute is before the BMI rate court, the parties to the rate proceeding frequently cite prior PRO licenses and other marketplace deals to serve as benchmarks in order to aid the rate court in setting reasonable license fee rates for the applicant music user.

While this rate court structure may have served a purpose in the traditional, stable broadcast marketplace, the process is ill-suited to the rapidly evolving digital licensing world. In short, the BMI rate court (and the parallel ASCAP rate court) federal litigation process has become unwieldy, expensive and slow, and it has produced what we believe are below-market rates that are not responsive to changes in the value of repertoire.

We believe that replacing the current rate court with arbitration in New York under the American Arbitration Association rules would be a faster, less expensive, and a more market-responsive mechanism for all parties to obtain fair, market-value rate decisions. Congress already enacted legislation to provide an expedited litigation structure for individual proprietors in Section 513 of the Copyright Act. This can perhaps be a template for a streamlined process, (albeit with replacing federal rate courts in the various federal circuits with arbitrations). We do not believe that moving BMI to compulsory licensing before the

Copyright Royalty Board ("CRB") would be a solution to this problem, as it would replace one expensive, slow system with another.

Under the current BMI consent decree, any business that wants to use our music just has to send BMI a letter asking to do so. If businesses can get instant access to our music, it is only fair that they pay us *something* from the moment they use the music, even if it may take a while to come to a final agreement on terms. Under the current decree, if the parties cannot agree on an "interim" fee, BMI must bring a motion in the BMI rate court – again, slow and expensive –to have the court set the rate. For an interim fee to be paid from the outset would require a change in the consent decree to become a reality.

D. The BMI Decree Should Be Periodically Reviewed or Sunset

In addition to these reform ideas, BMI also believes that the DOJ should re-examine the basis for a perpetual consent decree governing and restricting the rights of music content owners. In this regard, we should move toward a sunset of the current decree in its entirety if its existence can no longer be justified overall or partial deregulation in any digital market in which BMI may lack the market power that was the predicate for its original regulation.

The substantive provisions of BMI's current consent decree were negotiated and entered into in 1966, with the lone change since then being the addition of the compulsory license/rate court mechanism in 1994. This nearly 50-year span is several generations in human years, but measured in digital years, it is eons removed from the current marketplace. The current BMI consent decree assumes that BMI has significant market power that needs to be curbed, but those assumptions are questionable now that digital technology has exploded in the past two decades. The Internet's worldwide reach, combined with increasing computing power and decreasing storage costs, now affords both owners and music users far greater tools and capabilities to identify, monitor and license music use than was the case a half century ago. There are many rights licensing agencies and services competing to meet the rights clearance needs in an unregulated market.

However, even if regulation still has some place in the modern era, a likely future is one in which one or many major publishers may partially withdraw their digital rights from BMI (in the event that partial grants are permitted or recognized by the courts to be available under the decree), or large publishers may have left the PROs entirely. In any market sector in which this occurs, BMI would lack the market power presupposed as a basis for its consent decree restrictions. Why then should BMI continue to be regulated for those licensees? In short, the competitive landscape has changed so substantially that the DOJ should reexamine the justifications for the decrees and seek termination if they are no longer found to be warranted by original assumptions.

If record labels and major publishers can license in the unregulated marketplace, PROs should also be able to compete on the same playing field so that legions of smaller songwriters and publishers will not be disadvantaged. Competition from the collective body of smaller songwriters and publishers will benefit the public welfare. At a minimum, the decree should be subjected to mandatory periodic review, perhaps every five years, and terminated at a stipulated point in the future.[5]

As you may be aware, the DOJ has in the last week called for public comment on whether the PROs' consent decrees are fulfilling their purposes. We look forward to this process and are optimistic that DOJ will agree that the time has come to bring the consent decrees into the modern age in order to address the current needs of the marketplace.

III. THE SONGWRITER EQUITY ACT SHOULD BE ENACTED

BMI has joined with ASCAP, SESAC, Inc., the National Music Publishers' Association and the National Academy of Recording Arts and Sciences in support of the Songwriter Equity Act ("SEA"). The SEA is a modest bill which would help songwriters and publishers obtain fair market value royalties for public performance and mechanical licensing of digital services.[6] The SEA contains an amendment to Section 114(i) that could serve to reduce the current inequitable disparity between the low public performing rights fees paid by Internet music webcasters (such as Pandora) to songwriters and publishers for the public performance of musical works, and the far higher, fair market value fees paid by these same Internet music services to recording artists and record labels for the public performance of sound recordings.

The goal of the SEA, insofar as it relates to PROs, is simple: it removes the prohibition against the PRO rate courts' consideration of the fair market value rates set by the CRB as benchmarks. The bill, by removing the evidentiary prohibition, establishes a process that permits the rate courts to consider all relevant benchmark deals (including the CRB rates). The statutory fix would not only apply in a rate court but also in arbitration of rates if the BMI decree is amended as we propose herein.

While we believe this may lead to a more reasonably comparative valuation for music compositions, the bill is silent on the appropriate rate, and leaves all aspects of rate determination to the rate court; it does *not* mandate rate increases for the PROs or digital music services, nor does it even require the rate courts to give *any* weight whatsoever to sound recording rates. Rather, by modifying Section 114(i) in this way, Congress would afford rate courts the ability to address the rates for musical works based on a more complete examination of marketplace factors.

The reason we seek passage of this bill is because we believe that a PRO rate court, given all relevant benchmarks, would set rates that would reduce the current disparity. There is a roughly 12-to-1 disparity in the license fees paid to SoundExchange by large digital music services like Pandora compared to the license fees paid to songwriters and PROs by those same services. While ASCAP's rate court recently announced a blanket license rate of 1.85% of Pandora's net revenues to be paid to ASCAP (for its approximate 45% share of music performances), the same licensee is paying approximately 50% of its revenues for sound recording performing rights to SoundExchange.[7] BMI has its own rate proceeding pending against Pandora and we are seeking a reasonable rate increase.

There is no basis in law or economics for the current disparity. We believe that one of the causes for this disparity is the language in Section 114(i). Indeed, this section was cited by the ASCAP rate court decision as expressly forbidding the court from even *considering* as benchmarks the fair market value rates paid or set by the CRB for sound recording performance rights.

Indeed, this gap in the value of sound recording and musical work copyrights is out of sync with global music licensing norms. Internationally, performance rights in sound recordings are considered "neighboring" rights that are not the same as "authorship" rights under copyright. Rights of authorship vested in such creative works as musical compositions are viewed as having equal or greater value since they represent the foundational creative elements upon which other intellectual property is derived. This approach recognizes the undeniable truth that there can be no sound recording without an underlying musical composition.[8]

IV. THE PUBLIC PERFORMING RIGHT SHOULD BE UPDATED FOR THE DIGITAL AGE, RECOGNIZING THE "MAKING AVAILABLE" RIGHT IN THE WIPO COPYRIGHT TREATY

In the digital era, the future of content distribution is customized programming. Consumers want their programming on any device and available at any time. They will no longer accept having to be in front of their television sets at an appointed time to watch their favorite programming.

The worldwide copyright organization, WIPO, recognized in the WCT that the number of individuals who receive a particular content transmission simultaneously is not important. Rather, the WCT acknowledged that content will be consumed individually as a result of it being made available for consumption and therefore recognized that its "making available" right covers interactive, one-to-one transmissions commonly made by Internet and mobile services. In addition, the "making available" right in both the public performing right and public distribution rights includes liability for the "mere offering" to transmit works, without the need to demonstrate that a transmission to a particular listener took place.

To be clear, BMI believes that the current U.S. public performing right already includes the full scope of wired and wireless transmissions, as well as the full scope of interactivity, and that the "making available" right is an inherent part of current copyright law.

However, two recent court decisions have concluded that at least some individually-accessed content is *not* protected by the public performance right, suggesting that Congress should explicitly clarify that the concepts embodied in the "making available" right are applicable to public performances. Specifically, the Second Circuit's *Cartoon Network* and *Aereo* decisions have called into question whether the public performing right even applies to certain kinds of interactive transmissions.[9]

Together, these decisions have curtailed the public performing right, by declaring that one-to-one transmissions of a copyrighted work to individual members of the public are "private" (i.e., outside the scope of the public performing right, and the reach of copyright law) if they are made from so-called "private locker copies." This technology-based loophole is at odds with the wide application of the performing right to one-to-one, on-demand (or interactive) transmissions. Recognizing the importance of this issue, the U.S. Supreme Court granted certiorari in the *Aereo* case (and heard oral argument on the matter on April 22, 2014). BMI submitted an amicus brief as part of a music industry coalition and we are optimistic that the high court will reverse the Second Circuit's decision.

The future of commercial music content delivery lies with highly-customized and individualized content streaming offered by cloud music services, and many of these services are already claiming to make "private" performances, in reliance on *Cartoon Network*. I would like to emphasize that cloud computing services will not be threatened by a robust public performing right. Content rights should be licensed and the marketplace will respond to the legitimate needs of cloud locker services. By contrast, if these court decisions remain the law of the land, or are not cured by legislation, we face the potential for a growing range of uses of copyrighted content that will not compensate the content's creators. Together, these decisions threaten to eviscerate the value of creativity through a technological gaming of the system, enabling engineers to configure a performance as "not public" in order to avoid paying for the use of such content.

BMI therefore believes that the "mere offering" of performances for transmission is applicable to both the public performing right and the distribution right.

In light of these recent developments, we believe that the U.S. public performing right should be clarified or confirmed to include the full scope of the "making available" right.[10]

CONCLUSION

Music always starts with a song, and without songwriters, there would be no music. If music licensing reform is to reach fruition, protecting the economic interests of songwriters should be a paramount concern of Congress. The laws of the United States, enacted pursuant to an express constitutional clause, are rooted in a fundamental principle that authors should be incentivized to create. PROs are key players, as they present efficient marketplace licensing solutions that deliver performing rights to users and performing right royalties to songwriters and publishers.

We believe the keys to a continuing, vibrant music rights landscape are: (1) modernizing the consent decrees to permit partial rights withdrawal, enabling BMI and ASCAP to handle the licensing of mechanical and synchronization rights to digital music services, and streamlining and otherwise modifying the rate-setting mechanism; (2) enacting the SEA to enable rate courts (and any successor arbitration panels) and the CRB to establish fair market value rates for performance and mechanical licenses; and (3) if necessary, legislatively correcting the judicial decisions limiting the public performing right by clarifying that all interactive, on-demand transmissions to the public are public performances. These goals are achievable and will promote creativity and a robust music marketplace.

Mr. Chairman, BMI looks forward to working with you, your staff, and other Members of the Subcommittee. Under your leadership and that of the Ranking Member, BMI will continue to work closely with all sectors of the music industry in order to develop music licensing reform solutions. We are grateful to the Subcommittee for the effectiveness of the Copyright Act, which permits BMI to function, and songwriters, composers and publishers to be compensated – not only to make a living but to create small businesses in a free enterprise system. Thank you for your many years of strong leadership on these issues which has had such a beneficial impact on the livelihoods of the hundreds of thousands of individuals we represent.

End Notes

[1] Neither I nor BMI have received any funds, grants, contracts (or subcontracts) from any federal agency or proceeding of any kind during this fiscal year or the preceding two fiscal years that would have any relevancy to this hearing or my testimony.

[2] For example, as part of BMI's standard publisher affiliation agreements all publishers have for decades withheld the right to license "grand" performing rights from BMI because the market for musical theater is one that they can easily license themselves and for greater value.

[3] For example, if a publisher withdrew from BMI, it would either have to incur the costs of licensing, monitoring, and collecting royalties from tens of thousands of restaurants and many thousands of broadcasters, or forgo licensing them and the royalties to which it would otherwise be entitled.

[4] BMI has included limited sync licenses to the broadcast television networks as part of its longstanding blanket license agreements.

[5] On March 28, 2014, the DOJ streamlined its review process for considering modifications and terminations. See Antitrust Division Manual (5th ed., March 2014), available at http://www.justice.gov/atr/public/division manual/atrdivman.pdf (last visited, Apr. 14, 2014).

[6] BMI is very pleased that this joint effort culminated in the introduction of the Songwriter Equity Act of 2014 (H.R. 4079) ("SEA") on February 26, 2014 by Rep. Doug Collins (R-GA), joined by original cosponsor Rep. Marsha Blackburn (R-TN).

[7] License rates for "non-interactive webcasting" of sound recordings are subject to a statutory license. In the absence of a voluntary negotiation, they can be set by the CRB under Section 114 using a standard that reflects. This standard is referred to as the "willing buyer/willing seller" standard. Voluntarily-negotiated interactive licenses have been considered as benchmarks in CRB proceedings. Digital music services like Pandora are thus required to pay license fees to SoundExchange for the right to stream the sound recordings containing the underlying musical works at a fair market value. These fees are in addition to separate license fees to the PROs and/or music publishers for the right to stream the musical works contained in the sound recordings.

[8] The SEA also seeks to shift the rate standard for mechanical royalties from a hodgepodge, multi-factor test to a market-based willing buyer/willing seller standard. We fully support this goal of the bill.

[9] See Cartoon Network, LP v. CSC Holdings, Inc., 536 F.3d 121 (2d Cir. 2008); WNET v. Aereo, Inc., 712 F.3d 676 (2d Cir. 2013), cert. granted, ABC v. Aereo, Inc., 187 L. Ed. 2d 702 (U.S. 2014).

[10] On April 4, 2014, BMI joined ASCAP, SESAC, Inc. the National Music Publishers' Association and The Songwriters' Guild of America in submitting a response to the U.S. Copyright Office's Notice of Inquiry regarding its study on the Right of Making Available. See Joint Comments of American Society of Composers, Authors and Publishers, Broadcast Music, Inc., The Songwriters' Guild of America, SESAC, Inc., and the National Music Publishers' Association, Study on Right of Making Available, Docket No. 2014-2 (Apr. 4, 2014).

Chapter 6

TESTIMONY OF ROSANNE CASH, SINGER, SONGWRITER, ON BEHALF OF THE AMERICAN MUSIC ASSOCIATION. HEARING ON "MUSIC LICENSING UNDER TITLE 17 PART TWO"[*]

Chairman Goodlatte, Chairman Coble, Ranking Members Conyers and Nadler, Members of the Subcommittee, thank you for the opportunity to testify today.

I am a singer/songwriter, author and performer. I wanted to be a songwriter from the time I was a teenager. I thought songwriting was an honorable, even noble profession. I believe that songwriting is far beyond just self---expression, but a powerful means of service: we, songwriters and musicians, help people to understand themselves better by helping them to feel— through music. We shine light on the dark corners of the soul. We help reveal the nooks and crannies of our shared humanity. We provide a community for the language of the heart. As Hans Christian Andersen said, where words fail, music speaks.

From the age of 18, I put myself to work. I 'showed up for the Muse', as my friend, writer Steven Pressfield says. I sat quietly around great songwriters to listen to their conversations about process, refinement, editing, rhyme schemes, chord progressions, lyric structure, narrative arcs, and on and on. I was full of passion and ambition, and I made myself an apprentice to some of the greats.

I have been a singer/songwriter and a sound recording artist now for over 30 years and I feel the same passion I felt as a teenager.

I have enjoyed acknowledgment, and much encouragement. I've won a Grammy, and been nominated for that award twelve times. I have charted 21 Top 40 singles, including 11 number one singles. I attribute most of this to very hard work and wonderful opportunity, as well as some native talent and tremendous collaboration with other creative individuals over the course of my career. I have had the great fortune of wonderful mentors and incredible fans, who have stayed with me for 35 years. I now share what I have learned by teaching songwriting and creative process. I have been a guest teacher in both English and Music programs at many colleges and universities, including New York University and Harvard. I

---

[*] This is an edited, reformatted and augmented version of testimony presented June 25, 2014 before the House Judiciary Committee, Subcommittee on Courts, Intellectual Property and the Internet.

am also a writer of prose, and have published four books, including my memoir, 'Composed', in 2010. I have kept my head down and shown up for work.

But the right beginnings, hard work and talent have NEVER been enough in my business. Creating music is, for the most part, a collaborative effort. Musicians are a tight---knit group. In the creation of recorded music, co---writers, producers, fellow musicians, recording engineers, background singers and various support people all come together with a single purpose: to create ONE work. For example, my new album The River and The Thread, from conception to a finished product took almost two years of writing and recording by myself and my husband and writing partner John Leventhal. It was arranged and produced by John, and co produced by Rick DePofi over that period. Then a team of creative and business professionals committed to 18 solid months of promotion and touring with me to support it. I am in the sixth month of that promotion.

With good fortune, a musician may also enjoy, as I do, the confidence and financial investment of a record label. I have been signed to major labels since 1978 and I'm honored to be on the esteemed label of Blue Note Records now. I am also a member of BMI, my performing rights organization, a member of two unions— SAG---AFTRA and the Musicians Union, of an artists advocacy group called Content Creators Coalition, and I'm a member of the Americana Music Association on whose behalf I am privileged to testify today.

I tell you these things to underscore that to me as a singer/songwriter, a recording artist, and a participant in many other parts of the music business it seems painfully obvious that all creative people deserve fair compensation when their work is used by others. For various reasons, that does not seem to be happening in the marketplace today, and we need a realignment.

I am a fan of new technology, both as a consumer and an artist. I am active in social media and do it myself, and I love it— I love the connection and the conversation. I'm also excited about the potential I see in the multiple new means of distributing music digitally that are being offered to music lovers, but my enthusiasm is tempered by the realization that these new business models are all cast against the backdrop of at least two decades of crushing digital piracy. This is important, because the royalties we are often offered as a result seem non--- negotiable. We can license services on the terms they offer. The alterative is piracy.

My father, Johnny Cash, testified before this committee in 1997 in support of the Digital Millennium Copyright Act. He told the committee then how challenging and dispiriting it was to find one of his biggest hits, 'Ring of Fire', being sold by someone in Slovenia on an illegal website and that he hoped the DMCA would aid in solving that. What an innocent time that was. Isolated illegal websites have morphed into a multi---national juggernaut that threatens to decimate the livelihoods of *all* musicians, songwriters and performers. There is a team at my record label devoted to issuing takedown notices to pirate sites. It is an absolutely futile gesture. The most popular search engines list pirate sites on the opening page of a search.

I have been publicly critical about the payment structures streaming services currently offer artists. For example, for an 18 month period, there were nearly 600,000 streams of my songs on a popular subscription site. I was paid $114.00 for those streams. I am not a lawyer or a politician or a policy wonk, and I couldn't begin to parse the incredibly complex, outdated, pre---Internet laws regarding licensing and copyrights but I CAN tell you that I see young musicians give up their dreams Every Single Day because they cannot make a living, they cannot survive doing the thing they most love, the thing they just might be on the planet to do.

There are various legal obstacles that currently hinder creative people in the music business from making a fair living from their work.

Among those are:

The lack of a public performance right for terrestrial radio play for sound recording artists. The United States is among a small number of countries that lack a broad sound recording performance right for artists. The others are China, North Korea and Iran. That list speaks for itself. The failure to recognize a broad public performance right for sound recording artists means that performers cannot collect royalties for their work even when it is broadcast abroad in countries where the right exists, because the treaties the U.S. has signed work on a reciprocal basis. Besides being fundamentally at odds with the principles this country was founded on – that we value the creations of the mind as much as we value what we create with our hands --- since we export more music than we import, the continued failure to recognize a performance right for terrestrial radio play makes no economic sense.

Issues concerning how rates are set for compulsory and collective licenses songwriters offer for their work. Songwriters and composers typically collectively license their work for public performance through performing rights organizations (PROs). This makes it easier for services like digital music services, satellite radio, television and other users of music to get the rights they need in one place, rather than having to license them directly from songwriters on an individual basis. Rates for these licenses generally end up being set by a federal court in New York. A provision of the copyright act prohibits the court from considering sound recording royalty rates as relevant evidence when setting rates for performances of compositions. Courts should be free to consider all evidence they find relevant to set the fairest rates.

As songwriters, we are also required to allow anyone who wishes to make a reproduction of our songs to do so in exchange for paying a statutory royalty rate. That rate was 2 cents per song in 1909 and today is only 9.1 cents per song.

The Songwriter Equity Act, introduced by two members of this Committee --- Congressmen Collins and Jeffries – would address these issues by allowing the courts to consider all relevant evidence when setting rates, and by directing the government body that sets the rate for the compulsory license for making reproductions of songs to reflect market value for the songs.

The lack of federal copyright protection for pre---'72 sound recordings. There is a gap in copyright protection for sound recordings created before 1972 which allows digital streaming services to refuse to pay older artists even for digital performances of those sound recordings. Works recorded prior to 1972 are protected by state laws so they don't enjoy the digital sound recording performance royalty provisions of the federal copyright act. I thank Ranking Member Conyers and Congressman Holding for introducing the RESPECT Act to treat the work of older musicians fairly by addressing this payment disparity. To put a personal perspective on this, if my father were alive today he would receive no payment for digital performances of his song 'I Walk The Line', written and recorded in 1956, but anyone who re--- recorded that song WOULD receive a royalty. This makes absolutely no sense, and is patently unfair.

Bottom line: Copyright law should not discriminate among different types of creative workers in affording them basic rights to compensation for their work. The creation and delivery of music to audiences requires the collaboration of many individuals and businesses including songwriters, performers, producers, music publishers and record labels. All of these individuals and entities should be appropriately compensated for their role in crafting and bringing work to audiences. At the moment in various important circumstances, some artists have no rights to royalties at all when their work is used by others to generate income. Other creators, like songwriters, have the compensation for the use of their work regulated by outdated laws and regulations.

These are just a few of the issues facing the music community. I understand that other legislation may be proposed by Ranking Member Nadler, from my home state of New York, thank you Mr. Nadler, to address music issues more comprehensively, and I will look forward to that bill with interest.

The complex system of music licensing that exists today should not be used to pit colleagues one against the other. I value all the contributions other creative people have made to my work and my career, and I have felt fortunate to be able to contribute and collaborate with others in return. The current dissonance we hear over music licensing issues does not stem from any ill will amongst colleagues or business partners, but solutions need to be found that realign incentives so that artists and songwriters can succeed together with existing and new music platforms.

Violinist Pablo Casals, one of the greatest musicians ever to live, said 'Music will save the world.' I believe that with all my heart. Where there are great differences among people, where misunderstanding and conflict are entrenched and seem impenetrable, there is a commonality, a language we all understand that resonates outside the arena of dispute and bitterness, outside linear time, a language that creates community and joy, and that is beyond words: Music.

Thank you.

In: Copyright and the Music Marketplace
Editor: Keith Turner
ISBN: 978-1-63482-869-7
© 2015 Nova Science Publishers, Inc.

Chapter 7

STATEMENT OF CARY SHERMAN, CHAIRMAN AND CEO, RECORDING INDUSTRY ASSOCIATION OF AMERICA. HEARING ON "MUSIC LICENSING UNDER TITLE 17 PART TWO"[*]

INTRODUCTION

Chairman Coble, Ranking Member Nadler, Chairman Goodlatte, Ranking Member Conyers, and members of the Subcommittee, my name is Cary Sherman and I serve as the Chairman and CEO of the Recording Industry Association of America. RIAA is the trade organization that supports and promotes the creative and financial vitality of the major record companies (often called the "majors"). Its members include iconic incubators of musical talent such as the Columbia, Motown, Capitol and Atlantic labels, to name a few, that together comprise the most vibrant record industry in the world. I greatly appreciate the opportunity to participate in this continued hearing on music licensing.

RIAA's members have worked hard over the past two decades to build a viable, diverse and consumer-friendly digital music marketplace. Millions of music lovers now listen to billions of recordings every single day. They can find whatever music they want, whenever and wherever they want it, in whatever format they choose. Undoubtedly, we have come a long way. Digital models now account for more than two thirds of our U.S. revenue. There are numerous new business models that could not even exist just a decade ago. We are light years ahead of other content-based industries in fully adapting to digital models.

But despite our efforts to meet consumers' demands in the modern music space, there remain serious systemic issues to address before the music marketplace can realize its full potential in the 21st Century. I would like to discuss what we see as our role in this evolution and highlight the challenges that remain.

---

[*] This is an edited, reformatted and augmented version of a statement presented June 25, 2014 before the House Judiciary Committee, Subcommittee on Courts, Intellectual Property and the Internet.

THE ROLE OF THE SOUND RECORDING IN THE MUSIC LICENSING SYSTEM

Record labels are the venture capitalists of the music industry. They invest tremendous resources in developing, marketing and promoting artists, and serve as the industry's economic engine. Yesterday, we released a report that details the major record companies' investment in music. As the report states, major record companies have embraced the digital age in every facet of the music business, giving recording artists, and the songwriters whose works they record, broader reach, finding new ways for them to earn a living from their craft, and helping fans take full advantage of innovative ways to find, access and enjoy their favorite music. Consumers have told record labels how they want to access music, and they have listened, with offerings on numerous platforms from downloads, to on-demand streaming services with low subscription fees to ad-supported video streaming models that are free-to-the-consumer.

In the process of embracing digital distribution, record labels have revolutionized the business, streamlining their operations and allocating a higher proportion of their revenues to investing in artist career development. Record labels provide the investment on which everyone in the music value chain depends, "seeding" the entire music ecosystem with $22.6 billion in U.S. talent investment – including artists, songwriters and music publishers - in just the last decade (and that's just from the major labels). The majors also invested an additional $6 billion over the same period to market recordings in the U.S.

There can be no doubt that songwriters and music publishers are our partners in this business. As Lee Miller, one of today's most prolific songwriters and the President of the Nashville Songwriters Association International stated at the first session of this music licensing hearing on June 10th, "I do not succeed if my songs are not recorded, sold and played." The job of record labels is to help creators succeed, by investing in them and their talent, marketing and promoting the recording and the artist, while at the same time partnering with today's and tomorrow's music service providers to expand the existing marketplace for music. Record labels make heavy investments in the artist's brilliant way of bringing a song to life, and ensure that this creativity reaches and captivates generations of fans, allowing everyone to reap the rewards of their contributions.

And even in tough times, our investments in creators have been significant. As a percentage of U.S. net sales revenue, over the last decade major label payments for artist advances and royalties have increased by 36% and mechanical royalties for songwriters and music publishers have increased by 44%.

Records are the economic engine that drives the entire music industry, from songwriter/publisher royalties to earnings from broadcasters and music services. If the song isn't recorded, and invested in by record companies through marketing and promotion, there is no real revenue for a songwriter, for an artist, for a broadcaster, for a digital music service. And many other types of income, from concert ticket sales to merchandising and endorsement opportunities, rely on the risks taken by record labels through investments that benefit not just well-known recording artists and songwriters but engineers, background musicians and many others.

Needless to say, investing in the careers of artists is an inherently unpredictable business, given the elusive nature of consumer taste. According to data from Nielsen SoundScan, 80%

of new albums sell less than 100 copies and 94% sell less than 1,000 copies. Out of 8 million digital tracks sold in 2011, 7.5 million sold less than 100 copies. In 2011, only one-half of one percent of all albums that sold even a single copy sold more than 10,000. Professor Anita Elberse has concluded that most record companies "recovered their investments in only one out of every five or six new albums." And it goes without saying that record labels must be able to receive a fair return on their investment, or they cannot take the necessary risks. If record labels cannot license their products widely and efficiently, they cannot sustain the investment needed to keep the economic engine running smoothly. Impediments to licensing – be they rights that are more limited than other copyrighted works, rate-setting processes that result in less than fair market value, or inefficient systems for licensing musical works – all impact the ability for record labels to drive the future of the music business for the benefit of all stakeholders.

OVERALL GOALS

So why are we here today? Why is this Subcommittee holding a hearing on the system for *music* licensing and not movie licensing, or book licensing, or software licensing? Well, because behind the seamless experience provided to consumers lurks an antiquated, inefficient and, frankly, broken system. Modern media must pair with today's and tomorrow's technologies to meet consumers' demands and expand consumer choice; foster rapid and frictionless innovation; and provide fair market value to creators, entrepreneurs and investors across the ecosystem. Unfortunately, the current music licensing system is not achieving these goals.

ISSUES

Music licensing is uniquely a product of its history – a series of legislative, regulatory and industry measures designed to address particular needs at particular points in time. Each of these measures may have made sense when enacted but, taken together, they now make little sense. The resultant fraying patchwork has produced a number of anomalous consequences. For example:

- Recordings, inexplicably, and unlike any other copyrighted work, are excluded from a full performance right, which means AM/FM radio does not pay for their use;
- Recordings are protected by Federal copyright law only if made after February 15, 1972, and some large digital radio services that benefit from a compulsory license are refusing to pay for recordings created before that date;
- Three digital radio services which are each now more than 20 years old still pay for recordings based on a below-market rate standard that was first established on the theory they were start-ups in need of a break;
- Unlike any other kind of copyrighted work delivered to consumers, the considerable investments in recordings are encumbered by a complicated regulatory regime for licensing musical compositions incorporated in the recording;

- Separate licensing entities exist for each of the underlying rights in musical compositions (i.e., performance, reproduction/distribution), so that digital music services that want to use our music are encumbered by the need to obtain multiple licenses from multiple sources for the same commercial use; and
- Musical compositions can be simultaneously subject to (1) free market negotiations, (2) compulsory licensing, and (3) judicial consent decrees, all at the same time, for inclusion in the same product or for the same commercial use.

It's no wonder everyone finds music licensing arcane and complex and dysfunctional. The system is simply not fit for the needs of the current marketplace. If we were to devise a licensing system from scratch, the one we've got today would not even be on the table. So we've got to rethink the system to more closely resemble other modern licensing frameworks, and we need to do it together – to achieve consensus from recording artists, record labels, songwriters and music publishers, along with the rest of the music community.

What specifically do we need to achieve? Our music licensing system should:

- Ensure that everyone in the value chain receives fair market value for their works, and for all of uses of their works, regardless of platform;
- Simplify musical work licensing by aggregating works under a blanket license, such as those already offered by ASCAP and BMI and the Section 114 compulsory license for recordings.
- Cover all the rights needed to bring to market all modern music releases, not just the audio-only products of yesterday.

SOLUTIONS

Fortunately, we do not need to reinvent the wheel to come up with a system that could actually achieve these specific priorities, and the overall goals listed above. We can simply look to the rights and licensing regimes already in place for most other copyrighted works.

First, grant a broadcast performance right for sound recordings. Every other copyrighted work has the same full set of rights. Only recordings have been denied the comprehensive rights enjoyed by every other copyrighted work – namely the right of public performance. That's why AM/FM radio is able to profit from the public performance of recordings without paying artists or record labels a dime. This has to be fixed.

This loophole in the law, which is unique among developed nations, costs artists and rights holders – and the U.S. economy – millions of dollars as foreign countries refuse to pay for radio performance of U.S. music since the U.S. doesn't pay. This anachronistic exemption didn't make sense in the past, and it certainly doesn't make sense in the current broader music industry landscape. If we're talking about modernizing music licensing, it only makes sense to finally put an end to the nearly century-old economic government subsidy provided to terrestrial broadcasters.

Second, make sure artists who recorded before 1972 are paid. Compulsory licenses in the law apply to copyrighted works regardless of when they were created. Only sound recordings are paid, or not paid, under a compulsory license depending on the date of their creation. This too has to be fixed.

While recordings made on or after February 15, 1972 are covered under Federal copyright law, those made before that date are protected by state law. Unfortunately, some digital radio services operating under a compulsory license have abused this bifurcation by refusing to pay for use of "pre-72" sound recordings under either state or federal law. The result is that many legacy artists are not compensated for the classic music that not only stands on its own (and inspires entire dedicated stations like Sirius XM's "60s on 6"), but helped pave the way for the hits of today.

Reps. Holding and Conyers have proposed legislation, H.R. 4772, the RESPECT Act, that would create a condition for use of the compulsory license. Services that benefit by using the compulsory license to stream sound recordings without permission and by paying one check for all music to one entity, would have to also pay for pre-72 music under the same system. Modernizing the modern music landscape cannot overlook and leave behind these cherished artists and their invaluable contributions to our country's musical heritage.

Third, allow rights to be bundled and administered together. Those who develop and own every other type of copyrighted work are able to license all the copyright rights necessary for the uses to be made by the licensee. A movie streaming service doesn't have to go to one entity to license the performance and a different entity to license the making of a server copy. So it should be with musical compositions.

Right now, the antiquated consent decree under which ASCAP operates prohibits that organization from offering licenses to any rights other than the public performance right, and another consent decree prohibits BMI from offering other rights such as synchronization licenses. That may have made sense in the 1940's, but in an age where multiple rights are implicated when music is downloaded and streamed online or consumed on video services like YouTube and Vevo, these restrictions have become an impediment. This must be changed. All licensing entities must have the ability to license all the rights needed for the use of the musical composition.

Fourth, create an across-the-board market-based rate standard. It goes without saying that every rights holder deserves fair market value for their work. Their livelihoods depend on it. We should have one rate standard for uses of music that remain under a compulsory license.

For example, three mature digital radio services – Sirius XM, Music Choice and Muzak – have enjoyed below-market royalty rates for their use of sound recordings. Rather than using the "willing buyer/willing seller" rate standard that applies to every other service, these three services still operate under the "801(b)(1)" standard that they were "grandfathered" into before 1998. For these services, that standard has been interpreted to set royalty rates that are less than fair market value, effectively forcing artists and record labels to subsidize these services' business models on a continuing basis.[1] They were "grandfathered" into the lower rate standard because of concern for the business expectations of start-up companies, but Congress never intended this to produce permanent below-market subsidies on the backs of artists and record labels. These services are no longer nascent businesses. All services that take advantage of the statutory licenses should be subject to the same willing buyer/willing seller rate standard.

Similarly, musical work owners must be guaranteed fair market value for their works by basing royalty rates on the same "willing buyer/willing seller" rate standard when mechanical royalty rates are set under Section 115 of the copyright law. We support the revision of that provision to reflect the fair market value standard as part of comprehensive revision of music licensing law (which would include updating the standard for the "grandfathered" services under Section 114).

The consent decrees under which ASCAP and BMI operate must also be revisited to ensure that musical work rights holders are paid fair market value for their compositions.

Finally, consider a one-stop shop for musical work licenses. We have filed with the Copyright Office (in response to their request for comments) an idea laying out one possible way to license music in this manner. It would have the music publishing and recorded music sides of the industry negotiate, in the free market, an overarching allocation of royalties between them for the exploitation of sound recordings. It is a potential path toward simplifying the complicated way musical works must be licensed today.

The goals of any solution should be to align the economic interests and incentives of music creators; ensure that songwriters and publishers receive a fair portion of revenue from the licensing of the sound recording; avoid competition between record labels and music publishers for the same dollars from licensees; vastly simplify and speed the licensing process, making it quicker and easier for consumers to enjoy new music services; and make royalty payments to songwriters and publishers more efficient and more transparent.

There are undoubtedly many approaches to address today's broken system, and we are ready to discuss them with our industry colleagues.

Ultimately, what remains at the center of this exercise is music and its intrinsic value in our lives. Music – and fans' engagement with music – is more important than ever in this digital age. Music is at the core of our culture and it is often the connective tissue of the Internet. The most talked about topic on social media is music, the most watched videos on YouTube are music videos, the most followed people on Twitter are recording artists, and iTunes is still called iTunes. Just last week, Mashable published a story documenting how music is the essential draw for advertisers, for charitable organizations, for technology companies, for social media, you name it. Technology firms recognize they need to be part of the music space because they know that's where their customers are. Our members are proud to invest in the development of a diverse array of products that are so universally enjoyed, and they want to continue to be the engine behind this cherished art form. The music business has reinvented itself, but our work is not done. It can only be made easier if our complex licensing system is simplified and music creators are paid fairly.

Again, we thank the Subcommittee for holding this hearing and for its interest in modernizing music licensing. It's not easy to reform a system as deeply rooted as our music licensing system, and undoubtedly there will have to be give and take by every interested party if we are to succeed. But we believe, given the increasing dysfunction under our current system, that the time is ripe to make the changes that can truly transform music licensing for the better. And we hope, by working together with our music community colleagues, that we can find the consensus we think is necessary to establish a system that works for everyone.

Thank you.

End Note

[1] See, e.g., SDARS II, 78 Fed. Reg. at 23,058 (rejecting marketplace benchmark for preexisting subscription services as "so far from the current rate" and basing new rates on below-market rates previously established; selecting a lower SDARS rate because of cost structure); SDARS I, 73 Fed. Reg. at 4087 (selecting a lower SDARS rate because of concerns about profitability and cash flow); Determination of Reasonable Rates and Terms for the Digital Performance of Sound Recordings, 63 Fed. Reg. 25,394, 25,399-25,400, 25,405-09 (May 8, 1998) (rates to be based on policy considerations, not the marketplace; sustaining low rate based on service risk exposure and perceived precarious financial position).

Chapter 8

STATEMENT OF CHARLES M. WARFIELD, JR., SENIOR ADVISOR, YMF MEDIA, LLC. HEARING ON "MUSIC LICENSING UNDER TITLE 17 PART TWO"[*]

I. INTRODUCTION

Good afternoon, Chairman Coble, Ranking Member Nadler and members of the Subcommittee on Courts, Intellectual Property, and the Internet. Thank you for inviting me to testify today. My name is Charles Warfield, and I am currently the Joint Board Chair of the National Association of Broadcasters, and a Senior Advisor to YMF Media. I am testifying today on behalf of the more than 6,000 free, local, over-the-air radio members of the NAB.

My career in broadcast radio has spanned more than 36 years. Over that time, I served as President and COO of one of the first wholly minority-owned radio station groups, ran the day-to-day operations of some of America's top radio stations, and even spent several years as an executive on the record industry side of the business. Many of my radio stations directly served your constituents, and continue to do so today. These included WJLB-FM/WMXD-FM in Detroit, WEDR-FM in Miami, and WBLS-FM/WLIB and WRKS-FM in New York, which became "the most listened to radio station in America" under my watch.

I am uniquely situated to testify on the issues before this Committee today for two reasons. First, NAB is an Association comprising both creators and users of copyrighted works, so it has a distinct interest in advancing the cause of both sides in this debate. Second, I was personally involved on the recording industry side of the business, so I recognize the opportunity and challenges that industry faces as well.

II. THE OVERRIDING OBJECTIVE OF COPYRIGHT IS THE PUBLIC GOOD

As you undertake your review of the music licensing laws, it is worth highlighting at the outset that the Supreme Court has repeatedly held that the core objective of copyright law is

---

[*] This is an edited, reformatted and augmented version of a statement presented June 25, 2014 before the House Judiciary Committee, Subcommittee on Courts, Intellectual Property and the Internet.

the public good.[1] Not the creator's interest. Not the user's interest. But the interest of the public at large.

While stakeholders on each side have manipulated the text of the Constitution and subsequent case law in attempts to justify their own arguments and agendas; Congress and the Court have always strived for a copyright regime that balances the rights of creators and users to maximize this public good. The aim of this Subcommittee's Copyright Review should be no different.

Unfortunately, two weeks ago, when this Subcommittee held its first of two hearings on music licensing, groups representing artists, music publishers and songwriters seemingly ignored this incontrovertible objective. Instead, each industry made its case for fixes to copyright law that served a very different goal – ensuring that their individual constituencies receive greater compensation for their work at the expense of music licensees and listeners. Nowhere in their arguments did they emphasize the need for "balance", the interest of "consumers", or the impact on "competition" – any of which would promote the public good.

Today, I am going to take a different approach, and will briefly explain why I believe that broadcast radio, and the current legal framework that enables it, unquestionably promotes the public good. While unfortunately, the laws governing webcasters fail this test.

III. THE LEGAL FRAMEWORK GOVERNING BROADCAST RADIO PROMOTES THE PUBLIC GOOD

For over ninety years, broadcast radio has impacted the lives of Americans in many beneficial and significant ways. Radio broadcasters inform, educate, and alert our listeners to important events, topics, and emergencies. We introduce them to new music. We entertain them with sports, talk, and interviews. We are local, involved in our communities and proud to serve the public interest.

There is much to criticize regarding the complexity of the laws governing the music industry. But viewed through the lens of the public good, there should be little question that the specific laws governing the relationship between the music and broadcast industries have been a resounding success in three ways.

First, the current law has enabled a locally-focused, community-based broadcast industry that is completely free to listeners. This free service is unique among entertainment media, and doesn't require a subscription, a broadband connection, or an expensive wireless data connection for access. Instead, it is completely free to anyone with an AM/FM antenna. Combined with an architecture that ensures that broadcast radio is always on in times of emergency, even when other forms of communication fail, broadcast radio has played a critical role in communities across America for decades.

But make no mistake, maintaining this completely free model in an increasingly competitive and costly industry is a delicate balance. Like all other businesses, local radio stations represent brands created and maintained at great expense – from on-air talent and content-production costs to staffing and equipment. Radio broadcasters' ability to continue offering their product under a completely free model is directly premised on the existing legal framework and resulting cost-structure.

Second, the resulting popularity of broadcast radio – due to its cost (it's free!), community-focus, and of course the product, which often includes music – has contributed to a U.S. recording industry that dwarfs the rest of the world both in terms of size and scope. This output of diverse and high quality musical works and sound recordings unquestionably benefits the public and flows from the current legal regime.

The existing U.S. system of "free airplay for free promotion" has served both the broadcasting and recording industries well for decades. The U.S. is the most significant exporter of music and the largest creator for recorded music sales world-wide. Further, the mutually beneficial relationship between broadcasters and the music industry, enabled by the existing law, has incentivized a U.S. recording industry is larger than that of the U.K, Germany, France and Italy combined, all of which impose performance royalties on over-the-air sound recordings.

Both empirical[2] and anecdotal[3] evidence suggest that the U.S. radio industry – the equivalent of which exists nowhere else in the world and which is directly attributable to the existing legal framework – contributes to this commercial success by providing significant benefits both to performing artists and recording companies. Indeed, listeners identify FM radio as the place they first heard the music they purchased. With an audience of 242 million listeners a week, the radio audience dwarfs the listenership of satellite radio and Internet music services.[4] The fact is, the recording industry invests money promoting songs in order to get radio airplay, and earns revenues when radio airplay leads to the purchase of the music listeners hear. Contrasted with the varying legal regimes governing sound recordings in other countries, the U.S. system has unquestionably been a win for the U.S. recording industry, artists and the public.

Third, radio broadcasting has a profoundly positive impact on the economies and spirits of local communities. A recent study found that local radio generated a total of more than half a trillion dollars in GDP and over one million jobs in 2012 across the United States.[5] In North Carolina and New York, local radio is responsible for generating close to 32,000 and 67,000 jobs in these states, respectively.[6] But perhaps more importantly, the fundamental community-based nature of local broadcasting has driven extraordinary levels of public service that make our medium unique. The following are recent representative examples of local broadcasters serving their communities:

- When deadly tornadoes ripped through parts of Nebraska, Oklahoma, Arkansas, Alabama, and Mississippi in late April 2014, broadcasters stepped into their important lifeline roles as first informers, stopping the music and interrupting regularly scheduled programming to provide live, wall-to-wall storm coverage;[7]
- Hundreds of radio stations across the country have helped raise more than $385 million for the life-saving work of St. Jude, and the St. Jude family of partner stations continues to expand. Radio Cares for St. Jude Kids is one of the most successful radio fundraising events in America;[8]
- The North Carolina Association of Broadcasters, in a partnership with the USO North Carolina, hosted the Welcome Home Vietnam Veterans Celebration for more than 70,000 attendees including veterans, their families and community members;[9]
- In the wake of Hurricane Sandy, one of the hardest-hitting natural disasters to strike the northeast, WQHT/Hot 97's Hip Hop Has Heart Foundation was a life-line,

responding to the overwhelming needs of the community. During the storm, Hot 97 broadcast steadily throughout the multiple power outages, providing for some the only connection to news and information. In the days following, Hot 97 ran continuous informational announcements providing critical information about disaster-relief locations and assistance;[10]
- Fifteen radio stations across Chicago are currently helping to spread a message of antiviolence with "Put the Guns Down," an initiative to promote safety through the local communities and help to lessen the senseless gun violence that has plagued Chicago. Mayor Emanuel explained why he is now using local radio stations in his fight, saying: "We do policing. We do prevention. We do penalties. We also need parenting. We're going to add a fifth "P" today... pop culture;"[11]
- WACO-FM Waco, Texas, morning program, The Zack and Jim Morning Show, broadcast live from Afghanistan for a week in February to show support for members of the military who are stationed overseas;[12]
- Every August, WSLQ-FM Roanoke, VA, hosts its annual Pack the Bus campaign distributing school supplies to children in more than 21 school systems;[13]
- WSNW-FM, Greensboro, NC and its listeners raised over $200,000 to send more than 80 children intimately affected by illness to Victory Junction Gang Camp," a medically equipped place where children with chronic conditions get to just be kids;"[14]
- KLAC-FM Denver hosted the 13th annual Children's Miracle Network radiothon in 2014 to benefit the organization's local hospital, raising $1.87 million over three days and $14 million over 13 years;[15]
- When wildfires hit San Diego in May, prompting at least 23,000 evacuations, local radio stations including KBZT, KIFM, KSON, and KFMB, jumped into action with around the clock evacuation updates, wildfire reports, school closings, and traffic information;[16]
- And next week, the Virginia Association of Broadcasters – with the support of more than 150 local radio and television stations – will begin a year-long campaign Feeding Virginia to support all seven regional food banks in Virginia through fundraising and donation drives.[17]

These are not isolated incidents of public service. Rather, these are only a handful of examples of what radio stations do across the country, every day, every week, every year, for their local communities.

IV. THE LEGAL FRAMEWORK GOVERNING WEBCASTING STIFLES IT AND UNDERMINES THE PUBLIC GOOD

I would like to echo the previous testimony of DiMA Executive Director Lee Knife which underscored the significant problems created by the current legal framework governing the webcasting space. The current webcasting compulsory license contained in section 114 of the Copyright Act has failed to achieve the balance between music licensor and licensee that is necessary to benefit the public interest. To the contrary, the current compulsory license and resulting webcasting rates work to prohibit effective competition in the webcasting space and limit consumer choice.

Under the current law, it has proven impossible to run a profitable, stand-alone, non-interactive webcasting business. The largest player in the space, a company with 70% of the non-interactive streaming audience is losing money with every listener – and that service is paying license fees at a rate that has a 45% discount compared to the fees that the Copyright Royalty Board (CRB) set as the so-called market rate that others must pay. If Pandora had to pay the rate set by the CRB, it would have closed its doors long ago. That is not truly a competitive market rate.

As a result, this space lacks effective competition to maximize consumer choice. Make no mistake – today, the only companies that can attempt to challenge this service are companies that are successful in other industries – whether it be broadcasting, Internet search, or consumer electronics – and as a result can leverage that success to subsidize a long-term investment in streaming. But that leaves a limited pool of competitors in this space, and little opportunity for new entrants. Moreover, history shows that even those competitors eventually will tire of losing money and leave the field. It is not a recipe for long-term health.

For broadcasters in particular, the digital space offers an opportunity to expand the footprint of the public benefits highlighted above. But the current rate-setting standard and procedures used at the CRB have resulted in license fees that make webcasting cost prohibitive. Today, whether you are a large broadcaster or small broadcaster, or your station is based in Washington, DC or Charlotte or Casper, the revenue that can be generated from streaming simply does not, and cannot, offset the costs.[18] This imbalance is impeding the growth of Internet radio among local radio broadcasters, which ultimately is not to the benefit of artists, songwriters, or most of all consumers.

Broadcasters favor abandoning the "willing buyer/willing seller" standard and transitioning to the fair value "801(b)(1)" standard for setting sound recording performance royalty rates. The 801(b)(1) standard (so named because it is found in that section of the Copyright Act) has effectively, efficiently, and equitably balanced the interests of copyright owners, copyright users, and the public for decades, in various contexts and proceedings.[19] Further, changes in law that would promote increased transparency in copyright ownership, enhanced record-keeping requirements on the part of Performance Rights Organizations and other collectives, and reforms to the CRB process, would benefit webcasters and consumers, and serve the public good.

Conclusion

Thank you for inviting me to testify before this Subcommittee today. I am confident that as this Subcommittee undertakes its review of music licensing, it will find that laws which promote a vibrant and competitive broadcast industry – now and in the future – benefit the public good.

I am pleased to answer any questions you may have.

ATTACHMENT A

Members of the recording industry at the artist and label levels confirm the promotional impact of radio airplay:

- "Thank you to radio...This record ['Stay'] never would have been this big if it wasn't for radio" says @rihanna at @iheartmusic Awards.20
- "You can see a direct correlation. If you looked at a terrestrial radio audience chart and at the iTunes top 10 singles chart, I would say 75 percent of it matches up." - RCA Records Executive Vice President & General Manager Joe Riccitelli,21
- Radio "still has massive reach in the local community" and "the top of the food chain" for making hits. - Island Def Jam's Steve Bartels22
- "Radio connects the world together. It's my friend and it's everyone's goal to have a big hit song on the radio." - Lady Gaga producer and songwriter/producer and label executive RedOne23

End Notes

[1] See, e.g., Fogerty v. Fantasy, Inc., 510 U.S. 517 (1994) ("The primary objective of the Copyright Act is to encourage the production of original, literary, artistic, and musical expression for the good of the public"); Twentieth Century Music Corp. v. Aiken, 422 U.S. 151, 156 (1975) ("Creative work is to be encouraged and rewarded, but private motivation must ultimately serve the cause of promoting broad public availability of literature, music, and the other arts").

[2] Empirical analysis demonstrates that artists and record labels derive significant value from local radio airplay, ranging from $1.5 to $2.4 billion annually. Dertouzos, Radio Airplay and the Record Industry: An Economic Analysis 5 (https://www.nab.org/documents/resources/061008_Dertouzos_Ptax.pdf).

[3] See Attachment A.

[4] 2013 NAB Annual Report at 13.

[5] Woods & Poole Economics, Local Broadcasting: An Engine for Economic Growth 2 (http://www.nab.org/documents/newsRoom/pdfs/Local_Broadcasting_Engine_for_Growth_Publication.pdf).

[6] Id. at 41, 40.

[7] http://www.nab.org/documents/newsRoom/PSI/052014LTS.html

[8] http://www.radiocaresforstjude.org/programsites/v/index.jsp?vgnextoid=8431d8edea413210Vgn VCM1000001e 0215acRCRD

[9] http://www.nab.org/documents/newsRoom/pdfs/032812_NCBA_Vietnam_release.pdf

[10] http://www.nabef.org/documents/newsroom/pressRelease.asp?id=2918

[11] http://chicagoradioandmedia.com/news/6539-chicago-radio-stations-asking-listeners-to-put-the-guns-down

[12] http://www.nab.org/xert/2014emails/publicservice/032014LTS.html

[13] http://www.broadcastpublicservice.org/story.asp

[14] id.

[15] http://www.nab.org/xert/2014emails/publicservice/032014LTS.html

[16] http://www.allaccess.com/net-news/archive/story/129665/radio-responds-to-san-diego-fires

[17] http://www.vabonline.com/news/vab-announces-campaign-against-hunger/

[18] This economic reality has engendered several innovative direct licensing deals between radio broadcasters and record labels that include revenue sharing agreements for both streaming and terrestrial airplay. See, e.g., Press Release: Big Machine and Cox Media Group Seal Direct Licensing Deal, June 12, 2014 (http://www.coxmediagroup.com/news/cmg-press-releases/bigmachine-and-cox-media-group-seal-direct-licens/ngJ9z/). These agreements signify that efforts to impose a performance royalty on terrestrial broadcasters are better resolved through individualized marketplace agreements rather than a one-size-fits all legislative government mandate.

[19] Instead of determining rates for the a statutory license through a hypothetical marketplace, 17 U.S.C.§ 801(b)(1) sets forth four objectives to be considered: (A) To maximize the availability of creative works to the public; (B) To afford the copyright owner a fair return on his or her creative work and the copyright user a fair income under existing economic conditions; (C) To reflect the relative roles of the copyright owners and the copyright user in the product made available to the public with respect to relative creative contribution, technological contribution, capital investment, cost, risk, and contribution to the opening of new markets for creative expression and media for their communications; (D) To minimize any disruptive effect on the structure of the industries involved and on generally prevailing industry practices."

[20] https://twitter.com/InsideRadio/status/462048988997648385?refsrc=email

[21] September 26, 2013, http://www.radioink.com/Article.asp?id=2704233&spid=24698

[22] NAB Radio Show, September 18, 2013, http://www.allaccess.com/net-news/archive/story/122418/the-2013-radio-show-kicks-off-in-orlando

[23] SXSW "Navigating The Waters Of Radio To Your Benefit" panel, http://www.allaccess.com/netnews/archive/story/116420/radio-s-clout-hailed-at-sxsw

Chapter 9

STATEMENT OF PAUL WILLIAMS, PRESIDENT AND CHAIRMAN OF THE BOARD, AMERICAN SOCIETY OF COMPOSERS, AUTHORS AND PUBLISHERS (ASCAP). HEARING ON "MUSIC LICENSING UNDER TITLE 17 PART TWO"[*]

Mr. Chairman, thank you for this opportunity to present testimony before the Subcommittee on Courts, Intellectual Property, and the Internet of the U.S. House of Representatives Committee on the Judiciary on the important subject of the future of music licensing.

I am the President and Chairman of the Board of the American Society of Composers, Authors and Publishers ("ASCAP"), the oldest and largest performing rights organization ("PRO") in the United States. But first and foremost, I am a songwriter. For 100 years, ASCAP has defended and protected the rights of songwriters and composers, like myself, and kept American music flowing to millions of listeners worldwide. Today, our 500,000 songwriter, composer and music publisher members depend on ASCAP for their livelihoods, by negotiating licenses, tracking public performances, distributing royalties and advocating on their behalf. Through a century of innovation, ASCAP's collective licensing model has served as the primary gateway to music for businesses seeking to perform copyrighted music, ensuring that they may efficiently obtain licenses to perform the millions of works in ASCAP's repertory. As we consider our next 100 years, I firmly believe that ASCAP's collective licensing model is the most effective, efficient and compelling model to serve the needs of music creators, businesses that perform music, and music listeners everywhere.

New technologies, however, have dramatically transformed the way people listen to music, a transformation that, in turn, is greatly changing the economics of the music business, particularly for songwriters and composers, who do not share the same revenue streams as recording artists, such as concert and merchandise revenue. Streaming music through services such as Pandora, Spotify, and iTunes Radio is growing at a fast pace as physical music sales and digital downloads decrease in popularity. Digital audiovisual services such as Netflix and

---

[*] This is an edited, reformatted and augmented version of a statement presented June 25, 2014 before the House Judiciary Committee, Subcommittee on Courts, Intellectual Property and the Internet.

Amazon are revolutionizing the ways in which the world watches television and movies, changing the traditional media landscape. Music is now enjoyed by more people, in more places and over more devices, and ASCAP and our members embrace these new services as means to bring our music to the public. But the regulatory system that governs how ASCAP can license such new services has failed to keep pace, making it increasingly difficult for music creators to realize a competitive return for their creative efforts and for PROs such as ASCAP to appropriately serve the needs of their members (music creators), customers (music licensees) and the music listening public. A time for change has come.

In my testimony, I will describe how collective licensing by PROs such as ASCAP and Broadcast Music, Inc. ("BMI") plays an essential function in the music marketplace and continues to do so in the face of a digitally transformative economy. I will then describe how regulatory oversight through negotiated consent decrees and the U.S. Copyright Act has failed to meet those changes in the marketplace. Finally, I will suggest modifications to the consent decrees that will address such shortcomings and emphasize how Congress may assist in ensuring that ASCAP's songwriter, composers and music publisher members realize competitive prices that reflect the true value of their music.

I. COLLECTIVE LICENSING IS CRUCIAL TO THE MUSIC LICENSING MARKETPLACE

On February 13, 1914, a group of visionary songwriters convened at the Hotel Claridge in New York City to address the problem facing songwriters and composers of that day – how to efficiently obtain compensation for the widespread use of their copyrighted music by thousands of businesses performing their music countrywide. The solution was the creation of ASCAP, the first PRO. ASCAP would negotiate and administer bulk licenses for the non-dramatic public performance rights in works of its members on a collective basis, monitor music usage by and collect fees from licensees, distribute royalty payments to its members and protect from infringement of its members' exclusive public performance rights. A bulk license offered by ASCAP would provide efficiencies for both rights holders, who would otherwise struggle to individually license or enforce the millions of performances of their works by thousands of individual users on an individual basis, and licensees, who would otherwise find it impossible to efficiently clear the rights for their performances if forced to negotiate separately with each individual copyright owner. Most crucial to its success, ASCAP's collective licensing would permit its members to spread the costs of licensing and monitoring music usage among the entire membership, thereby reducing costs to a manageable level and ensuring that more of the money collected is paid to songwriters and publishers as royalties. As a testament to ASCAP's collective efficiencies, ASCAP – *which operates on a non-profit-making basis*, distributing all license fees collected, less operating expenses, as royalties to its members – today distributes to our members as royalties approximately 88% of all fees we collect, on account of performances made by over 700,000 different entities, making it the most efficient PRO in the world.

Moreover, PROs like ASCAP offer their members another crucial benefit – transparency. Unlike other relationships, such as that found with many record labels and recording artists where royalties are distributed on a pass-through basis, hinging on complex contracts, ASCAP's relationship with its members is direct and transparent. Every dollar that ASCAP receives is divided into two – fifty cents is allocated to songwriters and composers and fifty cents to music publishers. ASCAP distributes separately each allocation directly to our songwriter and composer members, and to our music publisher members, regardless of their separate contractual agreements. This direct relationship provides much needed transparency and is crucial to the continued ability for songwriters and composers to earn a competitive return for the use of their music.

A century ago, ASCAP's efforts were directed towards the music users of that day – performance venues and other public establishments that play music, such as bars, restaurants, hotels and retail stores. With the progression of technology over the years, ASCAP innovatively met the demands of the marketplace, ably negotiating licenses on a non-exclusive basis for the public performance rights in the musical works in our repertory of millions of works, as well as the repertories of nearly 100 foreign PROs with which ASCAP has reciprocal agreements, to a wide range of licensee industries. In the 1920s through the 1940s, ASCAP met the needs of the radio marketplace devising licenses that today serve thousands of radio stations. In the 1950s through the 1970s, ASCAP engineered licensing for the developing local and network television industry. In the 1980s and 1990s, ASCAP provided solutions to the emerging cable and satellite industries. In each decade, despite challenges posed by new technologies and business models, ASCAP was able to work with user industries to provide efficient licensing solutions that would provide a much needed stream of income to ASCAP's members for the use of their works – royalties such songwriters and publishers might otherwise be unable to collect. The consent decree did not impede ASCAP's ability to serve our members, who for decades were able to earn a living writing and composing music, largely due to the royalties collected by ASCAP on their behalf.

Today, ASCAP's role remains unchanged, despite the seismic changes confronting the music industry by virtue of the advent of the Internet and other digital technologies. If not for PRO collective licensing, the billions of performances made by digital music services such as Pandora, Spotify and Apple's iTunes Radio would require clearance on a copyright-owner-by-copyright-owner basis – exactly the problem faced by ASCAP's founders years ago, but on a magnitude far greater. Indeed, such services herald PRO collective licensing as a model of licensing efficiency to be emulated throughout the market, without which licensing – and their businesses – would suffer.[1] In fact, the U.S. Copyright Office and its current and past Registers of Copyright have attested to the success of and need for the PRO collective licensing model, and its potential as a model for other rights.[2]

Today's robust marketplace for performing rights is built on the foundation provided by collective licensing. Indeed, competition in the collective licensing marketplace has expanded widely. ASCAP now competes with two other PROs in the U.S. – BMI and SESAC, Inc. (a private unregulated PRO) – as well as new profit-making market entrants.

The role of the PRO therefore remains vital to the future of the music marketplace – both for ASCAP songwriter, composer and publisher members, who depend on the performing right royalties collected by ASCAP as a major source of income, particularly as digital music streaming services account for an increasingly larger portion of music revenues in the U.S. and other sources of royalties (such as those from the sale of compact discs and digital downloads) decline, as well as for digital content services, who depend on the efficiencies of PRO collective licensing to compete in the market. However, it has become clear – as I explain below – that the consent decree regulating ASCAP has failed to properly adjust to meet those changes, leaving ASCAP's members in much the same place as they were a century ago at the Hotel Claridge – searching for a solution to the problem of how to achieve a competitive return for the widespread use of their copyrighted music. And, much like its forebears concluded then, the solution is a vibrant ASCAP that provides collective licensing in an efficient manner. However, to maintain the feasibility of that solution, the consent decree must, too, adapt. A time for change has indeed come.

II. THE ASCAP CONSENT DECREE AND U.S. COPYRIGHT LAW REQUIRE ADJUSTMENT

In 1941, ASCAP settled a lawsuit brought by the Department of Justice and entered into a consent decree (the "Consent Decree" or "Decree") that prohibited ASCAP from receiving an exclusive grant of rights from its members and required ASCAP to charge similar license fees to music users that are "similarly situated." The ASCAP Consent Decree has only been amended twice – first in 1950 and, subsequently in 2001, prior to the biggest developments of the digital music era, including the introduction of Apple's iPod. In its current form, the Decree requires ASCAP, after receiving a request for a license from a music user, to negotiate a reasonable license fee or seek such a determination from a "rate court." Pending the completion of any such negotiations or rate court proceeding, the Decree grants the music user the right to perform any or all of the musical works in the ASCAP repertory.

Additionally, among other things, the Decree prohibits ASCAP from acquiring or licensing rights other than for the public performance of musical works, such as mechanical or synchronization rights. As I discuss below, it is now apparent that the Decree has failed in these and other respects to accommodate the rapid and dramatic changes in the music licensing marketplace brought about by the extraordinary evolution in the ways in which music is now distributed and consumed. As a result, the collective licensing model that has, for the past century, benefited music creators, licensees and consumers alike, and which is necessary for a viable music licensing system in the future, is at risk.

A. The Automatic License Requirement

Under the Decree, a music user is entitled to begin performing any or all ASCAP music as soon as a written license application is submitted, without the threat of infringement, before fees are negotiated by the parties or set by the rate court. However, the Decree does not currently compel either ASCAP or an applicant to commence a rate court proceeding in the absence of agreement on final license terms, nor does it establish a definite timeline for the negotiation of a final fee – elements of the licensing process that certain users have begun to exploit as a dilatory tactic to avoid paying competitive prices to perform the ASCAP repertory.

For many years, the license application process was merely a procedural step leading to eventual final licenses for established industries. ASCAP traditionally negotiated licenses with industry committees or associations representing entire classes of licensees. For example, ASCAP negotiates with the Television Music Licensing Committee, which testified before you on June 10th, to reach license agreements for the entire local broadcast television industry. Established relationships and courses of conduct, as well the development of traditional media business economies – such as the radio and television broadcast economies – led generally to continued payment of fees, even without a negotiated final license in place.

In today's marketplace, however, digital services without a history of negotiating licenses and paying fees, and often without any proven business model, utilize the Decree license process to their benefit. As ASCAP licenses are compulsory and fees can be set retroactively, certain music users have strategically delayed or extended the negotiating process, choosing to remain applicants or interim licensees indefinitely—in some cases a decade or longer—without paying fees to ASCAP or providing ASCAP with the information necessary to determine a reasonable final fee. In some cases, music users have decided that interim license rates are more favorable than anticipated rate increases, and have made strategic choices to stay on interim terms for as long as ASCAP permits. In other cases, new applicants have applied for a license – claiming the shelter of the Consent Decree's guarantee of a right to perform ASCAP members' music while an application is pending – while simultaneously disclaiming the need for such a license and refusing to provide the information ASCAP needs to formulate a fee proposal.

In the scenarios above, ASCAP has limited choices. It can do nothing and permit users to remain as applicants or interim licensees longer than would be preferred without paying any fees. Or, it can accept what it believes is a sub-optimal outcome and, open the door for other users to argue that ASCAP must offer to them the same sub-optimal license due to the Decree's mandate to offer the same license rates and terms to similarly situated licensees. Or, ASCAP can decide whether to use its limited resources to pursue a lengthy, expensive and arduous rate court proceeding, which, as I describe below, can result in below-market rates. ASCAP's members consequently often find themselves placed between a rock and a hard place.

This problem is particularly pronounced with regard to new digital services or other new media services that are particularly susceptible to changing market conditions. As compared to traditional music users like terrestrial radio stations or television broadcasting networks, the potential scale and type of music use can now vary widely among new media licensees, complicating the process through which ASCAP values the requested license. Moreover, the speed with which new media licensees enter and exit the market has increased. As a result, ASCAP's need for information from an applicant regarding its plans for a particular service has increased, both to calculate a reasonable fee, but also – in the event that the applicant refuses to provide information – to assess the potential costs and benefits of petitioning the rate court to set a reasonable fee. When applicants ignore ASCAP's requests for information, ASCAP can lack even the basic information necessary to determine whether rate court litigation is justified. These problems might be mitigated somewhat if the new media services were amenable, and able, to negotiate on an industry-wide basis like other industries do. However, as these new media services elect not to (or simply cannot) negotiate collectively, ASCAP is forced to go down the same path with each service separately at a huge cost to ASCAP's members.

B. The Rate Court Process

Until the advent of the digital era, the rate court process was rarely invoked. Established industry groups and ASCAP were generally able to reach license agreements outside of the rate court. However, as I described earlier, the compulsory license application process under the Decree has led to licensing deadlock with many digital services, forcing greater resort to the rate court. Indeed, of the 30 or so rate court proceedings to date over the past half century, more than half were initiated since 1995.

While the ASCAP rate court was meant to provide a forum for the efficient and timely determination of rate disputes, in practice, rate court litigation has resulted in great expense and prolonged uncertainty for both ASCAP and license applicants. The Decree mandate to commence the trial within one year of the filing of the initial petition is rarely met, largely because the parties are permitted the full range of costly pretrial motion practice and discovery afforded by Federal rules; post-trial appellate proceedings or possible proceedings on remand further delay the determination of a final fee even beyond the original expiration date of the license at issue.

Rate court proceedings have proven to be extremely expensive for the parties involved. In addition to enormous internal administrative and labor costs, ASCAP and applicants have collectively expended many tens of millions of dollars on litigation expenses related to rate court proceedings, much of that incurred since only 2009. Of course, each licensee bears only the expense of its own ASCAP rate court proceeding; ASCAP must bear the expense of them all.

C. Rate-Setting Standards

In addition to making the rate-setting process administratively faster and less expensive, there is a dire need to establish a clear rate-setting standard that looks to competitive free-market benchmarks. Under the Decree, the rate court must set a "reasonable fee." However, the Consent Decree does not define "reasonable;" thus, ASCAP and our members are burdened by the lack of clarity regarding what factors the rate court should consider when setting a reasonable fee and the weight given to those factors. The rate court has often looked to the concept of fair market value, looking at the price that a willing buyer and a willing seller would agree to in an arm's length transaction, and finding that this value can best be determined by the consideration of analogous licenses or benchmark agreements from a competitive market. However, many of the licenses presented as benchmarks – those between ASCAP or BMI and various licensees – are inherently different from the licenses that would be obtained in a competitive market. This is because a seller's ability to refuse to sell is a key requirement for a true market transaction, and neither ASCAP nor BMI are free to refuse to license their repertories under their respective consent decrees.

But the last few years have seen an increase in the number of direct licenses negotiated between music publishers and music users outside of the compulsory licensing regime imposed by the ASCAP and BMI consent decrees – licenses that can be used as a measure of competitive pricing in the market for public performance rights. As certain publishers withdrew their digital rights from ASCAP and BMI and negotiated licenses in the free marketplace outside of the constraints of consent decrees (a phenomenon I will describe below), the rate court was, for the first time, supplied with actual competitive market benchmarks. However, the rate court signaled in its most recent decision that it would not rely on the most recent licenses negotiated by copyright owners in the free market – rates that were widely known to be higher than what applicants were willing to pay the PROs – a result that means that ASCAP's members will be paid lower rates than what other copyright owners are receiving from the same licensee.

In addition, the rate court is not permitted to look to other relevant marketplace indicia when it sets rates. Section 114(i) of the Copyright Act prohibits the rate court in setting fees for the performance of musical works from looking at fees paid *by those same services* to the recording industry for the performance of sound recordings, leading to rate disparities in favor of sound recordings in the order of 12 to 1. This problem has been addressed by the introduction of the Songwriter Equity Act, which I discuss below.

It is clear that the legal and regulatory restrictions imposed on ASCAP by the Consent Decree and the Copyright Act severely limit ASCAP's members from achieving competitive market rates for their works.

D. Flexibility in Licensing Is Imperative

The option for copyright owners to directly license works has long been a key feature of ASCAP membership. Because ASCAP can accept grants of rights only on a non-exclusive basis, ASCAP's members are free to issue licenses directly to users, and many have done so over the years. Of course, due to the efficiencies afforded through ASCAP's collective licensing system, most ASCAP members, however, have licensed all of their works through ASCAP all of the time. However, certain ASCAP publisher members recently developed concerns that, due to the constraints imposed by the Decree and the inability to achieve competitive market rates through the rate court process, licensing their songs through ASCAP in the new media marketplace did not allow them to realize the full value of their copyrights. Moreover, some ASCAP members wanted increased flexibility to manage their own rights and negotiate contractual scope and terms directly with particular music users (terms which the Decree might prohibit). These members questioned whether their only option to achieve these licensing goals was to withdraw their membership from the PROs altogether.

To ensure that our members would be able to exercise the rights granted to them under the copyright law as copyright owners, but not be forced to surrender all of the benefits of PRO collective licensing by withdrawing from ASCAP completely (after all, licensing tens of thousands of music users individually is practically impossible for any copyright owner), ASCAP struck a balance: we decided to permit our publisher members to withdraw rights on a limited basis, giving such members the flexibility to license digital services on their own in the free marketplace while retaining the blanket efficiencies afforded by collective licensing for all other uses for the benefit of owners and users alike. BMI took a similar approach. However, the ASCAP and BMI rate courts both denied copyright owners this flexibility, ruling that the ASCAP and BMI respective consent decrees did not allow for a partial grant of rights, but instead require copyright owners to be either "all in" as PRO members or "all out."

As a result, copyright owners are currently forced to choose to either remain PRO members and reap the benefits of PRO collective licensing, but through a regulated system that does not compensate them for the true value of the performances of their works or leave the PRO system altogether, achieving competitive rates in the marketplace, but losing the efficiencies of collective licensing and leaving unlicensed performances by thousands of music users they cannot affordably individually license. The crucial problem with this second choice is that the efficiencies of collective licensing depend on the PRO's ability to spread the costs of licensing and monitoring music usage among the entire membership, thereby reducing costs to a manageable level; the loss of major members from the PROs would severely limit such efficiencies for the remaining members, perhaps so much so that the PROs could not efficiently operate anymore. If that happens, and the collective system consequently collapses, we all lose – songwriters, music services and consumers alike.

Furthermore, the Decree denies ASCAP the flexibility to construct the licenses its digital music users seek. The public performance right licensed by ASCAP on behalf of its members is only one of several exclusive rights provided to copyright holders of musical compositions. Others include the right to reproduce and distribute musical works as phonorecords (the "mechanical right"); the right to use a recording of a musical work in timed relation with visual images, such as part of a movie or television program (the "synchronization" or "synch right"); and the right to print or display a composition's lyrics (the "print right"). Each of these rights are licensed separately; at the moment, services typically license performance rights through a PRO and mechanical rights and synch rights directly from the copyright owner, administrator or a designated agent, often on a song-by-song basis.

This division of licensing was sufficiently convenient in the traditional analog world in which licensees rarely needed licenses for multiple rights. The introduction of digital technology, however, has changed the traditional licensing environment, requiring digital users to often clear multiple rights for the same use. Digital music services that stream music on an on-demand basis need a public performance license as well as a mechanical license. A wide variety of digital music services display lyrics as songs are streaming, necessitating both public performance and print licenses. Services utilizing audiovisual content are now required to clear synchronization rights on a large scale basis, which must be obtained from the publishers directly, again on a song-by-song basis. Separate licensing of these rights is inefficient and may discourage new media users from properly licensing their services.

These complexities inherent in a multiple rights clearance system have triggered music users to vocalize their desires for collective licensing solutions. ASCAP, of course, offers that collective blanket licensing solution, but is prohibited under the Consent Decree from licensing rights in musical compositions other than public performance rights. Other PROs in and outside of the U.S. are able to do so. Indeed, many foreign PROs are already engaged in the process of licensing multiple rights. ASCAP's inability to offer licenses for multiple rights not only creates licensing inefficiencies for music users to the detriment of consumers who ultimately bear the transactional costs, but it also places ASCAP's members at a competitive disadvantage in the licensing marketplace if other organizations can license those rights.

E. U.S. Copyright Law Must Be Technology Agnostic

While music businesses have been built upon a rights model largely unchanged in 100 years, the drastic changes in the means by which copyrighted content is used and transmitted on a global scale means copyright law must be modernized to ensure that copyright owners are protected in the future. Consumers no longer rely upon a passive, pre-scheduled means of experiencing content. Rather, digital content is made available in a myriad of ways that permit consumers flexibility in the means by which they experience such content. The old strict divide between user-uncontrolled, non-interactive webcast streaming and full download transmissions that took minutes (or hours) to complete has evolved into hybrid technologies that do not lend themselves to traditional content delivery labels. Users care little how they obtain content – the simply wish to access it, whenever and wherever they choose. Technologies have evolved to meet those consumer expectations.

While the differences in technologies and user experience may be reflected in the ultimate compensation paid for those experiences, it is clear that artificial legal differentiation between what is and what is not compensable under U.S. law is no longer justified. ASCAP has always believed that our Copyright Act grants to copyright owners the broadest protection for the offering of their works to the public, and does so in a manner that brings our law in compliance with various international treaty obligations.[3] However, a number of recent cases have interpreted the public performance right in such a manner so as to limit the reach of a copyright owner's rights. First, courts have held that transmissions that result in content downloads do not meet the statutory definition of a performance, even though it is clear that such technologies have evolved to make any such distinction irrelevant.[4] More recently, decisions have further limited the extent of the performance right by holding that the transmissions of certain individually-accessible content on a one-to-one basis at the request of consumers are not "public" performances, thus denying copyright owners the right to authorize and be compensated for those transmissions.[5]

If these decisions and their rationale are permitted to stand, the narrowing of the public performance right based on loophole-exploiting technological engineering will lead to the increased use of music without due compensation to its creators. And, considering that countries around the world do not make these technological distinctions in their laws, and we now exist in a borderless digital economy, U.S. rights holders are further disadvantaged. Continued access to creative output depends on competitive compensation to creators for the use of their works, without which, again, ultimately the consumers lose.

III. PROPOSALS FOR CHANGE

Maintaining ASCAP as the effective licensing solution it has been for the past century requires change – changes to update the Consent Decree, as well as change to the copyright law. Specifically, I propose the following modifications.

A. Modifying the Consent Decree

Maria Pallante, current Register of Copyrights and Director of the U.S. Copyright Office, stated recently that "the time has come to review the role of the consent decrees governing ASCAP and BMI".[6] That time is now. In order to alleviate the significant limitations placed on ASCAP and our members by the Consent Decree, I propose four ways in which the Decree should be modified.

1) *Permitting Limited Grants of Rights.* The Decree should permit PROs to accept partial grants of rights from copyright holders. Allowing ASCAP to maintain the compromise already struck with our members would preserve the benefits of collective licensing for users and owners in many situations, while allowing copyright holders to pursue direct non-compulsory licenses when they felt it was economically efficient and beneficial to do so. This approach would also afford greater latitude in structuring license arrangements, ultimately benefiting copyright owners and music users alike. Further, by encouraging the negotiation of direct licenses by truly willing buyers and willing sellers who are not under any compulsion to grant licenses, this approach would result in competitive market transactions that would then provide informative benchmarks for the rate-setting tribunal. Finally, members would be encouraged to remain within the PRO system, thereby effectuating collective efficiency for, and benefiting, all other members, music users and consumers alike.

2) *Expedited Rate-Setting Process.* The Consent Decree's rate-setting process should be replaced with an expedited arbitration process with focused discovery that would be significantly faster and substantially less costly. Expedited arbitration proceedings would serve two purposes. First, both music creators and music users would benefit from a more definite timeline and cheaper resolution of license fee disputes. Second, it would discourage applicants for automatic Decree licenses from indefinitely resting on mere license applications or remaining on interim licenses, and impose on applicants an obligation to pay for their use of ASCAP members' music.

3) *Competitive Market Rate Standards.* The establishment of an evidentiary presumption that direct non-compulsory licenses voluntarily negotiated by copyright holders provide the best evidence of reasonable rates would ensure that rates are based on competitive market transactions. Such a presumption would provide more certainty for all parties involved and also encourage more out-of-court negotiations, by providing the parties a reliable preview of the rate court's ultimate benchmark analysis and discouraging the strategic use of rate court proceedings to avoid the influence of market rates.

4) *Licensing Multiple Rights.* ASCAP should be permitted to extend the benefits of collective licensing through aggregated licensing to music users that could negotiate with ASCAP for multiple rights – namely, mechanical, synchronization and print rights in addition to public performance rights – in a single transaction. This would finally create a "one-stop shop" for musical work rights. Modifying the Consent Decree in this way would respond to licensee demand for simplification of the licensing process and administration of multiple rights. In addition, the flexibility to structure licenses that aggregate rights would greatly reduce transactional costs and

administrative expenses for owners and music users, which would benefit their customers, and, ultimately provide music creators with a greater monetary return for the use of their works. This would also allow ASCAP to compete more effectively in both the domestic and international licensing marketplace with owners or PROs that can, and do, aggregate rights.

B. Modifications to the Copyright Law

1) *Songwriter Equity Act.* ASCAP, along with other PROs and music publisher and songwriter groups, have joined to support the Songwriter Equity Act ("SEA"), a bill that would further the goals of providing competitive market rates to songwriters and composers. The SEA would provide for the setting of competitive market rates under the outdated pre-World War One era Section 115 mechanical license, and would remove the unfair barriers placed by Section 114(i) upon rate courts from considering license rates and fees paid by services for the public performances of sound recordings in setting fees for the same public performances of the underlying musical works. Significantly, the SEA does not mandate the rate-setting bodies to increase rates. Rather, it will permit them to finally be able to examine and take into account all relevant market evidence in setting rates. It is our hope that the passage of the SEA will further the ability for songwriters and music publishers to achieve competitive prices for the use of their works and lessen the inequitable disparity currently in place between payment for sound recordings and musical works. ASCAP and our members thank Representative Doug Collins and Hakeem Jeffries for their leadership in introducing this bill, and thank the many subcommittee members who have joined them through their co-sponsorship.

2) *Making Available Right.* The Supreme Court, understanding the significance of the issues raised in the *Aereo* case regarding Internet retransmission of broadcast signals to individual users, is reviewing the lower court's decision and will thereby shed further light on the reach of the performance right. ASCAP hopes and expects the Court to rule in favor of a broad reading of the performance right. However, regardless of the ultimate decision, U.S. law should remain agnostic regarding how copyrighted content is made accessible to users, and should extend protection to cover all means by which copyrighted content is made accessible to the public. This principle of neutral treatment is the basis for the broad "making available" right required upon signatories to the two WIPO Internet Treaties, the WIPO Copyright Treaty and WIPO Performances and Phonograms Treaty, which were intended to provide a broad technology-agnostic exclusive right to encompass all manner and form of providing and disseminating copyrighted works to the public regardless of the manner of such transmission. Congress must ensure that the U.S., as a signatory to those treaties, provides a copyright law that respects this principle, and to the extent necessary, amend the Copyright Act to confirm that copyright owners should receive due compensation for the use of their works regardless of the means of delivery.

IV. CONCLUSION

For 100 years, PRO collective licensing has served as the solution to an efficient licensing marketplace, and it remains the solution today. However, new innovations in the marketplace demand that the outdated regulations governing the ability of the PROs to license on behalf of their songwriter, composers and publisher members evolve to meet those changes in order to provide competitive remuneration for the use of those members' musical works. Without those changes, copyright owners may abandon the collective PRO system in hope of achieving competitive rates on their own, potentially tearing apart our collective licensing system. If that were to occur, everyone loses. Withdrawing copyright owners lose the efficiencies offered by the PROs, leaving unlicensed many performances of their work. Other copyright owners lose the ability to license their work on a blanket basis. Songwriters and composers lose the transparencies and services provided by the PROs. Services lose the ability to license on an efficient and transactional cost saving basis. And the ultimate losers would be those for whom the music is intended – the consumers. A time for change has indeed come.

Mr. Chairman, ASCAP and I look forward to working with your committee and staff to achieve these changes, and ensure that the music licensing marketplace works for all.

End Notes

[1] See, e.g., Comments of Sirius XM Radio Inc., U.S. Copyright Office, In the Matter of Music Licensing Study: Notice and Request for Public Comment, Docket No. 2014-3 ("Music Study") at 5 ("[T]he efficiencies of the blanket licenses and one-stop shopping may justify the PROs' existence"); Comments of the Digital Media Association, Music Study at 27 ("[T]he blanket licenses (among other forms of licenses) offered by ASCAP, BMI and SESAC provide a framework that promotes licensing efficiencies and reduced transaction costs for both licensors and licensees alike.")

[2] See U.S. Copyright Office, LEGAL ISSUES IN MASS DIGITIZATION: A PRELIMINARY ANALYSIS AND DISCUSSION DOCUMENT 32 (2011); Maria Pallante, Remarks at the Copyright Matters program of February 25, 2014 ("Pallante Remarks") ("[I]t is clear there will always be an important role for the collective licensing paradigm, which was innovative when ASCAP was founded 100 years ago and remains innovative today."); Statement of Marybeth Peters, The Register of Copyrights, Before the Subcommittee on Intellectual Property, Committee on the Judiciary, United States Senate 109th Congress, 1st Session, July 12, 2005, Music Licensing Reform ("The United States also has collective licensing organizations, such as ASCAP, BMI and SESAC, which appear to function quite successfully. These performing rights organizations license the public performance of musical works – for which there is no statutory license – providing users with a means to obtain and pay for the necessary rights without difficulty. It seems reasonable to ask whether a similar model would work for licensing of the rights of reproduction and distribution.")

[3] See Joint Comments of the American Society of Composers, Authors and Publishers, Broadcast Music, Inc., The Songwriters Guild of America, SESAC, Inc. and The National Music Publishers' Association, U.S. Copyright Office, Study on the Right of Making Available, Docket No. 2014-2.

[4] U.S. v. ASCAP, In the Matter of the Application of America Online, Inc., 627 F.3d 64 (2d Cir. 2010).

[5] WNET, Thirteen v. Aereo. Inc., 712 F.3d 676 (2d. Cir. 2013); Cartoon Network LP v. CSC Holdings, Inc., 536 F.3d 121 (2d Cir. 2008)

[6] See Pallante Remarks.

In: Copyright and the Music Marketplace
Editor: Keith Turner

ISBN: 978-1-63482-869-7
© 2015 Nova Science Publishers, Inc.

Chapter 10

TESTIMONY OF CHRIS HARRISON, VICE PRESIDENT, BUSINESS AFFAIRS, PANDORA MEDIA INC. HEARING ON "MUSIC LICENSING UNDER TITLE 17 PART TWO"[*]

INTRODUCTION

Thank you, Mr. Chairman and ranking Member Nadler. Pandora appreciates this opportunity to testify at this important hearing. Pandora applauds Chairman Goodlatte and this Committee for your leadership in initiating a comprehensive review of the current Copyright Act. The subcommittee's hearings of June 10th and today are particularly important as they bring focus to the many thorny issues related to how copyright law impacts the licensing of music. Music is a vital part of our vibrant culture that enriches our lives and connects us to places, times and people; Pandora is proud of the constructive role we play in the music ecosystem.

Pandora is confident that members of this Committee, as well as the full House and Senate, will bear in mind that any changes to the Copyright Act that impact the licensing of music must be advanced with the interests of the primary intended beneficiaries of copyright firmly in mind: the hundreds of millions of Americans who listen to, delight in, and benefit from their *legal* consumption of music.[1] Pandora supports any efforts to make the current system work better and smarter, so long as such efforts adhere to the following foundational principles:

1. The interests of all stakeholders in the music ecosystem must be balanced, not just the interests of big copyright owners;
2. Statutory blanket licenses enable broad participation in the music marketplace and must be preserved; and
3. The music ecosystem must be protected from anticompetitive licensing behavior.

---

[*] This is an edited, reformatted and augmented version of testimony presented June 25, 2014 before the House Judiciary Committee, Subcommittee on Courts, Intellectual Property and the Internet.

While Pandora believes that there are important improvements that can be made to the music licensing process, the existing statutory blanket licensing structures[2] for non-interactive Internet radio services such as Pandora are largely achieving copyright's primary goal.

Pandora Is Radio

Although delivered over the Internet and not the airwaves, Pandora is radio. Advertising supported, free-to-the-listener radio like Pandora has been a critical part of the cultural fabric of America for nearly 100 years. In establishing nonsubscription services in the DMCA, Congress recognized that advertising supported radio is a democratizing force, enabling shared cultural expression across the entire socioeconomic spectrum. Radio is also the preferred mode of music consumption; research shows that 80% of time spent listening to music is a "lean back" radio experience, in which the listener selects the style or genre of music and the radio service selects which songs to play.

Although it is the newest form of radio, non-interactive Internet radio has quickly become a significant platform of legal music consumption. Seventy-seven million Americans (nearly 1 in 3 Americans over the age of 13) tuned into Pandora last month and listened for an average of more than 22 hours. Every month, Pandora performs more than 1.5 million songs by more than 100,000 recording artists, 80% of whom were not played on terrestrial radio.

In addition to exposing this wide variety of artists to tens of millions of listeners, Pandora also contributes hundreds of millions of dollars to a new royalty stream that did not exist twenty years ago. Today, Pandora pays more than $1,500 in total royalties per 1 million performances on our service. In the language of terrestrial radio, 1 million performances on Pandora is equivalent to 21 performances on 102.7 KIIS FM in Los Angeles or just 16 performances on 100.3 WHTZ FM in New York. Just nine years after launching, Pandora is on track later this summer to pass the milestone of $1 billion in total royalties paid.

Pandora's Technology

The public's embrace of Pandora is the result of a massive investment in its unique intellectual property. Tim Westergren, Pandora's founder, had the idea that all music could be categorized against a single taxonomy, and created the most powerful tool for discovering music: the Music Genome Project. Fourteen years later, Pandora's music analysts, most of whom have degrees in music composition or music theory, have devoted as much as 333,000 hours - the equivalent of 38 years - listening to and cataloging the musicological traits of each song in the Genome across as many as 450 different characteristics. The result of this process is that each song in Pandora's Music Genome Project exists as a single point in a multi-dimensional space at the intersection of all of that song's characteristics or "genes." Pandora then uses as many as 50 proprietary mathematical algorithms to determine how geometrically "close" one song is to another. It is Pandora's creation of, and investment in, its intellectual property that enables a listening experience that empowers tens of millions of listeners to discover new music that they love.

Non-interactive Internet radio, however, is not just about discovering new music; it's also about being able to experience music that is culturally relevant regardless of whether a local broadcaster operates a station in a particular format. Pandora routinely receives emails from listeners like Chris who tuned into Pandora after his local jazz station changed formats or Jen who listens to Christian Rock on Pandora because no local station carries that genre.

Pandora's Investments in Monetization

To help generate our 120-plus percent average annual revenue growth over the last three years, Pandora has invested more than $440 million in resources and initiatives to monetize our tens of millions of monthly listeners. Pandora now employs more than 800 people (and growing) in sales and sales support operations across the country, including salespeople selling in 37 local advertising markets, going head-to-head with terrestrial radio for local advertising dollars. Pandora's investment in monetization has produced remarkable results, both in magnitude and in the pace of growth. For example, Pandora is behind only Facebook and Google in revenue generation from mobile advertising sales, with $366 million in mobile advertising revenue last year, representing a growth rate of approximately 1,200% in just three years.

IS LICENSING REFORM NEEDED?

As this Committee considers changes in music licensing regimes, Pandora hopes that the Committee will appreciate the salutary aspects of our current system that encourages innovation through simplified licensing procedures, protects music users from the anticompetitive behavior of big copyright owners, and assures that artists actually receive their fair share of the hundreds of millions of dollars in royalties that services like Pandora pay each year. In order to understand the need to maintain but improve upon the status quo, we must consider the current music licensing environment.

The Music Industry Is Too Concentrated

Our music industry is a highly concentrated one, in which major record labels do not really compete against one another for distribution on digital platforms[3] but attempt to use their market power to decide which services win and lose,[4] in many instances because that major record label has a direct financial interest in a digital music service.[5] Unfortunately, the loudest voices in the debate about music licensing are these big copyright owners who assert that what is good for them is good for all.[6]

Copyright Ownership Is Too Fragmented

While the music industry is highly concentrated, copyright ownership is extremely fragmented. For example, the 2013 Grammy winner for best song, "We Are Young" recorded by fun.[7] has four different songwriters and seven different music publishers.[8] Although the

Copyright Act provides that a co-author may grant a non-exclusive license to a joint work such as "We Are Young," the custom and practice in the music industry has developed such that each co-owner will only license its proportionate share in the underlying work.[9] Therefore, absent the availability of a statutory blanket license, the more than 1.5 million tracks that Pandora plays in a given month may implicate separate licensing negotiations with tens of thousands of individual copyright owners.

Copyright Ownership Information Is Too Opaque

There is no authoritative database of copyright ownership information to which a service such as Pandora could turn if it had to license directly these millions of copyrights owned by tens of thousands of copyright owners. Those databases that are available (e.g., ASCAP, BMI and some music publishers maintain online databases that can be searched on a title-by-title basis) often contain conflicting information. For example, the ASCAP database indicates that Universal Music Publishing owns the composition for the song "Somebody that I Used to Know" co-written and recorded by Gotye; however a search of the Universal Music Publishing website results in no matches for the title "Somebody that I Used to Know" or songs recorded by Gotye.[10]

Statutory Blanket Licenses Are Necessary to Alleviate Concentration, Fragmentation and Opacity

In a concentrated industry with fragmented and opaque copyright ownership, statutory blanket licensing can be an efficient means for digital music services to license the millions of copyrights owned by tens of thousands of copyright owners that are necessary to offer a compelling service to consumers.[11] As the Future of Music Coalition recently stated, "The incredible growth of Internet radio, for example, would have been inconceivable had fledgling webcasters been compelled to negotiate with all of the music publishers individually. Without an easier way to obtain permission to play songs, Internet radio might never have happened."[12]

1. Statutory Blanket Licenses Provide Transparency for Songwriters and Recording Artists

In addition to ease of licensing, statutory blanket licenses, as practiced by ASCAP and BMI and required of SoundExchange, provide extremely valuable transparency into the royalty payments of songwriters and recording artists.[13] For example, in her opinion in Pandora's rate proceeding with ASCAP, Southern District of New York Judge Denise Cote described how "Songwriters, and at least some independent music publishers, were concerned about the damage that might be wrought from ... the partial withdrawal of rights from ASCAP" because "Songwriters were concerned about the loss of transparency."[14] In almost every case under a statutory blanket license, a songwriter or recording artist can determine the royalty rate applicable to a particular performance to ensure that payments received accurately reflect royalties earned.[15]

2. Statutory Blanket Licenses Provide Direct Payment of Royalties to Songwriters and Recording Artists

Not only do statutory blanket licenses provide transparency of how royalty payments are calculated, they allow songwriters and recording artists to participate directly in the receipt of royalties. Under the Section 114 license, recording artists are directly paid by SoundExchange for performances of their music on services such as Pandora.[16] Likewise, ASCAP and BMI directly pay songwriters their share of the royalties collected.[17] These direct payments are important because they bypass the traditional royalty accounting whereby royalties flow through a record label or music publisher, where unrecouped advances are deducted and a much smaller percentage of the royalty collected—if any—is passed through.

3. Anticompetitive Behavior Must Be Constrained

Collectively licensing an aggregation of copyrights owned by different copyright owners, however, creates the very real market power problems from which anticompetitive behaviors can emerge.[18] It is the consent decrees in the case of ASCAP and BMI and the statutory provisions of Sections 112 and 114 in the case of record labels that protect music users from the potential abuse of market power created by collective licensing. Notwithstanding recent calls to do away with consent decrees because, for example, they were last modified before the advent of the iPod, the same joint selling agency among horizontal competitors that gave rise to the anticompetitive behavior that the government felt needed to be constrained in the 1940s still exists today. In fact, it is ironic that it was the reactions of ASCAP and big music publishers to the advent of terrestrial radio, when ASCAP attempted to increase royalty rates by 375%, that caused the government to sue ASCAP for engaging in an "unlawful combination and conspiracy in restraint of ... commerce in radio broadcasting."[19] Today, ASCAP, BMI and the major publishers appear to be saying that the consent decrees that resulted from this prior anticompetitive behavior against terrestrial radio broadcasters needs to be amended so that they can repeat this same anticompetitive behavior against Internet radio services.

The recent experiences of Pandora and other music licensees reflect the very real and continued anticompetitive behavior of various music publishers and the performing rights societies for which continued government intervention is required. SESAC, the one performance rights society in the U.S. that does not operate under a consent decree or statutory license, is currently being sued in two separate antitrust lawsuits. In one case, federal District Court Judge Engelmayer found that the "evidence would ... comfortably sustain a finding that SESAC ... engaged in an overall anticompetitive course of conduct designed to eliminate meaningful competition to its blanket license."[20] In the other case, federal District Court Judge Jones found that the Radio Music License Committee was likely to prevail on the merits of its antitrust case because, in part, SESAC was deliberately concealing the contents of its repertoire to effectively stifle competition to its direct license.[21]

Pandora's Recent Experience with Anticompetitive Behavior by Major Music Publishers

As this Committee is no doubt aware, over the last two years major music publishers, allegedly motivated by a perceived inequity between the amount of royalties Pandora pays to record labels and the amount publishers collect, sought to withdraw from ASCAP and BMI the right to license digital music services such as Pandora. When the major music publishers purportedly withdrew their digital rights from ASCAP and BMI in 2012 and 2013, they were supposedly operating in the "free market," the expected benefits about which you have heard so much from the publishers themselves. When given the chance to compete, however, the major publishers and ASCAP choose not to. Instead, they quickly reverted back to exactly the type of anticompetitive behavior the consent decrees are meant to mitigate. As Judge Cote concluded, "the evidence at trial revealed troubling coordination between Sony, UMPG, and ASCAP, which implicates a core antitrust concern underlying [the ASCAP consent decree]."[22]

Judge Cote's 136 page opinion is replete with the details of this coordinated and anticompetitive behavior. For example, the major publishers and ASCAP refused to provide Pandora with the list of repertoire purportedly being withdrawn,[23] thereby depriving Pandora of the ability to exercise self-help and take down content it could not or did not want to license.[24] The major publishers "each exercised their considerable market power to extract supra-competitive prices" from Pandora.[25] The major publishers "interfered" with Pandora's negotiations with ASCAP at the end of 2012, preventing ASCAP from signing a deal Pandora believed it had reached with ASCAP management.[26] A major publisher even used the press to leak the confidential terms of their agreements with Pandora.[27] In sum, "ASCAP, Sony, and UMPG did not act as if they were competitors with each other in their negotiations with Pandora. Because their interests were aligned against Pandora, and they coordinated their activities with respect to Pandora, the very considerable market power that each of them holds individually was magnified."[28]

Statutory Blanket License Rate-Setting Process Can Be Improved

While Pandora believes that because of its procompetitive benefits statutory blanket licensing should remain a central feature of licensing non-interactive Internet radio, there are steps that Congress can take to improve the efficiency of determining the reasonable fees for statutory blanket licenses and mitigate against the kind of continued anticompetitive behavior Pandora recently experienced.

During Pandora's rate setting proceeding with ASCAP, Judge Cote welcomed thoughts from all interested parties "about ways that the litigation could be conducted in a more cost-effective way" and asked "to talk ... with ASCAP and the right set of music users" about ways to "set up some streamlined procedures for appropriate discovery." Judge Cote indicated that a revision to the consent decree would not be required to implement these types of cost-saving efficiencies. Instead of rushing into a decree modification process, ASCAP and BMI should engage with music users around process changes to which all parties could agree.

Several respondents to the Copyright Office's recent notice of inquiry regarding music licensing commented on the expense and burden of the current Copyright Royalty Board

("CRB") rate-setting proceedings.[29] The current process involves a bifurcated proceeding during the first phase of which the parties submit their written direct cases, including their rate proposals and all testimony and evidence they intend to introduce at the hearing, without the benefit of any discovery from other participants. Because the record labels, which share information with their representative SoundExchange, have access to all of the direct licenses that typically serve as benchmarks in these proceedings, but individual licensee-participants only have access to direct deals into which they have entered, if any, the current procedure significantly favors the copyright owner participants. Recently, Pandora and the National Association of Broadcasters attempted to ameliorate this problem by filing motions for the issuance of subpoenas with the CRB in connection with the current rate-setting for non-interactive webcasting, commonly referred to as Web IV.[30] The CRB, however, denied these motions.

The common themes among these respondents are (1) the need for the application of the federal rules of civil procedure and federal rules of evidence to apply to CRB proceedings, (2) the establishment of a unitary proceeding with ample time for discovery and presentation of evidence, and 3) the application of the so-called 801(b) standard. Even the Recording Industry Association of America recognizes that the application of the 801(b) standard can result in rates that reflect fair market value.[31]

A Database of Record Would Mitigate Anticompetitive Behavior

Just as statutory blanket licenses provide much needed transparency for songwriters and recording artists, in order to foster more transparency for music users such as Pandora, we recommend the creation of a single database of record, hosted by the Copyright Office, that would house all relevant music copyright ownership information.[32] Participation in such a database need not be mandatory, but Congress could create the proper incentives for robust participation. For example, just as Chapter 4 of the Copyright Act prevents a copyright owner from seeking statutory damages unless the work at issue is registered, Congress could include a further requirement that entitlement to statutory damages was contingent on registering and keeping accurate copyright ownership on this database. Because this database would be the database of record, copyright owners would only have to enter their ownership information a single time, reducing the current situation where information is often entered and reentered across multiple databases. A single reliable and fully searchable database of record, coupled with ineligibility of statutory damages for works not in the database, would prevent copyright owners from holding services such as Pandora 'hostage' during negotiations, threatening massive copyright infringement penalties while refusing to disclose their repertoire.[33] By enabling services to quickly ascertain who owns which rights to a work, a single database of record would also enable services to identify, on a catalog-by-catalog basis, the owners of the songs it performs, which would encourage real competition among copyright owners for distribution on digital platforms. While the transparency provided by such a database would mitigate the anticompetitive behavior Pandora recently experienced, it would not alleviate such behavior entirely, reaffirming the need for the protection of statutory blanket licensing structures.

Thank you again for your leadership on this issue and the opportunity to testify. I look forward to answering your questions.

End Notes

[1] Both the intent of Congress behind the Copyright Act and decades of jurisprudence from U.S. Courts of Appeals and our Supreme Court instruct that copyright is intended to "stimulate activity and progress in the arts for the intellectual enrichment of the public." Cariou v. Prince, 714 F.3d 694, 705 (2d Cir. 2013) (quoting Pierre Leval, Toward a Fair Use Standard, 103 Harv. L. Rev. 1105, 1107 (1990)) (emphasis added); see also H.R. Rep. No. 2222, 60th Cong., 2d Sess. (Report on the Copyright Act of 1909) (noting that copyright exists "primarily for the benefit of the public.").

[2] For ease of reference, we refer to both statutory licensing of sound recordings under Sec. 114 and blanket licensing under the ASCAP and BMI consent decrees as "statutory blanket licensing."

[3] "Because each Major currently controls recorded music necessary for these streaming services, the music is more complementary than substitutable in this context, leading to limited direct competition between Universal and EMI." Statement of FTC Bureau of Competition Director Richard A. Feinstein, In the Matter of Vivendi, S.A. and EMI Recorded Music, September 21, 2012.

[4] "Power is the ability to stop new services. Power is the ability to create new services. That's power." Billboard Power 100: Lucian Grainge Q&A, by Bill Werde, February 07, 2013 8:55 PM EST http://www.billboard.com/biz/articles/1538532/billboardpower-100-lucian-grainge-qa; See Paul Resnikoff, "Sony/ATV 'Now Has the Power to Shut Pandora Down...,'" Digital Music News, Jan. 17, 2013, available at http://www.digitalmusicnews.com/permalink/2013/20130117pandora (quoting publishing sources as saying, "The 25 percent bump is going to get higher after the first year deal," "They aren't squeezing Pandora now, but they will," and "Sony now has the power to shut Pandora down, that's your negotiating power"); Paul Resnikoff, "Universal Music Publishing 'Now Has the Power to Shut Pandora Down...'," Digital Music News, Feb. 5, 2013, available at http://www.digitalmusicnews.com/permalink/2013/20130205umpg (quoting source saying, "I said it to you on Sony/ATV and it's the same with Universal. They can shut Pandora down if they want to. So that's your negotiating power.").

[5] Universal Has A Big Stake In Beats That's Worth Nearly $500 Million, by Peter Lauria posted on May 8, 2014, at 6:11 p.m (Universal Music's investment in Beats, recently sold to Apple, may yield $500 million) http://www.buzzfeed.com/peterlauria/universal-music-will-make-nearly-500-million-on-apples-beats; The Major Labels Are Trying to Sell Spotify for $10 Billion, Sources Say, by Paul Resnikoff Wednesday, June 11, 2014 (Major labels own a 20% stake in Spotify) http://www.digitalmusicnews.com/permalink/2014/06/11/major-labels-trying-sell-spotify-10-billion-sources-say.

[6] Two foreign-owned multinationals now dominate music publishing and recorded music; e.g., the so-called "Majors." Sony Corporation, headquartered in Japan, controls the largest music publishing catalog along with the second largest record label. Vivendi, headquartered in France, through its Universal Music Group subsidiary, controls the second largest music publishing catalog and the largest record label. While music publishers complain about the disparity of royalties they receive compared to record labels for performances on Pandora, in many cases Pandora is paying same company for both performance rights.

[7] The band's name is stylized as fun.

[8] The songwriters are Jack Antonoff, Jeff Bhasker, Andrew Dost, and Nathaniel Ruess and the music publishers are Bearvon Music, FBR Music, Rough Art, W B Music Corp., Shira Lee Lawrence Music, Sony/ATV Songs, and Way Above Music.

[9] 1 Melville B. Nimmer & David Nimmer, Nimmer on Copyright § 6.10[A][2] (2013).

[10] The Universal Music Publishing website contains the following disclaimer: "UMPG makes no warranties or representations whatsoever with respect to its accuracy."

[11] "Collective licensing has enormous benefits for the music market and consumers. It provides broadcasters and services with a one stop license for the world's repertoire under compulsory statutory licenses with rate setting by the Copyright Royalty Board. ... The non-interactive compulsory statutory licensing regime ensures equity and fairness for all copyright owners and allows greater music service marketplace access resulting in greater consumer choice." American Association of Independent Music ("A2IM") President Rich Bengloff's letter to the Federal Trade Commission Chairwoman Edith Ramirez and Director Bureau of Competition Deborah L. Feinstein regarding Google/YouTube Notice-Independent music labels and their artists' content to be blocked on the YouTube music website (June 4, 2014) available at (http://www.a2im.org/ downloads/ FTC LetterJune42014.pdf)

[12] The Blanket 'Problem': Balancing the Needs of Songwriters with New Forms of Radio (Guest Post), By Casey Rae, April 21, 2014 12:59 PM EDT available at (http://www.billboard.com/biz/ articles/news/ radio/6062737/the-blanket-problem-balancingthe-needs-of-songwriters-with-new)

[13] "Direct deals on the publishing side also raise concerns about transparency. Outside of the framework made possible by oversight, what guarantees do songwriters and composers have that their share will be fairly apportioned?" Comments of Future of Music Coalition in Response to the Copyright Office's Music Licensing Study, Docket No. 2014-3, May 16, 2014 at 16; "The trend toward direct licensing to copyright users by music publishers of performing rights in musical compositions is one that is causing grave concern to the music creator community because of the utter lack of transparency in the direct licensing process." Comments of Songwriters Guild of America, Inc., U.S. Copyright Office Study on Music Licensing, Docket No. 2014-3, May 16, 2014 ("Comments of Songwriters Guild") at 7; "The statutory licenses are also transparent." Comments of SoundExchange, Inc., U.S. Copyright Office Study on Music Licensing, Docket No. 2014-3, May 16, 2014 at 4.

[14] Songwriters "were concerned as well that the publishers would not manage with as much care the difficult task of properly accounting for the distribution of fees to multiple rights holders, and might even retain for themselves certain monies, such as advances, in which writers believed they were entitled to share." In re Petition of Pandora Media Inc., 12 civ 8035-DJC (SDNY March 18, 2014) (hereinafter "In re Pandora") at p. 97).

[15] For example, the rate that Pandora pays for the public performance of sound recordings is part of the Federal Register and is prominently displays on SoundExchange's website.

[16] "An important feature of the Section 114 statutory license is that artists directly and immediately participate in the royalty stream." Comments of SoundExchange, Inc., U.S. Copyright Office Study on Music Licensing, Docket No. 2014-3, May 16, 2014 at 3.

[17] "This system has ... provided music creators with the crucial assurance that an important source of revenue will be paid directly to them by the PRO." Comments of Songwriters Guild, p 7.

[18] As the U.S. Copyright Office recently concluded, "there is a significant risk that the collective may exploit its market power by charging supra-competitive rates or discriminating against potential licensees" U.S. Copyright Office STELA § 302 Report 95-96 (August 29, 2011).

[19] Original Complaint filed by the Department of Justice in U.S. v. ASCAP, 41 civ. 1395 (SDNY February 26, 1941).

[20] Meredith Corp. v. SESAC LLC, 9 civ 9177-PAE (SDNY March 3, 2014).

[21] Radio Music License Comm., Inc. v. SESAC, Inc., 12 civ 5807-CDJ (ED Pa. February 20, 2014).

[22] In re Pandora at p. 97.

[23] "Pandora also asked ASCAP for the list of Sony works in ASCAP's repertoire. It would have taken ASCAP about a day to respond to Pandora's request with an accurate list of the Sony works. But, ASCAP, like Sony, stonewalled Pandora and refused to provide the list." In re Pandora, p. 67.

[24] "Without that list, Pandora's options were stark. It could shut down its service, infringe Sony's rights, or execute an agreement with Sony on Sony's terms." In re Pandora, p. 98.

[25] In re Pandora p. 97.

[26] "They also interfered with the ASCAP-Pandora license negotiations at the end of 2012. UMPG pressured ASCAP to reject the Pandora license ASCAP's executives had negotiated, and Sony threatened to sue ASCAP if it entered into a license with Pandora." Id.

[27] "[D]espite executing a confidentiality agreement with Pandora, Sony made sure that UMPG learned of all of the critical terms of the Sony-Pandora license. And LoFrumento admitted at trial that ASCAP expected to learn the terms of any direct license that any music publisher negotiated with Pandora in much the same way." In re Pandora, p. 98.

[28] In re Pandora pp. 98-9.

[29] See, e.g., Comments of Sirius XM Radio Inc., pp. 15-17; Comments of the National Association of Broadcasters, pp. 19-22 (noting that the "current CRB procedural rules applicable to rate cases have resulted in proceedings that are at least as, if not more, expensive than analogous litigation in the federal ASCAP and BMI rate courts, but also provide less complete evidentiary records and therefore less satisfactory results"); Comments of Music Choice, pp. 29 – 32, and Comments of Digital Media Association, pp. 37 – 39 (noting that "CRB rate proceedings are actually more expensive (or certainly no less expensive) than federal court proceedings before the ASCAP and BMI rate courts, but they are far less efficient.").

[30] In re Determination of Royalty Rates and Terms for Ephemeral Recording and Digital Performance of Sound Recordings, Docket No.14-CRB-0001-WR (2016-2020).

[31] See Comments of the Recording Industry Association of America, U.S. Copyright Office Study on Music Licensing, Docket No. 2014-3, May 16, 2014, p. 25. In the context of Section 115 licenses, in over 35 years that the 801(b) standard has applied, there have been only two litigated proceedings. Compare this record of compromise to the history of the application of the so-called "willing-buyer, willing-seller" standard. Each of

the webcasting rate-setting proceedings have been fully litigated, including appeals, and, on at least two occasions, Congress felt compelled to intervene.

[32] "Identifying and locating the co-authors of each of millions of copyrighted musical works is a daunting task that is hampered significantly by, among other things, the lack of a modern and publicly searchable database identifying the current owners of musical works and the contact information for such copyright owners." Comments of Spotify USA Inc., U.S. Copyright Office Study on Music Licensing, Docket No. 2014-3, May 16, 2014 at 4.

[33] One cannot search the ASCAP or BMI databases by publisher and receive a list of all works owned by that single publisher.

INDEX

#

21st century, 197

A

Abraham, 146, 165
abuse, 241
access, 2, 35, 39, 40, 41, 48, 67, 71, 74, 76, 77, 78, 84, 85, 89, 101, 111, 121, 148, 149, 155, 164, 196, 198, 199, 200, 210, 218, 233, 243, 244
accessibility, 109, 118, 123
accountability, 58, 81
accounting, 54, 58, 59, 62, 85, 86, 144, 150, 158, 241, 245
adjustment, 64
administrators, 15, 16, 36, 59
adverse effects, 108
advertisements, 163, 169
advocacy, 206
Afghanistan, 220
AFM, 17, 44, 61, 68, 125, 129, 137, 150, 152, 159, 162, 171, 172
age, 12, 18, 90, 109, 148, 179, 187, 189, 195, 201, 205, 210, 213, 214, 238
agencies, 36, 60, 99, 166, 168, 180, 200
aggregation, 182, 241
aloe, 150
America Online, 236
annual rate, 25
antitrust, 2, 3, 8, 11, 16, 22, 23, 24, 25, 26, 27, 31, 45, 47, 50, 52, 71, 75, 77, 78, 79, 81, 82, 83, 101, 111, 119, 140, 143, 151, 153, 155, 159, 166, 172, 175, 176, 241, 242
appetite, 12
apples, 244
appointees, 19
arbitrage, 52

arbitration, 25, 55, 151, 156, 167, 176, 199, 201, 203, 234
assessment, 182
assets, 3, 78, 98, 142
attachment, 70, 109, 118, 123
audit(s), 6, 21, 58, 59, 67, 68, 87, 92, 108, 148, 158, 162, 171
authority, 3, 7, 9, 20, 26, 32, 54, 55, 64, 73, 75, 83, 84, 85, 92, 96, 97, 99, 102, 108, 110, 170, 184

B

background information, 195
ban, 62
banks, 220
bargaining, 11, 62
barriers, 196, 235
barter, 174
base, 148, 166, 184
behaviors, 241
benchmarks, 21, 25, 26, 51, 52, 75, 76, 81, 83, 92, 170, 199, 201, 204, 230, 231, 234, 243
beneficiaries, 182, 237
benefits, 2, 12, 44, 58, 60, 64, 72, 74, 84, 90, 104, 191, 195, 196, 219, 221, 229, 231, 234, 242, 244
blame, 44, 45
blogs, 144, 163
bonuses, 148, 173
breakdown, 58
Brittany, 126, 145, 157, 161, 162, 163, 174
broadcast television industry, 229
browser, 109, 118, 123
business model, 12, 71, 76, 91, 105, 193, 196, 206, 209, 213, 227, 229
business partners, 208
business processes, 163
businesses, 46, 86, 182, 190, 192, 196, 200, 207, 213, 218, 225, 226, 227, 233

Index

buyer(s), 3, 11, 23, 31, 45, 46, 47, 57, 61, 63, 67, 73, 75, 76, 78, 91, 95, 107, 113, 159, 160, 165, 173, 177, 184, 204, 213, 221, 230, 234, 245

C

cable television, 22, 75
Capitol Hill, 191
career development, 210
case law, 218
cash, 215
cash flow, 215
CBS, 25, 140, 141, 166
census, 68
certification, 58
challenges, vii, 13, 25, 56, 58, 73, 90, 106, 111, 182, 209, 217, 227
Chamber of Commerce, 129, 130
chaos, 85
charitable organizations, 214
Chicago, 220
children, 220
China, 177, 182, 207
city, 13, 24, 76, 79, 118, 226
clarity, 51, 95, 230
classes, 11, 17, 36, 71, 73, 163, 228
clients, 16, 78, 79, 151, 166
CNN, 149, 150
coffee, 151
collaboration, 97, 98, 173, 205, 207
colleges, 205
collusion, 155
color, 94
commerce, 23, 37, 179, 241
commercial(s), 18, 22, 32, 34, 79, 80, 82, 84, 97, 111, 140, 143, 173, 191, 196, 202, 212, 219
common law, 33, 48, 178
common sense, 167
communication, 20, 39, 218
communities, 102, 196, 218, 219, 220
community, 53, 66, 68, 69, 105, 153, 169, 185, 195, 205, 208, 212, 214, 218, 219, 220, 245
comparative advantage, 167
compensation, 2, 4, 10, 26, 45, 48, 49, 54, 63, 68, 71, 74, 78, 87, 121, 147, 152, 163, 170, 174, 182, 183, 187, 190, 191, 192, 206, 207, 218, 226, 233, 235
competition, 19, 25, 33, 42, 55, 69, 76, 78, 82, 140, 141, 174, 196, 199, 214, 218, 221, 227, 241, 243, 244
competitive advantage, 49, 52, 62
competitors, 55, 77, 79, 81, 197, 199, 221, 241, 242
complement, 7, 29, 61, 95, 198

complexity, 12, 18, 35, 59, 60, 99, 218
compliance, 29, 58, 62, 96, 104, 175, 233
composers, 15, 36, 38, 52, 69, 110, 111, 114, 119, 120, 121, 138, 141, 148, 170, 180, 181, 182, 184, 195, 196, 203, 207, 225, 226, 227, 235, 236, 245
composition, 14, 18, 110, 145, 148, 163, 165, 168, 179, 180, 188, 189, 196, 202, 213, 232, 238, 240
comprehension, 64
compulsion, 234
computer, 167
computing, 200, 202
conception, 206
confidentiality, 67, 245
conflict, 190, 208
congress, 3, 4, 7, 10, 12, 14, 19, 22, 23, 27, 28, 29, 31, 32, 48, 49, 61, 64, 66, 70, 73, 74, 75, 76, 77, 79, 90, 94, 95, 96, 97, 100, 107, 108, 109, 110, 112, 115, 116, 117, 122, 124, 137, 139, 142, 144, 148, 151, 152, 163, 164, 168, 170, 172, 175, 176, 177, 180, 182, 185, 187, 188, 189, 190, 191, 193, 195, 196, 199, 201, 202, 203, 213, 218, 226, 235, 236, 238, 242, 243, 244, 246
congressional hearings, 29
connective tissue, 214
consensus, 1, 2, 39, 71, 120, 155, 212, 214
consent, 4, 11, 16, 23, 24, 25, 26, 27, 43, 45, 47, 50, 51, 52, 53, 54, 55, 56, 63, 71, 75, 76, 77, 78, 79, 80, 81, 82, 83, 84, 87, 96, 101, 111, 112, 113, 119, 137, 140, 153, 154, 155, 156, 163, 165, 166, 168, 169, 171, 175, 176, 180, 185, 190, 191, 192, 193, 195, 197, 198, 199, 200, 203, 212, 213, 214, 226, 227, 228, 230, 231, 234, 241, 242, 244
consolidation, 53, 168, 199
conspiracy, 23, 166, 241
constituents, 217
constitution, 181, 218
consumer choice, 211, 221, 244
consumer taste, 210
consumers, 12, 18, 34, 41, 42, 49, 50, 71, 78, 89, 90, 110, 192, 193, 196, 209, 211, 214, 218, 221, 228, 232, 233, 234, 236, 240, 244
consumption, 40, 42, 115, 182, 189, 202, 237, 238
consumption patterns, 40
continental, 124
contingency, 84
controversial, 32, 45
convention, 139
conversations, 205
conviction, 11
cooking, 161
cooperation, 66, 148, 196
coordination, 242

Index

Copyright Act, vii, 1, 3, 12, 14, 18, 19, 20, 23, 27, 28, 29, 34, 45, 47, 48, 58, 73, 74, 76, 77, 78, 106, 108, 109, 110, 111, 112, 116, 130, 136, 138, 139, 140, 142, 144, 161, 164, 176, 177, 182, 188, 189, 195, 199, 203, 206, 220, 221, 222, 226, 231, 233, 235, 237, 240, 243, 244
copyright law, vii, 3, 4, 11, 12, 15, 19, 31, 39, 46, 47, 48, 73, 74, 76, 110, 152, 177, 180, 187, 190, 192, 193, 195, 198, 199, 202, 211, 213, 214, 217, 218, 231, 233, 235, 237
Copyright Office, v, vii, 1, 2, 3, 4, 7, 8, 9, 10, 11, 12, 19, 20, 21, 29, 32, 33, 37, 48, 49, 59, 66, 70, 72, 75, 83, 84, 85, 86, 97, 104, 108, 109, 110, 113, 115, 116, 117, 118, 122, 123, 136, 138, 139, 142, 144, 145, 146, 154, 157, 160, 162, 163, 164, 166, 168, 169, 170, 173, 176, 177, 178, 183, 192, 204, 214, 227, 234, 236, 242, 243, 245, 246
correlation, 222
cost, 12, 20, 21, 26, 37, 47, 55, 63, 64, 86, 104, 119, 121, 143, 150, 151, 155, 158, 161, 164, 172, 177, 215, 218, 219, 221, 223, 229, 236, 242
cost saving, 47, 64, 236
cost structures, 119, 121
cough, 180
counsel, 89
Coup, 148
Court of Appeals, 31, 94
covering, 24, 29, 38, 60, 73, 92, 150, 164, 170, 172, 174, 176
creative process, 187, 205
creativity, 192, 196, 197, 203, 210
creditworthiness, 59
creep, 151
culture, vii, 1, 10, 52, 179, 214, 220, 237
cure, 90
customers, 53, 197, 198, 214, 226, 235

D

damages, 22, 57, 59, 66, 243
database, 8, 9, 21, 36, 37, 38, 65, 66, 67, 97, 98, 101, 102, 103, 104, 147, 148, 161, 162, 167, 173, 240, 243, 246
deduction, 158
deficiencies, 38
deflate, 51
Department of Agriculture, 165
Department of Commerce, 140, 150, 155, 169, 176
Department of Justice (DOJ), 4, 24, 25, 47, 50, 53, 54, 55, 77, 78, 79, 80, 81, 83, 84, 111, 130, 137, 138, 140, 141, 153, 155, 156, 166, 171, 190, 191, 197, 198, 200, 204, 228, 245
depth, vii, 14, 16, 26, 82

deregulation, 200
developed nations, 212
differential treatment, 76
digital revolution, vii, 1
digital technologies, 18, 227
direct payment, 7, 30, 63, 95, 174, 175, 241
disaster, 220
disclosure, 121, 161
discrete data, 37
discrimination, 111
discs, 10, 110, 227
dissatisfaction, 56
dissonance, 208
distribution, 5, 11, 13, 14, 17, 18, 19, 21, 27, 40, 50, 56, 62, 63, 68, 69, 71, 75, 76, 79, 86, 91, 97, 99, 102, 111, 112, 113, 115, 117, 119, 121, 122, 139, 142, 143, 152, 157, 159, 163, 164, 168, 169, 172, 173, 174, 190, 192, 199, 202, 203, 210, 212, 236, 239, 243,245
distribution function, 102
district courts, 4, 24, 79, 119
District of Columbia, 25, 31
diversity, 199
DNA, 181
due process, 166

E

earnings, 16, 73, 210
economic incentives, 46
economic power, 23
economics, 4, 31, 47, 83, 201, 225
ecosystem, 44, 155, 185, 198, 210, 211, 237
effort level, 171
election, 21
electricity, 165
emergency, 218
encouragement, 172, 205
endorsements, 189
enforcement, 2, 30, 71, 77, 80, 83, 153
engineering, 233
entrepreneurs, 211
environment, 12, 69, 70, 72, 80, 110, 116, 118, 123, 150, 152, 195, 232, 239
equipment, 218
equity, 8, 32, 44, 68, 100, 120, 121, 151, 174, 180, 244
EST, 244
Europe, 36, 56, 198
evacuation, 220
evidence, 46, 49, 62, 64, 65, 75, 85, 107, 139, 150, 153, 155, 165, 176, 184, 191, 192, 207, 219, 234, 235, 241, 242, 243

evolution, 167, 209, 228
examinations, 171
exclusion, 56, 177
exercise, 7, 54, 58, 153, 163, 187, 214, 231, 242
expertise, 4, 83, 106
exploitation, 10, 18, 34, 43, 54, 60, 84, 152, 214
exporter, 219
exposure, 28, 49, 215
extinction, 153

F

Facebook, 239
fair use, 33, 48, 74
fairness, 47, 57, 58, 244
faith, 59
families, 179, 180, 191, 219
fear, 47, 54, 55
federal agency, 204
federal courts, 166, 192
federal government, 115
federal judiciary, 153
federal law, 33, 73, 74, 144, 213
Federal Register, 12, 108, 245
films, 23, 110, 112
financial, 10, 44, 104, 167, 173, 174, 206, 209, 215, 239
financial resources, 173
financial support, 10, 104
fingerprints, 37
fires, 222
fixed rate, 170
flaws, 55
flexibility, 31, 54, 105, 108, 175, 193, 231, 232, 233, 234
flour, 151
flowers, 180
FMC, 16, 54, 55, 66, 124, 128, 130, 151, 152, 153, 155, 156, 161, 164, 171
food, 191, 220, 222
food chain, 222
force, 19, 158, 159, 238
formula, 47, 62, 93, 99
foundations, 82
framing, 12
France, 219, 244
free will, 180
freedom, 163
friction, 100, 196
funding, 9, 104, 105, 175
fundraising, 219, 220
funds, 9, 10, 21, 30, 68, 99, 103, 105, 175, 204

G

GAO, 142, 152, 153, 164, 183
GDP, 219
genes, 238
genre, 196, 238, 239
Germany, 219
global scale, 233
google, 145, 151, 173
government intervention, 3, 90, 91, 241
government policy, 78
government regulation, vii, 1, 11, 70, 77, 87, 180, 187, 188, 192
grants, 24, 152, 200, 204, 228, 231, 233, 234
grounding, 70
growth, 73, 149, 150, 158, 197, 221, 239, 240
growth rate, 239
guidance, 84, 98, 140, 170
guidelines, 77, 154, 198
guiding principles, 1

H

hamstring, 170
harbors, 33, 45, 74, 151
harmony, 66, 199
health, 221
history, 14, 43, 58, 140, 144, 159, 160, 176, 196, 211, 221, 229, 245
hobby, 193
hotels, 22, 162, 196, 227
House, 12, 90, 128, 159, 170, 176, 179, 181, 187, 195, 205, 209, 217, 225, 237
House of Representatives, 195, 225
hub, 9, 102, 147
human, 19, 200
husband, 206
hybrid, 174, 233
hypocrisy, 183

I

ideal, 163
identification, 12, 35, 36, 65, 67, 88, 99, 102, 115
identity, 66, 120, 121
image, 109, 118, 123
imitation, 88
improvements, 6, 10, 120, 159, 238
income, 7, 10, 20, 35, 40, 41, 42, 43, 44, 48, 49, 86, 92, 105, 111, 114, 115, 121, 145, 148, 149, 151, 161, 180, 188, 189, 191, 196, 208, 210, 223, 227
income tax, 180

increased competition, 42, 55, 149
individual rights, 88, 103
individuals, 36, 117, 119, 202, 203, 205, 207
industrialized countries, 73
industries, 15, 20, 75, 137, 148, 171, 190, 209, 218, 219, 221, 223, 227, 228, 229
industry, vii, 8, 11, 12, 16, 17, 18, 20, 21, 23, 28, 29, 31, 35, 39, 40, 41, 42, 44, 49, 50, 52, 53, 55, 58, 73, 75, 76, 77, 80, 82, 83, 85, 87, 89, 90, 97, 98, 111, 117, 119, 136, 137, 142, 148, 149, 152, 157, 164, 168, 182, 185, 190, 191, 195, 196, 197, 209, 210, 211, 214, 217, 218, 219, 221, 222, 223, 227, 228, 229, 230, 231, 240
inefficiency, 45, 63, 65
inequity, 46, 49, 57, 153, 187, 242
inflation, 57, 138, 189
infrastructure, 12, 54, 76
ingest, 97, 102
initiation, 106, 108
institutions, 70
integration, 91
intellectual property, 78, 152, 166, 182, 184, 188, 189, 191, 192, 193, 202, 238
intellectual property rights, 182, 188, 193
interface, 38, 109, 118, 123
intermediaries, 34, 44, 57, 69, 110
interoperability, 98
intervention, 11, 76
intrinsic value, 214
investment(s), 20, 98, 114, 117, 143, 165, 177, 192, 206, 210, 211, 221, 223, 238, 239, 244
investors, 211
Iowa, 139
Iran, 50, 142, 164, 177, 182, 207
isolation, 70
issues, 4, 11, 12, 13, 22, 32, 48, 52, 56, 61, 64, 70, 71, 74, 79, 81, 87, 89, 90, 99, 100, 107, 108, 109, 114, 115, 116, 118, 120, 121, 122, 148, 163, 165, 168, 175, 185, 191, 192, 203, 207, 208, 209, 217, 235, 237
Italy, 219

J

Japan, 244
judicial interpretation, 88
judiciary, 136
Judiciary Committee, 12, 21, 170, 176, 179, 181, 187, 195, 205, 209, 217, 225, 237
jurisdiction, 47, 74
justification, 3, 7, 28, 76, 96

K

kicks, 90, 223

L

landscape, 11, 53, 65, 110, 117, 122, 187, 200, 203, 212, 213, 226
laws, 2, 3, 12, 25, 71, 140, 153, 164, 182, 188, 203, 206, 208, 217, 218, 221, 233
laws and regulations, 208
leadership, 196, 203, 235, 237, 243
learning, 179
legislation, 10, 19, 32, 46, 49, 70, 74, 75, 90, 100, 107, 152, 159, 163, 174, 176, 180, 183, 185, 187, 188, 199, 203, 208, 213
lens, 75, 218
license fee, 24, 51, 56, 111, 119, 175, 176, 196, 197, 199, 201, 204, 221, 226, 228, 234
licensing system, vii, 1, 5, 6, 8, 10, 39, 40, 58, 60, 71, 88, 89, 90, 92, 93, 100, 102, 108, 119, 151, 155, 168, 169, 192, 211, 212, 214, 228, 231, 236
light, 4, 5, 7, 12, 25, 39, 55, 56, 60, 66, 79, 81, 89, 96, 97, 108, 109, 116, 170, 171, 203, 205, 209, 235
litigation, 10, 25, 26, 31, 33, 34, 51, 64, 77, 79, 80, 82, 84, 105, 107, 112, 120, 140, 141, 151, 154, 158, 165, 173, 176, 199, 229, 230, 242, 245
lobbying, 75, 182
local community, 222
local television stations, 25, 26, 52, 166
logistics, 6, 92, 121
longevity, 77
love, 70, 171, 181, 206, 238

M

magazines, 188
magnitude, 227, 239
majority, 10, 41, 62, 80, 83, 104, 182
man, 158
management, 35, 38, 39, 53, 67, 87, 242
market failure, 6, 87, 89
market share, 8, 16, 77, 81, 82, 101, 137, 161, 180
marketability, 152
marketing, 36, 165, 210
marketplace, vii, 1, 3, 6, 8, 11, 12, 13, 17, 18, 19, 21, 31, 34, 35, 38, 39, 44, 47, 50, 51, 55, 60, 62, 66, 70, 72, 74, 75, 76, 77, 78, 82, 84, 87, 91, 97, 98, 108, 111, 113, 114, 115, 117, 119, 121, 139, 147, 148, 149, 153, 154, 155, 156, 164, 169, 177, 180, 182, 184, 185, 187, 190, 193, 195, 197, 198, 199,

200, 201, 203, 206, 209, 210, 212, 215, 222, 223, 226, 227, 228, 229, 230, 231, 232, 235, 236, 237, 244
Maryland, 129
mass, 57, 170
matter, vii, 5, 18, 30, 31, 41, 48, 50, 51, 79, 82, 91, 94, 97, 143, 166, 169, 170, 178, 185, 202
measurement, 68
media, 17, 20, 39, 54, 100, 111, 130, 137, 142, 148, 149, 150, 162, 167, 171, 173, 196, 197, 206, 211, 214, 218, 222, 223, 226, 229
mediation, 55
medicine, 180
melody, 20, 88
membership, 16, 18, 226, 231, 232
merchandise, 40, 44, 189, 225
Miami, 217
Microsoft, 109, 118, 123
Microsoft Word, 109, 118, 123
middle class, 44, 148, 150
military, 220
mission, 195, 196, 197
misunderstanding, 208
misuse, 25
mobile telecommunication, 167
models, 44, 71, 78, 91, 94, 101, 105, 114, 115, 122, 153, 170, 189, 193, 197, 209, 210
modernization, 56, 153, 155
modifications, 12, 13, 65, 107, 204, 226, 233
mole, 45
monopoly, 19, 55, 59, 76, 77, 78, 154, 165, 166, 179, 189
monopoly power, 55, 59, 77
motivation, 23, 222
MRI, 16, 86, 125, 127, 129, 130, 137
music creators, vii, 3, 22, 39, 40, 68, 69, 76, 88, 100, 120, 148, 154, 163, 174, 185, 196, 214, 225, 226, 228, 234, 235, 245
music industry, 12, 18, 35, 36, 37, 42, 53, 58, 67, 99, 116, 138, 149, 168, 170, 173, 187, 188, 190, 192, 202, 203, 210, 212, 218, 219, 227, 239
music licensing, vii, 2, 4, 7, 10, 12, 13, 18, 27, 34, 38, 39, 40, 45, 47, 50, 56, 65, 66, 70, 71, 78, 79, 86, 95, 97, 103, 104, 107, 109, 114, 115, 116, 117, 118, 120, 121, 122, 123, 136, 147, 169, 180, 181, 184, 185, 187, 188, 191, 192, 195, 198, 201, 203, 208, 209, 210, 211, 212, 214, 217, 218, 221, 225, 228, 236, 238, 239, 242
music marketplace, vii, 1, 3, 11, 12, 17, 35, 38, 60, 70, 72, 77, 98, 113, 114, 115, 117, 147, 148, 154, 169, 193, 203, 209, 226, 227, 237
music videos, 6, 34, 60, 89, 120, 121, 145, 191, 214
musicians, 16, 17, 29, 43, 62, 68, 93, 100, 146, 150, 166, 171, 172, 177, 181, 182, 183, 205, 206, 207, 208, 210

N

National Public Radio (NPR), 17, 62, 63, 125, 129, 130, 142, 159, 160, 172, 173
natural disaster, 219
natural gas, 165
negotiating, 8, 25, 53, 60, 75, 80, 94, 101, 150, 154, 157, 163, 167, 225, 227, 229, 244
negotiation, 26, 28, 31, 34, 55, 63, 64, 66, 79, 80, 81, 82, 87, 151, 165, 170, 173, 204, 228, 234
neutral, 235
new media, 26, 53, 54, 80, 81, 85, 88, 119, 229, 231, 232
niche market, 169
Nimmer on Copyright, 244
North Korea, 50, 142, 164, 177, 182, 207

O

obstacles, 39, 207
offenders, 151
Oklahoma, 219
operations, 9, 93, 103, 197, 210, 217, 239
opportunities, 10, 52, 148, 170, 196, 198, 199, 210
opt out, 4, 5, 8, 46, 72, 85, 88, 100, 101, 169
oral presentations, 77
outreach, 30
overlap, 14
oversight, 2, 7, 9, 11, 13, 16, 52, 55, 57, 72, 77, 80, 82, 83, 89, 92, 95, 101, 112, 121, 140, 153, 156, 188, 245
ownership, 5, 9, 17, 35, 36, 37, 38, 39, 57, 65, 66, 67, 68, 70, 73, 74, 82, 87, 97, 101, 102, 103, 104, 120, 121, 149, 154, 173, 174, 175, 189, 221, 239, 240, 243

P

parallel, 4, 72, 79, 92, 199
parenting, 220
parents, 179
parity, 2, 71, 72, 74, 91, 95, 117, 145, 155, 163
participants, vii, 2, 5, 8, 11, 12, 13, 21, 22, 39, 40, 45, 47, 48, 54, 55, 57, 61, 67, 69, 71, 76, 77, 78, 90, 97, 98, 106, 107, 117, 118, 120, 136, 154, 157, 161, 176, 184, 243
penalties, 26, 220, 243

performance rate, 11, 32, 51, 53, 56, 61, 151, 158, 167
performers, 16, 50, 68, 96, 143, 177, 181, 182, 206, 207
performing artists, 44, 49, 139, 172, 219
permission, 50, 78, 88, 148, 152, 163, 182, 213, 240
permit, 5, 20, 24, 31, 43, 54, 59, 82, 85, 87, 92, 95, 113, 170, 203, 226, 229, 231, 233, 234, 235
phonograph, 14, 19
piano, 14, 19, 76, 77, 179, 189
piracy, 44, 45, 150, 183, 206
platform, 117, 152, 163, 212, 238
playing, 14, 46, 71, 89, 179, 184, 192, 200
police, 96, 182
policy, 3, 4, 18, 20, 30, 32, 46, 50, 55, 63, 71, 74, 75, 76, 77, 82, 83, 92, 97, 151, 166, 206, 215
pools, 28, 55, 161
precedent, 94
predicate, 200
predictability, 63
preparation, 14
preservation, 32, 48, 74, 164
president, v, 19, 138, 143, 170, 179, 181, 187, 210, 217, 225, 244
prevention, 220
primary function, 4, 82
principles, 2, 8, 12, 23, 39, 70, 71, 101, 109, 207, 237
private sector, 98
procedural rule, 106, 107, 245
producers, 7, 16, 23, 30, 63, 95, 96, 181, 184, 185, 206, 207
product market, 23
production costs, 218
professionals, 16, 173, 206
profit, 3, 15, 16, 22, 29, 45, 49, 66, 69, 76, 85, 102, 159, 196, 212, 226, 227
profitability, 61, 215
programming, 22, 30, 62, 77, 94, 97, 138, 196, 197, 202, 219
project, 16, 38, 89, 144, 169, 184
proliferation, 112
property rights, 188, 193
proposed regulations, 168
protection, 3, 11, 14, 22, 32, 33, 47, 49, 54, 59, 69, 74, 103, 112, 114, 139, 144, 152, 153, 164, 177, 178, 187, 207, 233, 235, 243
public broadcasting, 27, 96, 97, 172
public domain, 144
public interest, 13, 46, 77, 156, 166, 172, 190, 218, 220
public policy, 45
public radio, 17, 62

public service, 219, 220
public welfare, 200
publishing, 15, 21, 29, 44, 47, 53, 54, 80, 101, 102, 137, 138, 141, 145, 148, 155, 167, 168, 170, 178, 189, 197, 198, 199, 214, 244, 245

Q

qualifications, 31
quality of service, 62
questioning, 56
quotas, 153

R

radio, 2, 6, 10, 11, 12, 17, 18, 22, 26, 27, 28, 29, 30, 31, 32, 33, 42, 43, 46, 49, 50, 52, 53, 61, 62, 68, 69, 73, 74, 75, 76, 79, 80, 84, 91, 93, 94, 95, 106, 110, 111, 112, 113, 119, 140, 141, 142, 152, 153, 162, 164, 165, 167, 174, 177, 179, 180, 182, 183, 190, 191, 195, 197, 207, 211, 212, 213, 217, 218, 219, 220, 221, 222, 223, 227, 229, 238, 239, 240, 241, 242, 244
ratification, 168
reactions, 241
reading, 33, 176, 235
reality, vii, 44, 105, 157, 163, 200, 222
reasoning, 19, 33, 164, 165
recession, 41
reciprocal relationships, 54
reciprocity, 29, 50, 54, 156, 177
recognition, 12, 19, 96, 105, 139, 163, 164
recommendations, vii, 1, 2, 3, 4, 5, 8, 70, 71, 164
reconciliation, 102
recovery, 22, 92
reform(s), vii, 2, 21, 22, 71, 87, 131, 137, 138, 139, 165, 168, 174, 176, 183, 197, 200, 203, 214, 221, 236, 239
regenerate, 149
Register of Copyrights, 21, 31, 73, 86, 109, 115, 116, 117, 118, 122, 123, 138, 139, 142, 164, 165, 168, 171, 176, 190, 234, 236
registries, 39, 66
registry, 39, 130, 147
regulations, 30, 59, 86, 92, 108, 139, 154, 155, 162, 163, 174, 180, 187, 193, 236
regulatory oversight, 8, 76, 102, 226
reimburse, 80
relaxation, 107
relevance, 75
relief, 52, 61, 78, 220
rent, 191

repair, 12, 197
reproduction, 5, 11, 13, 14, 18, 19, 27, 34, 40, 56, 62, 72, 75, 76, 79, 85, 86, 96, 113, 119, 122, 138, 139, 150, 157, 164, 169, 172, 189, 190, 192, 198, 199, 207, 212, 236
requirements, 16, 29, 33, 58, 61, 62, 65, 92, 94, 95, 96, 102, 108, 158, 171, 221
reserves, 196
resistance, 90
resolution, 55, 73, 92, 151, 174, 180, 183, 185, 234
resources, 5, 8, 9, 34, 45, 53, 62, 64, 65, 86, 91, 97, 98, 103, 105, 164, 173, 199, 210, 222, 229, 239
response, 12, 13, 21, 24, 26, 45, 65, 69, 107, 113, 115, 118, 120, 136, 167, 169, 204, 214
restaurants, 22, 54, 79, 111, 119, 162, 190, 196, 204, 227
restrictions, 5, 18, 55, 62, 64, 83, 185, 197, 198, 200, 213, 231
restructuring, 60
retail, 41, 196, 227
revenue, 19, 20, 22, 32, 40, 41, 42, 47, 48, 49, 69, 76, 82, 95, 119, 143, 145, 146, 148, 149, 150, 153, 155, 162, 163, 165, 174, 177, 182, 183, 191, 196, 209, 210, 214, 221, 222, 225, 239, 245
rewards, 91, 210
ringtones, 20, 28, 110, 139, 169, 170
risk(s), 20, 51, 57, 59, 60, 66, 143, 155, 161, 177, 210, 211, 215, 223, 228, 245
royalty, 3, 4, 7, 10, 15, 16, 19, 20, 24, 25, 27, 30, 31, 32, 42, 44, 45, 46, 47, 51, 53, 54, 55, 56, 58, 59, 60, 61, 62, 63, 64, 66, 68, 71, 73, 79, 81, 84, 86, 90, 92, 95, 96, 99, 100, 102, 104, 106, 111, 112, 113, 114, 117, 119, 121, 137, 139, 144, 147, 148, 153, 156, 157, 158, 159, 160, 162, 163, 164, 165, 167, 171, 172, 173, 174, 175, 176, 182, 183, 184, 188, 189, 197, 207, 213, 214, 221, 222, 226, 238, 240, 241, 245
rules, vii, 13, 26, 52, 87, 92, 99, 106, 107, 108, 142, 153, 156, 167, 171, 173, 180, 197, 199, 230, 243

S

safety, 220
sample survey, 68
satellite service, 31, 46, 142, 177
savings, 64
SCAP, 54
school, 220
science, 181
scope, 3, 11, 19, 23, 39, 45, 49, 60, 90, 100, 114, 143, 152, 169, 202, 203, 219, 231
SEA, 46, 56, 83, 131, 151, 156, 165, 167, 184, 188, 192, 201, 203, 204, 235

security, 78
seeding, 210
self-employment, 180
seller(s), 11, 21, 23, 45, 46, 47, 51, 57, 61, 67, 63, 73, 75, 91, 95, 159, 160, 165, 173, 204, 213, 230, 234
Senate, 236, 237
service provider, 12, 33, 39, 56, 61, 119, 121, 146, 148, 150, 151, 156, 161, 210
settlements, 31, 64, 107, 120, 160, 176
shape, 70
shelter, 229
Sherman Act, 25
shortfall, 64
showing, 23, 40
signals, 77, 235
singers, 206
small businesses, 203
social benefits, 77
society, 54, 153, 155, 156, 241
software, 211
solution, 8, 48, 73, 87, 97, 98, 148, 169, 175, 196, 200, 214, 226, 228, 232, 233, 236
sound recordings, vii, 1, 2, 3, 7, 8, 9, 10, 11, 12, 13, 14, 15, 16, 17, 19, 27, 28, 29, 30, 31, 32, 33, 34, 35, 36, 37, 38, 39, 43, 45, 47, 48, 49, 51, 55, 56, 57, 60, 61, 62, 63, 65, 67, 70, 71, 72, 73, 74, 76, 78, 87, 90, 92, 95, 96, 97, 98, 99, 101, 102, 103, 104, 106, 110, 112, 113, 114, 115, 116, 117, 118, 120, 121, 123, 137, 139, 142, 143, 144, 146, 152, 153, 154, 164, 165, 166, 167, 176, 177, 178, 183, 185, 191, 201, 204, 207, 212, 213, 214, 219, 231, 235, 244, 245
species, 13, 18
specifications, 108
specter, 80
spending, 41
spin, 169
stability, 155
staff members, 175
staffing, 175, 218
stakeholders, vii, 1, 12, 31, 39, 41, 44, 45, 46, 47, 48, 49, 51, 53, 56, 58, 60, 63, 64, 65, 67, 71, 74, 85, 90, 97, 98, 106, 107, 119, 151, 159, 163, 167, 176, 185, 211, 218, 237
standardization, 98
state(s), vii, 3, 11, 32, 33, 47, 48, 49, 74, 99, 112, 144, 149, 154, 164, 178, 207, 208, 210, 213, 219
state laws, 32, 33, 48, 112, 207
statutory provisions, 16, 63, 96, 97, 107, 241
storage, 33, 200
stress, 10, 45

structure, 1, 7, 9, 20, 29, 39, 61, 69, 73, 75, 91, 97, 102, 148, 164, 190, 192, 196, 199, 205, 215, 218, 223, 234
structuring, 234
style, 30, 34, 76, 103, 112, 170, 176, 196, 238
subscribers, 112
subsidy, 212
supervision, 2, 55, 71, 81, 82, 106, 112, 153, 154
supervisors, 34
supplier(s), 84, 151
supply chain, 67
Supreme Court, 19, 23, 25, 40, 77, 166, 202, 217, 235, 244
survival, 137
synchronization, 6, 18, 23, 24, 34, 35, 40, 57, 89, 119, 145, 149, 192, 198, 203, 213, 228, 232, 234
synchronize, 13, 18

T

tactics, 26, 81, 82, 150, 155, 158, 192
talent, 114, 205, 206, 209, 210, 218
target, 26
tariff, 49, 55, 73
Task Force, 150, 169, 198
taxes, 183
taxonomy, 238
techniques, 173
technological advances, 19
technological developments, 35, 42
technologies, 11, 14, 49, 64, 69, 98, 99, 109, 139, 148, 211, 227, 233
technology, 13, 18, 55, 137, 148, 150, 166, 173, 182, 192, 193, 196, 200, 202, 206, 214, 227, 232, 235
telephone, 109, 116, 118, 123
television stations, 17, 22, 23, 26, 52, 80, 220
temporary jobs, 179
tension, 94
tenure, 190
thoughts, 242
time frame, 97, 99
tobacco, 179
tornadoes, 219
total revenue, 22
tracks, 29, 36, 101, 103, 146, 211, 240
trade, 15, 17, 23, 24, 137, 149, 181, 187, 209
traits, 238
transaction costs, 53, 66, 121, 236
transactions, 2, 13, 35, 51, 71, 89, 92, 98, 102, 234
transcripts, 136
transformation, 225
transmission, 14, 19, 28, 30, 94, 110, 112, 139, 141, 151, 163, 165, 170, 202, 203, 235

transparency, 7, 8, 11, 44, 54, 55, 58, 66, 81, 99, 100, 120, 121, 148, 155, 174, 180, 221, 226, 240, 241, 243, 245
treaties, 207, 235
treatment, 2, 32, 45, 48, 52, 70, 71, 72, 81, 97, 98, 117, 172, 185, 235
trial, 24, 26, 51, 74, 107, 120, 170, 230, 242, 245
trustworthiness, 59

U

U.S. economy, 212
unhappiness, 75
uniform, 3, 33, 65
unions, 17, 172, 206
United Kingdom (UK), 38, 147, 168
United States (USA), vii, 1, 3, 10, 15, 17, 24, 29, 31, 36, 40, 50, 54, 73, 81, 108, 110, 122, 125, 127, 129, 130, 137, 140, 142, 146, 151, 165, 169, 170, 176, 177, 187, 195, 196, 197, 199, 203, 207, 219, 225, 236, 246
universe, 78, 97, 199
universities, 196, 205
updating, 95, 195, 214
Uruguay, 144
Uruguay Round, 144

V

vacuum, 47
validation, 148
valuation, 65, 175, 201
variations, 16
vein, 46
venture capital, 210
venue, 18, 159, 167
vested interests, 12, 75
Vice President, v, 222, 237
video games, 34, 110, 112, 145, 188
videos, 6, 34, 35, 60, 72, 89, 111, 145, 149, 170, 214
Vietnam, 219, 222
violence, 220
vision, 16, 97, 182, 185
visual images, 232
vote, 170, 176

W

walking, 179
Washington, 116, 184, 221
watches, 226
Watt, Melvin L., 164

web, 39, 150, 198
websites, 38, 66, 68, 163, 206
White House, 183
White Paper, 146
wholesale, 85
wildfire, 220
withdrawal, 4, 26, 38, 53, 54, 66, 80, 81, 85, 100, 119, 121, 155, 168, 174, 198, 203, 240
witnesses, 161

workers, 207
World War I, 77, 180, 189, 191
worldwide, 38, 200, 202, 225
worry, 42, 44, 81, 99

yield, 72, 105, 155, 244